Varieties of Psychohistory

George M. Kren is associate professor of history at Kansas State University and contributing editor of the *History of Childhood Quarterly*. Dr. Kren (Ph.D., University of Wisconsin) brings to *Varieties of Psychohistory* a longstanding scholarly concern with how past events may be illuminated through psychological interpretation of the key personages involved. In addition to this volume, he has published numerous articles in this rapidly growing, interdisciplinary area of scholarship, many of them written jointly with his present co-author.

Leon H. Rappoport is professor of psychology at Kansas State University. Like his co-author, Dr. Rappoport (Ph.D., University of Colorado) draws on extensive research on aspects and methods of psychohistory. Two-time recipient of fellowships from the National Institute of Mental Health, he is a frequent contributor to periodicals. Among his books are *Personality Development* and *Human Judgment and Social Interaction* (with co-editor David Summers).

Varieties of Psychohistory

EDITED BY

George M. Kren and Leon H. Rappoport

Springer Publishing Company
NEW YORK

ACKNOWLEDGMENTS

Lloyd deMause has been a major source of help, encouragement, and support throughout this project, as well as in our other efforts in psychohistory. We are most appreciative of Ellen Tumposky's excellent editorial suggestions and her careful scrutiny of the manuscript.

Springer Publishing Company, Inc.
200 Park Avenue South
New York, N.Y. 10003

76 77 78 79 80 / 10 9 8 7 6 5 4 3 2 1

Library of Congress Cataloging in Publication Data
Main entry under title:

Varieties of psychohistory.

Includes index.
Contents: Kren, G. and Rappoport, L. Introduction.—The nature of psycho-history: Mazlish, B. What is psycho-history? Manuel, F. The use and abuse of psychology in history. Kren and Rappoport. Clio and psyche. [etc.]
1. Psychohistory—Addresses, essays, lectures.
I. Kren, George M., 1926- II. Rappoport, Leon.
D16.V282 155 76-225
ISBN 0-8261-1940-9
ISBN 0-8261-1941-7 pbk.

Printed in the United States of America

For Margo

Contents

Introduction:
Values, Methods, and the Utility of Psychohistory 1

PART ONE
The Nature of Psychohistory

1 What Is Psycho-history?
Bruce Mazlish 17

2 The Use and Abuse of Psychology in History
Frank E. Manuel 38

3 Clio and Psyche
George M. Kren and Leon H. Rappoport 63

PART TWO
Psychobiography

4 On the Uses of Psychology:
Conflict and Conciliation in Benjamin Franklin
Richard L. Bushman 81

5 The Legend of Hitler's Childhood
Erik H. Erikson 99

6 Woodrow Wilson and Colonel House: Research Note
Alexander L. George and Juliette L. George 111

PART THREE

The History of Childhood

7 The Evolution of Childhood
Lloyd deMause 123

8 Developmental Perspectives on the History of Childhood
John Demos 180

9 Childhood and Adolescence among the Thirteenth-Century Saints
Michael Goodich 193

10 The Psychohistorical Origins of the Nazi Youth Cohort
Peter Loewenberg 219

PART FOUR

Group Processes and Historical Trends

11 Stranded in the Present
Kenneth Keniston 251

12 The Making of a Murderer
Herman P. Langner 257

13 Death-Profit, "Evil," and the Chinese Feminist Movement
Leslie E. Collins 264

14 Violence without Moral Restraint: Reflections on the Dehumanization of Victims and Victimizers
Herbert C. Kelman 282

15 Groupthink among Policy Makers
Irving L. Janis 315

16 On America
Carl G. Jung 330

17 The Ethics of a Therapeutic Man
Clarence J. Karier 333

Index 365

Contributors

Richard L. Bushman teaches history at Boston University. He has focused primarily on the colonial and early national periods in America, and has written articles on Jonathan Edwards.

Leslie E. Collins is a Ph.D. candidate in sociology at Yale University. He did research in China and is particularly interested in cross-cultural perspectives on women's roles.

Lloyd deMause is broadly trained in psychoanalysis, history, and political science. He is the founder and editor of the *History of Childhood Quarterly*, and has played a central role in the development of that field.

John Demos of Brandeis University is primarily an American colonial historian. His *A Little Commonwealth: Family Life in Plymouth Colony* (1970) is considered a pioneering study in the history of the family.

Erik H. Erikson, the eminent psychoanalyst, is the author of several groundbreaking studies, including *Young Man Luther* (1958), *Gandhi's Truth* (1969), and *Childhood and Society* (1964).

Alexander L. George was trained as a political scientist and *Juliette L. George* was originally a sociologist. In addition to their Wilson-House biography—the best known of their collaborative efforts—they have written *Psycho-McCarthyism: The Kennedy Neurosis* (1973). Alexander George was awarded the 1975 Bancroft Prize for his *Deterrence in American Foreign Policy*, co-authored by Richard Smoke.

Michael Goodich is a medieval scholar and member of the history faculty at the University of Haifa, Israel.

Irving L. Janis is a widely published social psychologist. A professor of psychology at Yale University, he is best known for his book on group decision processes, *Victims of Groupthink* (1972).

Clarence J. Karier teaches at the University of Illinois (Urbana), specializing in the history of education. He is author of *Shaping the Educational State in America* (1975) and many articles on the development of American education.

Herbert C. Kelman teaches social relations at Harvard University and is an authority on attitude research and intergroup processes.

Kenneth Keniston is widely known for his work on alienation among college students (*The Uncommitted*, 1965). He is based at Harvard University and has studied family life patterns in relation to sociocultural changes.

Herman P. Langner is a practicing analyst who served as an Army psychiatrist in Vietnam.

Peter Loewenberg is on the history faculty of the University of California, Los Angeles. His writings include psychoanalytically oriented studies of Theodore Herzl and Heinrich Himmler. He is now working on a study of Otto Bauer.

Frank E. Manuel, a professor at New York University, is mainly interested in European intellectual history. Among his most important publications are *Shapes of Philosophical History* (1964), *The Eighteenth Century Confronts the Gods* (1959), and *Portrait of Isaac Newton* (1968).

Bruce Mazlish teaches at the Massachusetts Institute of Technology. Among his publications are *The Western Intellectual Tradition* (with J. Bronowski, 1960), *The Riddle of History* (1966), *In Search of Nixon* (1972), and *James and John Stuart Mill* (1975).

Varieties of Psychohistory

Introduction
Values, Methods, and the Utility of Psychohistory

> The inclination of modern times tends rather to trace back the events of human history to more hidden, general, and impersonal factors—the forcible influence of economic circumstances, changes in food supply, progress in the use of materials and tools, migrations caused by increase in population and change of climate. In these factors individuals play no other part than that of exponents or representatives of mass tendencies which must come to expression and which found that expression as it were by chance in such persons.
>
> —Sigmund Freud, *Moses and Monotheism*, 1939.[1]

> There is, however, still ample scope for penetration in depth, and I personally have no doubt that the "newest history" will be more intensive and less extensive. I refer more specifically to the urgently needed deepening of our historical understanding through exploitation of the concepts and findings of modern psychology.
>
> —William Langer, in his presidential address to the American Historical Association, December 1957[2]

Writing in 1975, it is quite safe to say that psychohistory has finally arrived as a substantive new area of social science. It is instructive to see that almost two decades had to pass before Freud's expression of the need for psychohistorical perspectives on history were taken up by the distinguished historian William Langer. Furthermore, just as Freud's colleagues in psychology were generally indifferent to his historical-philosophical views and speculations, so the great majority of Langer's scholarly constituents were also indifferent. It was not until the late

1960s that a new generation of scholars, undoubtedly influenced by the chaotic social changes surrounding them, began to find important meaning in the promise of psychology applied to history and history applied to psychology.

This is not to say, of course, that no major work in psychohistory was accomplished prior to the sixties. On the contrary, as the articles in part one of this book clearly demonstrate, a firm body of relevant psychohistorical material has been accumulating for some time.

But in scholarly academic circles the wheels of change grind exceedingly slowly. Although various individual studies in psychobiography, for example, could be recognized and applauded for their intrinsic value, the idea that psychology and history could be intimately joined together for anything more than occasional idiosyncratic investigations was hardly acceptable: Does the lion lie down with the lamb? As some of us know to our pain, there is no primate more jealous of its territory than ***homo scholasticus***.

Yet there is now firm evidence demonstrating that the intimate relationship between history and psychology has yielded a thriving academic offspring. Thus:

1. According to a recent survey, courses in psychohistory are currently offered at approximately thirty major colleges and universities, and this number is growing rapidly.[3]

2. At national professional meetings of the American Historical Association, the American Psychological Association, and Cheiron, an increasing amount of time is being devoted to matters of psychohistory.

3. Two scholarly journals (*The History of Childhood Quarterly* and *The Journal of Interdisciplinary History*) are devoted in full or in part to psychohistorical research, and a newsletter is issued regularly by the Group for the Use of Psychology in History.

4. An increasing number of books is available, containing either specific studies in psychohistory or general perspectives on the field itself.

The present volume falls in the latter category. It has grown out of our collaborative efforts, beginning in 1967, both to conduct original research in psychohistory and to develop appropriate courses for interested students. As will be made clear in detail later, the book provides newcomers to psychohistory with a broad introduction to the various branches of this field: theory and methods, psychobiography, childhood history, and group processes.

A more primary issue, however, concerns the basis for interest in psychohistory. Why does it attract professional scholars and laymen alike? What are the potential benefits that people see in it? These and similar commonsense questions deserve serious consideration because they involve the practical as well as abstract meaning of psychohistory; they deal with its larger cultural significance. And like all such questions, they lead directly into the domain of human values. This is not a domain that lends itself to easy discussion, and it would be much more convenient to go immediately to concrete subject matter. But the controversies that have accompanied the growth of psychohistory make it all the more imperative—as a matter of professional integrity—to begin with a general, straightforward perspective on the values problem.

It is well-recognized by scholars and philosophers of contemporary culture that during the past century, the accumulating power of western science has gradually destroyed or discredited all competing sources of human values. This state of affairs shows itself in many ways; for example, divinity school graduates frequently seek advanced degrees in some branch of social science, but social science graduates hardly ever turn up in divinity schools. Yet when people come to any branch of science seeking values, they ironically find themselves immersed in methods instead.

Those who persist in science despite this apparent value-method contradiction may slowly come to realize that it is false. There is no genuine distinction between values and methods to be made in science because they are one and the same; the values of science inhere in the logic of its methods; the methods *are* the values. Briefly, this assertion rests on the established philosophical premise that the subject (observer) cannot be separated from the object (whatever is being observed). As indicated by the philosopher of science Patrick Heelan, the concepts and tools employed by the observer determine what will be seen; scientists experience the world through their instruments just as a blind man experiences it through the tip of his cane.

Implicitly or explicitly, such understandings are widely accepted in modern science; indeed, they permeate Western culture, where the only remaining *absolute* value is *utility*—that is, the practical capacity to bring about change, to make a significant difference. Of course, this is not a terribly new idea. The young Karl Marx (ahead of his time like all men of genius) expressed it very well in 1845 in his famous eleventh thesis on Feuerbach: "The philosophers have only *interpreted* the world in various ways; the point is, to *change* it."

Indeed, science dominates the modern world because of its ability to change it. The potent utility of physical science may be seen through the tools it produces (dynamite, computers) that change the physical world, and the utility of social science may be seen through the tools *it* produces (intelligence tests, public opinion surveys) that change the social world.

Viewed in this general context, psychohistory demands recognition not only as a new method or tool of social science, but also as a vehicle for change. The fundamental theme of this discussion follows quite directly: How is it possible to understand the potential utility of psychohistory?

Such a thematic question will seem premature or irrelevant to those scholars still not prepared to acknowledge psychohistory as a legitimate new field of social science. Geoffrey Barraclough, for example, has been eloquent in his condemnations:

> For my part, I regard "psychohistory" as a murky quagmire, unredeemed even by its more comical extravagances. But it has also to be said that its proliferation is a sad reflection on the state of historical study today. If historians cannot find something more profitable to argue about than Hitler's motivations—or William the Conqueror's, or anyone else's—they have only themselves to blame if they waken up one morning and find their place taken by the psychiatrist's couch.[4]

Yet the very terms of this denunciation emphasize a kind of competitive utility. Barraclough claims that historians must find something more *profitable* to study than motivations; and if they do not, then they may *lose* their place to psychiatry.

These statements also imply that historians have better alternatives to follow than psychohistory, but give no hint that the methods of history are themselves historical, and that changing ways of doing history reflect changes in the society or culture surrounding historians. The meaning of any history is only understandable in terms of the sociocultural dynamics surrounding its creation; one can no more judge the validity of psychohistory apart from its milieu (the idea of the therapeutic n. b.) than one can judge Old Testament history apart from the idea of Jehovah.

The history of historical writings provides very clear illustrations of how cultural values and historical methods have been locked together. Some examples:

1. Thucydides' account of the Peloponnesian war specifically reflected the dialectical culture of the Athenian *polis* by centering upon the drastically different perspectives that men of good will could bring to discussion of public policy. Persuasive rhetoric and political debate, not gods or military power, were the causal focus of this history.

2. Renaissance writers projected the values of personal ambition and secular power. Machiavelli's political essays and Shakespeare's dramas both portray man as the dominator of nature and other men. The key to their work may be seen in their unswerving search for the nexus between human frailty and the pursuit of power.

3. Eighteenth-century scholars translated the values of the enlightenment into a view of history that was quite independent of the ambitions of great men. Gibbon saw the Fall of Rome as dictated by the slow triumph of Christianity; Montesquieu offered climate as a decisive explanatory principle. In this fashion, historical events were perceived to be the consequence of autonomous processes beyond human control.

4. Applying his revised Hegelian philosophy to the events of the industrial revolution, Karl Marx developed the theory and methods of economic determinism. History could now be seen as a function of the organization of production. If labor was the critical variable establishing value, then dialectical materialism had to be the correct method to grasp history.

5. Emerging in the chaos of Weimar Germany, the sociology of knowledge made suspicion and distrust into a paradigm for historical inquiry by maintaining that ideas can only be understood in terms of the special, selfish interests that they serve. In these terms, therefore, every socioeconomic grouping was seen as producing its own unique truth.

Many more examples could be cited, but the principle at issue here hardly requires further illustration. Indeed, the idea that the methods of history evolve out of cultural values is so apparent as to seemingly preclude debate, except when knowledgeable writers pose contradictory arguments in their zeal to dispose of psychohistory.

As Clarence Karier has noted in his elaborations of the Rieffean thesis, this is the age of the therapeutic; from kindergarten to graduate school, from *Mr. Roger's Schoolhouse* to Dick Cavett, from Spock on child-rearing to *The Joy of Sex*, our culture is thoroughly saturated with watery versions of Freud, Skinner, and the effluvia of sensitivity training. It is a culture in which Nixon's psyche attracts as much interested attention as his violations of law. And in this sort of cognitive environment, the use of psychology in history cannot be viewed as anything other than a valid reflection of cultural values.

On the other hand, to understand and acknowledge the cultural legitimacy of psychohistory is only a first step toward recognition of its utility. For, as the examples listed above testify, the methods of history not only grow out of cultural values; they also feed back upon culture, exerting a dialectical force towards change.

This forward thrust of history has always been rather obscure, probably because from time immemorial historians have generally preferred to masquerade as simple storytellers, only occasionally giving mild warnings that those who do not know the mistakes of the past are condemned to relive them. Hidden underneath such platitudes is the fact that historians create the mirrors in which a culture or society may gaze upon itself, confront its own image. In this fashion, acting as interpreter and all-around representative or impressario of the past, the historian arranges the conditions for dialogue between a people and their history. Metaphorically, at least, the historian is master of ceremonies at such cultural dialogues just as the psychotherapist is master of ceremonies at the personal history dialogues of his patients.

The real utility of history, therefore, is not to be found in the busywork and polemics of most professional historians, but rather in the character of the dialogue and confrontations that historians contribute to the ongoing cultural processes of the society they serve. The utility of history lies in its capacity to influence the future by reflecting images of the past to generations inhabiting the sociocultural present.

Marxists, of course, have always taken this as a primary article of faith. Hence their diverse efforts to control the production of history, including the brutally awkward Stalinist attempts to "rewrite" it. In western democracies, with much less conscious effort we nevertheless do much better. Instead of changing history by counterfeiting source material, we restructure our images of history by applying new methods. The source material remains inviolate, but our new methods change its meaning.

As indicated earlier, the history of history-writing clearly shows that this is to be expected: if historical methods are truly rooted in culture, and cultures change, then so will histories.

Placed in this general context, any serious inquiry about the utility of psychohistory leads inevitably to questions concerning its present and future implications: How does the use of psychology in history influence our image of the past? What kinds of cultural dialogues are likely to be created by psychohistorical studies? As this new method of history becomes more prevalent, can its impact on the future be seen in tangible sociopolitical and economic terms? In sum, and from a slightly different perspective, our fundamental thesis is that important questions about the utility of psychohistory can be intelligently explored through examination of its current theory and practice.

It is clearly impossible to specify the future significance of psychohistory in advance. But the work already accomplished in this field is substantial enough to indicate how it is bound to develop during the forseeable future. Accordingly, the contents of this book are arranged in four general sections corresponding to the major branches growing out of the work of contemporary psychohistorians.

Part one is devoted to discussions of psychohistory as an academic, philosophical, and cultural enterprise. The articles presented here are all in one way or another concerned with definitions of form and substance. They represent efforts to gain a firm conceptual perspective on psychohistory; to construe the field in such a way as to clarify ambiguities, answer critics, and thus permit further intelligent development.

What most strikes the reader of these articles is the unity in their diversity. Mazlish writes mainly from the standpoint of an academic man of action, a bold pioneer whose recent work on Richard Nixon points the way toward psychobiographical studies of contemporary figures. His theoretical paper ("What Is Psycho-history?") divides psychohistorical research according to whether it emphasizes individual or group processes, and he discusses questions of theory and method in terms of the concrete problems facing working scholars.

In rather sharp contrast to Mazlish, Manuel's "Use and Abuse . . ." paper offers a broadly discursive philosophical inquiry on the origins and present status of psychohistory. The thrust of this discussion is toward discovery of a secure place for psychohistory in the general arena of competing social science disciplines.

Finally, our own historiographical "Clio and Psyche" essay contains a critical review of the relationships between history, Freud's psychoanalytic theory, and non-Freudian academic psychology. This paper also explains in some detail why it has been judged necessary to group together different kinds of studies in separate categories.

Apart from similarities of reference—the three articles mention the same outstanding events in the history of psychohistory—the unitary theme emerging is that no fully representative picture of the human condition can be achieved unless psychological understandings are properly incorporated into historical studies. History must be informed by psychology. No writer has been able to pinpoint how this goal can be rigorously and systematically attained. But it is this very uncertainty, the recognition that different problems in the field require different approaches, that produces the exciting, creative tension in scholars determined to expand the existing boundaries of their disciplines.

Part Two offers representative studies in psychobiography. Although one might look back to Plutarch and the Greek playwrights for origins, modern psychobiography is generally conceded to have begun with

Freud's book on Leonardo DaVinci, published in 1910. Widely promulgated almost fifty years later through the more popular works of Erik Erikson, particularly his study of Martin Luther, psychobiography has been and still remains the chief enterprise of psychohistory. Indeed, psychobiography is too often considered to be all there is of psychohistory, a view that we aim to correct in this volume. Yet the area deserves careful attention because it has served as the primary vehicle for the entry of psychology into history.

The articles reproduced in this section range from a didactic discussion of how psychological insights may be employed to understand some of the more important characteristic behavior patterns of Benjamin Franklin, to a pioneering psychobiographical portrait of Adolf Hitler. Aside from their intrinsic quality, these papers were deliberately selected for their diverse subject matter. This variety should be particularly helpful to those making their first acquaintance with psychobiography, enabling them easily to see how the techniques of analysis generalize across the particular objects of analysis.

Part Three, "History of Childhood," is obviously close to psychobiography insofar as the latter typically involves extensive study of childhood experience. But the psychobiographer is usually only engaged with the specific childhood of his subject, whereas the historian of childhood focuses on the conditions of children per se: the normative socializing experiences of whole generations in particular historical epochs. Childhood history may also be set apart from other areas of psychohistory because it is the most recent addition to the field.

The historical significance of childhood was not widely recognized prior to the 1960 publication of Phillipe Ariès' *Centuries of Childhood.* In this ground-breaking work, he argued that up through the medieval period, European civilization contained no formal conception of childhood as a distinct developmental era of human growth and education, and, further, that ever since the Middle Ages, the evolution of the idea of childhood has been a key factor in the evolution of European civilization. Ariès' book contained enough concrete information, including separate chapters on discipline, clothing, games, and education, to demonstrate forcefully how previously neglected primary sources could provide new perspectives on important social, political, and economic events.

Important as it is, however, Ariès' book by itself does not fully explain the rise of scholarly interest in history of childhood. At least three additional factors deserve mention. First, on a purely psychological level, studies of childhood attract a great deal of attention because they ultimately focus upon a very basic human question: are children intrinsically good or evil? Should they be seen as barbarous representatives of the devil or angelic messengers from heaven? Even a casual review of European history indicates that the answer varies depending upon the social conditions prevailing in different historical periods. Consequently, childrearing may be influenced by important historical events, and, as generations of children come of age, their early experience will in turn influence adult behavior patterns of historical significance. The popularity of psychobiography also tends to draw attention to history of childhood, for the unique characteristics of a great person's early experience can be better understood when a normative standard is available to serve as a basis for comparison. The logic of their work thus compels students of psychobiography toward concern with the history of childhood. Finally, and perhaps most important of all, childhood history has gained rapid acceptance because it fits into a general scholarly trend emphasizing study of how ordinary people lived in the past.

The considerations noted above help explain the plausibility of childhood history as a distinct field of study, but critical readers may still quite properly ask for an accounting: "What has been accomplished? What does history of childhood have to offer in the way of tangible results?" The articles in this section were selected because they provide strong answers to these questions.

Thus, in his "The Evolution of Childhood," Lloyd deMause first shows that contrary to common belief, the record of child treatment in western civilization is abominable. Based on evidence accumulated in over five years of research on thousands of sources, this conclusion is further supported by an analysis of the psychological factors governing adult-child relationships.

DeMause then goes on to suggest that historical change results from the gradual evolution of psychological processes across generations spanning the centuries. Most striking in this connection is his taxonomic framework for categorizing parent-child relations through twenty-four centuries of recorded history. His work can only be described as a bold effort to integrate historical and psychological knowledge in a uniquely new way.

The second article, "Developmental Perspectives on the History of Childhood" by John Demos, examines Erikson's personality development scheme as an instrument for the analysis of childhood history. Applying Eriksonian ideas to history, Demos shows how the childrearing practices of the Puritans produced important psychological effects on new generations.

In "Childhood and Adolescence among the Thirteenth-Century

Saints," Michael Goodich suggests that the new religious orders of this period were rather like the radical communes of our own time. Many of the saints were either emotionally deprived as children or were raised completely apart from their parents. On entering adolescence, these young people experienced profound conflicts emanating from what we today would call a "generation gap." Their reaction was to replace the parental authority they could not accept with a more individualized metaphysical authority.

Peter Loewenberg's "The Psychohistorical Origins of the Nazi Youth Cohort" offers a new perspective on the meaning that National Socialism provided for a whole generation of ordinary Germans. Loewenberg's article is exceptionally appropriate as the final component of this section because it presents both a specific analysis of an important problem and an incisive general discussion of how such analyses can contribute to the making of a new kind of history: ". . . a history that tells us how men responded to and felt about the great political and economic events that shaped their lives, a history that gives due place to the irrational, the unconscious, and the emotions not only of men, but also of the child in the man."[5]

Like deMause, Demos, and Goodich, Loewenberg sees the normative events of childhood as a critically important factor leading to historical change, but he also argues for attention to the linkages between generations that give a society its historical continuity. These generalizations all receive careful consideration in his substantive work on the generation of Germans born between 1900 and 1915.

Part Four, entitled "Group Processes and Historical Trends," must be acknowledged as the most loosely-knit and controversial of the general areas constituting the field of psychohistory. It might be argued cogently that the works of philosophy, social psychology, and history included here would be better left alone on the fringes of their parent disciplines, or else be identified simply as notable efforts toward interdisciplinary understanding. There can be no perfect answer to such views; however, any robust definition of psychohistory will inevitably include "history informed by psychology"; "psychology informed by history"; and "philosophy informed by both history and psychology." These are not mere catchphrases; they represent the qualitative character of much serious work that must be assimilated into the mainstream of psychohistory in order to round out its potential for analysis of important contemporary affairs. That scholars from various disciplines have concerned themselves with problems directly relevant to the purposes of psychohistory is, therefore, more than sufficient cause for including their work in this volume.

How are ordinary persons connected with the group processes and historical trends of their time? A reversal of the traditional "great man" theory of history, this question is the underlying problem addressed in the first two papers by Keniston and Langer. In very different ways, both articles suggest the powerful dominance of history over the psychology of everyday life.

Keniston shows that rapid technological and sociopolitical changes in American culture may leave the middle-aged and elderly confused about the meaning of their lives. As his title suggests, to be "Stranded in the Present" is to be without strong personal anchors holding the past to the future. How such situations may arise quickly and dramatically for young people is described in Langer's "The Making of a Murderer," a brief case study of a young man whose sense of connection with his friends and family was shattered by the stress of combat in Vietnam.

Historical events also influence group activities in ways not clearly perceived by individual group members. The articles by Kelman, Janis, and Collins indicate some of the diverse, historically relevant qualities of group processes that have only recently begun to receive careful attention.

Kelman's "Violence without Moral Restraint" reviews what has been learned about the social and psychological factors associated with "sanctioned massacres" or atrocities. Although he does not employ specifically historical dimensions in his analysis, the major causes of atrocious group behavior that Kelman identifies—authorization, routinization, and dehumanization—all have obvious historical origins in western civilization.

In "Groupthink among Policymakers," Janis suggests that the social psychological character of high level decision-making groups may become so powerful a form of reality for group members that the ultimate human consequences of their decisions tend to be ignored. Based on psychological reconstructions of group processes among elite policymakers caught up in such important historical situations as the Cuban missile crisis, the Janis study is a novel type of psychohistorical investigation because analysis is focused on the group as a whole rather than on individuals.

Group processes at the family level are examined in Leslie Collins' "Death-Profit and the Chinese Feminist Movement," an aritcle providing psychological interpretations of the traditional social role imposed on women in Asia. Hemmed in by a complex structure of duties to parents, husband and children, Chinese women could only achieve a significant degree of freedom to govern their own lives upon the death of their husbands. This condition, in which the wife profited both personally and materially from death, is identified as an important source of the moral ambivalence that runs through the Chinese feminist movement.

When psychohistorical analysis of group processes is carried to its final, logical extreme, it serves as a vehicle for the study of whole cultures and long-term historical trends in their development. Works of this kind are rare, however, because in pursuing them one inevitably must enter that uncharted domain of protean scholarship where art, science, and philosophy all intermingle.

Conventional academic disciplines generally cannot cope with such works as Freud's *Civilization and Its Discontents*, Spengler's *Decline of the West*, or Marcuse's *Eros and Civilization*. Books of this scope tend to remain on the shelf, serving more than anything else as awesome icons representing the boldest kind of intellectual adventures. Carl Jung is a preeminent figure in this special category; certainly no psychological writer can be said to rely more directly than Jung does on unique premises tying the human psyche to history. His theory of a powerful "racial unconsciousness" that expresses itself in culture as well as individual human behavior is perfectly displayed in a short excerpt from a book not available in English. Titled for editorial purposes "Jung on America," the excerpt contains his unusual view of American social behavior as a compound of elements assimilated from racial qualities he assumes to be present in African Negroes and American Indians.

The final article in the book, which fittingly enough includes a strong critique of Jung's conduct in Nazi Germany, is Karier's "The Ethics of a Therapeutic Man." Working across the whole spectrum of modern European and American culture, Karier portrays therapeutic man as a prototypical creature of the twentieth century. Based on a model of the alienated, sensitive artist-intellectual who can find no meaning other than disgust or purposeless heroism in the major events of this century, therapeutic man struggles to transcend the sterilizing effects of alienation by probing his psyche with instruments ranging from classical psychoanalysis to arcane oriental religions. Karier's discussion of the problem of meaning in this century not only concerns psychohistory as an *object* of study, but also quite properly carries implications for psychohistorians as *subjects*, the agents of a therapeutic culture.

The essay reprinted at the end of this collection circles back upon our initial thematic question: What is the utility of psychohistory? Insofar as therapeutic concerns stand as a primary aspect of contemporary culture, the attractions of psychohistory should be obvious. Founded on a growing body of theory and methods sufficient to permit new interpretations of important human events, this hybrid discipline promises to discover and reveal certain of the hitherto obscure roots of such events.

More specifically, psychohistorical studies have the cumulative effect of *repersonalizing* history for many scholars and laymen alike, who have felt themselves to be caught up in an impersonal, unknowable, and capricious flux of happenings. It offers at least a preliminary cognitive map or guide to some of the fundamental human elements influencing important historical events. Thus, by grasping at complex, opaque, and consequently frightening situations, and pulling them apart until they may be seen on a comprehensible human scale, psychohistorians may accomplish for their society what the early Greek storyteller-historians did for theirs: make inscrutable fate personal.

Very concretely, then, the utility of psychohistory is that it adds a new human dimension to great events, thus enriching our understanding of these events, and also, at least by implication, our understanding of ourselves. That which had once seemed mystery—Hitler's appeal to the youth of Germany, Richard Nixon's moral failure, the atrocious killings at My Lai—may be comprehended through application of psychoanalytic and social psychological knowledge. Phenomena of modern psychology involving the dynamics of unconscious needs and their origins in early life experience appeared baffling, if not downright bizarre, to an earlier generation of scholars; to a new generation, however, they have already become a familiar set of working tools for the *de*-mystification of history.

It must be acknowledged, of course, that abstract arguments over the validity of psychohistory still go on, viz: is it a mystification or a demystification to understand Hitler's hatred of the Jews as having had its emotional sources in the circumstance of his mother's death? A nice philosophical problem, this, with much heuristic value. But like so many other abstract questions, it may never receive a definitive answer. In the case of Hitler, for example, the fact of his mother's death while under treatment from a Jewish physician must be considered along with the whole history of anti-Semitism in Germany before one can grasp the nature of his feelings toward the Jews. On the other hand, it cannot be denied that psychohistorians perform a useful service when they explain how the contours of a leader's thinking were shaped by certain events of his childhood. Moreover, growing public and professional interest in such matters should not be dismissed merely as idle curiosity, for it may reflect an important new awareness of the intimate relationship between politics and personality.

In our present situation of uncertain public morality and widespread economic distress, with even more rapid movement down the path of uncertainty likely to occur in the future, people need to know as much as they possibly can about the interpenetration of public and private life, personality and history—the psychological side of history and the historical side of psychology. It is arguable that such knowledge offers at least one important basis for coming to grips with the profound evolutionary changes that are now quite apparent in much of contemporary western civilization.

Notes

1. Sigmund Freud, *Moses and Monotheism* (New York: Vintage Books, 1955), pp. 136–137.

2. William Langer, "The Next Assignment," *American Historical Review* 63 (1958), p. 284.

3. Personal communication from Dr. John Fitzpatrick, advanced scholar, Menninger Foundation, Topeka, Kansas.

4. Geoffrey Barraclough, "Psycho-history Is Bunk," *The Guardian*, March 3, 1973. Note also other critics such as Robert Coles, "Shrinking History," *New York Review of Books* 20 (February 22 and March 8, 1973), pp. 15–21, 25–29; Jacques Barzun, *Clio and Her Doctors: Psycho-history, Quanto-history, and History* (Chicago: University of Chicago Press, 1974).

5. Peter Loewenberg, "The Psychohistorical Origins of the Nazi Youth Cohort," *American Historical Review* 76 (December 1971), p. 1460.

PART ONE

The Nature of Psychohistory

1

What Is Psycho-history?

BRUCE MAZLISH

Do men or circumstances make history? That is the perennial philosophical question that all aspiring professionals are taught to ask and can never forget. Mazlish places this question in a new perspective, suggesting that the dichotomy may be a false one and that the discipline of psychohistory may enable scholars to bridge the gap between biography and general history. Although his own major works have been limited to psychobiographical studies (most recently an analysis of John Stuart and James Mill), in this article he points to the need for greater understanding of group processes and of collective acts in mass settings.

I have entitled my paper "What Is Psycho-history," in obvious imitation of an illustrious predecessor in analyzing Clio's nature and character. For reasons that will be clear later, I have come to think that psycho-social history may well be a better title than psycho-history for the inquiry that seems to be emerging, but since "tradition," that is, about ten years of effort by historians and psycho-analysts, has gone on under the latter rubric, I shall retain it here.

A previous effort of mine to deal with the present subject appeared in the "New Approaches to History" issue of *The Times Literary Supplement* (28 July 1966). At that time, I claimed that my seminar at M.I.T. in "History and Psycho-analysis" was unique for an historian (Erikson, at Harvard, is a psycho-analyst); since then, a number of other historians have begun to give similar courses, showing that the field is beginning to flourish. In any case, *The Times Literary Supplement* at

From *Transactions of the Royal Historical Society*, Series 5 (1971), 79–99. Read at the Society's Conference 22 September 1970. Reprinted by permission of the publisher.

the time gave to my piece the title, "Inside the Whales." Perhaps this was for its profundity, but more likely because they thought a whale plumbs great depths and comes up spouting a lot of air. There is always the danger, in fact, that that is what I shall do here. However, I hope at least it will be ecologically suitable, that is, clear air.

Having established my title and made my *apologia,* let me make one other general point before I come to grips with my subject per se. It is simply that any discussion of the use of psycho-analysis by historians in their work must take place in the context of a broad movement in the profession towards greater use of *analysis in general.* No one, I trust, wishes to deny the usefulness of what I shall call "traditional" history: a basic reliance on the chronological and descriptive approaches, usually limited by choice of a subject set in a definite period and territoriality, e.g., the nation state. Nevertheless, such an approach has certain severe limitations. Thus, increasingly, historians have turned to explicit theory, usually leaning heavily on related disciplines, to comparison, and to what I am calling analysis, and have chosen as subjects a particular social or political phenomenon, a structural feature of historical change, a "problem" rather than a "given." This is the spirit in which, increasingly, I have found my own work in intellectual history, for example, leading me to psycho-history.

II

Psycho-history, in my view, divides rather sharply into two kinds: that treating of individuals and that treating of groups. The first, under the inspiration of its founding father, Erik Erikson, has taken on the name life-history, and it focuses on great men. The second, as yet, has no characterizing name—we do not talk frequently of "group history," although we do refer to group psychology—and has no acknowledged mentor. Though Erikson has sought to build a bridge between these two kinds of psycho-history, starting from his side, the connection is still precarious and insufficient for the traffic historians might like to see it carry.

In life-history, we are primarily concerned with the motives of an individual, suitably psycho-analyzed, of course, and the way in which these personal motives are shaped by the culture and society as well as by his genetic factors, etc. We then seek to understand how the individual interrelates with and helps further to shape his surrounding culture and society. In what I shall now call group history, for want of a better term, we are concerned with groups driven or inspired by common motives. In both cases, individual or group, motives will be complicated, ambivalent, and so forth; in the case of groups, of course, the complications can be expected to be of a higher order. Both kinds of psycho-history enjoy common methodological and historiographic problems, but each, I shall submit, has special problems of its own, and may therefore require rather different approaches.

My purpose here is briefly to explore some of the problems, or aspects, of the two kinds of psycho-history. To facilitate my task I shall introduce some consideration of an intermediary social form: the family. Further, I take it as a fundamental premise that without a thorough grounding of the individual or group analysis in the social, political, economic, and other historical developments of the time, such inquiry is vitiated, and becomes mere pathology. For this reason, I have suggested earlier my personal preference for the title "Psycho-social history."

III

It has been the genius of Erik Erikson to establish the basic theory and practice of life-histories. In *Childhood and Society*, and other works, he developed his theories concerning the psycho-sexual developmental stages of individuals in general, always carefully relating these genetic stages to the enveloping culture and society, e.g., child-rearing among the Sioux Indians differing from modern Americans. Then, in *Young Man Luther*, and what his friends affectionately call *Middle-Aged Mahatma* (otherwise known as *Gandhi's Truth*), Erikson both applied and developed these theories in relation to an actual historical individual, thus establishing the theory and practice of psycho-history at one and the same time.

So emerged the life history of great leaders. Following Erikson, psycho-historians have returned to the Great Man in History approach. There is a curious paradox here. As I have recorded elsewhere, "In the more halcyon times of the late nineteenth and early twentieth centuries . . . the quiet summer of parliamentary democracy was relatively undisturbed by charismatic figures: a Giolitti, a Waldeck-Rousseau, was more suitable. Historians reflected the political scene of their time, and focused more on long-range, impersonal forces in history." Then came World War I, and the very massification of politics, or politicization of the masses, if one prefers the political scientist's term, which would have seemed to favor an increasing impersonalization of history brought forth its opposite—the great leader: Lenin, at first, and then Il Duce, Der Führer, and Stalin as Vodzd. So, too, emerged Gandhi and Nehru in India, and later Mao in China.

Such leaders seem to be Rousseau's god-like legislators, unmoved but moving everything around them. Although many of them spoke in the name of Marx's ideology, with its stress on material forces in history, or else, as with a Hitler, the impersonal forces of racism, they operated in terms of voluntarism and a "cult of personality." Here, indeed, was a problem and a challenge to the psycho-historian, who quickly discovered that the great leader was not "unmoved," but "moved" instead by recognizable human motives that could frequently best be analyzed by psychological theory. So, too, the way in which the leader "moved" his followers could also be illuminated by the same theory, though here the aid of an insufficiently developed group psychology had to be called upon.

Erikson himself claimed that understanding the great man in depth allowed us to understand the masses around him, and what moved them, as well as the events that unrolled from their actions. As Erikson put it, the great man in solving his personal problems helps to solve those of his fellow men, and does so in the highest and most illuminating terms. Naturally, the great man solves the problems set for him by the history into which he is born, but his particular solutions then set the way in which future problems will be met. As some critics have also emphasized, the great man's solutions then produce special ways of acting, of dealing with problems, until another great man comes along to shatter the existing political and personality paradigm.

Karl Jaspers, though appealing to a different sort of psychology from that used by Erikson, puts the case for the sort of knowledge that results from the procedure just described:

> Comprehension in depth of a single instance will often enable us, phenomenologically, to apply this understanding in general to innumerable cases. Often what one has once grasped is soon met again. What is important in phenomenology is less the study of a large number of instances than the intuitive and deep understanding of a few individual cases.[1]

Historians, shy of generalizations, should be happy with such a result. At least in this aspect of the matter, the historiographic beliefs of Eriksonian-like psycho-historians and traditional historians coincide.

Up to this point, I have tried to hint at some of the reasons for the emerging interest in Eriksonian-like life histories, and the sort of knowledge that might result from its practice. Now, with equal brevity, I would like to offer a few further historiographic observations. The first is that psycho-history can usefully be seen as an extension of sociology of knowledge. It offers, in this sense, a fusion of Freud with Marx. In the sociology of knowledge that he pioneered, Marx, as is well known, suggested that the overt beliefs and values held by men comprised merely a superstructure, based on the more fundamental substructure of economic and social conditions. The latter, the "material conditions of production," can then be thought of as the causal determinant of or influence on conscious ideas. Now comes Freud, to suggest that the overt, conscious ideas, reflecting the material conditions, are themselves strongly determined by deeper, unconscious impulses, fundamentally biological and libidinal in nature. Both Marx and Freud, then, seek to go behind and below appearances, the "veil of illusion" to use Marx's phrase, to a deeper, "realer" reality.

Psycho-history in its best moments tries to combine both insights. It attempts to understand the social conditions shaping the development of the individual (and group) psyche, and then the psychological factors forming the social conditions. Linear language forces me to present these as separate operations; in fact, the processes coexist, and correspond, rather than one being the "cause" of the other. Hence, sociology of knowledge is broadened to include "psychology of knowledge."

But not only the subjects of history are to be regarded in this new light. The historian himself becomes subject to the new discipline. We are all familiar with the historiographic studies of recent times, in which the ways in which historians view, for example, the French Revolution or Napoleon, are analyzed in terms of their political, or social, or economic positions. Liberal historians "see" only from that vantage point; Conservatives from another. Now, we are being asked to study the way in which the historian's own psychology—his *hitherto unconscious* processes—may affect his work.

Such a study, needless to say, is fraught with difficulty, and assertions such as that a particular historian chose to write about Cromwell and the regicides because of his own unresolved Oedipal complex are as trivial and simple-minded in relation to the historian as they would be if made about his subject itself. It is Erikson once again who has pioneered in this problem. Painstakingly, almost tediously so (though utterly necessary and thus a measure of Erikson's courage), in the Gandhi book—and this marks one of its significant advances over the earlier work—Erikson has sought to understand his own involvement with his subject. How have his own transferences, or "countertransferences," defined as the transfer of emotions stemming from figures and events of early infancy onto a present figure, no matter how "realistically" inappropriate, e.g., for a patient, emotionally, the analyst "becomes" the mother, or the father—how have these affected Erikson's perception or *lack of perception* of the data? What kinds of ambivalences does Erikson bring to his inquiry? By asking and seeking to answer such questions, Erikson forces a whole range of *self-observations* on the historian, and these must touch on the hitherto *unconscious* part of his self, as well as the conscious part. Henceforth, it is not only philosophers and physicians who must take unto themselves the Socratic injunction: "Know Thyself." It must become the oath of the historian as well. [2]

Now, this sort of self-knowledge is not a cure-all, or a guarantee that the historian will emerge with deep and penetrating knowledge of himself and his fellow men, which he can then apply to historical explanation. Here, as elsewhere, the quality of the historian is crucial. One man, such as Erikson, may have much of this gift; another little. Of such men as the latter, we may have to admit, as Peter de Vries scathingly remarked, "Down deep, he's shallow." Or, if I may put it in less witty terms, from such an historical well, the waters may run still, but not deep.

Will the knowing psycho-historian, as just defined, be prompted to discover new historical materials, or will he merely reinterpret data already noticed, but discarded by other historians? The answer is, clearly, both. Let me cite a few instances of each effort. For example, Erikson noticed that Gandhi, in his autobiography, touched on a labor strike of 1918, in Ahmedabad, in which he was involved, and then rapidly moved on to other matters. Erikson, believing that this strike was crucial for the manifestation of Gandhi's personality and his development of Satyagraha, or nonviolence, asked living survivors about it—thus "making" history—and sought for documentary accounts of the events. His fascinating and difficult chase through Indian and British archives will gladden the heart of any historian given to *Schadenfreude*. "At the end," he tells us, "my best friends were the British spies of the Criminal Intelligence Division of the old Home Department, who dutifully reported what they had observed, in documents which had been marked 'to be burned' but, of course, had escaped this fate." Here, Erikson at last found what he was looking for: "a crumbling number of the *Bombay Chronicle* of March 1918" and "back among the letters to the editor a long epistle signed M. A. Gandhi," commenting on the strike. In this epistle, Gandhi "revealed" what Erikson was looking for: himself. [3]

I offer another instance. A psycho-historian interested in the family will unearth child-rearing manuals and dusty medical books, hitherto buried in some back room or family trunk. (Parenthetically, it is an interesting experience to try to obtain early nineteenth-century books on birth control, such as Knowlton's *Fruits of Philosophy:* still, in 1968, when I asked for this at the British Museum, it could only be obtained from the "forbidden" books section!) Occasionally, the psycho-historian will meet active opposition, as when I asked for some of the Mill-Taylor volumes, part of which have been excerpted to such good purpose by F. A. Hayek, and was told by the librarian: "Oh, you wouldn't want *those* volumes; they're only about his trivial personal affairs." It took quite a bit of argument to persuade her that that was exactly what I was interested in; and that, nevertheless, I was a "respectable" historian, to be trusted with the sacred documents.

New material will undoubtedly be brought to public attention by the psycho-historian. Nevertheless, the bulk of his work depends on the re-examination and interpretation of materials already familiar to other historians and frequently ignored by them in deliberate fashion. Thus, Erikson makes much of Luther's anal language. Renzo Sereno refuses to pass by without comment a forgery by Machiavelli of a letter purporting to emanate from Caesar Borgia; and the Georges (Alexander and Juliette) refrain from treating a recurring pattern of behavior in Woodrow Wilson, culminating in his actions concerning American ratification of the League of Nations covenant, as merely accidental and meaningless.[4]

Who, or what, is a fit subject for a life-history? How does a life-history help us explain large-scale historical events? The first is a relatively easy question to answer; the second of enormous complexity. On the first question, I will offer some rule of thumb suggestions. My criteria for choosing the subject of a life-history would be that he truly matters in some way important to me and history. I will come back to this point in a moment. Next, there must be sufficient available materials; this is most often dependent on the subject himself being psychologically aware. For example, Lenin seems to me a subject who matters but the materials are simply not available for a full life-history because he has left us so little concerning his intimate personal life. And last, I must have some initial understanding, or gain it quickly, of my personal involvement with my subject; i.e., my transferences. What feelings does a Lenin, if I were to choose him, awaken in me, on the hitherto unconscious level? Must I be able to emphathize with him? On the assumption that we are, as psycho-analysis shows, "human, all too human," *in theory*, we should be able to treat even Hitler "sympathetically" as a life-history.[5]

Now, back to the question of how a life-history helps us explain historical events. Is it merely biography, now made psycho-biography? This in itself would be sufficient justification, as the writing of historical biographies is an ancient and accepted part of Clio's domain. Psycho-history, however, places its claims even higher, and considers itself part of general history, just as is social or economic history. By itself, of course, psycho-history does not offer total explanation; that would be sheer *reductionism*. It does claim, however, that where a great man occupies a unique position allowing him *personally* and *significantly* to shape history in a given direction—e.g., a Lenin or a Hitler—understanding of *his* life-history gives us increased understanding of *our* history.

For example, Bolshevism without Lenin, or Nazism without Hitler, is almost impossible to imagine. Men such as these shaped their movements, and the movements shaped general history. Unlike, say, a Secretary of State in the United States, or, in the good old days, even a President of the United States, whose position and power were sharply limited by traditional interests and policies, by entrenched bureaucracies, and moreover were self-selected, so to speak, to play by the rules of the game, charismatic figures such as Lenin and Hitler lead to a large extent *by force of their personality,* astonishingly unfettered by the usual limiting factors. It is naive to think that a life-history could explain why Hitler invaded the Rhineland exactly when he did; it is equally naive to believe that without a depth analysis of Hitler's anti-semitism, we can satisfactorily explain the intensity, and thus the nature, of his policy that led to the extermination of six million Jews. In short, life-history does not automatically offer us historical explanation; it merely raises in somewhat new terms the problem of historical explanation as we have always known it.

Life-history, then, to summarize, is a part of psycho-history that reintroduces the great man theme in history in a new and deeper sense; that promises us an addition to the sociology of knowledge, which I propose we call "psychology of knowledge"; that makes the historian look much more carefully at the previously unconscious part of himself and his choice of subject; that leads him either to new materials, or to reinterpretation of familiar ones; and, lastly, that promises no "final" historical explanations, but only deeper, more complicated problems of historical interpretation. If, however, as E. H. Carr suggests, history is a matter of human *meaning,* then life-histories certainly make the story of our past much more *meaningful.*

IV

Nevertheless, in spite of all the contributions, and more, that I have suggested for life-histories, even those historians who are persuaded of its virtues seek something additional from psycho-history. We historians are most used to working with large groups of men, with social institutions, and with mass events. Can psycho-history help us in these matters? There is a serious challenge posed to Eriksonian life-history in the comments of Clifford Geertz. In a review of *Gandhi's Truth,* he said of Gandhi,

> In attempting again and again to re-enact this family drama [in the 1918 strike] on the national stage his career revealed both the intrinsic power of attraction that a view of politics as a process of inward change possesses—its ability to move men—and its radical inability, having moved them, to deal with the issues—whether workers' wages or the threat of Partition—thereby raised. The contrast which appeared already at Ahmedabad between Gandhi's extraordinary ability to shape the personal lives of those immediately around him and his inability to control the direction of the strike as a collective act grew greater and greater as he extended himself across India and into larger and larger mass settings. . . . Nehru was wrong. Gandhi did not psycho-analyse India, he (though of course not alone) politicized it; and having politicized it could not . . . in the end control it.[6]

In part, I believe, Geertz is wrong: Gandhi *did* psycho-analyse India, i.e., understand part of its psyche, which was why he was able to politicize it. And Erikson brilliantly shows us *how* Gandhi's own psychological development fitted with India's, so that he was able to politicize it. Geertz is right, however, when he says that Gandhi could not then control his politicized subject. Why not? First, because as with an individual patient in therapy, one can understand the unconscious dynamics and still not always be able to control, i.e., cure them. Second, because our psychological understanding of a "collective act," of "mass settings" is embryonic, to say the least, even in comparison to life-histories, themselves in their infancy. And last, because in the very nature of the subject, psycho-history, like history in general, may be mainly, if not completely, restricted to retrodiction rather than prediction, and thus control.

The desire to understand, psycho-historically, collective acts and mass settings—which I shall henceforth call group history—is, then, primarily an intellectual yearning for deeper understanding of past events, and only incidentally, and hopefully, a wish for greater control over them. Only after we have a satisfactory theory of group history might we turn to the problem of using such knowledge in the future. Our immediate problem, needless to say, is to develop such knowledge. In what follows, I shall suggest certain probes in this direction.

V

The family, potentially, is where psychological and sociological theories can best intersect. It can serve as a mid-point between life-history and group history. In doing a life-history, we can analyze relations in an individual family, e.g., Hitler's family. In working towards group history, we can analyze "the German family," as an ideal type or model family. Obviously, the individual family, e.g., Hitler's, its typicality and uniqueness, can only be understood in terms of our understanding of the model family, e.g., the German; and vice versa.

The family is, additionally, of crucial importance in working towards group history because it establishes the nuclear social and psychological relations from which all others spring.[7] Loving and hating, giving and receiving, obeying and commanding, controlling and being controlled all take their origin here. By transference, they become the basic patterns on which are erected such abstract political problems as Authority, Liberty, Equality, and so forth. *How* the transferences take place, and *in what ways* they are shaped by social, political, and economic forces, for example, is an empirical question. Until now, the key approaches to these problems have been in terms of child-rearing practices and socialization processes; and it is these that psycho-historians, along with social anthropologists and social psychologists, have attempted to study.

So far, I have talked of the family and its nuclear relations, as if this were a "given," affecting history but not affected by it. Clearly, this is not so. The very structure of the family is historically shaped. Its size may be the result of religious beliefs, or economic changes, or war, or demographic shifts. Its authority structure may be affected by a French Revolution and by a Napoleonic Code; its tasks by the provision of public education, by a change from rural to urban settings. New medical knowledge can affect the procreation of children and the way in which they are reared. And so forth. All of these changes, in turn, interact and correspond with changes in the personality formation of members of the family.

What does psycho-analysis offer in this setting? It claims to call our attention to certain recurrent and universal features of *all* familial situations: infantile sexuality, and the ways in which these drives are allowed expression or given repression, and then encouraged to develop in mature forms; the Oedipal relations in particular, and the means by which it is resolved; the toilet training of the child, and the manner in which control over his own movements and eventually over himself and others is permitted to the infant, and attitudes towards what is clean and what is dirty inculcated in him—these and numerous other aspects that then underlay the entire political and social structure of group behavior are first played out and trained for in the family.

Once again, these aspects are themselves historically affected. To take merely one example: the Oedipus complex. Not only is this strongly influenced by the particular family structure, laid down by history, whereby a South Italian family differs from a North American one, but its very elements are affected by historic forces.[8] Thus, puberty is the stage for the reawakened Oedipal feelings; but puberty may emerge in different societies and historical periods at an earlier or later time, dependent, for example, on diet. For instance, one of the striking facts of our time is that the onset of menstruation for girls, say, in America, is now, on the average, at age 13; whereas in the seventeenth century it is estimated to have been at 16 (we can assume comparable changes for boys)! It does not take much imagination to realize that the Oedipal struggle can take on a different outcome and perhaps have a different meaning when it occurs in conjunction with the young person being in different work, educational, or emotional situations. Even more important, as we shall touch on later, is the setting of an Oepidal, i.e., a generational conflict, in a time of rapid economic and technological change.

In the psycho-historic understanding of the family, sociology is as important as psychology. To speak of a model family is probably nonsense. Child-rearing practices, for example, seem to differ drastically among different classes in society. So do sex and marital attitudes. Rural and urban, working and middle class (not to mention upper class), Northern and Southern family practices, and their possible admixtures, vary greatly one from another. And, to further complicate our study, they do so over time, i.e., each one changes in various historic periods.

In spite of the complexity of studying the family psycho-historically, and I have only touched on a few of the problems, progress has been made, and more, much more is promised. The psychological theory appears to be at hand, and the historical materials available for the diligent searcher (e.g., one may have to use the iconography of paintings in order to understand some of the attitudes to children in the fifteenth century). There seem to be no insurmountable methodological problems, though the work will be hard and long. Philippe Ariès has shown what can be done in his *Centuries of Childhood.*[9] While its use of psycho-history is low-keyed and implied, even hostile, rather than explicit, and its validity now under question, its heuristic value is unquestionable. Thus, it has stirred a young American historian, David Hunt, both to test the universality of Erikson's theory of developmental stages and to re-examine Ariès's theses, to the advantage of the former and the disadvantage of the latter, in his book *Parents and Children in History: The Psychology of Family Life in Early Modern France.*[10] More recently (March 1970) a conference on "Childhood and Youth in

History," held at Clark University (scene of Freud's initial public triumph in America, in 1909), produced an astounding number of stimulating and provocative papers: on Puritan child-rearing customs; on youth and identity in the Great Awakening (*c.* 1720 in America); on "discovery" of childhood and youth in nineteenth-century America; on the crisis of modern youth and the modern family in historical perspective; and so forth.

If the family can be considered the transmission belt between the individual and society, then, as studies such as those just mentioned above show, we are at least beginning to try to understand the precise mechanism involved; and to do so in psycho-historic terms. Such studies are of critical importance in themselves as well as the indispensable basis for all further work in psycho-history, both of life-histories and group history. They are essential, and, fortunately, feasible. Individually, they are joined to demographic, sociological, and economic history. They promise much. Yet when all is said and done, I suspect that they will not supply the key to the lock of group history which still stands as our outstanding problem in psycho-history. Family history, so to speak, merely indicates the door through which we must enter.

VI

Back in 1958, before the bulk of Erikson's work and before the interest in family history, William Langer gave his famous Presidential address, "The Next Assignment," to the American Historical Association.[11] He suggested that what we needed was "elaboration of a theory to bridge the gap between individual and collective psychology." "As historians," he challenged us, "we must be particularly concerned with the problem whether major changes in the psychology of a society or culture can be traced, even in part, to some severe trauma suffered in common. That is, with the question whether whole communities, like individuals, can be profoundly affected by some shattering experience."[12] As his example, Langer took the Black Death and described some of its characteristic effects.

> The age was marked by a mood of misery, depression, and anxiety, and by a general sense of impending doom. Numerous writers . . . have commented on the morbid preoccupation with death, the macabre interest in tombs, the gruesome predilection for the human corpse . . . But the most striking feature of the age was an exceptionally strong sense of guilt and a truly dreadful fear of retribution, seeking expression in a passionate longing for effective intercession, and in a craving for direct, personal experience of the

> Deity, as well as in corresponding dissatisfaction with the Church and with the mechanization of the means of salvation as reflected, for example, in the traffic in indulgences.

Langer concludes this description by turning to Freud, and paraphrases the latter's theory that "disaster and death threatening the entire community will bring on a mass emotional disturbance, based on a feeling of helpless exposure, disorientation, and common guilt."

With a few changes in content and emphasis, how contemporary this all sounds! We shall see just how contemporary it is a little later, when I shall deal with our twentieth-century fears of destruction and genocide as my particular example of group history. Here, however, let us look more closely at the methodological problems raised by Langer. He talks of a communal "shattering experience," of a "mood," and of a "general sense of impending doom." How does one establish the existence of a "mood"? What sorts of materials does one use to prove that an experience was "in common" and "shattering"? What kind of sample is necessary to serve as acceptable evidence for a "general sense" of doom?

Time and space do not allow me to enter into an extended discussion of such problems. They are, fortunately, not unfamiliar; indeed, they are the staple questions asked by all intellectual historians, who speak of "moods" and "spirits" in friendly ambiguity. It goes without saying that both psychologists and intellectual historians are well advised to root their "moods" and "spirits" in specific social strata, where possible, e.g., the Russian peasantry did not share the "mood" of the Russian intelligentsia in the nineteenth century, as well as to press home the question whether their sample is illustrative of a "cutting edge" of thought and feeling, or representative of a broad mass of opinion. And so forth.

Here, I shall take for granted that the group historian will face all the problems confronting intellectual historians—perhaps more—but will eventually be able to establish the existence of his "mood." (Parenthetically, I shall be prepared to allow for a large measure of initial "intuition" in this procedure.) What are the consequences for psycho-history? In the first place, it means that instead of working from an individual, a great man, out to the psychological history of a period, we move the other way, and go from the general mood, or *Geist,* back to ordinary individuals. In the second place, though building on the theories of individual psychology and life-history, as well as family history, we need to bring these into a correspondence with newly developed theories of collective psychology and group history. Alas, I make only small pretense to knowing exactly how this should be done; we must stumble towards our results.

My example will be our twentieth-century fears of destruction and genocide, expressed most poignantly by our youth, or rather by a selected group of students among them. The evidence, it seems to me, is quite clear. My own students, for example, especially the more radical among them, talk incessantly about the impending doom of the human race. Ten years, they tell me, is all we have left as a species. Initially, what they have in mind is nuclear destruction. And in this vision of apocalypse, they have had prophets among their elders, such as C. P. Snow and many others in the scientific community. More recently, the voices warning of ecological destruction—by pollution and over-population—have also risen in chorus, to remind the young that even if they escape the Bomb they will be overwhelmed by another disaster in, say, twenty years.

Now, my personal evidence, I believe, is abundantly supported by public data. Thus, a copy of the Harvard undergraduate newspaper, *The Crimson*, last year had headlines proclaiming the inevitable and unavoidable end of the world in ten years. To take another example, Tom Hayden, one of the founders of SDS, was speaking for many of his followers when he said, "Our work is guided by the sense that we may be the last generation in the experiment with living." Additional such evidence is easily available, and I shall take the point as proven.

Is there a "severe trauma suffered in common" behind such fears of destruction? Have they been raised to the level of fantasies of destruction? Or joined hands with such fantasies? And what are the effects of such fears and fantasies? The first question is easy to answer; the others enormously difficult. The dropping of the first Atomic Bomb, on Hiroshima, in my judgment, has had a delayed spreading effect, psychologically as well as physically; indeed, more so. Physical poisoning from the Bomb frequently manifested itself only months and months later, and then death followed thereafter. The psychological poisoning, if I may use that phrase, has taken years to manifest its true virulence and is still with us.

Most of us who were young, or adult, back in 1945 have blocked or numbed the terrible threat contained in the Bomb.[13] Else we could not go on living stable lives. Moreover, coming as it did in response to the grotesque horrors of World War II, alas, displaced from the Nazis onto the Japanese, the Bomb seemed to many a "good thing," "justified." In fact, it could be thought of as "saving" lives (American and Allied, of course), as "preserving" the "way of life" that alone was worth living.

The young of today cannot react in this way. From the day they were born, the ominous mushroom cloud has hung over their cradle. Strontium 90 is in their bones. The world into which they entered had the smell of doom all about it. The "criminals" in all of this were their elders, and especially the scientists and technologists who had "perfected" the Bomb. Is it any wonder that these "latent" feelings, when called into play by the correct historical stimuli, should produce dramatic reactions?

I wish to call attention to three consequences of what I have just described. The first is the *feeling*, and not merely the intellectual awareness, among the young students that science and technology are not cornucopias producing beneficial progress but rather poisonous boxes spreading death and destruction. Our young radicals are all becoming Rousseaus, rejecting the "arts," that is, science and technology, in the name of a purer, simpler world.

The second consequence, as I have already noted, is that they feel their elders are the "criminals" responsible for this mess. In former times, apocalypse was tied to religious conceptions, and a Black Death was seen as God's punishment for man's evilness. Now, the threat of world destruction is perceived as coming directly from man's own hands, not God's. Thus, man is doubly guilty for his own impending doom. The young share in this double guilt to the extent that they go along with the "system," instead of actively opposing it—as they say, "If you are not part of the solution, you are part of the problem." In order to deny to themselves that the sins of the father are inherited by the sons, they must throw off completely any allegiance to their "criminal" elders.

The third consequence is that world destruction fears rapidly become associated with fantasies of genocide. In a different context, Norman Cohn, for example, has shown how fantasies concerning the wicked Elders of Zion worked themselves out as a belief in the genocidal tendencies of the Jews, which then became a warrant for the extermination of the latter. I suspect that something similar may be taking place with some of our more radical young with paranoiac tendencies (and I definitely do not intend this judgment to apply to the bulk of the moderate radicals).

Clearly, in this case, the fantasies take their cue from certain reality factors; it is the extent to which they depart from the reality that makes them into genocidal fantasies. Thus, for example, in America, radicals are inspired by the empathy for Blacks, and the fears of some of the latter that white America seeks not only to suppress or maltreat them, but to destroy them. The rhetoric of "The only good nigger is a dead nigger" used by a lunatic fringe of racists is matched by the Black Panther rhetoric of "The only good pig [that is, policeman] is a dead pig." White radicals then pick up this theme and perceive the older generation trying to destroy the young (identified, of course, with the Blacks, since both are "oppressed" groups). It is, of course, mainly in the realm of the unconscious that a statement such as the following by Abbie Hoffman makes sense: "We present America with her most difficult problem. For America to burn innocent countries abroad is no problem, for America to commit genocide on the blacks that live in her cellar is no problem, for America to kill her children, that is her most difficult problem." Anyone who has seen the recent American movie *Easy Rider* will realize that Hoffman's genocidal fantasies are not unique to him, but represent a pervasive, conscious as well as unconscious, feeling among the radical young. Behind this feeling, of course, in the American case, is the reality of the Vietnam War, which seems to confirm the belief that the older generation, who alone make the decision to wage the war, are waging a genocidal war, "destroying" both their own children and the people of Vietnam.

Let me pause for a summary at this point. My thesis has been that, as Langer suggested, there is a "severe trauma suffered in common" in our time. The trauma originated in the dropping of the Bomb. Spreading out from that moment, a pervasive sense of doom and destruction has hovered over mankind, manifesting itself, as Freud claimed it would, in a "mass emotional disturbance, based on a feeling of helpless exposure, disorientation, and common guilt." I have also emphasized the feelings of incipient destruction, and their connection with the criminality of the older generation and the genocidal fantasies of the militant young. With this resaid, we can now tackle certain methodological considerations.

The first relates to the problem of evidence. Am I right that these feelings are widespread? That is a relatively simple problem to deal with, in ways to which historians are quite accustomed.

The next is far more difficult. How can we bring this "collective feeling" into touch with existing psychological theory? How can we "prove" that it is the Atomic Bomb that has given rise to the collective feeling? I can only hint at the starting point for an answer. We know that the individual, according to Freudian theory, has personal fantasies involving destruction of others and himself. These are intimately bound up with his feelings of aggression and violence (and, parenthetically, it is the aggressive impulses that occupy the center of psycho-analytic interest today, rather than, as in the nineteenth century, the libidinal impulses). Such feelings, although present in all of us, are made highly apparent in the fantasies of psychotics. One would expect that an analyst, treating patients (many of whom would be youths) normal and abnormal, might be able to tell us if the universal predisposition to destruction fantasies indeed takes on the particular shapes that I have indicated.

What of creative literature? Can the "fantasies" so richly supplied to us in them be further analyzed? Should the psycho-historian be trained in what my friend, Norman Holland, called the "Dynamics of Literary Response"? [14]

Another body of data exists. These are the studies of reactions to the assassination of a President, or to a natural disaster.[15] While they do not involve depth analysis, they do offer us empirical evidence, psychoanalytically informed, as to mass reactions to a particular, immediate event. Can such evidence supply indirect support for the sort of psychological linkages that I have been talking about? Would such previous studies justify new ones, directly designed to shed light on the validity of my thesis?

Any and all of these approaches, I suggest, must be explored; each and every one of them may fail us. Moreover, in moving from individual psycho-analysis to group psycho-analysis there is a special problem. Let me illustrate in terms of some work done on the character traits of young radicals, by Kenneth Keniston.[16] According to Keniston, the young radicals whom he was analyzing are inclined to, among other things, unusual emotional openness and ideological flexibility. Yet, experience by others with them in groups suggests that they are highly intolerant, yearning for total commitment, and closed to compromise or other views. How can this be (assuming both observations correct)? The answer seems to be that there is an alchemy involved in groups, which transmutes individual feeling into something different in the collective. Some sort of "contagion" seems to set in, some sort of "animal magnetism," which, in spite of the work of Freud, Le Bon and others more recent, we know very little about.

Ernst Simmel has given us an example of the sort of contagion about which I am talking in his analysis of anti-semitism, where he tells us of the way in which individual paranoiac fears are transmuted into vicious Jew-baiting in the presence of a group.[17] Now, I am suggesting that individual destruction fears are taking the specific form of genocidal fantasies, and, by the process of contagion, spreading into collective and common emotions which, when assembled in a group, have consequences beyond the original intentions, conscious or unconscious, of the individuals composing it. In the group, tolerant students give way to their destructive anxieties, and become fanatics.

Exactly how the contagion spreads brings us back to sociological theory and general history. Once again, I shall use my example of destruction fears among the young. My thesis has been that the present generation of the young are manifesting a severe reaction to the threat of annihilation posed by nuclear war. They are coloring their entire mental horizon with their fears. But who are these young? At this point, we must turn, for example, to demography and social structure. It is, obviously, not all the young, but only a small portion of them, who are students. Of this small proportion, even a smaller portion of them are radical; and are students in the advanced countries; and are in the advanced countries where politics are propitious (e.g., not in the Soviet Union).

How have they been able to exert such a force on public opinion, as we can well certify? The startling fact about "youth" (defined here as those between 15 and 29) is that, as a proportion of total population, they are only about half as large today in the advanced countries as at the time of the American and French Revolutions![18] Yet they exert an enormously disproportionate force. The reasons are partly as follows: a larger proportion of this proportion are now concentrated in the universities, where they stay for longer times than before; they are unusually independent, because of existing in an affluent society; they have been able, largely because of increased communications possibilities, to create a youth "culture," thus giving them a rallying point; and again because of communications, and all the factors previously mentioned, they are easily mobilizable for political ends.

It is only through demography and sociology—and I have only sketched the way these disciplines must be appealed to—that I would be able to establish the importance of my group—young students—as the carriers of my contagion. Not only do they affect one another, for the reasons given, but through the exposure of TV, movies, and other media they communicate their message to the rest of us in exponentially increasing doses.

At this point, too, I ought to refer back to family history. How were these young people reared and socialized in the family setting? We have all heard about permissive parents. Did these parents over-restrain their own aggressive and violent feelings, while conveying to their children their repressed fears of a world about to destroy them all? What attitudes to authority were conveyed? Is father merely a "buddy" to his children, and thus the way paved for peer group relations as the only meaningful ones? Is liberty a form of license in the modern family? And, looking ahead, what sorts of feelings and attitudes will the present generation of young convey to *their* children?

Now, it would be the height of absurdity to pretend any of the following: that this anxiety was transmitted solely through the family; that other factors than the Atomic Bomb and the ecological danger do not also animate this anxiety—indeed, with more time, I would try to show that it is "over-determined," that is, determined from many other sources as well; that abundant reality factors for the fears do not exist; and perhaps most important, that much good may not also emerge from the upheavals forced upon us by student radicals. I have chosen to ignore such matters here because I am concerned with using one small part—youthful fantasies of genocide and destruction—of our present mood and problems as my proving ground for certain thoughts on the possibilities of group history.

This small part presumably takes on general historical importance when, for example, it justifies student extremists in using any means to try and change the situation which, as they see it, gives rise to their anxieties. Many of them have said to me: since the world will be destroyed anyway ten years from now if we do not change its direction, any action, no matter how violent and destructive, is justified. Arson, bombings, riots, and ultimately urban guerrilla warfare all become part of the historical record as a result, in large part, of such a feeling. It may be that even larger such events will follow. In short, my particular collective fantasy, as with the choice of a Lenin or Hitler as a topic, "matters" as a part of historical explanation. How, exactly, it matters is a problem that, as a psycho-historian, I would be expected to work out in greater detail if I were to choose it as a major subject rather than merely as an example.

As an example, however, let me summarize what I hope it has accomplished. It has allowed us to see that, in principle at least, we can start from a common psychic convulsion and work back to the individuals who comprise the group manifesting it. The particular group, of course, must be carefully identified by appealing to related disciplines, such as sociology. Group moods are not the sum of individual fears and fantasies but take on a life and character of their own. One need only look at small children to see how powerful in man are the forces of imitation, suggestibility, and transference. These forces produce the group convulsion.

What sorts of collective psychological moods can best be studied in group history? I took, as one example, fears of death and destruction among our present young. Another scholar, Lucian Pye, recently has taken the role of hate in Chinese society.[19] Feelings about aggression and violence in different societies and periods might profitably be studied. In short, all of the basic Freudian mechanisms can themselves be analyzed in terms of specific historical contexts. Naturally, in group history, the "symptoms" must be manifested by an identifiable group, and related to particular historical occurrences. In this way, then, historians can begin responsibly to discharge themselves of Langer's assignment.

VII

Group history, family history, life history: these are new dominions in Clio's empire. As yet, relatively unexplored, they need conquistadores of the historic spirit to explore and help settle them. Such imperialism, I hope, is acceptable, even in today's atmosphere, for we seek to conquer only knowledge. This knowledge for which we seek is of ourselves, and the ways in which we behave as historical creatures. A significant part of that knowledge, I have suggested, is best sought in terms of psycho-history, or what I have preferred to call psycho-social history. Perhaps it is such knowledge that will help in eliminating other forms of conquest. In any case, I believe that we must press on, in whatever time is left us—and here at last I show my own anxieties—in the effort to understand the strange kind of being we call the human; that is to say that animal of the planet Earth who characteristically is at one and the same time historical and psychological in nature.

Notes

1. Karl Jaspers, *Psychopathologie générale,* French translation by Kastler and Mendousse, quoted in Franz Fanon, *Black Skin, White Masks,* translated by Charles Lam Markmann (New York, 1967), pp. 168–69. Cf. Michael Polanyi, *Personal Knowledge* (London, 1958).

2. For a further instance of Erikson's efforts to establish the historian's self-knowledge, see Erik H. Erikson, "On the Nature of Psycho-Historical Evidence: In Search of Gandhi," *Daedalus* (Summer, 1968).

3. Erik H. Erikson, *Gandhi's Truth* (New York, 1969), pp. 50-51. This particular instance should remind us that evidence and inference in psycho-history are, necessarily, defined by the needs and theoretical concepts of the discipline itself. A datum may be evidence for a psycho-historian that would quickly be passed over by the general historian as of no value. Similarly, inferences from a range of evidence may be sound or untenable in terms only of a given psycho-analytic theory; obviously, only a historian conversant with the latter is able properly to judge the particular inference. (Of course, this still leaves entirely open the question as to whether the particular psycho-analytic theory, or indeed any and all such theories, is itself acceptable and valid.)

4. For these matters, and/or a discussion of them, see *Psychoanalysis and History*, ed. Bruce Mazlish (Englewood Cliffs, New Jersey, 1963). (A new version of this volume is being prepared.)

5. For a tentative effort in this direction, see, for example, Erik H. Erikson, "The Legend of Hitler's Childhood," in *Childhood and Society* (New York, 1963). Some of the straightforward historical material that might be used in

such a psycho-historical study can be found in Bradley F. Smith, *Adolf Hitler: His Family, Childhood and Youth* (Stanford University, 1967).

6. *New York Review of Books* (20 November 1969), p. 4.

7. Of course, other than "family" arrangements can be made by a society to socialize and bring up its young. In some societies, kinship groupings or communal nurseries may hold the commanding role in these processes. However, for most of Western, and certainly modern, history, the family may be generally assumed to be the key unit in establishing the nuclear social and psychological relations with which psycho-history is concerned.

8. For a splendid exemplification of this point, see Anne Parsons, "Is the Oedipus Complex Universal? The Jones-Malinowski Debate Revisited and a South Italian 'Nuclear Complex'," *The Psychoanalytic Study of Society*, iii (1964).

9. Translated from the French by Robert Baldick (New York, 1962).

10. New York, 1970.

11. Langer's address is reprinted in *Psychoanalysis and History*, ed. Mazlish.

12. Parenthetically, one might note that Freud himself, and psycho-analytic theory after him, later began to underplay the entire notion of trauma as an explanatory device.

13. For one examination of ways of dealing with feelings about death and survival, see Robert Jay Lifton, *Death in Life: Survivors of Hiroshima* (New York, 1967).

14. See Norman N. Holland, *The Dynamics of Literary Response* (New York, 1968).

15. See, for example, some of the essays in *Children and the Death of a President*, ed. Martha Wolfenstein and Gilbert Kliman (New York, 1966), and *The Threat of Impending Disaster*, ed. George H. Grosser, Henry Wechsler and Milton Greenblatt (Cambridge, Mass., 1964).

16. Kenneth Keniston, *Young Radicals* (New York, 1968).

17. See Ernst Simmel, "Anti-Semitism and Mass Psychopathology" in *Anti-Semitism: a Social Disease*, ed. E. Simmel (New York, 1946) and the valuable discussion on this point in Norman Cohn's chapter, "Case-Study in Collective Psychopathology," in his excellent book, *Warrant for Genocide* (New York, 1969).

18. For an interesting study of the demographic and social situation of modern youth, see Herbert Moller, "Youth as a Force in the Modern World," *Comparative Studies in Society and History* x. 3 (April 1968).

19. Lucian W. Pye, *The Spirit of Chinese Politics* (Cambridge, Mass., 1968).

2

The Use and Abuse of Psychology in History

FRANK E. MANUEL

This essay has become a standard reference in the contemporary literature on psychohistory because it accomplishes two significant objectives for serious students. First, the author provides a quite detailed discussion of the more remote, pre-Freudian origins of psychohistory. In this connection, he not only mentions the ancient Greek forebears of all social science, but also focuses on the lesser-known French psychologizing historical tradition—a line of scholarship extending from Michelet through Lefebre and Foucault. Furthermore, in his discussion of the German idealist tradition he succinctly evaluates the significance for history of Wilhelm Dilthey's phenomenological psychology.

Manuel shows that, contrary to the beliefs of many scholars, these traditions are not opposed to modern Freudian thought. In fact, the latent similarities are most impressive.

The second achievement of this essay is to bring forward for careful discussion the critical reservations that thoughtful scholars have expressed about psychohistory. Paying special attention to the work of Erikson, Manuel addresses these criticisms forthrightly and sensibly, offering a summary perspective that has proven itself to be of real value to current efforts in psychohistory.

Almost a century ago Friedrich Nietzsche, that history-intoxicated son of the German philological school, delivered a tirade against the hypertrophy of history in the life of his times. In appropriating the title

From *Daedalus*, Journal of the American Academy of Arts and Sciences, Boston, Massachusetts (Winter 1971, *Historical Studies Today*), 187-213. Reprinted by permission.

An earlier version of this essay was presented as the Rabbi Irving M. Levey Lecture at Princeton University, April 29, 1970.

of his essay, I confess to a similar ambivalence respecting the modern uses of psychology in historical studies. After some years of history-writing I have begun to fear that I may be losing my way in the jungles of psychologism. In my predicament I could of course appeal to the analytical philosophers and ask them to enlighten me about the implicit assumptions of my work; but having read their interpretations of the writings of my colleagues I am obdurately resistant. Instead, I shall seek a way out of my perplexity by hearkening to the advice of Alfred North Whitehead, who once said that when a man is lost, he should not ask where *he* is, but where the *others* are. And so, advancing behind a chronological shield, I intend to locate myself by passing in critical review the experience of historians and psychologists whenever they have come into close proximity. After skimming over the eighteenth-century origin of their relationships, I shall concentrate on the last hundred years and even more especially on the recent period, when both disciplines have become mammoth academic enterprises, whose cohabitation, some might say, is doomed to sterility from the outset, like the improbable mating of a whale and an elephant. What my presentation lacks in depth and subtlety, I hope it may achieve in breadth. Perhaps at the end I may find a place for myself, and, who knows, others might be willing to join me even if it means standing midstream in rather shallow waters.

My level of discourse will not be hard-nosed and analytical but descriptive of the goals and achievements of those who sensed the rich potentialities of a new field of expression and proceeded to cultivate it. Men have been prospecting for a long time in this region, and I am less interested in the scientific theories they brought with them than in what they have carried back from their expeditions. Though I have not made an actual body count, I suspect that of late there has been more hortatory exposition of what might or should be done than perspective on what has in fact been going on. Commenting on the topos, on the content, of psychological history-writing may prove more illuminating than either dissecting benighted historians who enjoy the *Narrenfreiheit* of blithely going their narrative way, or issuing manifestos on what would constitute a perfect psychological history.

In the past three centuries major attempts have been made to recover not only the written thoughts of men of other times but their thinking; not only the record of their actions but the secret purposes and hidden, even unconscious, feelings that spurred and accompanied the *res gestae;* not only the literary and artistic objects but the sensibility that was expressed and the emotions aroused in the creators as well as in their contemporary audiences. When there are Pyrrhonists about who question the veracity of recorded history in its most commonsensical usage, how must they regard an undertaking that presumes to re-create inner experiences, which do not usually manifest themselves in clear-cut fashion through specific and forthright documents! And yet this is what psychological history has self-confidently set out to do. Admittedly, this wild intention has always been a minor element in historical narrative since the first Persian chronicles, echoed in the Book of Esther, where we are told what a personage "speaks in his heart." Greek and Roman historians used a variety of devices to disclose the secret purposes and unfulfilled desires animating their protagonists; and the Renaissance historians who imitated them availed themselves of a rich psychological vocabulary in describing the wellsprings of human conduct. It is only since the early eighteenth century, however, that some historians have committed themselves to making the re-creation of inner experience the core of their work, shifting the focus from the deed to the psychic events that transpired in the doer.

I

More and more I see in Giambattista Vico, that lone Italian who lived in Naples from 1668 to 1744, the bold conceptualizer of this novel form of historical consciousness. In its exterior aspect his *Scienza Nuova* was a rather conventional theology of history with a cyclical pattern. But if we look beyond the structure, we are amazed to find that he wrote of "tre spezie di natura," three kinds of human nature, and postulated that in each stage of a *ricorso* men had quintessentially different modes of perceiving reality, that not only the physical conditions but the feeling tone of existence was profoundly different in each one, that the very capacity for expression assumed radically different shapes: signs and emblems at one time the only way for mute humans to externalize feelings; poetry the only speech of barbaric men; and not until the rational epoch the voice of reason in prose. Every stage in the cycle was marked by its own balance between rational faculties and aggressive violence, between terror of death and a desire for convenience, between robust imagination and calculated punctiliousness. In sum, the nature of living—of thinking, feeling, and willing, the three traditional faculties—had undergone revolutions in time. And the changing quality of existence was discernible in the history of language, in literature and laws, and in visual arts like painting.

How was it possible for Vico, a man of the early eighteenth century, to interpret that evidence, to recapture the emotions and spirit of the age of heroic barbarism? His answer was that the cycle of history was imbedded in the human soul. Understanding of the transformations was possible because men in fact themselves lived through the whole of the cycle from primitivism to rationality in the course of their development from earliest infancy through adulthood. And all about in the world there remained vestiges of primitive mentality in savage countries and perhaps in the behavior of women.

The great French romantic historian of the next century, Jules Michelet, translated and commented on the works of Vico when they were hardly known in Western culture. Michelet's voluminous history of France can be conceived as an effort to explore the changing consciousness of Frenchmen in their thousand years of national life. His dramatization of the Renaissance as a new way of perceiving the world was an innovation in the uses of psychology in history entirely in the spirit of Vico's "New Science." By mid-nineteenth century Michelet had at his disposal more refined psychological tools, some inherited from the utilitarian tradition of the Enlightenment, others derived from the works of Jean-Jacques, that great revealer of the previous age, who had made himself transparent and bared his own complex private world as a model for every man.

In the latter part of the eighteenth century the Germans had a parallel to Vico in Herder, who imagined that through the course of world history an infinite number of human aggregates would be fashioned in isolation by the physical and climatic conditions of their living-space and that each one, in a totally unique way, would forge for itself an idiosyncratic balance of sense perceptions which no other *Volk* could imitate. This *Volk*-genius was early embodied in a mythology, a religion, a poetry, in short a *Volk* culture, within the confines of which men of that *Volk* were forever fixed. In the later efflorescence of a culture, elements of reason might appear, but for all time every work of literature, art, and music was in its essence a reflection of the primitive, affective *Volk* psyche. Herder's universe pullulated with *Volk* cultures at different stages in their life-cycles; and though he made feeble efforts to establish connexities among them in an overriding concept of *Humanität*, he was the founder of a particular type of German historicism that emphasized the search for concrete psychological "specificity"—the word is his friend Goethe's—in time and place. For both Vico and Herder the nature of things was hidden in the emotional differences among human collectives.

Hegel's contribution to psychological history does not, in my judgment, lie primarily in his characterization of the stages in the history of spirit, but rather in his power to grasp and present the phenomenological fullness of crucial human relationships—for example, his insightful diagnosis of the contrarieties of the master-slave bond, and his depiction of *Entfremdung*, alienation, which was passed on to Marx and Kierkegaard and has since been inflated as the central psychological distinction of modern consciousness.

II

In the last decades of the nineteenth century, there was a substantive discontinuity in the history of psychological history, a breakthrough. Psychology began to achieve a measure of recognition as an autonomous science in the German academic world. Though it had had a long literary and philosophical past—the name itself was invented by Rudolf Goclenius of Marburg in the sixteenth century—when psychology first appeared as an independent form of knowledge at the university it underwent a crisis of adolescence. What was it? A physical science in quest of uniformities? Or did it belong to humanist studies and could it be subsumed under history? Almost simultaneously with the rise of experimental psychology, new schools of psychiatry were founded, and the unconscious itself was baptized around the 1880s. This date then becomes a convenient starting-point for taking a prospect of the modern relationship of history and psychology.

In the German and French schools there were two early significant moves in the direction of fusing these disciplines, the older one under Wilhelm Dilthey, born in 1833, and another under Lucien Febvre, born in 1878. Dilthey's first important writing was published in 1883, and twenty-five years later he was still at work on a critique of historical reason, some fragments of which appeared posthumously after World War I.[1] A professor of philosophy in Berlin, he strongly influenced Troeltsch and Meinecke, Heidegger, and a whole generation of German academic historians of ideas. He even left his mark on Spengler, who would have spurned any identification with him. Lucien Febvre ultimately became a professor at the College de France and one of the founders of *Annales*, a journal that was to propagate his ideas. Though both Dilthey and Febvre were dedicated to exploring the relationship of psychology and history, they were virtually unaware of each other's existence, separated as were their intellectual worlds by a generation gap and by the then insuperable barrier of the Rhine. And they meant rather different things by psychology. Both, of course, were totally untouched by such outrageous novelties as the doctrines of their contemporary, Sigmund Freud. As for the historical forays of Freud himself and his immediate disciples, they rarely came within the purview of the academic historians of any country at this period. (Preserved Smith, of Cornell University, was one of the exceptions.) Dilthey and Febvre represent two different versions of an initial stage in the emergence of psychological history in recent times.

Though Dilthey's testament remains unfinished, his essays on the towering figures of western European thought, above all his Schleiermacher and his young Hegel, leave no doubt about his purposes.[2] He would have had all studies of man absorbed into intellectual history and would have allowed no independent status to either psychology or sociology. Rejecting the feasibility of any connected world history in a traditional sense and scornful of the Rankean state as the primary object of historical knowledge, Dilthey was convinced that the history of man could best be presented as a series of psychological world outlooks, more significantly emotive than rationalist, embodied mainly in the writings of literary, religious, and philosophical geniuses. For all his ambition to seize the essence—in a phenomenological sense—of entire ages and to interrelate economico-social and philosophico-religious trends, he always seemed most comfortable with biographical studies of creative men in whom he saw the various psychic currents of an age criss-cross and ultimately assume a manageable structure. His heroic figures are vessels for the dominant passions, cosmic attitudes, and deep-rooted beliefs of a whole epoch. Through the study of the historical varieties of human psychic experience he found an affirmation of freedom, an emancipation from dogmatism, a humanist deliverance. Though he belittled Nietzsche, it is now easy to recognize that with a far less arresting rhetoric and with none of Nietzsche's moral fervor, Dilthey was developing a parallel conception of monumental world personages the expression of whose spiritual, form-imprinting natures was the stuff of history. Resurrecting and consorting with these overmen was virtually the sole justification for historical knowledge.

Rarely, if ever, did Dilthey descend from the heights of exalted intellectual history sprinkled with affects. In theory he was committed to relating the individual psychological natures of his heroes with the grand world outlooks which they had evolved, to lay before us the fullness of his subject's lived experience. But it is always lived experience as a closeted Wilhelmine professor of philosophy conceived it. His histories are elitist dramas of the passions of great men's souls. Dilthey studied the manuscripts of his protagonists and provided us with glimpses of their social status, of their intellectual friendships, occasionally of a great love. Their search for God is always apprehended with a deep sympathy and understanding of the intricacies of the Western religious tradition. But nothing below the navel was mentionable. Economic and social reality may penetrate his narrative, but only as part of a world-view, and political revolutions are quickly transformed into abstract ideas. Incapable of grappling with total psychic breakdown, when confronted by Hölderlin's madness Dilthey dissolves into utter banality and depicts the dying poet as sitting in

Tübingen, his mind "wandering, wandering."[3] If this is *Erlebnis,* it is the *Erlebnis* of soap opera. On the other hand, the nuanced description of Schleiermacher's religious experience attains universality. Dilthey was aware of the depths of the unconscious, but for him it was accessible only in the form of an artistic creation.

Dilthey has testified to the impression made upon him by Hüsserl's phenomenology, and in his turn Heidegger in *Sein und Zeit,* which historicized the categories of cognition, described his view of the historical world as dependent on the philosophical implications of Dilthey's writings. To the extent that pure intellectual biography is still being written and there are still attempts to present *Weltanschauungen* in literary psychological terms, Dilthey endures as a living if limited influence. Karl Jaspers, who began his career as a student of psychiatry as practiced in Germany in the first decade of the twentieth century, untouched by Freud, was less restrictive in his studies of Swedenborg, Hölderlin, Strindberg, and Van Gogh, in which he combined a phenomenological psychology with an attempt to communicate the varieties of world historical outlooks.[4] His pathographies were even intended to show the neurotic drives of his characters as allies in their creative achievements, an insight which Freudian psychohistorians have sometimes claimed as their unique discovery. But when he sought to encompass the whole psychic universe in his *Psychologie der Weltanschauungen* of 1919, a work that caused quite a stir in its day, his typologizing remained on the same intellectualist plane as Dilthey's.[5]

The French historical tradition since Michelet has been rich in the study of religious and other forms of emotional expression; but it was not until Lucien Febvre that a declaration was made on the centrality of *histoire psychologique.* Febvre summoned his colleagues to devote themselves to histories of *mentalité* and *sensibilité.* I would loosely translate *mentalité* in this context as what was "thinkable" in a human collective at a given moment of time. While the Germans tended to be impressionistic in their psychological portraits, Febvre insisted on great technical, one might say positivistic, rigor.

The heritage he bequeathed is nonetheless problematic. After we have been assured in the opening of his *Luther* that the underlying preoccupation of his study was the relationship between the individual and the mass, between personal initiative and public necessity, we are left dangling. Whether or not one agrees with the conclusions of Erikson's *Luther,* published as a study in psychohistory thirty years later, it does propose answers to the initial query set by Febvre, whose *histoire psychologique* flatly refused to engage with what he dismissed as the hypothetical Luther of the youthful period. "Let us frankly abandon the effort to reconstruct Luther's early surroundings; their effect on his ideas and sentiments could never be estimated. . . . It is better even to hold out against the seductions of the psychoanalysts for whose taste no theory is too facile. . . . A Freudian Luther is so easy to imagine that one feels not the least curiosity or wish to prosecute the acquaintance when an investigator undertakes to delineate him. For, in fact, might one not with an equal facility conjure up a Lutheran Freud, and observe how completely the illustrious father of psychoanalysis exemplifies permanent traits of the German national genius, of which Luther in his day was so notable an exponent?"[6] This is the voice of a French nationalist of the twentieth century, relying on a fatuous, *ad hominem* argument against Freud, with whose writings he had only the most casual acquaintance.

Febvre's *Rabelais* is the work in which his particular skill in communicating what another epoch "willed, felt, and thought" established the school's prototype of *histoire psychologique*, its virtues as well as its limitations. When Febvre concentrated upon an interpretation of his subject's religious beliefs, he was able to demonstrate with a plethora of empirical evidence that Rabelais' *plaisanteries courantes* and *malices d'Eglise* could be read as proof of atheism only by committing the historical sin of sins—anachronism.[7] Febvre moved in ever-extending circles to define the limits of what was thinkable and what could have been experienced in one's relationship to the supernatural in sixteenth-century Europe. Far from a herald of the new rationalism, Rabelais appears as a kind of Erasmian Christian, as do his giants. In passing, Febvre developed a character for the age in standard literary psychological terms, and he proposed the identification of the discrete elements of a collective historical psychology as the historian's primary mission. But the "mental structure" of the age is confined to the conscious level—the manifest content of ideas and beliefs, the style of their expression, where the line was drawn between the natural and the divine, or the intensity in the externalizing of emotion as compared with men of the twentieth century. In the world of the sixteenth he found imprecision, lack of historical awareness, absorption with the senses of smell and hearing rather than sight. This sort of workmanlike history of ideas and sensibility is still practiced in France both in the literary and in the historical faculties, and is yielding a steady flow of respectworthy Gargantuan dissertations on subjects like the idea of nature or of happiness in various epochs.

But Febvre pointed out one of the greatest obstacles in the way of any attempt to define the history of sensibility in a segment of past time. In the course of a review of Johan Huizinga's *Waning of the Middle Ages*, he asked skeptically whether in fact it could ever be determined that some periods were characterized by more love, fear, cruelty, or violence than others in their over-all feeling tone, and he cautioned against reading into other epochs a psychology derived from contemporary sensibility. How would it be possible, he wondered, to apply psychological models of the comfortable twentieth century to ages that knew endemic famine, awoke and went to sleep with the sun, suffered extremes of heat and cold as a norm. He mocked biographies of Pharaohs that were merely portrayals of moderns gotten up in the stage costumes of ancient Egyptians. Cooperative research in which historians and psychologists would be joined—and he referred to French academic psychologists like Dr. Henri Wallon—was the only safeguard he could propose against such follies. But though conscious of the pitfalls, Febvre held to the very end that capturing the unique *sensibilité* of a past age was the ultimate goal of the historian to which all his other efforts were subordinated. "It is true that to presume to reconstitute the emotive life of a given epoch is a task at once extraordinarily seductive and terrifyingly difficult. But what of it? The historian does not have the right to desert."[8] Stirring declamation, *de l'époque*.

One of Febvre's disciples, Robert Mandrou, who adheres to the pure tradition, spent years in the detailed study of the judicial aspects of witchcraft in seventeenth-century France, and has recently produced an exhaustive history to show the transformation in the mentality of the judges of the *Parlement* of Paris that made a belief in witchcraft, still acceptable to so sophisticated an intelligence as Jean Bodin's early in the century, virtually impossible by the end.[9] This is a classical, multifaceted diagnosis of an important change in the mentality of a ruling group and of the political, social, and scientific forces that effectuated the revolution. Mandrou is a superb craftsman, who does not presume to plumb lower depths. His methodology is positivistic and its conclusions hardly to be faulted, except for neglect of the general question—which may be the critical one for a historian with a psychological bent in 1970—of what the change signified on an unconscious psychic level. Recent American studies of white racism, perhaps an analogous phenomenon, which sometimes call themselves psychohistorical and may be pretentious and methodologically sloppy, nevertheless give an inkling of how a historian might explore collective obsessions related to excremental and oedipal fantasies.[10] Such ideas are untouchable in the purist French school of *histoire psychologique*, though there has been a growing intrusion of psychoanalytic concepts in recent issues of *Annales*.

When the elaborate outside scaffolding of Michel Foucault's theoretical model is stripped away, there still remain elements of

Febvre's original program in Foucault's brilliant and well-documented definitions of seventeenth- and eighteenth-century concepts of madness and reason, and perhaps even in his attempts, in *Les mots et les choses,* to grasp the content of mental structures of various epochs.[11] His analysis is more intricate and formally constructed, if less readily demonstrable, than Febvre's approach to a historical mentality. Freud, who belatedly made the scene in France after World War II, has forced Foucault's generation to peer into the underground recesses that were still forbidden to the previous one. Though I frequently lose Foucault along the way of his argument, I find his work the most exciting new event in French *histoire psychologique,* though not as unrelated to the original master of the school as might be imagined.

III

Apart from the continuation of the Dilthey and Febvre traditions, the years between the World Wars brought novelty in two important respects. First, a number of brilliant young Frenchmen of the Ecole Normale, military class of 1905, Raymond Aron and Jean-Paul Sartre among them, in the most daring intellectual adventure since Mme. de Stael's, traveled to faraway Berlin and submitted themselves to the influence of German sociology and the phenomenological philosophy. At about the same time, the advent of Hitler and a Jewish exodus from Central Europe brought to America men of the generation of around 1900 who had in various ways come within the orbit of Freud's doctrines. I refer to thinkers like Herbert Marcuse and Erik Erikson, not to speak of a large contingent of psychoanalysts who made the United States the world center of Freudian thought and practice. Then, in the loose, free-wheeling intellectual atmosphere of the post-World War II period in America, a host of theories were formulated with an intimate though problematic link to Freud. Marcuse tried to amalgamate a philosophical interpretation of Freudian texts—often excerpted ruthlessly without regard to the main body of the work—with a Marxist-Hegelian world-view that on the face of it is totally alien to Freud. Erikson, joining forces with Freudian ego psychologists, struck off in a truly new direction of psychological history, and in the sixties popularized the term "psychohistory." And in the same postwar period Sartre attempted a monumental syncretism in which phenomenological philosophy, Marxist dialectical materialism, and, of late, Freudian psychoanalysis—*quelle galère*—are made to lie together in existential unhappiness. His *Critique de la raison dialectique,* now a decade old, does not yet seem to have made a breach in the historical ramparts of either Europe or America.[12] In France a new generation of structuralists writes about him as if he has long since been, as they say, transcended; but the announcement of his demise is premature.

When Freud finally married the unconscious after the long flirtations conducted by other men (the *mot* is his), the ground was laid for a fundamental innovation in the employment of psychological concepts in history, though, as I have indicated, virtually no historian was aware of it at the time. The therapeutic technique devised by Freud resulted in the accumulation of literally hundreds of thousands of personal histories. Perhaps Erik Erikson exaggerated when he once said that in the twentieth century we have learned more about individual human development than in all previous ages put together; but the clinical histories have surely provided us both with new types of data and with a flood of material that are not of the same order as the literary and philosophical reflections of the past. After all, every classical analysis produces about 10,000,000 words that in some fashion reveal the inner life of a man. From now on out, human conduct can no longer be explained in terms of plain utilitarian motives, as it was by nineteenth-century writers, and even Augustinian churchmen are today willing to complicate the war of the two cities by adopting tactical suggestions on the ways of the devil from the great disbeliever.

Freud himself made a number of applications of psychoanalysis to history. Though he retained a certain diffidence, shying away from the interpretation of Descartes' famous dreams, for example,[13] at times he boldly ventured brief psychobiographical hypotheses about creative men, as in his essays on Leonardo and Dostoevsky, where paintings and novels were used as illustrative documents.[14] In this manner he could support his conceptions with objective materials that were public property and did not require disguise, as did his own self-analysis and the case histories of his patients. Aside from his interpretations of literary documents, he invented for us a macrohistorical myth on the origin of civilization; he advanced an extravagant psychological hypothesis about the beginnings of Jewish monotheism (he once called his *Moses and Monotheism* a "historical novel"[15]); and he interspersed his writings with analogies between primitive and neurotic behavior. The identification of phylogeny and ontogeny was axiomatic with Freud. The psychological history of civilized mankind probably did not differ substantively from one period to another. Wars and revolutions, whatever their genesis, could be viewed in general terms as changing opportunities for the manifestation of aggression. From time to time there were massive social outbursts against the excesses of instinctual repression in civilized society. But history as a whole meant only the recurrent, eternal conflict of Eros and death.

While Freud's historical essays were attacked for errors in detail, his analytic method of gaining access to the unconscious opened a vast new area to historical inquiry. The followers of Freud, in imitation of the master, but often without his reticence, or at least ambivalence, proliferated psychobiographies. In the beginning their efforts were devoted almost exclusively to the pathography of literary figures—an example would be Marie Bonaparte's *Poe*, which enjoyed the imprimatur of the master in a few introductory remarks.[16] The writings of poets and novelists lent themselves to plausible readings as symbolic representations of the inner states of their authors, their deep loves and hates, their longings and terrors. Fictional incidents were analyzed as disguised materials or fantasy wish-fulfillment of neurotic drives, all by analogy to the dream-work of patients. A similar method of symbolic interpretation was extended to painters by Ernst Kris, a psychoanalyst who was trained as an art historian, and to composers by Editha and Richard Sterba.[17] Except for obiter dicta, until very recently it has not been attempted with physical scientists—though some of us may be creeping up on them, casting doubt on the autonomous development of science itself. The effect of all this on historical evidence in the traditional sense is disconcerting, and sometimes constrains the more hide-bound professionals to avert their eyes from the glass, like the eminent contemporaries of Galileo. Henceforth the plainest affirmations in memoirs, dispatches, letters, and secret confessions may require intricate psychological interpretation in the light of the Freudian model. The unconscious demands a hearing and will not be silenced.

Though some psychoanalytic biographers formulated hypotheses about the nature of creativity as a universal phenomenon, in general their artistic subjects were approached as self-contained little monads sufficient unto themselves. This kind of discrete treatment was superseded, however, when political scientists and historians, trying to explain historical developments on the grand scale, applied Freudian personality theory to world-historical actors. An American professor of political science, Harold Lasswell, was one of the first to come up with a formula relating the individual and the collective, something to the effect that the great politician displaces private affects upon public objects.[18] The merit of the political studies has varied enormously; Woodrow Wilson has received a sophisticated treatment at the hands of Alexander and Juliette George and a vulgar one in William Bullitt's analysis, which Freud may or may not have approved.[19] Despite scandalous instances of overinterpretation, immense new vistas have been opened up on the behavior of the monumental figures of world history; and if one is repelled by the grossness of some analyses, one has only to look back on such pre-Freudian compilations as Augustin Cabanes' *Grands névropathes, malades immortels* to appreciate the enormous strides that have been taken.[20]

This, I believe, is the perspective from which to examine the work of Erik Erikson. With Erikson, who has written both programmatic statements and two biographical studies of politico-religious figures, the analytic method applied to history has received its most subtle exemplification.[21] Yet the basic problem raised by Lucien Febvre remains unresolved. We are obliged to ask: Is the ideal psychological model of human development in eight stages, constructed by Erikson, universally applicable? Is this not a summary of twentieth-century psychoanalytic experience, whose relevance to other cultures and periods is open to question?

Clearly, in epochs where the composition of the family, its spiritual and economic character, and life expectancy are very different from ours, definitions of the successive crises of life would have to vary. Erikson might say they would need modification. But a historian confronted, for example, with data on Florence 1426–1427 indicating that the average age differential of husband and wife was twenty years and that fathers died early in their children's lives could feel that in this instance the schema would have to undergo drastic alteration.[22] A historian may hold with Plato and Aristotle, Locke and Descartes, yes, and Freud and Erikson that the earliest experiences are far and away the most potent. (We remember Descartes' analysis of his predilection for cock-eyed girls based on an early fixation.) And he will surely welcome Erikson's shift from exclusive emphasis on infancy and the early family romance to a more extensive view of ego development including periods of life that are better documented and hence more accessible to historical treatment. But can he accept without debate the proliferation of later "crises" in the Eriksonian design, or Erikson's assignment of weight to each of eight crises? The historian should be warned that the selection of materials to fill the boxes of the eight stages may make of the schema a self-fulfilling prophecy. I find wholly credible the crises of adolescence and what early nineteenth-century psychiatrists like Philippe Pinel called the male climacteric, for these are vocal, articulate periods whose anguish is attested by cries and confessions. The rest of the eight stations of life appear rather arbitrary; the traditional divisions of the Church Fathers or Dante's four or Vincent de Beauvais' six may be quite enough. Before I can seriously evaluate the Eriksonian model as a historical tool, I feel that the history of the epigenetic cycle itself, diversified in time and place, needs to be written—and initial soundings in this direction have been made.[23] These reservations aside, however,

Erikson's stress upon the total epigenetic cycle, whatever its form, seems to me a permanent acquisition of historical consciousness.

In the two studies of men he calls politico-religious geniuses, Luther and Gandhi, Erikson found a motive drive to heroic action in the need of the sons to outstrip their fathers and compensate for their failures. When he generalizes these conjectures about a small and special sample to all geniuses, he is speaking as a theorist of psychoanalysis, eager to find uniformities, and a historian's judgment must remain suspended. His catalogues of the common characteristics of geniuses—a secret foreboding that a curse lies upon them, a tie to the father which makes open rebellion impossible, a sense of being chosen and carrying a superior destiny, a feeling of weakness and shyness and unworthiness, a precocious conscience in childhood, an early development of ultimate concerns, a brief attempt to cast off the yoke of their fate, and a final settling into the conviction that they have a responsibility for a segment of mankind—is troubling even to a historian who has wandered far from the all-too-commonsensical positivists. As a description of Gandhi's and perhaps Luther's experience, yes; as a historical typology, no.

In his Gandhi, Erikson closely scrutinized the manner in which a group of followers resonated to their hero, identified with him in terms of their own life cycles. The skill and imagination with which he handles their recollected dreams, fantasies, and symbolic acts is unmatched in contemporary psychological history-writing. On the other hand, the general relationship between the world historical figure and his age is not advanced much beyond Hegel's lectures. There is no theory of social change in Eriksonian psychology, any more than in Freud's, except for the assumption that each new generation strives to surpass the older one, to innovate upon its works, risking oedipal ambivalence in the process. Erikson does not offer us any help in comprehending either the tempo or the direction of change beyond the categorical assertion that at certain moments mankind is prepared for epoch-making transformations—an epochal identity vacuum is created, he tells us[24]—and the hero comes along and sounds the clarion-call. Each such moment has its potentialities for new creation and redemption from historical psychic blocks that inhibit a society from embarking on a course for which it is ripe and which it desires in its innermost being. The genius leader first releases himself from psychic bondage or points the way to a release for others which he may not have personally achieved.

There is too much of the sacred drama for me in this model of the historical moment. That the hero responds sharply to forces in his world, that he has antennae in his head giving him prescience, foreknowledge, is metaphoric language that German *Zeitgeist* historians have resorted to for many decades. Though he does not mention him, I cannot help hearing the overtones of Hegel's world-historical person, who incarnates the ongoing history of absolute spirit. I am left unenlightened as to what brought about the historical crisis and unconvinced that the hero's prescience is the force that resolves it. On occasion there is a prophetic quality to Erikson's heralding of the next stage in world history, with its ever-broadening area of common identities, that leaves the agnostic behind. The austere and rigorous criteria for "psychohistorical evidence" that he set forth in a theoretical statement are not always observed in practice.[25]

Deriving from a totally different tradition is Sartre's existentialist amalgam of psychology and history. He has at least one thing in common with Eriksonian psychohistory, and that is a humanist emphasis upon personality in history and the freedom of, shall we say, ego-will—though Sartre is now prepared to give greater weight to the fetters of inherited psychological conditioning than he was previously.

Sartre renders existential the legacy of a psychologized Marxist framework, fills in the interstices in the history of socioeconomic development with choices of human wills as he presumes Marx would have done, and subjects the action of these wills to psychological analysis. A general Marxist class determinism is postulated, but, in addition, he believes that a humanist history can show how it is possible for individuals with a variety of class and psychic identities to sacrifice their lives in common historic actions. He has fleshed out a Marxist historical dialectic based on production relations and class structure with an existential account of how men who in an inert state have a relationship of mere seriality to one another—like people waiting in a queue—come, in a given historical crisis, to assume ties that entail responsibilities of life and death in action. His convoluted argument is less interesting for a historian than the kinds of questions he addresses to his materials. Rereading histories of the French Revolution, the Revolution of 1848, and the Commune, he asks: What really happens when a crowd moves on an objective? What is the nature of the secret psychological commitments and pacts they have made with one another? How in fact does collective historical action come about? Though Sartre's passion for phenomenological totalization will put many of us off, historians may be able to adapt to other times and places his method of extracting the full existential implications of isolated events. In his treatment of individuals, Sartre has created prototypes for the fusion of social and psychological knowledge. The published fragments of his Flaubert, a work in progress, are a brilliant synthesis of Marxist and Freudian insights.[26]

The penetration of the outer social and ideological world into the intimacy of the family and the psychological history of the individual in this primary field of confrontation are for Sartre the first and perhaps most significant of a whole sequence of developments. In the introduction to his *Critique de la raison dialectique*, he criticized his Marxist friends for concerning themselves solely with adults: "Reading them one would believe that we are born at the age when we earn our first wages. . . . Existentialism, on the contrary, believes that it can integrate the psychoanalytic method which discovers the point of insertion for man and his class—that is, the particular family—as a mediation between the universal class and the individual."[27] I have considerable sympathy for this viewpoint. At the present time writers who call themselves psychohistorians are forced to use, *faute de mieux*, crude and misleading affirmations about both the economy and the interpsychic relationships of the Western family. A measure of our poverty is the frequency with which Philippe Ariès' history of childhood is cited as Holy Writ.[28] Whenever I have tried to interpret the family relations of historical figures I have felt on shaky ground in relying on old-hat, impressionistic utterances about this nuclear institution. But the possibilities for research are open and the materials cry for exploitation. There seems to be a consensus among social historians, prosopographers, and historians with an interest in psychological phenomena that the history of the family represents a gaping lacuna in our knowledge to which a new generation of historians should give significant priority.

History can now be individuated and particularized in a way that Leopold von Ranke never dreamed of. The economic and social existence of individuals and aggregates today can be seen reflected in the family alongside the psychic pattern set by this primal reality at a crucial period in life. The insights of Marx and of Freud can thus be brought together not in the sibylline macrohistorical rhetoric of Herbert Marcuse or Norman Brown but in concrete historical works where life situations are depicted.

IV

A certain imperialistic character attaches to a major intellectual discovery such as psychoanalysis. When a new instrument for the study of man is developed, believers in its potency tend to conceive of it as a panacea, a solution to a wide range of problems, ultimately including the historical. If it is a successful and persuasive technique that wins assent in one area of the study of man, why should it not be introduced elsewhere? Proclamations are issued raising high hopes and staking out large claims. The new technique is often applied with a heavy hand. Revolutionary results are awaited, as it pretends to answer questions for which there already exist explanations more elegant and plausible or more nuanced. It becomes totalitarian. Under attack the proponents of the new technique may withdraw from their most advanced outposts: their position was misunderstood, their theory was not meant to be all-embracing. It is only the most important interpretive device and does not quite account for everything. The original formulation has been misrepresented, misconstrued.

The initial negative reaction of official historians—and there is such a body of academic mandarins in every country—to a new method like psychoanalysis in history is equally fervid. The new technique is based on a series of false assumptions; it is not acceptable even in its own discipline; depending upon it is leaning upon a weak reed. Psychology and history are declared to be different in their essence—as if either of them had an "essence" that enjoys even a partial consensus. The human phenomena that psychological analyses are presumed to illuminate are too elusive, or if they can be grasped they are insignificant and irrelevant as far as the true vocation of the historian is concerned. The evidence brought forth by these techniques is obfuscatory, raising more problems than it resolves—as if the opening up of new problems were not in itself a virtue instead of a fault.

As studies multiply—good, bad, and indifferent—the proponents cite the best as examples and the opponents the most ill-conceived and outlandish specimens. With time, however, both extreme positions are eroded. The imperialists of the new technique pull in their horns, and the absolute deniers of its usefulness permit it a humble place in the republic of knowledge. Eventually the new perceptions insinuate themselves into the most normative orthodox history-writing, often without the author's awareness, and the controversy joins the ranks of those "appearance problems" that at intervals have shaken the intellectual world and that one later reads about with some incredulity. This has been the historical fortune of Marxist conceptions and seems a fair prognosis of what will happen to Freudian ideas in the process of their assimilation by historians.

Despite serious misgivings about some of the uses of psychology in history, I feel we have come a long way from the intellectualist psychological history of the earlier part of the century. I still cast my lot with the Freudian "psychologizers." A historian can scarcely compose a narrative line without committing himself, implicitly or explicitly, to some theory of personality and motivation. In various periods since the late seventeenth century there have been dominant psychologies, like those of Locke and Descartes, that seeped into the literary language as well as into everyday speech, and through these media constrained the historian to employ their motivational terminology. Today a historian must feel at least some uneasiness about adhering to the traditional nineteenth-century patterns of motivation. A skeptic may rightly be uncertain that the more novel systems are intrinsically superior or truer in an absolute sense than those handed down by the past; but it is eccentric in 1970 to go about in satin knee-breeches or wear a Prince Albert frock-coat, even if one likes the style. The historian is probably always obliged to accept and express himself in the psychological language of his times; and thus, as I see it, there is no escape from Freud's conceptions in some form, orthodox or heterodox.

Although there may have been a general appreciation of the long interdependency of history and psychology in a wide variety of shapes and forms, on both a theoretical and a practicing level, most members of the American historical profession, positivists and relativists alike, were nevertheless ill-prepared for the bombshell that fell into their midst on December 29, 1957, when William Langer in his presidential address before the American Historical Association in New York announced that the historian's next assignment was an application of the findings of psychoanalysis to history. There were visible stirrings among members of the audience that a behavioral scientist of any school would have identified as consternation. This was the most unkindest cut of all, from a scholar who had produced an impressive array of impeccably solid works of diplomatic history. Since then, there are indications that the stubborn resistance of a phalanx of historians generally suspicious of what they considered random psychological associations is being overcome. Papers dealing with psychology and history, presented at a number of recent meetings of the American Historical Association, have attracted large audiences. In 1963 Bruce Mazlish assembled an impressive group of theoretical statements on psychoanalysis and history, and urged the historian to acquaint himself with the relevant texts.[29] Stuart Hughes reiterated the general sense of Langer's manifesto and added a programmatic statement of his own in *History as Art and as Science* (1964), where he called for historical research into the "shared anxieties and aspirations [of various epochs] which may be all the more decisive for being only partially conscious." Experiences such as these, he maintains, cut across the conventional delimitations of class or elite groups, and he has voiced confidence in the feasibility of arriving at valid historical generalizations about "deep-seated fears and ideal strivings."[30] While it is probable that the American historical profession has produced in the last decade more articles about the desirability of establishing a bridge between history and psychology than works animated by the new ideas, that there has been far more talk about the subject than actual performance, some younger historians are beginning to incorporate the findings of the new psychology into the body of their work. For example, the June 1970 issue of the *American Historical Review* contained an article by a young historian, John Demos, "Underlying Themes in the Witchcraft of Seventeenth-Century New England," that was informed by psychoanalytic concepts judiciously introduced.[31] In this respect, however, American historians have lagged behind the political scientists, who have more eagerly embraced the new ideas in their studies of dominant contemporary political figures—witness the *Daedalus* issue on "Philosophers and Kings" (Summer 1968).

The collaborators of the French *Annales*, which has lately shown itself hospitable to articles on psychoanalysis and history, are beginning to explore the psychological aspects of demography, of which they are today the outstanding school in the world. The Russians for Marxist ideological reasons and the official English historians for traditionalist ones are likely to hold out longest against the new trend.

Any contemporary use of psychology in history must postulate the existence of the unconscious, a belief that the unconscious of past epochs has left behind visible traces, and a conviction that these traces are decipherable. About the interpretation of the documentary vestiges of psychic experience there will inevitably be controversy, as there has been over the reading of dead and forgotten languages, and at present the historian is faced with rival and contradictory theories of human development from among which he must choose an initial hypothesis if he is to avail himself of the new techniques. The lack of consensus among psychologists and psychoanalysts is bound to perplex him. Once even a tentative commitment is made, however, to some psychoanalytic theory—and the historian may permit himself the luxury of being eclectic and pluralist—the results can vastly enrich our understanding of historical experience. The investigation of psychological phenomena in past epochs not only will alter historical conceptions about other ages, but could lead to an appreciation of the historical dimensions and limitations of present-day psychological doctrines.

Accusations of dilettantism are commonly made against those who are introducing modern psychology into history, and the problem of professional training in two disciplines, psychology and history, is admittedly nettlesome. Yet is it not precisely at the crossroads of two forms of knowledge that the most fertile conceptions in present-day historiography are emerging? The idea of an *équipe*, of the teaming of a psychologist and a historian, is a too-facile solution; an ultimate synthesis must take place within the mind of the historian if the work is to have a wholeness.

On the use of a specialized vocabulary and the borrowing of technical terminology, as contrasted with concepts, my position is rather conservative. I find the psychological jargon, with infrequent exceptions, too ugly for narrative history, and am convinced that one can adopt the concepts without the nomenclature, which derives from a parochial scientistic tradition. After all, no therapist worth his salt will resort in his consultation room to technical terms because of the obvious danger that they may be confused with common and vulgar usage. If the historian eschews technical words, he is less likely to be seduced into dogmatism. His explanations of historical phenomena can be ambiguous, multifaceted, possible, or probable; he can write suggestively, propose solutions by indirection. Psychological labels are unnecessarily restrictive; historical figures are not patients admitted to a hospital who have to be categorized for housekeeping convenience.

Acceptance of psychoanalytic concepts in history-writing presupposes, of course, a somewhat different set of criteria for historical proof than those to which traditional historians are accustomed. For some, the evidence is not concrete enough, and the element of conjecture more obtrusive than they can countenance. While the quantitative school of history continues the Galilean tradition of mathematicizing knowledge with the instruments of a new technology congenial to our age, psychology in history still has a tendency toward the sample of one and the search for uniqueness. Any prospect of quantification seems remote, though not entirely to be excluded as an element in analyses of the behavior of groups.[32]

On the whole I feel that psychological knowledge is at this stage more useful in description than in explanatory system-making. When two disciplines are locked into the same cage, the historical keepers tell me, cannibalistic tendencies well up from their unconscious and they sometimes try to devour each other. Recent attempts to merge psychology and history in a clumsily labeled psychohistorical process do presume the sort of grand monist thesis to which history has always been refractory. Since so many historico-psychological problems have not been mapped even in a crude manner, I am reluctant to embrace elaborate theoretical structures. In the end I conceive of psychology as playing a more modest role, adding a set of vivid psychedelic colors to the historian's palette, offsetting the mournful black-and-white of structure and number that in this technological age will inevitably suffuse a large part of the historical.

The new psychologies can open up whole areas of inquiry by encouraging the historian to ask some direct, perhaps impertinent questions. The restriction of the method to biography, where it has enjoyed at least partial acceptance, should not be a lasting confinement. Historians will have to wrestle anew with symbolic representation on a broad scale. There are central problems in the history of ideas that cannot be treated adequately on an intellectualist and conscious level of expression alone and that invite the use of new psychological tools: the history of feelings about time, space, utopia, myth, love, death, God. The "unconscious mental habits" that Arthur Lovejoy hoped to analyze in his history of ideas had little or nothing to do with Freud's unconscious. Perhaps the fundamental shortcoming of his work and that of the Febvre school was their exclusive intellectualism. We all know that the experience of love and death and aggression has changed through the centuries. If a professor dared to propose a course on the history of love he would certainly take a ribbing from his colleagues. Yet this emotion has been as protean in its forms and as vital to human existence as, let us say, shipping or banking, whose respectability as subjects for historical treatment in university teaching is quite unchallenged. When a psychologist investigating contemporary attitudes toward death looks for historical comparisons, we can only provide him with impressions and isolated, sparse instances. Particularly dramatic intrusions of death, such as great plagues, have been studied by historians in their psychological as well as their economic, political, and artistic consequences; Millard Meiss's study of the Black Death is a prototype.[33] But there is need for an exploration of the long-term, changing meaning of death on the unconscious as well as on the conscious level. Death in the eighteenth century had its special character, but I think we know far less about it than we do about the diplomatic relations between Parma and Venice in that period.

The particular forms of psychic repression have a history and so do the forms of sublimation—their instrumentalities differ widely in time and place. The overt manifestations of neuroses have changed, as any sampling of case histories over the past seventy years will show. As far back as 1913 Karl Jaspers in a section of his *General Psychopathology* entitled "Social and Historical Aspects of the Psychoses and the Personality-Disorders" recognized that "the neuroses in particular have a contemporary style."[34] Few historians have yet coped with the intricacies of presenting to their readers the varying patterns of libidinal satisfaction in different epochs. You can read that grand masterpiece of provincialism, the *Cambridge Modern History*, in its newest version, without even suspecting the existence of these transformations.

The histories of fashion, clothes, sexual and marital customs, punishments, style, and a hundred other questions which have traditionally belonged to *la petite histoire* and to the antiquarians need to be explored for their symbolic content. Freud's second most important legacy to a historian may well be the dissolution of a hierarchy of values among historical materials. If all things can become vehicles of expression for feelings and thoughts, then the state document, grand philosophical affirmation, and scientific law may lose some of their prestige to other more intimate records of human experience. The day of Dilthey's elitist psychological history is over. Conversely, classical psychoanalysis, with a dubious future as a therapy, might be reborn as a historical instrumentality. The dead do not ask to be cured, only to be understood.

A great expansion in our comprehension of the past might be effected through the rereading of old or neglected documents with a different apperception. Notebooks and scribbles that seemed destined for the ashheap of history may be rescued and made to live again—as exciting a reconquest of the past as a new archaeology. A great body of dream literature and of fantasies of past ages is unexplored. In Western Europe and in America there are voluminous materials—legal, political, medical, literary—in manuscript and print, to say nothing of representations by the plastic arts, that have not been researched for their psychological meaning. The questions have not been asked, and therefore historians have not been on the *qui vive* for the answers that lie concealed in the texts.

Economic history has become respectable, and who would now demean the history of labor, or the history of consumption patterns? I merely advocate adding to them a history of other needs and expressions of living. In defense of his idealist history of Spirit as the definition of human existence, Hegel once wrote with utter contempt of nutritive history. Now that we have, in spite of Hegel, recognized the claims of hands and stomach to a share in human history, let us make ready to welcome the other more secret and hidden parts of man into the temple.

Notes

1. Wilhelm Dilthey, *Einleitung in die Geisteswissenschaften: Versuch einer Grundlegung für das Studium der Gesellschaft und der Geschichte* (Leipzig: Duncker and Humblot, 1883), I (no more volumes published). A second edition with additions from unpublished manuscripts forms vol. I, ed. Bernhard Groethuysen (1923), of Dilthey's *Gesammelte Schriften* (Leipzig: Teubner). With the exception of vol. II, *Weltanschauung und Analyse des Menschen seit Renaissance und Reformation* (1914), the collected works appeared from 1921 to 1936. *Der Aufbau der geschichtlichen Welt in den*

Geistenswissenschaften. Studien . . . ., pt. I, was published in the *Abhandlungen der Königlich Preussichen Akademie der Wissenschaften: Phil.-hist. Klasse* for 1910; a new edition with additions from unpublished manuscripts forms vol. VII, ed. Bernhard Groethuysen (1927) of the *Gesammelte Schriften.*

2. Wilhelm Dilthey, *Die Jugendgeschichte Hegeles*, which appeared in the *Abhandlungen der Königlich Preussischen Akademie der Wissenchaften* in 1905, now vol. IV, ed. Herman Nohl (1921) of the *Gesammelte Schriften; Leben Scheiermachers*, published with *Denkmale der inneren Entwicklung Schleiermachers, erläutert durch kritische Untersuchungen* (Berlin, 1870), I (no more volumes published).

3. Wilhelm Dilthey, *Das Erlebnis und die Dichtung*, 13th ed. (Stuttgart: Teubner, 1957; original ed., 1905). p. 289.

4. Karl Jaspers, *Strindberg und Van Gogh: Versuch einer pathographischen Analyse unter vergleichender Heranziehung von Swedenborg und Hölderlin* (Bern: E. Bircher, 1922).

5. Karl Jaspers, *Psychologie der Weltanschauungen* (Berlin: J. Springer, 1919; 4th ed., 1954).

6. Lucien Paul Victor Febvre, *Un destin: Martin Luther* (Paris: Rieder, 1928); quotation is from *Martin Luther: A Destiny*, trans. Roberts Tapley (New York: E. P. Dutton, 1929), pp. 33, 35.

7. Lucien Febvre, *Le problème de l'incroyance au XVIe siècle: La religion de Rabelais* (Paris: A. Michel, 1947; original ed., 1942), p. 163.

8. Lucien Febvre, *Combats pour l'histoire* (Paris: A. Colin, 1953), p. 229.

9. Robert Mandrou, *Magistrats et sorciers en France au XVIIe siècle: Une analyse de psychologie historique* (Paris: Plon, 1968).

10. See, for example, Joe Kovel, *White Racism: A Psychohistory* (New York: Pantheon, 1970).

11. Michel Foucault, *Histoire de la folie à l'age classique* (Paris: Plon, 1961), *Les mots et les choses* (Paris: Gallimard, 1966).

12. Jean-Paul Sartre, *Critique de la raison dialectique, précédé de Questions de méthode* (Paris: Gallimard, 1960).

13. Sigmund Freud, "Brief an Maxim Leroy über einen Traum des Cartesius" (1919), in *Gesammelte Schriften*, XII (Vienna: Internationaler Psychoanalytischer Verlag, 1934), pp. 403–405; for English translation, see the *Standard Edition of the Complete Psychological Works of Sigmund Freud*, ed. James Strachey with the collaboration of Anna Freud (London: Hogarth Press), XXI, 203–204.

14. Sigmund Freud, *Eine Kindheisterinnerung des Leonardo da Vinci* (Leipzig: F. Deuticke, 1910; for English translation see *Standard Edition*, XI, 63–137); *Der Wahn und die Träume in W. Jensen's "Gradiva"* (Vienna: F. Deuticke, 1907; English translation in *Standard Edition*, IX, 3-95); "Dostojewski und die Vatertötung" (1928), published as a preface to *Die Urgestalt der Brüder Karamasoff* (a supplementary volume in the German edition of Dostoevsky's works by René Fülop-Miller and F. Eckstein) and

republished in the *Gesammelte Schriften*, XII, 7-26 (English translation in *Standard Edition*, XXI, 177–196).

15. Sigmund Freud, *Der Mann Moses und die monotheistische Religion, Drei Abhandlungen* (Amsterdam: A. de Lange, 1939; parts 1 and 2 published in German in *Imago* in 1937; English translation by Katherine Jones, *Moses and Monotheism*, New York: Knopf, 1939); Ernst L. Freud, ed., *The Letters of Sigmund Freud and Arnold Zweig*, trans. Elaine and William Robson-Scott (New York: Harcourt, Brace and World, 1970), p. 91, Freud to Zweig, September 30, 1934.

16. Marie Bonaparte, *Edgar Poe: Etude psychoanalytique*, 2 vols. (Paris, 1933).

17. Ernst Kris, *Psychoanalytic Explorations in Art* (New York: International Universities Press, 1962; original ed., London: Allen and Unwin, 1953); Editha and Richard Sterba, *Beethoven and His Nephew: A Psychoanalytic Study of Their Relationship*, trans. Willard R. Trask (London: Dennis Dobson, 1957).

18. Harold D. Lasswell, *Psychopathology and Politics* (Chicago: University of Chicago Press, 1930), pp. 75–76.

19. Alexander L. George and Juliette L. George, *Woodrow Wilson and Colonel House: A Personality Study* (New York: John Day, 1956); Sigmund Freud and W. C. Bullitt, *Thomas Woodrow Wilson, Twenty-Eighth President of the United States: A Psychological Study* (Boston: Houghton Mifflin, 1967).

20. Augustin Cabanes, *Grands névropathes, malades immortels*, 3 vols. (Paris: A. Michel, 1930–1935).

21. Erik H. Erikson, *Childhood and Society* (New York: Norton, 1950); *Young Man Luther* (New York: Norton, 1958); *Identity and the Life Cycle: Selected Papers* (New York: International Universities Press, 1959); *Insight and Responsibility* (New York: Norton, 1964); *Gandhi's Truth* (New York: Norton, 1969).

22. D. Herlihy, "Viellir au Quattrocento," *Annales: économies, sociéties, civilisations* (November–December 1969), pp. 1338-1352.

23. Creighton Gilbert, "When Did a Man in the Renaissance Grow Old?" *Studies in the Renaissance*, 14 (1967), 7–32, is an example of what needs to be done on a broad scale.

24. Erikson, *Insight and Responsibility*, p. 204.

25. Erik H. Erikson, "On the Nature of Psycho-Historical Evidence: In Search of Gandhi," *Daedalus* (Summer 1968), pp. 695-730.

26. Jean-Paul Sartre, "La conscience de classe chez Flaubert," *Les Temps Modernes*, 21st year, no. 240 (May 1966), 1921-1951, and no. 241 (June 1966), 2113-2153; "Flaubert: Du poète á l'artiste," *Les Temps Modernes*, 22nd year, no. 243 (August 1966), 197-253; no. 244 (September 1966), 423-481; no. 245 (October 1966), 598–674.

27. Jean-Paul Sartre, *The Problem of Method* (prefatory essay of *Critique de la raison dialectique*), trans. Hazel E. Barnes (London, Methuen, 1963), p. 62.

28. Philippe Ariès, *L'enfant et la vie familiale sous l'Ancien Régime* (Paris: Plon, 1960).

29. Bruce Mazlish, ed., *Psychoanalysis and History* (Englewood Cliffs, N.J.: Prentice-Hall, 1963).

30. H. Stuart Hughes, *History as Art and as a Science* (New York: Harper and Row, 1964), pp. 61, 62.

31. John Demos, "Underlying Themes in the Witchcraft of Seventeenth-Century New England," *American Historical Review*, 73 (1970), 1311-1326.

32. An interesting attempt to deal with the psychology of a social aggregate that raises the problems of quantification is Marc Raeff, *Origins of the Russian Intelligentsia: The Eighteenth-Century Nobility* (New York: Harcourt, Brace and World, 1966).

33. Millard Meiss, *Painting in Florence and Siena after the Black Death* (Princeton: Princeton University Press, 1951).

34. Karl Jaspers, *General Psychopathology*, trans. J. Hoenig and Marian W. Hamilton (Chicago: University of Chicago Press, 1963; original German ed., *Allgemeine Psychopathologie*, 1913), p. 732.

3

Clio and Psyche

GEORGE M. KREN AND LEON H. RAPPOPORT

If it is at all legitimate for authors to write introductions to their own work, it is in order to note its origins. Having been at work on some psychohistorical studies, we felt the need to examine the state of the discipline, and this led us to review the history of the use of psychology by historians. Critical examination of past efforts indicated a steady widening of horizons—going beyond earlier Freudian psychobiography toward a concern with issues and questions whose significance had previously not been understood.

The primary purpose of the disciplines of history and psychology is to increase understanding of human behavior. Though historians tend to work with larger events extending through longer time periods, the two disciplines share a similar logic: by reconstructing and analyzing the past, a better understanding of the present may be gained. Despite such apparent grounds for close collaboration, however, the two disciplines have generally ignored each other.

Any review of the relationship between history and psychology must recognize that, secure in its status as the senior discipline, history has until very recently maintained a cavalier, paternalistic attitude toward the substance of modern psychology; tolerant at best, simply xenophobic at worst. Apart from *hubris*, one primary explanation for this lies

From *History of Childhood Quarterly* (Summer 1973), 151–163. *History of Childhood Quarterly: The Journal of Psychohistory*, 2315 Broadway, N.Y., N.Y. 10024. Reprinted by permission.

Author's note: An earlier version of this paper was presented at the fourth meeting of Cheiron at the University of Calgary, Calgary, Alberta, Canada, June 29, 1972. We wish to thank Professor Al Hamscher for his critical readings of this material.

in a tradition of historiography that extends back to Herodotus and Thucydides: namely, that by definition the good historian is a good psychologist, good enough, at any rate, to use his own emotional and cognitive sensitivities as a means of elucidating the psychological functioning of remote historical figures. The historian's argument here comes down to a claim for the sufficiency of intuitive, common sense psychology, and can only be supported by rejecting (or ignoring) the counterintuitive findings of modern psychoanalysis and other branches of psychology.

A further reason for the disjunction between history and psychology derives from the historian's stubborn (and not altogether misplaced) allegiance to a methodology and a language of common sense. Hayden White observed that historians have not only been unable to meet the criteria of "hard" science, but also have failed to "probe the more arcane strata of human consciousness."[1] This state of affairs has not gone unrecognized. In his presidential address to the American Historical Association in 1957, William Langer called upon historians to learn from psychoanalysis.[2] During the past several years, however, young historians have shown growing interest in psychology (psychohistory, as it has come to be known), and the fact that such work has emerged as a legitimate element in the historical profession is evidenced by significant new publications and burgeoning interdisciplinary courses in many universities.

If a new trend toward interdisciplinary work is indeed developing, it seems all the more important to scrutinize prior achievements and failures and to place the use of psychology and psychoanalysis by historians into a historical context. Almost a century ago, Wilhelm Dilthey introduced the phenomenological concept of *verstehen* (understanding) as a tool for the analysis of historical events: he demanded that the historian immerse himself in his source material in order to gain an intuitive understanding of the past. At the same time he called for a psychology that rejected the methods of the natural sciences. He envisioned a psychological discipline that would not restrict itself to the investigation of sensations and feelings, but would attempt to comprehend the "structures by which the various functions of the human mind are organized." For this purpose introspective autobiographies, literature, poetry, and historiography could be used as primary source material.[3] Dilthey's works are characterized by discriminating perceptions and an uncanny sensitivity which is used to understand another person's thought. They are in Frank E. Manuel's words "elitist dramas in the passion of Great men's souls."[4] Yet Manuel cogently observed that "nothing below the navel was mentionable."[5] None of the perceptions of modern psychoanalysis which seek the sources for adult behavior in early experiences and which make sexual development central are used by Dilthey. His colleagues in the historical profession agreed with his rejection of positivism and empiricism, but had little use for any kind of psychology.

Most German historians accepted Heinrich Rickert's classification of scholarship; on the one hand, there were the natural sciences and those new disciplines that attempted to imitate their methods, such as sociology; on the other, the *Kulturwissenschaften*, which were not interested in discovering general laws, but sought to understand the unique experience—whether found in a work of art or in an historical event.

This concern for individuality and uniqueness by German historians was a defensive reaction to a perceived threat to conservative values. By emphasizing the constant flux of historical movement and seeing all values as relative to time and place, they maintained a philosophical posture opposed to democratic premises of the Enlightment. [6]

Following Dilthey's unsuccessful effort to join history and psychology, the disciplines went in opposite directions. History remained true to its time-honored commonsense traditions, while psychology modeled itself on the methods of the exact sciences. The result has been that most historians have found academic psychology too narrow and simplistic to be useful in explaining historical events, while psychoanalytic theory appeared too speculative to be helpful in providing historical explanations.

For their part, most psychologists, usually trained either as natural scientists or as medical doctors, have rejected history as irrelevant to their concerns because it lacks both empirical standards of validity and a commitment to hypotheticodeductive methodology. Yet when it suits them, they have not hesitated to appeal to history. Thus, one may encounter the inconsistent but familiar arguments that Freud's ideas are only relevant to persons raised in the Victorian morality of *fin-de-siècle* bourgeois society, and that the human psyche has been unchanging through the ages. Academic psychologists have focused on those kinds of problems that would permit narrow quantitative solutions—precise study of the capacity of the eye to differentiate color, exact analysis of responses to pinpricks.

Interdisciplinary efforts conducted in the psychoanalytical tradition—never quite respectable in academia—stand in sharp contrast to "scientific" psychology. Two levels of analysis are involved: the sociocultural and the individual. Psychoanalytic efforts at the sociocultural level originate with Freud's works on religion and the origin of civilization. These metapsychoanalytical works have generally been rejected by anthropologists and other scholars in "traditional" disciplines. Clinically oriented analysts trained to treat individual patients, but not to understand culture, regard *Moses and Monotheism, Future of an Illusion,* and *Totem and Taboo* as sources of embarrassment, and of little or no value to their therapeutic concerns. There is a certain logic in the fact that the most exciting speculative works done in the Freudian tradition have been written by non-analysts: Norman O. Brown, author of the daring metapsychoanalytical and philosophical works *Life against Death* and *Love's Other Body*, is a classicist; Herbert Marcuse, whose *Eros and Civilization* is the most sophisticated attempt to join Marx and Freud, comes to these questions from previous concern with the philosophical issues raised by Marx and Hegel.[7]

At the individual level, Freudian theory has been employed to explain the actions of great men. Freud himself started this line of development with his study of Leonardo da Vinci. Numerous significant psychoanalytical biographies of historical figures are now available.[8] But until very recently most efforts to apply psychology and particularly psychoanalysis to history have at best been interesting failures, largely because their authors have given insufficient weight to the various elements defining the historical context. Such phenomena as shared life patterns and modal experiences, present at diverse levels of society, have typically been ignored in favor of psychodynamic interpretations of the individual. The historical personage is treated as if he were a patient in analysis, with crucial diplomatic and political situations viewed only as triggers for some form of individual pathology.

Before 1914, when Freud wrote most of his seminal works, the world seemed so "normal" that a feeling of persecution had to be explained as a delusion. Most psychologists today still operate in accordance with this nineteenth-century perception of reality, having failed to realize that in the twentieth century persecution, torture, and arbitrary imprisonment have become normative for a large portion of the world. Many persons feel persecuted because they are. Consequently, the first question that needs be asked about behavior patterns that conform to the textbook version of paranoia is whether the felt persecution is real or imagined. This is a historical and not a psychological question.

In their discussion of adjustment problems among blacks, for instance, Grier and Cobbs cite paranoid feelings associated with a sense of powerlessness to be typical.[9] Other researchers report that blacks more often indicate weaker feelings of fate control—they see their lives dominated more by external than by internal events.[10] Yet it is clear from their historical and contemporary status in our society that among blacks such perceptions are eminently reasonable. In fact, it may be those blacks who do not show some denotatively paranoid behavior who are out of touch with reality.

The close weave between historical events and nominally pathological descriptions of behavior is dramatized in Lifton's analysis of Japanese who survived the nuclear attack on Hiroshima.[11] He reports that psychiatric examinations reveal them to be relatively alienated, and suffering from a kind of unique nuclear "survivor complex" marked by paranoid overtones. But in a critique of Lifton's work, Paul Goodman asks, "Why shouldn't they?"[12] Should not alienation be understood as a healthy reaction among people who have reason to fear themselves damaged genetically and subject to other disorders associated with intense exposure to radiation? Should not paranoid suspicions characterize their adjustment to a larger society which on the one hand sets them on a pedestal with assurances that they are not forgotten while on the other hand treating them as lepers? The fundamental issue here is that the definition of paranoia is not fully defined by behavior, but requires historical analysis to determine whether the feeling of persecution has an actual basis.

Some works have in varying degrees suggested how a sophisticated application of psychology can increase substantially the understanding of a historical event or process. In a hitherto neglected study published in 1931, Fedor Vergin analyzed the major political and social forces of the 1920s and 30s within a psychoanalytic framework. Particularly significant is his discussion of the subconscious anal-sadistic forces influencing Hitler.[13]

The experience of national socialism fascinated many. A book of 1943 expounded the thesis that Germany was suffering from paranoia.[14] Both Leo Alexander and Elie Cohen attempted to explain the behavior of the SS by using such concepts as "tribal superego" and "criminal superego."[15] Following World War II, a number of studies appeared offering psychoanalytic interpretations of German anti-Semitism.[16] They attempted to explain anti-Semitism as a compensation for real or imagined inferiorities. The basic problem with much of this work is that the relationship between individual psychopathology and mass political behavior is generally not convincing. Kurth, for instance, found the origins of Hitler's anti-Semitism in the treatment that his mother was given by a Jewish physician, arguing that the dynamics of an unresolved Oedipus complex led Hitler to generalize his hostile emotions from his father to the physician, and from the physician to Jews in general.[17] Some twenty years later, Waite has elaborated the theme that Hitler's fear of incest energized his hatred of the Jews.[18] Valuable as they may be for heuristic purposes, studies of this type do not make a major contribution to the understanding of Nazi anti-Semitism, much less the "final solution," because they ignore the gross historical and situational factors that must inevitably influence relationships between individual psycho-dynamics and political action.

Two important works addressed themselves to the problem of the relationship between individual psychology and modern totalitarian movements.[19] Published in 1950, *The Authoritarian Personality* stands as one of the most ambitious attempts to relate Freudian personality theory to politics at the level of everyday individual behavior. This study is not concerned with the "great man" but addresses itself to the relationship between early family experiences and personal adjustments and attitudes towards minority groups, war, democracy, and childrearing.

The work was all the more impressive because it offered a convenient empirical tool—the F (for Fascism) scale—which allows easy identification of those who hold a certain cluster of rigidly conservative and ethnocentric beliefs. This was shown by illustrative material in the original book. Subsequent studies demonstrated that many forms of retrograde political behavior can indeed be accurately predicted for persons with very high scores on the F-scale. Christianson reported that such persons held extremely conservative views of international affairs.[20] Henry Dicks's interviews with captured German soldiers and SS men also supports the reality of a basic authoritarian personality pattern.[21] At the same time, however, studies showing that the F-scale could not be employed to predict the behavior of persons with moderate or low scores have given the original work an ambiguous status in contemporary social science. It is relevant, in this connection, to observe that Nevitt Sanford, one of Adorno's co-authors, now suggests that authoritarianism should be viewed as a ". . . psychohistorical concept, a pattern of personality and ideology that belonged to its time."[22] Indeed, with the benefit of hindsight, it is clear that the 1950 work on authoritarianism says little about situational factors which establish the basis for relationships between personality and sociopolitical behavior. Hence the problem of understanding how personality dynamics can lead large numbers of people into a mass movement is at best only partially illuminated by this work.[23]

Compared with *The Authoritarian Personality*, Fromm's *Escape from Freedom* gives much more consideration to historical events mediating the relationship between personality and politics. Although it is explicitly concerned with the psychological basis for modern mass movements, particularly German National Socialism, Fromm's work is founded upon a broad interpretation of the psychological effects of the industrial revolution. Much of it is designed to give a psychological dimension to the Marxian concept of alienation. He provides a variant of Reich's *Psychology of Fascism*, with the Reichian radicalism now made palatable to middle-class sensibilities. (Reich had suggested that Fascism was a psychological escape from sexual repression.)[24]

Fromm's fundamental thesis is that since the Reformation, and particularly since the rise of modern capitalism, the trend of European history has had two related effects observable at the everyday level of individual adjustment. People have gained increasing freedom from various communal institutions—the family, the guild, the church, etc.—but the cost of this freedom has been individual insecurity and loneliness. Western Man seeks substitutes for the social support these communal ties had provided. As a result, Fromm argues, modern men join mass movements which promise a new sense of belonging, and which reduce the heavy burden of freedom.

Fromm's thesis has been criticized by historians who point out that it is more of a diagnosis of the effects of capitalism than an explanation of national socialism. His later work tends to confirm this critique because in conjunction with more explicit statements about the psychological costs of a capitalistic, competitive style of life, he offers utopian solutions of how to achieve a better life in a "sane society." Setting other criticisms aside, however (it has been said that Fromm is the Norman Vincent Peale of the intellectuals), his ideas suggest only an individual basis for the appeal of mass movements; they explain why some people are willing to accept a follower's role in totalitarian organizations, but do not explain how such organizations can acquire almost unconditional allegiance from people.

Some of these questions are examined by Sanford and Comstock in their anthology *Sanctions for Evil.*[25] Written under the shadow of the My Lai massacre, this work analyzes processes whereby members of one culture or group become persuaded that they may properly inflict injury or death upon people they regard as inferior to themselves. An important contribution of this material is the effort it makes to explain the meaning of historical factors both at the individual level and the policy-making level.

Whereas Sanford examines evil from the perspective of its perpetrators, Bruno Bettelheim, a Freudian psychoanalyst who was imprisoned in a German concentration camp, sees it from the perspective of a victim. His experience led him to modify traditional Freudian views:

> My experience in the camps taught me, almost within days, that I had gone much too far in believing that only changes in man could create changes in society. I had to accept that the environment could, as it were, turn personality upside down, and not just in the small child, but in the mature adult too.[26]

Bettelheim has applied his newly found insight in his work with severely disturbed children. He has developed a technique known as milieu therapy, which is relatively successful and which depends upon a fine-grained evaluation of the psychological meaning of social and physical factors in a child's immediate environment.[27]

Bettelheim's ideas are especially important because, while deploying psychological knowledge upon recent historical events, he breaks through the traditional pattern involving imitations or small extensions of Freud. Equally valuable here is the fact that Bettelheim's concern with the psychological properties of situations fits an increasingly broad stream of basic research. Thus:

1. Barker and Wright have produced a large volume of work showing how common "behavior settings" can be understood as constituting a psychological ecology which determines the meaning of much individual behavior.[28]

2. Mental health experts see great value in transitional facilities. Whether used to help narcotics addicts, alcoholics, or mental patients, increasingly popular "halfway house" operations all involve the same principle: they are environments specially designed for people with special problems.

3. Based on extensions of research findings concerning human learning, behavior modification therapists have shown that they can desensitize people to the threatening psychological properties of certain situations.

4. Various studies of international conflict show how decision-makers may be swept along by situations and events regardless of their personal inclination. De Rivera analyzes some of the diplomatic-military conduct of the Korean War from this perspective.[29] Osgood argues that the escalation and de-escalation of international tension depends upon the alteration of situational factors, while Anatol Rapoport has developed experimental evidence demonstrating the crucial role of situational factors which can determine whether or not persons will behave cooperatively or competitively.[30]

These emerging trends in psychology mark a major change from past concerns and offer promising new ground for fruitful interaction between history and psychology. More specifically, the key factor providing a new basis for interdisciplinary cooperation is at once both prosaic and profound: childhood. Direct awareness of this may be found in Erik Erikson's pioneer efforts in psychohistory. Reflecting upon the lessons of his work on Martin Luther, Erikson suggested in 1968 that:

> historical processes have already entered the individual's core in childhood. Past history survives in the ideal and evil prototypes which guide the parental imagery and which color fairy tale and family lore, superstition and gossip, and the simple lessons of early verbal training. Historians on the whole make little of this; they account only for the contest of autonomous historical ideas and are unconcerned with the fact that these ideas reach down into the lives of generations and re-emerge through the daily awakening and training of historical consciousness in young individuals: via the mythmakers of religion and politics, of the arts and the sciences, of drama, cinema and fiction—all contributing more or less consciously, more or less responsibly, to the historical logic absorbed by youth.[31]

A new generation of historians, many of them trained in psychology and history, are recognizing childhood as a genuine psychohistorical phenomenon. Summerville observed that "although professional historians have long neglected the history of the child, and of the cultural constructs of childhood, the publication record of the past several years is evidence of a surge of interest in this field."[32] Sessions at recent professional meetings devoted to the analysis of childhood and its historical setting have appeared with increasing frequency. The *Journal of Interdisciplinary History* has in the three years of its existence published a number of significant articles dealing with childhood and the family, while responses to the announcement of *History of Childhood Quarterly* provides further evidence of the increasing interest in childhood as a proper subject for historical investigation.

An analogous trend has emerged in the discipline of psychology. Here also, a dramatic rise in the empirical and theoretical literature concerning childhood has led to the publication of a new serial, the *Journal of Developmental Psychology.* Among contemporary psychologists, Jean Piaget's work on the intellectual development of the child is increasingly given the same high status that was once exclusively reserved to Freud.[33] There is, moreover, a serious recognition by many psychologists that understanding of human development requires a knowledge of its historical context.[34]

Dramatic new perspectives on the meaning of childhood are being provided by historians scrutinizing hitherto neglected primary sources.

For the first time, at least with reference to some historical periods in Europe and America, we are beginning to develop a detailed picture of how children were treated, and it is becoming quite clear that throughout most of Western history, childrearing practices were hardly more than brutal, often sadistic processes designed to break the child's will.

The studies of Ariès and Hunt form a vital center for current discussion.[35] First published in 1960, Phillipe Ariès's *Centuries of Childhood* is a groundbreaking analysis of changing childrearing practices in the family and in the schools, as they evolved from the Middle Ages to the seventeenth century. Ariès's study is in the tradition of descriptive historiography, aimed at explaining how the concept of childhood changed through time and came to be recognized as a distinct stage of human development. More recently David Hunt, in *Parents & Children*, examines similar phenomena in a more narrow chronological focus and in conjunction with a more self-consciously theoretical framework. Hunt's theme is the fundamental antithesis between Ariès's historical definition of childhood and current psychological theories of development that assume that parents are innately concerned with maximizing the welfare of their children. Acknowledging his debts to Ariès and Erik Erikson, he is critical of both. Ariès's work is judged to lack an explicit psychological dimension, while Erikson's theory of child development is criticized for lacking a serious historical context. Hunt specifically objects to Erikson's assumption of an innate generativity, a desire to look after small children, as a part of human nature.[36]

The historical evidence available at present certainly justifies Hunt's critique, but he himself does not offer important new theoretical integration between the historical and psychological dimensions of childhood.

Cruelty towards children is the main substance of Gordon R. Taylor's *Angel-Makers.*[37] Utilizing hitherto unexploited primary sources concerning childrearing practices in England during the period 1750–1850, he concludes that, caught up in the grip of puritan doctrine and ideology, many parents of this time almost literally sought to transform their children into angels, perpetrating some devilishly refined cruelties in the process. Parenthetically, it may be noted that R. D. Laing's writings on contemporary family life emphasize the frequency with which parents today do psychological violence to their children in the name of love.

The persistent pattern of cruelty and rejection of children—ranging from beating to ill-disguised forms of infanticide—is perhaps the main burden of all the salient psychohistorical childhood studies that are now current. This is in stark contrast to prevailing psychological assumptions taking parental love and concern for the child to be a universal norm. This new knowledge requires a theoretical integration which is not yet available, although a beginning may be found in a psychiatric study rarely mentioned in the literature: Joseph C. Rheingold's *The Fear of Being a Woman.*[38] Based on the author's clinical observations of parental cruelties, this work concludes that "a large part of [child] rearing practices and parental acts and attitudes is predicated on hate. . . . [the child] lives in a world of threat and he responds to it with fear; he learns to hate defensively and in turn becomes a destructive parent."[39] Rheingold also suggests a biosocial theoretical framework for his observations which might well serve as a basis for interpretation of the psychohistorical findings mentioned earlier.

Finally, Peter Loewenberg's "Psychohistorical Origins of the Nazi Youth Cohort" must be singled out for its ingenious analysis of the relationship between childhood events and subsequent political behavior.[40] Based on a psychoanalytic interpretation of prototypical events characterizing the childhood of Germans born between 1900 and 1915, such as prolonged father-absence, near-starvation diet, and the collapse of the old order, Loewenberg cogently argues that the Nazi movement satisfied needs arising from the early experiences of this age group. Seeking compensation for their "lost" childhood, this generation fell prey to Hitler's manipulation of their hopes for warmth, security, and power. But, as Loewenberg states, instead of achieving these conditions, they recreated ". . . a repetition of their own childhoods. They gave [to Europe] . . . precisely the traumas they had suffered as children and adolescents a quarter of a century earlier."[41]

In general, it should be clear that recent efforts toward the integration of history and psychology have progressed beyond promise and have begun to yield significant results. Sophisticated use of psychological perspectives by historians is already an accomplished fact, and among psychologists there is a growing awareness of the need for historical interpretations of human development. Perhaps Wilhelm Dilthey's dream of a new science of man that can comprehend "historical man" in all his manifestations may yet be fulfilled.

Notes

1. Hayden V. White, "The Burden of History," *History and Theory* 5 (1966): 111–34.

2. William L. Langer, "The Next Assignment," *American Historical Review* 63 (January 1958): 283-304. The most complete bibliography on the

relationship between history and psychology may be found in Hans-Ulrich Wehler, ed., *Geschichte und Psychoanalyse* (Kohn, Verlag Kiepenhur & Witsch, 1971), pp. 156–73. See also the important article by Frank E. Manuel, "The Use and Abuse of Psychology in History," *Daedalus* (Winter 1971): 187–213. A largely negative view is provided by Jacques Barzun, "History: The Muse and her Doctors," *American Historical Review* 77 (February, 1972): 36–64; rejoinders to Barzun's provocative article in Ibid. 77 (October, 1972): 1194–97. Patrick P. Dunn of the University of Wisconsin at La Crosse edits a newsletter for the Group for the Use of Psychology in History which reviews current trends and which is now in its second year of publication.

3. We owe the above summary of Dilthey's views to an important article by Hajo Holborn: "Wilhelm Dilthey and the Critique of Historical Reason," *Journal of the History of Ideas* 11 (1950): 93–118, which is also reprinted in Hajo Holborn's posthumously published collection of essays *History and the Humanities* (Garden City, New York, Doubleday and Co., 1972), pp. 125–52.

4. Manuel, "Use and Abuse," p. 162.

5. Ibid.

6. George M. Kren, "Political Implications of German Historicism," *Rocky Mountain Social Science Journal* (April, 1969): 91–99; Georg Iggers, *The German Conception of History: The National Tradition of Historical Thought from Herder to the Present* (Middletown, Conn.: Wesleyan University Press, 1968); Karl Mannheim, "Conservative Thought," *Essays on Sociology and Social Psychology* (London: Routledge & Kegan-Paul Ltd., 1953), pp. 74–164.

7. Norman O. Brown, *Loves's Body* (New York: Random House, 1966) and *Life Against Death: The Psychoanalytical Meaning of History* (New York: Random House, 1959); Herbert Marcuse, *Eros and Civilization: A Philosophical Inquiry into Freud* (Boston: The Beacon Press, 1955); cf. Paul A. Robinson, *The Freudian Left: Wilhelm Reich, Geza Roheim, Herbert Marcuse* (New York: Harper and Row, 1969); Philip Rieff, *The Triumph of the Therapeutic: Uses of Faith After Freud* (London: Chatto & Windus, 1966).

8. Otto Pflanze, "Toward a Psychoanalytic Interpretation of Bismarck," *American Historical Review* 77 (April 1972): 419–44; Peter Loewenberg, "The Unsuccessful Adolescence of Heinrich Himmler," Ibid. 76 (June 1971): 612–41; Gustav Bychowski, "Joseph V. Stalin: Paranoia and the Dictatorship of the Proletariat," Benjamin B. Wolman, ed., *The Psychoanalytic Interpretation of History* (New York/London: Basic Books Inc., 1971), 115–47; Robert G. L. Waite, "Adolf Hitler's Anti-Semitism: A Study in History and Psychoanalysis," in Ibid., 192–230; Alexander L. George & Juliette L. George, *Woodrow Wilson and Colonel House: A Personality Study* (New York: Dover Publications, 1964 (first ed., 1956); Erik H. Erikson, *Young Man Luther: A Study in Psychoanalysis and History* (New York: W.W. Norton & Co., 1962).

9. W. H. Grier and P. M. Cobbs, *Black Rage* (New York, Basic Books, 1968).

10. P. Gurin, G. Gurin, R. C. Lao, and M. Beattie, "Internal-External Control in the Motivational Dynamics of Negro Youth, *Journal of Social Issues* 25 (1969): 29–53; R. C. Lao, "Internal-External Control and Competent and Innovative Behavior Among Negro College Students," *Journal of Social Issues* 14 (1970): 263–70.

11. Robert Jay Lifton, *Death in Life: Survivors of Hiroshima* (New York, Random House, 1967).

12. Paul Goodman, "Stoicism and the Holocaust" (review of Lifton's *Death in Life*), *The New York Review of Books* 10 (March 28, 1968): 15–19.

13. Fedor Vergin, *Das Unbewusste Europa: Psychoanalyse der Europaischen Politik* (Vienna: Hess & Co., Verlag, 1931), 137–53.

14. Richard M. Brickner, *Is Germany Incurable?* (Philadelphia: J. B. Lippincott Co., 1943).

15. Leo Alexander, M.D., "War Crimes: Their Social-Psychological Aspects," *The American Journal of Psychiatry* 105 (August, 1948): 170–77; Elie A. Cohen, *Human Behavior in the Concentration Camp* (New York: Grosset & Dunlap, 1953). We believe that the concept of SS criminality causes more confusion than clarification. Cf. George M. Kren and Leon H. Rappoport, "Morality and the Nazi Camps: A Historical-Psychological Perspective on 'How Such Things Are Possible,' " *Western Humanities Review* 26 (Spring, 1972): 101-25.

16. Henry Loeblowitz-Lennard, "The Jew as Symbol," *The Psychoanalytic Quarterly* 16 (1947) 33-38; Rudolf M. Loewenstein, "The Historical and Cultural Roots of Anti-Semitism," *Psychoanalysis and the Social Sciences* 1 (1947): 313-56; Martin Wangh, "National Socialism and the Genocide of the Jew," *International Journal of Psychoanalysis* 45 (1964): 386-95. Max Horkheimer and Samuel H. Flowerman have been responsible for the publication of a series of books under the general title *Studies in Prejudice;* particularly relevant, T. W. Adorno, *The Authoritarian Personality;* Bruno Bettelheim and Morris Janowitz, *Dynamics of Prejudice;* Nathan W. Ackerman and Marie Jahoda, *Anti-Semitism and Emotional Disorder*. Freud himself has addressed himself to the problem. The literature is vast.

17. Gertrud M. Kurth, "The Jew and Adolph Hitler," *The Psychoanalytic Quarterly* 16 (1947): 11–32.

18. Robert G. L. Waite, "Adolf Hitler's Anti-Semitism: A Study in History and Psychoanalysis," Wolman, Ed., *The Psychoanalytic Interpretation*, pp. 192–230; R. G. L. Waite, "Adolf Hitler's Guilt Feelings: A Problem in History and Psychology," *The Journal of Interdisciplinary History* 1 (Winter, 1971): 229–49.

19. T. W. Adorno and others, *The Authoritarian Personality* (New York: Harper, 1950); Erich Fromm, *Escape from Freedom* (New York: Holt, Rinehart and Winston, 1941); the English edition is entitled *The Fear of Freedom*. A major critique of Fromm is provided by John H. Schaar, *Escape from Authority: The Perspectives of Erich Fromm* (New York: Harper and Row, 1964).

20. B. Christianson, *Attitudes towards Foreign Affairs as a Function of Personality* (Oslo: Oslo University Press, 1959).

21. Henry V. Dicks, *Licensed Mass Murder: A Socio-psychological Study of some SS Killers* (New York: Basic Books, Inc., 1972), pp. 68, 70-71.

22. Nevitt Sanford, "Some New Perspectives on Authroitarianism in Personality" (Presidential Address, Western Psychological Association, Portland, Oregon, 1972).

23. The Adorno tradition is continued and developed by a recent German work: Michaela von Freyhold, *Authoritarismus und Politische Apathie: Analyse einer Skala zur Ermittlung autoritätsgebundener Verhaltensweisen* (Frankfurt: Europäische Verlagsanstalt, 1971).

24. Wilhelm Reich, *The Mass Psychology of Fascism* (New York: Farrar, Strauss & Giroux, 1970). There has recently been a revival of interest in the work of Reich. Cf. the works of Rieff and Robinson cited in note 7.

25. Nevitt Sanford, Craig Comstock & Associates, *Sanctions for Evil: Sources of Social Destructiveness* (Boston: Beacon Press, 1971.)

26. Bruno Bettelheim, *The Informed Heart: Autonomy in a Mass Age* (Glencoe, Illinois: The Free Press, 1960), pp. 15-16.

27. This has been dealt with in a number of works, most notably Bettelheim, *Truants from Life: The Rehabilitation of Emotionally Disturbed Children* (Glencoe, Illinois: The Free Press, 1955); Bettelheim, *Love is not Enough: The Treatment of Emotionally Disturbed Children* (New York: Collier Books, 1965); Bettelheim and Emmy Sylvester, "Milieu Therapy—Indications and Illustrations," *The Psychoanalytic Review* 36 (1949) 54-68.

28. R. G. Baker and H. F. Wright, *The Midwest and its Children: The Psychological Ecology in an American Town* (Evanston, Illinois: Row Peterson, 1955).

29. J. H. de Rivera, *The Psychological Dimension of Foreign Policy* (Columbus, Ohio: Charles E. Merrill Publishing Co., 1968).

30. C. E. Osgood, *An Alternative to War or Surrender* (Urbana, Illinois: University of Illinois Press, 1962).

31. Erik Erikson, *Identity Youth and Crisis* (New York: W.W. Norton & Co., 1968), p. 257.

32. John Sommerville, "Bibliographic Note; Toward a History of Childhood and Youth," *The Journal of Interdisciplinary History* 3 (Autumn, 1972): 439-47.

33. Cf. Leon Rappoport, *Personality Development: The Chronology of Experience* (Glenview, Illinois: Scott, Foresman and Co., 1972), pp. 92-100.

34. See, for example, the publication of Wayne Dennis, ed., *Historical Readings in Developmental Psychology* (New York: Appleton-Century Crofts, 1972).

35. Philippe Ariès, *Centuries of Childhood: A Social History of Family Life* (New York: Random House, 1962); David Hunt, *Parents and Children in History: The Psychology of Family Life in Early Modern France* (New York: Harper and Row, 1972).

36. Hunt, *Parents and Children*, pp. 14–26.

37. Gordon Rattray Taylor, *The Angel-Makers: A Study in the Psychological Origins of Historical Change 1750–1850* (London: William Heinemann Ltd., 1958).

38. Joseph C. Rheingold, *The Fear of Being a Woman: A Theory of Maternal Destructiveness* (New York: Grune & Stratton, 1964).

39. Ibid., pp. 25–26.

40. Peter Loewenberg, "The Psychohistorical Origins of the Nazi Youth Cohort," *The American Historical Review* 76 (December, 1971): 1457–1502.

41. Ibid., 1502.

PART TWO

Psychobiography

4

On the Uses of Psychology: Conflict and Conciliation in Benjamin Franklin

RICHARD L. BUSHMAN

This article presents a practical exposition of what psychology has to offer the working historian. It might well be called "the reasonable and methodologically conservative historian's guide to psychobiography," for it makes no pretentious or dramatic arguments favoring psychology at the expense of more conventional historical methods, nor does it presume psychoanalytical training on the part of the historian.

Instead, after first discussing some of the more salient problems involved in direct application of psychology to history, Bushman carefully shows how he has been able to understand the psychodynamics underlying much of Franklin's important activity as a successful negotiator. Bushman also generalizes his discussion in a valuable way by suggesting six substantial rules or guidelines designed to help psychohistorical investigators work through their methodological difficulties. It is noteworthy, finally, that the author's studied avoidance of polemics is reminiscent of Franklin's own pragmatic, conciliatory behavior pattern; and his positive conclusions about the uses of psychology in history are all the more convincing for their general tone of reason and moderation.

Historians began to reflect on the applications of psychology when as a formal study it was still young. Mutual interest in the question of motivation made reciprocal borrowing seem natural and inevitable. Time has proven the interest more than a faddish attempt to be scientific or avant-garde. In 1957 William Langer, who had long been known for his meticulous, hardheaded scholarship, gave his blessing in his presidential address to the American Historical Association. Earlier, historical applications of psychology had intrigued historians with a psychological bent and psychoanalysts with an historical bent; but the Langer address stimulated practicing historians of all sorts to examine more carefully the possibilities of the younger discipline. Discussion has continued in crescendo ever since. [1]

In recent years, besides speculating on the uses of psychology, a number of historians have put psychological notions to work in substantive studies. [2] The results have had a mixed response. Many historians manifest considerable reluctance about embracing psychology or even accepting work where psychological conceptions are evident. Few are prepared to assimilate psychology in the way that many anthropologists accepted psychoanalysis in the 1930s. Professional conservatism, perhaps some lack of vision, but most important, the actual difficulties of applying psychology stand in the way. The great variety of personality theories and the fierce disagreements among psychologists discourage serious study. Although historians, of all people, can hardly blame any discipline for failure to arrive at a consensus, the forbidding task of sifting contending theories disposes even the most earnest seekers to wait for psychologists to set their house in order. [3]

Even those who do find a convincing theory still confront the crucial problem of evidence. In most personality theories—and particularly in psychoanalysis, with which this essay is concerned—explanations of motivation lead down into the unconscious or back toward early childhood. But the conscious mind is endeavoring to repress the memory of childhood traumas, and thus does not allow them into historical documents. Psychiatric interviews and various assessing instruments permit the psychologist to get at these unconscious materials. Then he tests each tentative hypothesis by trying it out on the person himself. Psychological formulations about dead men, by contrast, seem to be constructed from flimsy materials indeed: scattered items of aberrant behavior, the interpretation of a dream, and a comment or two about the subject's mother. Of course, the hypothesis can never be tested on the subject in the clinic. [4]

Another difficulty is that psychological speculations may fail to justify the effort and risk. Historians are accustomed to speculative hypotheses, but ones which earn their keep by ordering historical materials. Psychological hypotheses frequently serve to label rather than to illuminate a subject's conduct. Ernest Jones found Louis Bonaparte's relationship with his brother, Napoleon, marked by times of deep affection and special regard alternating with times of anger and disgust. Basing his judgment on clinical experience, Jones attributed this cycle to a latent homosexual relationship. Even if proven, the point would be little more than an interesting aside in an historical biography. The mere naming of well-known facts about Louis and identification in the psychoanalytic frame contributed little to historical knowledge. The historian wishes to order the great mass of data on Napoleon's life in all its connections. Until the hypothesis of Louis' latent homosexuality can be put to work in the historical materials, the notion is no more helpful than a resort to the *Zeitgeist*. [5]

These troubles may arise because many historians turn to psychology with a mistaken medical analogy in mind. The historian may think that he can go to a psychology text like a doctor to a pathology book to find out the nature and cause of the subject's symptoms. Difficulties over relevance and validity inevitably result. Assuming the quest is successful, the text will indicate that the symptoms show the subject was schizoid or paranoid; this discovery, as we have seen, often does nothing but bestow an imposing title on traits already identified. The cause given will likely be some unfortunate childhood experience, lack of affection in the mother, or concealed tension with the father, for which there is little evidence in the record. The historian may well conclude that his conscientious attempt to consult psychology was of little profit.

Believers in the medical analogy are mistaken for expecting both too much and too little from psychology, which cannot as yet deduce specific childhood causes for adult symptoms. Psychologists themselves do not operate this way. They infer that compulsive behavior in the patient resulted from compulsive behavior in the parent, but the actual configuration of childhood relationships and traumas is always unique. Moreover, even Freudians are inclining to the commonsense view that critical events throughout life reshape the unconscious. One's essential character is not laid down once and for all in the first five years. Erik Erikson has argued that early crises shape susceptibilities which develop into fixed patterns of widely differing form depending on the quality of later life. [6] The historian must relinquish his hopes for a handbook of single, simple causes of human conduct.

While less helpful in offering crisp diagnoses, psychology may be more helpful than expected in discerning a person's—or a group's—characteristic patterns of acting. Sometimes the historian himself notices the pattern before consulting the psychology book, but often he cannot; finding the pattern may be the most difficult part and the place where personality theory can be of greatest aid. Confronting his materials, the historian's task is to create a coherent picture.

Psychology sensitizes the researcher to new connections and draws into a pattern data normally regarded as insignificant. This may be its most important contribution, and one that is verifiable by historical criteria.[7]

Psychological theory raises a number of questions that might not normally occur. For example, how does the subject characteristically respond to authority? Does he perceive it as helpful and friendly, as cruel and domineering, or as distant and uninterested? Does he react to control by submitting, rebelling, reasoning, or pandering to authority? A similar set of questions might be asked about relations to women or to equals, about methods and success in achieving intimacy, about attitudes towards emotions of hate and love and towards the exercise of power. Merely pursuing the questions will often disclose patterns; knowledge of certain observed psychological syndromes will suggest others. Discovery that a subject's tendencies are schizoid adds little knowledge in itself, but one may learn that schizoid personalities have difficulty relating to other people and thus be alerted to conduct previously neglected. Similarly the somewhat outdated notion of an anal character, while not specifying a fixed set of qualities, may draw attention to a disposition to alternate strict restraint with periods of letting go. Even though the diagnosis of Louis Napoleon's latent homosexuality may be irrelevant, Jones' perception of an unnoticed pattern can be useful.

The patterns may be very simple, like those offered as examples, or they may be more complex; but they can be verified and made relevant to historical concerns. Suppose a person characteristically thinks of authority figures as cruel and domineering. This attitude will naturally manifest itself in his statements and actions. The researcher may discover that the person submits docilely, except when authority tries to deprive him of something; then a negative reaction occurs. By the medical analogy the historian would then look for the genesis of this trait and find himself in the historical no-man's land where nothing can be proved. The more rewarding course is to use the pattern itself as a cause in the explanation of other events. Predictions can be made that if a person characteristically submits to authority readily, except when deprived of something, government efforts to tax him unduly will engender resentment and accusations of tyranny. The explanation for the pattern, in childhood events or whatever, is historically irrelevant so long as facts are unavailable, but the role of the pattern in historical events—let us say, in a revolution—could be highly significant.

Nathan Leites's *A Study of Bolshevism* illustrates perfectly this method of using psychology. Among the rich variety of Bolshevik behavior patterns, Leites found the critical one to be a double terror.

The Bolsheviks anticipated an attack from external enemies believed to be determined to annihilate their foes; they also feared a loss of internal control that would make them more vulnerable to such attacks. Leites discovered this pattern in personal statements, in formal addresses to Party congresses, and in contemporaneous Russian literature. In his eagerness to demonstrate the empirical validity of his findings, he devoted nearly half the book to quotations.[8]

Although Leites's work is psychoanalytic political science, he never introduced theory merely to label the Bolshevik neurosis. Quite obviously psychoanalytic theory provided the questions and determined the juxtaposition of the quotations. Leites might have spoken of paranoia and latent homosexuality, but parading these terms was unnecessary for his purposes. Avoiding speculation about the childhood genesis of Bolshevik character traits, Leites concentrated on the validity of the patterns and their ramifications in Soviet strategy. He spoke to political scientists and to government policymakers and did not waver from his purpose to please psychoanalytic readers or to display his diagnostic virtuosity.

Leites's work stands as a finished product, with the materials on Bolshevik character reduced to an intelligible order, but the discovery and elaboration of a psychological pattern may still seem mysterious. I have attempted to explicate some passages from *The Autobiography of Benjamin Franklin* in the hope of illustrating how personality theory can sharpen informal observations and help shape up a testable hypothesis. The end in view is not a finished interpretation of Franklin's character, but a description of the process of applying psychology; the invitation is to observe an historian in the workshop trying out a new tool.

Every biographer looks for patterns that help explain his subject's life. Familiarity instills a more or less vague sense of a characteristic style. The problem is to crystallize these feelings into clear propositions which illuminate a large number of specific events. Beginning with a single passage or event, a close analysis using personality theory can often put together scattered impressions.

Theoretically any passage could be chosen. A comprehensive explanation should account for every word, every act. In fact, the biographer must content himself with a partial explanation. He should begin, therefore, with an episode that strikes him as representative. He may have to try a number before the outlines of a pattern begin to appear. The following passage was chosen because echoes of it are heard throughout the *Autobiography:*

When about sixteen years of age I happened to meet with a book written by one Tryon, recommending a vegetable diet. I determined to go into it. My brother, being yet unmarried, did not keep house but boarded himself and his apprentices in another family. My refusing to eat flesh occasioned an inconveniency, and I was frequently chid for my singularity. I made myself acquainted with Tryon's manner of preparing some of his dishes, such as boiling potatoes or rice, making hasty pudding, and a few others; and then proposed to my brother that if he would give me weekly half the money he paid for my board, I would board myself. He instantly agreed to it, and I presently found that I could save half what he paid me. This was an additional fund for buying of books. But I had another advantage in it. My brother and the rest going from the printing house to their meals, I remained there alone, and dispatching presently my light repast (which often was no more than a biscuit or a slice of bread, a handful of raisins or a tart from the pastry cook's, and a glass of water) had the rest of the time till their return for study, in which I made the greater progress from the greater clearness of head and quicker apprehension which generally attend temperance in eating and drinking. Now it was that being on some occasion made ashamed of my ignorance in figures, which I had twice failed in learning when at school, I took Cocker's book of arithmetic, and went through the whole by myself with the greatest ease. I also read Seller's and Sturmy's book on navigation and became acquainted with the little geometry it contains, but I never proceeded far in that science. I read about this time Locke, *On Human Understanding*, and *The Art of Thinking* by Messrs. du Port Royal. [9]

Different impressions, some ephemeral, some forceful, and doubtless varying for each reader, occur as one examines this passage. The phrase "happened to meet" in the first line suggests that Franklin was trying to say this was a casual meeting, not the result of an earnest search for the true way. In the same sentence, the words "by one Tryon" reinforce this impression. Tryon was not presented as an imposing authority whose word everyone must accept, but as a nobody whom Franklin ran across in a chance encounter.

In a somewhat carefree manner, then, he began his vegetable diet and was "frequently chid" for his "singularity." To extricate himself, he adopted a threefold stratagem: he planned to withdraw from the boardinghouse, he developed a cooking skill which enabled him to provide for himself, and he struck a bargain with his brother. And a very good bargain it was for both sides. The brother paid half as much for Franklin's food, and Benjamin in return, by practicing economy, saved half of this amount.

In the conclusion Franklin described how well he was compensated for his pains. He saved money and used it to purchase books; he saved time and used it to gain knowledge; and temperance clearing his head, he repaired earlier failures in arithmetic. Franklin implied a modest triumph over his brother as well: "I had another advantage in it. My brother and the rest going from the printing house to their meals, I remained there alone," and dispatching his light meal, moved ahead with his learning, while they, he seems to say, wasted time eating.

The reading omits much, and more must be disregarded to highlight a pattern. The very conception of pattern entails abstracting the essence from a welter of details. But the seeming arbitrariness will prove warranted if the resulting generalization can be applied to other episodes. The pattern thus far can be summarized as follows: (1) Franklin had a dispute over his singular ways of eating. (2) He withdrew from the situation and made himself independent by developing a skill and striking a mutually advantageous bargain. (3) He thereby obtained compensation in various forms and gained an implicit sense of triumph over his brother. It might be objected that not enough, rather than too much, has been omitted: the dispute, it might be said, is the essential item and the singular ways of eating incidental. The detail is retained because similar elements recur in *The Autobiography.* Franklin had an incredible memory for what he was fed, especially if the menu was skimpy, and so diet may turn out to be important. Its singularity remains for the same reason. Franklin often operated as a lone wolf standing against the common opinion. The skills and bargaining mentioned in point two also are repeated through the book. Franklin's skills as a writer, swimmer, and printer figured large in his success; and a single reading of *The Autobiography* will impress a reader with his extraordinary ability to make mutually advantageous bargains. Anyway, at this stage, an overabundance of detail is preferable to a lean generalization, for one cannot yet tell which elements will prove most nearly universal.

Although not apparent, psychological notions have already influenced the analysis. The idea of a compensatory skill is psychoanalytic, and the notion of withdrawal was suggested by Erik Erikson's conception of personality vectors as presented in Henry Murray's *Explorations in Personality.*[10] But the pattern is not yet satisfactorily developed, for its range is too limited. The sequence, which never reoccurs in just that form, must be related to a more general structure of which it is particular.

Personality theories suggest various methods of formulating general hypotheses. Among the most helpful are psychoanalytic conceptions about the formation of character in childhood, when the mind is most plastic. Freudians have related persisting attitudes, emotional styles, and preoccupations with food, money, or power to fundamental childhood experiences. Behavioral issues such as giving and taking, restraint and release, autonomy and subservience, creation and destruction, and intrusion and inclusion are traced to early crises of coming to maturity, when physical urges and capacities, especially those connected with body apertures, have had to adapt to the demands of a specific social setting. Analysts have observed a particular array of traits which seem to originate in each stage of development. These observations suggest general patterns to look for in a subject who displays some of the characteristic traits. To cite a classic example, a person obsessed with questions of restraint and release originating in the anal stage is likely also to be concerned about autonomy and subservience and about cleanliness and filth.[11] The importance of any complex for a given person depends on his inherited constitution and the treatment he receives. The best clue as to which stages of development were most significant for any individual is his persistent return to some of the related issues. The observer may then expect to find other qualities characteristically associated with this syndrome.

Perhaps the clearest way to conceive the import of these crucial social-physical experiences is to compare them to language. Before a child masters spoken language, he learns a language from his physical parts which ever after helps him to construe experience, just as ordinary language does. The idea of status-seeking, for example, imparts meaning to many observed facts. A car, a house, a style of speech may be interpreted as an effort to rise socially; and it may stimulate disgust or disdain in the observer. The mental construct determines the internal response to otherwise neutral facts. Similarly a child learns constructions from its body which become part of a basic vocabulary. Grasping objects with the hand enlarges to include grasping wealth or power or knowledge. The adult experience retains some of the emotional qualities associated in childhood with grasping—security, strength, or control. The child's environment imparts a particular form to the various critical episodes of infancy and accentuates some. These comprise his most fundamental vocabulary of emotional meanings, the broadest and most lasting frame in which he interprets life. Psychoanalysis helps the researcher to understand this vocabulary.

The episode which seemed most applicable to the passage from *The Autobiography* has been vividly portrayed by Erik Erikson. In the early months of life, a baby derives the most blissful satisfaction from nursing at its mother's breast. The combination of warmth, love, food, and pleasant sucking sensations impart a sense of perfect peace and union with its universe. The eruption of teeth disturbs this bliss, causing pain in the very place where pleasure previously centered. Teeth also disrupt the peaceful relation with the mother, for in biting to relieve its pain, the infant hurts the mother and causes her withdrawal. Erikson reports that clinical experiences shows this situation to be the origin of a dilemma: the yearning to bite conflicts with the yearning for nourishment and for the continuation of blissful well-being. The child must restrain the urge to bite and learn to obtain food without hurting. Its feelings are overshadowed by the anxiety of having been responsible for the destruction of the happy union with the mother. [12]

In time all of this is forgotten, often never to be recovered to consciousness. But for those especially affected by this crisis the problem of getting without hurting continues into adult life. The meaning of food expands to include all sustenance for the ego, praise or approval or love, which make a person feel pleased with himself and accepted in the world. The individual constantly encounters the question of how to get these "ego supplies" without hurting. Time after time he construes experience in terms of this body language and worries about his own responsibility for cutting off the source of supply.

No single element in the passage from *The Autobiography* pointed toward this reconstruction of Franklin's character. Any given fact can have various interpretations in a psychoanalytic system. A vegetarian diet might be more important in anal conflicts than in oral ones, signifying less the fear of hurting than, for example, of being polluted by corrupt substances. The appropriate analytical structure must correspond to a whole pattern of responses. In this instance, the concern about food, the discomfiture of the provider, and the effort to obtain compensating rewards without hurting anyone all seemed to fit. Throughout the book, giving and getting are prominent moral issues.

The snugness of the fit can be best appreciated when the pattern is reformulated in a set of propositions drawn from the psychoanalytic structure.

1. *Franklin was concerned about how to get supplies.* The quest for supplies is the central drive in the psychological model and also in the whole of *The Autobiography*. Franklin's point in the vegetarian episode and in virtually all that follows was that his methods of seeking gratification invariably brought rewards. Throughout the book this quest was assumed to be basic.

2. *Franklin feared he would hurt in the process of getting supplies and therefore avoided hostilities.* The psychoanalytic theory says a subject may unconsciously enjoy the sadistic pleasure of hurting and may also seek revenge on the provider who fails him, but he combats these

dangerous urges by consciously or unconsciously avoiding hurtful actions. Rather than fight for his rights, Franklin withdrew from the hostilities. Though sharp words may well have passed across the dinner table, in recounting the episode he presented himself as placid and utterly noncombative, preferring to withdraw rather than inconvenience anyone.

3. *Franklin looked for ways to obtain supplies without hurting.* In this episode the development of a skill and a mutually advantageous bargain are the chosen means, and the money, books, and so on are the supplies he obtained. The skill permitted him to get food on his own, without dependence on a temperamental and irritable provider. Later, deploying his various skills and devising clever bargains became standard methods of earning gratification without relying on anyone's fickle affection. The careful attention to the brother's interests reflected the concern that no one be hurt in the process.

4. *Franklin needed to justify his actions when involved in hostility*, or at least to determine how much to blame he was. According to the theory, the child wonders if he destroyed the "unity with a maternal matrix," and tries to assure himself that he was not guilty. This addition permits the inclusion of the initial observation, omitted from the first summary, about the casual nature of the meeting with vegetarianism. Franklin admitted that he "occasioned an inconvenience," but described himself as an innocent, free from any malice aforethought. His adoption of the vegetable diet was a lighthearted experiment, not wilful dogmatism calculated to disturb the boardinghouse table. [13]

In this form the propositions about Franklin's character have broad applications. While the earlier pattern suggested that Franklin would withdraw following disputes over eating, the new one postulates a general aversion to disputes where love and prestige are at stake and a desire to avoid them in whatever ways possible. The historian is also alerted to find Franklin seeking forms of compensation that will benefit and not hurt others, and to find him clearing himself of responsibility for instigating contention. Instead of working with a static sequence of reactions, the investigator has a dynamic model of motivation that is much more flexible and powerful.

This rather mechanical imposition of theory on the data may offend historians who conceive of their skill as an art. All the heavy machinery may seem to mangle Franklin beyond recognition. In defense, let it be said that the process is more cumbersome in the reconstruction than in the execution. The insights derived from personality theory emerge from reflection on the man exactly as any insights into motivation or purpose do. Both depend on a sensitive comparison of the subject's experience with experiences of our own or of people we know well. Both follow a path roughly like the one I have set down, though the assumptions and ramifications are usually not so well articulated. The difference in the psychologically informed and the ordinary observer is that the former calls upon the wider range of comparative experience provided by personality theory.

Of course the truth of the propositions is not yet established. The passage examined has led us to an hypothesis, not confirmed it. On first impulse one would search the reports of Franklin's childhood for evidence of tensions with his mother. Such a search bears little fruit, as might be predicted. It is a false quest because it misinterprets the meaning of the psychoanalytic construction. *The description of the infantile conflict was not primarily intended as an account of events, though there are grounds for believing they occurred, but as a symbolic representation of emotional structures present in the adult Franklin.* Childhood traumas created a lasting vocabulary of analogs by which Franklin construed experience. Evidence of this vocabulary in action is the proof we seek. The infantile crisis is recounted because that is the simplest and most coherent way of highlighting patterns which continue into adulthood.

The confirmation of the hypothesis coincides with the illumination of the text. The four propositions about Franklin's character should explain other episodes in *The Autobiography* and in his life. Whenever he sought gratification, he should characteristically have favored peaceful means, earning it by using his skills or entering into mutually advantageous bargains. Examination of every dispute should reveal in a high proportion of cases an aversion to contention and an effort to get his way without hurting others. The theory also predicts that he would try to prove his innocence; at least the question of responsibility for the dispute was one he must answer. These situations should appear frequently too, for Franklin would prize that kind of success.

Sometimes the hypothesis illuminates incidents where disputes are of small account. Apparently inconsequential details fall into place, as illustrated by a later episode in *The Autobiography*. Franklin omitted this story at first and then went out of his way to include it, indicating perhaps its importance to him.

> I believe I have omitted mentioning that in my first voyage from Boston to Philadelphia, being becalmed off Block Island, our crew employed themselves catching cod and hauled up a great number. Till then I had stuck to my resolution to eat nothing that had had life; and on this occasion I considered, according to my Master

Tryon, the taking every fish as a kind of unprovoked murder, since none of them had or ever could do us any injury that might justify this massacre. All this seemed very reasonable. But I had formerly been a great lover of fish, and when this came hot out of the frying pan, it smelled admirably well. I balanced some time between principle and inclination till I recollected that when the fish were opened, I saw smaller fish taken out of their stomachs. "Then," thought I, "if you eat one another, I don't see why we mayn't eat you." So I dined upon cod very heartily and have since continued to eat as other people, returning only now and then occasionally to a vegetable diet. So convenient a thing it is to be a *reasonable creature,* since it enables one to find or make a reason for everything one has a mind to do. [14]

The first summary of Franklin's behavior has no bearing on this passage. The incidental revelation of the reason for becoming a vegetarian—that "according to my Master Tryon, the taking of every fish" was "a kind of unprovoked murder"—stands outside the system, unexplained and neither confirming nor disproving. Reasons of health or economy would have fitted just as well. The apprehensions about killing animals, however, accord perfectly with the psychoanalytic proposition that "Franklin feared he would hurt in the process of getting supplies." Franklin gave up meat because he disliked destroying animals in order to eat them. The more general motivational statement accounts both for his acceptance of vegetarianism and his refusal to fight with the keeper of the boardinghouse.

The passage also tells how Franklin eventually decided to eat the fish. He recollected that the fish themselves had eaten smaller fish, and he reasoned that "if you eat one another, I don't see why we mayn't eat you." This rationalization confirms the notion that "Franklin needed to justify his actions when involved in hostility." Going back to the model, it will be remembered that the infant fears his own sadism has destroyed the unity with the source of supply. The discovery that the fish ate each other mitigated Franklin's responsibility.

Franklin passed off the episode lightly as an example of the ease with which reason opened the door for desire. A casual aside indicates he may have undergone more soul-searching before permanently abandoning vegetarianism. Afterwards he ate as other people, "returning only now and then occasionally to a vegetable diet." The ambiguities of feeling compelled him, even after this first departure, to reconsider the recitude of eating flesh.

Sometimes a sequence repeats the entire pattern, and the propositions illuminate the whole of it. After returning from England, Franklin went back to work for his old employer, Keimer, whom he served by training apprentices, engraving, making ink, and casting type.

> But however serviceable I might be, I found that my services became every day of less importance as the other hands improved in the business; and when Keimer paid me a second quarter's wages, he let me know that he felt them too heavy and thought I should make an abatement. He grew by degrees less civil, put on more airs of master, frequently found fault, was captious, and seemed ready for an outbreaking. I went on, nevertheless, with a good deal of patience, thinking that his incumbered circumstances were partly the cause. At length a trifle snapped our connection; for a great noise happening near the courthouse, I put my head out of the window to see what was the matter. Keimer being in the street, looked up and saw me, called out to me in a loud voice and angry tone to mind my business, adding some reproachful words that nettled me the more for their publicity, all the neighbors who were looking out on the same occasion being witnesses how I was treated. He came up immediately into the printing house, continued the quarrel; high words passed on both sides, he gave me the quarter's warning we had stipulated, expressing a wish that he had not been obliged to so long a warning. I told him his wish was unnecessary for I would leave him that instant, and so taking my hat, walked out of doors, desiring Meredith, whom I saw below, to take care of some things I left; and bring them to my lodging.

Franklin laid plans to go into the printing business with a friend, but for the time being was out of work,

> when Keimer, on a prospect of being employed to print some paper money in New Jersey which would require cuts and various types that I only could supply, and apprehending Bradford might engage me and get the job from him, sent me a very civil message that old friends should not part for a few words, the effect of sudden passion, and wishing me to return. Meredith persuaded me to comply, as it would give more opportunity for his improvement under my daily instructions. So I returned, and we went on more smoothly than for some time before. The New Jersey job was obtained. I contrived a copperplate press for it, the first that had been seen in the country. I cut several ornaments and checks for the bills. We went together to Burlington, where I executed the whole to satisfaction; and he received so large a sum for the work as to be enabled thereby to keep his head much longer above water.[15]

All of the elements of the pattern appear in this episode, perhaps most notably the avoidance of hostility. Franklin patiently bore Keimer's ill-temper for many weeks before the final blow-up. "High words" passed for a moment, but Franklin rapidly withdrew rather than remain to do battle, so rapidly that he left his possessions behind. At once he gave thought to means of earning a living independently by his skill. While waiting for equipment, he temporarily returned to Keimer in an arrangement which Franklin clearly specified was of mutual advantage. Keimer contracted for a lucrative job, and Franklin, while working on it—as he related subsequently—met high-placed individuals who later helped him. The withdrawal from hostility, the search for an independent source of supplies, the bargain all fit. So does the explanation in the first sentences where Franklin proved he was guiltless and Keimer entirely to blame for the outbreak.

The mounting evidence confirms the validity of the pattern, but it should never be mistaken for the whole of Franklin's personality. A full description would relate this portion of his character to his desire for recognition from important people, his disposition to lead, his pleasure in public service, and so on. Moreover, his identity matured gradually. By his own admission, Franklin as a youth enjoyed the attack, and suppressed his combative urges only as experience taught him better. His character was not permanently fixed by a single crisis at his mother's breast, assuming it occurred. At most this episode left him with dispositions that would have to be reinforced many times before assuming prominence in his personality.

Even a partial analysis, however, can help interpret public phases of his life as well as private incidents. The tenor of his lengthy career as an ambassador accords well with the profferred formulation. Franklin was above all a negotiator, an expert bargainer, inclined to reconcile conflicting parties on terms mutually beneficial. He so excelled in this role that at one time four colonies employed him as their London representative.[16]

Franklin lost his influence only as hostilities neared their climax. Not a revolutionary eager to resist authority in the stubborn manner of Samuel and John Adams, Franklin usually sheathed his criticisms of the mother country in wit. Even when attacking or defending he never lost his amiable manner. The vicious indictment by the solicitor-general, Alexander Wedderburn, for transmitting the Hutchinson letters to Massachusetts put Franklin's self-restraint to its most severe test, but his steely calm never broke. Eventually when relations with Britain became too strained, Franklin, it is proper to say, withdrew rather than revolted.[17]

Franklin's personality was only one among a number of determinants of his public actions. The influence of character shows up mainly in the overall shape of a career and in the style of operation. Franklin's abilities and predilections disposed him to select, and others to select him for, negotiating roles. From his first appointment as colonial agent until his last great public acts in the Constitutional Convention, Franklin bargained and reconciled in an effort to prevent overt hostilities. Always conciliatory, he was suspected of being soft when colleagues and constituents expected firmness. Near the outbreak of the Revolution, as bad feelings mounted, the colonial leaders grew suspicious because the old Doctor, for all his disgust with British policy and corruption, remained outwardly amiable. Again in Paris, John Jay and especially John Adams believed that Franklin sacrificed American interests to remain in the good graces of France and that he was, perhaps, too conciliatory with Britain. In reality Franklin never betrayed his constituents' interests. He simply preferred cordial relations, whether with friends or enemies, to any form of open hostility. As he wrote to another of the commissioners, "of all things I hate altercation." [18]

Of course Franklin, despite his personality, lived in revolutionary times. The critical point is that personal traits do affect public actions and deserve the historian's attention. So long as he concentrates on patterns of adult behavior and, where the evidence is skimpy, restrains the desire to find the origins of character, he can fruitfully use psychology. [19] Then insights derived from theoretical conceptions can be verified in the historical record. As an added advantage, this method does not require extensive, formal training. Obviously the better informed and more perceptive the researcher, the more readily will he relate behavior to theory. An awkward beginner will miss the nuances and perhaps even the main point. If the aim were to reconstruct the subject's past or his unconscious, the neophyte might go far astray. But if he carefully checks his results against the available facts, as historians are trained to do, he will not err grossly. His conclusions may lack subtlety, but they will not be unreal.

This empirical check will also inhibit dogmatism. The zeal of the convert could betray the researcher into an unwarranted faith in his new tools. The urge to explain the historical materials will keep him open to new theories and new analogies which better account for the facts. Quite possibly, another psychologist could fully explain the conflict and conciliation pattern in Franklin and assimilate still more of his conduct into a generalization drawn from a different source. Freudian notions of psychic topography—the relations of ego, superego, and id—Murray's theory of needs, Kelly's ideas about personal constructs, and others might prove more useful.[20] The historian who aims to illuminate his subject and not to confirm some notion of human nature will put to work whatever conceptions serve best.

A concluding summary may help to focus the suggested procedures.

1. The researcher becomes sufficiently familiar with his subject to recognize recurring actions, attitudes, and values. Usually a characteristic tone or stance will be vaguely sensed before its exact nature can be described.

2. The researcher absorbs theoretical constructs and works with them until they become extensions and refinements of his personal stock of common-sense notions. So long as psychological ideas stand apart as a strange body of "scientific" theories they will be employed awkwardly.

3. A passage or event from the subject's life is chosen for its characteristic qualities, based on the vague sense developed through familiarity.

4. The first step in the close analysis is to become familiar with all the components, the feelings of the participants, their responses to each other, and the moral as well as the plot of the story.[21] The second step is to try out various theoretical constructs until one seems to fit comfortably; that is, all or most of the components can be classed as particulars of the construct's generalities. Care should be taken to use the construct flexibly and with critical sensitivity. The sure sign of the beginner (much in evidence in my own work, I fear) is the rigid imposition of theory on facts, the cramming of data into the given categories without due regard for all the implications and wisps of emotional meaning emanating from it. Freudian notions especially, being more poetic than scientific in the use of metaphor, are meant to be suggestive, not iron-bound rules of human development.

5. From the theory, general propositions are formulated to describe the subject's motivation and behavior. At best these propositions are predictive and can be easily translated into the form, "if such and such conditions prevail, the subject will do thus and so."

6. The simplest form of confirmation is to test these if-then propositions. The most obvious predictive statement in the analysis of Franklin is that when faced with hostility, Franklin would seek to avoid it and achieve his ends peaceably. His autobiography offers a plentiful number of such instances. The more complex confirmation comes from the process I have called illumination. An odd fact, such as the adoption of vegetarianism to avoid killing animals, is seen to fit. Actually illumination is a form of prediction. It might have been predicted that if Franklin saw that vegetarianism avoided hostility in getting supplies, he

would adopt vegetarianism. But the specific circumstances of life are too complex for the researcher to think up all such possibilities in advance. Consequently, he must often content himself with after-the-fact understanding.

These final comments suggest that confirmation might be reduced to a rigorous procedure able to pass rather strict methodological tests. Few historians will go so far. Most will be satisfied with the generous amount of understanding which rewards the more informal pursuit of psychological insights.

Notes

1. There is a brief outline of the early speculations in Norman Kiell, ed., *Psychological Studies of Famous Americans: The Civil War Era* (New York, 1964). Langer's address was published as "The Next Assignment," *American Historical Review* 63 (1958), 283-304. Representative of recent discussions are Bruce Mazlish, ed., *Psychoanalysis and History* (Englewood Cliffs, New Jersey, 1963); II. Stuart Hughes, *History as Art and as Science: Twin Vistas on the Past* (New York, 1964), chapter III; and John A. Garraty, *The Nature of Biography* (New York, 1957), chapter 9. There is also a vast literature pertinent to the historian's interests written by psychologists, anthropologists, and political scientists.

2. Representative of recent work are: Stanley M. Elkins, *Slavery: A Problem in American Institutional and Intellectual Life* (New York, 1963); Alexander L. George and Juliette L. George, *Woodrow Wilson and Colonel House: A Personality Study* (New York, 1956); William B. Willcox, *Portrait of a General: Sir Henry Clinton in the War of Independence* (New York, 1964); Emery J. Battis, *Saints and Sectaries: Anne Hutchinson and the Antinomian Controversy in Massachusetts Bay Colony* (Chapel Hill, 1962). The most striking work is by a psychoanalyst: Erik Erikson, *Young Man Luther: A Study in Psychoanalysis and History* (New York, 1958).

3. As a consequence of diversity, no one can claim possession of *the* psychological interpretation or surround his work with an aura of scientific certainty. Even psychologists of the same persuasion disagree on significant points. Psychological conceptions must be employed with appropriate humility.

4. A psychologist discusses the problem of evidence in Frederick Wyatt, "Psychoanalytic Biography," *Contemporary Psychology* 1 (1956), 105–07.

5. Ernest Jones, "The Case of Louis Bonaparte, King of Holland," in *Essays in Applied Psychoanalysis* (London, 1951), 39-54. Jones said that his observations would have to be carried further to be historically relevant and left this task to the historians.

6. Erikson makes his case and gives examples in *Young Man Luther* and in *Childhood and Society* (2nd ed., New York, 1963).

7. A psychologist makes a similar point, though still giving somewhat too much attention to what is "psychologically interesting," in Fritz Schmidl, "Psychoanalysis and History," *Psychoanalytic Quarterly* 31 (1962), 532–48.

8. Nathan Leites, *A Study of Bolshevism* (Glencoe, Illinois, 1953). The most succinct summary of the pattern is on pp. 24–25.

9. Max Farrand, ed., *The Autobiography of Benjamin Franklin* [1818] (Berkeley, 1949), 20-21.

10. Henry A. Murray, et al., *Explorations in Personality* (New York, 1938), 102–105.

11. Many patterns are described in Erikson, *Childhood and Society.*

12. Ibid., 78–79.

13. The theory would also postulate the presence of an evil feeling about life underlying Franklin's prevalent optimism, but this quality could not be exhibited without a much more complicated demonstration than is feasible here.

14. *Autobiography*, 43-44.

15. Ibid., 67-69.

16. The standard source of biographical information is Carl Van Doren, *Benjamin Franklin* (New York, 1938). Information about Franklin's colonial agencies is on p. 359.

17. Van Doren treats the Wedderburn incident in chapter 17.

18. Van Doren, *Franklin*, 450-51, 480-81, 688-89, 694. The quotation is from a letter to Arthur Lee, April 4, 1778, in Carl Van Doren, ed., *Benjamin Franklin's Autobiographical Writings* (New York, 1945), 442.

19. I do not mean to say that childhood can never be reconstructed. The biographer is obliged to make the most of his evidence, however skimpy. But historians should not denigrate psychology because it seems to stress that part of life where the record is least complete. Psychological conceptions can illuminate adulthood as well. Moreover, a genetic reconstruction is of little use unless it sheds light on adult behavior.

20. Murray, *Explorations in Personality;* George A. Kelly, *The Psychology of Personal Constructs*, two vols. (New York, 1955). I have demonstrated to my own satisfaction the usefulness of the personality theories of Murray and Kelly by applying them to historical problems.

21. Formal inventories of components may be found in the manuals of the Thematic Apperception Test.

5

The Legend of Hitler's Childhood

ERIK H. ERIKSON

William Langer must be credited with sounding the call for a union between the disciplines of history and psychology, but it was left to Erik Erikson to respond to this challenge with a concrete achievement. Erikson's Young Man Luther *has served as the model for many psychohistorical studies. In this work—as in his later Gandhi study—Erikson employed his Freudian theory of developmental stages to explain historical personality.*

If psychobiography is the most widespread and certainly the most popular form of psychohistory, it is because sufficient evidence is available to provide a convincing psychological reconstruction of many historical figures. But psychobiography does not always succeed in making the crucial connection between individual personality and major historical trends. In this study of Hitler and Germany, Erikson convincingly relates the individual personality of Hitler to general trends of German history. He escapes the danger, to which so many psychohistorians fall prey, of resurrecting a great-man-in-history theory which insists that the great (or in some cases, the pathological) personality is the primary cause of all major events.

I shall take as my text the Brown Piper's sweetest, most alluring tune: the account of his childhood, in *Mein Kampf.*

> In this little town on the river Inn, Bavarian by blood and Austrian by nationality, gilded by the light of German martyrdom, there

lived, at the end of the eighties of last century, my parents: the father a faithful civil servant, the mother devoting herself to the cares of the household and looking after her children with eternally the same loving care.[1]

The sentence structure, the tone quality, indicate that we are to hear a fairy tale; and indeed we shall analyze it as part of a modern attempt to create a myth. But a myth, old or modern, is not a lie. It is useless to try to show that it has no basis in fact; nor to claim that its fiction is fake and nonsense. A myth blends historical fact and significant fiction in such a way that it "rings true" to an area or an era, causing pious wonderment and burning ambition. The people affected will not question truth or logic; the few who cannot help doubting will find their reason paralyzed. To study a myth critically, therefore, means to analyze its images and themes in their relation to the culture area affected.

Germany

"This little town. . . . Bavarian by blood and Austrian by nationality, gilded by the light of German martyrdom. . . ."

Hitler was born in the Austrian town of Braunau, near the German border. He thus belonged to the Austrian Empire's German minority.

It had been in Braunau, he records, that a man named Palm was shot by Napoleon's soldiers for printing a pamphlet: *In the Hour of Germany's Deepest Humiliation*. Palm's memorial stands in the center of the town.

There was, of course, no German Reich in Palm's time. In fact, some of the German states were Napoleon's military allies. But having used the all-inclusive, the magic term "Germany," Palm, when delivered to Napoleon by the Austrian police, became the idol of the nationalist movement calling for a greater Germany.

Having pointed to Palm's resistance to and martyrdom under the sinister *Bonaparte*, the story proceeds to describe young Adolf's heroic opposition to his *father*, and tells of the German minority's hatred of the Austrian *emperor*. Little Adolf belonged, so he says, to "those who in painful emotion long for the hour that will allow them to return to the arms of the beloved mother"—Germany.

It is here that his imagery begins to involve terms of family relations which openly identify his "oedipus" situation with his country's national problems. He complains that this "beloved mother, . . . the *young* Reich," by her "tragic alliance with the *old Austrian sham state* . . . herself sanctioned the slow extermination of the German nationality."

Hitler's mother was twenty-three years younger than his father; and, as we shall see, the mother, as a good woman of her day, valiantly stood up for the man who beat her. The father was a drunkard and a tyrant. The equation suggests itself that in Hitler's national as well as domestic imagery, the young mother betrays the longing son for a senile tyrant. Little Adolf's personal experience thus blends with that of the German minority which refuses to sing "God Save Emperor Francis" when the Austrian anthem is sung and substitutes for it "Germany over All." Hitler continues: "The direct result of this period was: first, I became a nationalist; second, I learned to grasp and to understand the meaning of history . . . so that at fifteen, I already understood the difference between dynastic patriotism and popular nationalism."

Such seemingly naive coincidence of themes lends itself easily—much too easily—to a psychoanalytic interpretation of the first chapter of *Mein Kampf* as an involuntary confession of Hitler's oedipus complex. This interpretation would suggest that in Hitler's case the love for his young mother and the hate for his old father assumed morbid proportions, and that it was this conflict which drove him to love and to hate and compelled him to save or destroy people and peoples who really "stand for" his mother and his father. There have been articles in psychoanalytic literature which claim such simple causality. But it obviously takes much more than an individual complex to make a successful revolutionary. The complex creates the initial fervor; but if it were too strong it would paralyze the revolutionary, not inspire him. The striking use of parental and familial images in Hitler's public utterances has that strange mixture of naive confession and shrewd propaganda which characterizes the histrionic genius. Goebbels knew this and he guided his barking master well—until very close to the end.

I shall not now review the psychiatric literature which has described Hitler as a "psychopathic paranoid," an "amoral sadistic infant," an "overcompensatory sissy," or "a neurotic laboring under the compulsion to murder." At times, he undoubtedly was all of that. But, unfortuately, he was something over and above it all. His capacity for acting and for creating action was so rare that it seems inexpedient to apply ordinary diagnostic methods to his words. He was first of all an adventurer, on a grandiose scale. The personality of the adventurer is akin to that of an actor, because he must always be ready to personify, as if he had chosen them, the changing roles suggested by the whims of fate. Hitler shares with many an actor the fact that he is said to have been queer and unbearable behind the scenes, to say nothing of in his bedroom. He undoubtedly had hazardous borderline traits. But he knew how to approach the borderline, to appear as if he were going too far, and then to turn back on his breathless audience. Hitler knew how to exploit his own hysteria. Medicine men, too, often have this gift. On the stage of German history, Hitler sensed to what extent it was safe to let his own personality represent with hysterical abandon what was alive in every German listener and reader. Thus the role he chose reveals as much about his audience as about himself; and precisely that which to the non-German looked queerest and most morbid became the Brown Piper's most persuasive tune for German ears.

Father

". . . the father a faithful civil servant . . ."

Despite this sentimental characterization of the father, Hitler spends a heated portion of his first chapter in reiterating the assertion that neither his father nor "any power on earth could make an official" out of him. He knew already in earliest adolescence that the life of an official had no appeal for him. How different he was from his father! For though his father, too, had rebelled in early adolescence and at the age of thirteen had run away from home to become "something 'better,' " he had, after twenty-three years, returned home—and become a minor official. And "nobody remembered the little boy of long ago." This futile rebellion, Hitler says, made his father old early. Then, point for point, Hitler demonstrates a rebellious technique superior to that of his father.

Is this the naive revelation of a pathological father-hate? Or if it is shrewd propaganda, what gave this Austrian German the right to expect that the tale of his boyhood would have a decisive appeal for masses of Reichs-Germans?

Obviously, not all Germans had fathers of the kind Hitler had, although many undoubtedly did. Yet we know that a literary theme, to be convincing, need not be true; it must sound true, as if it reminded one of something deep and past. The question, then, is whether the German father's position in his family made him act—either all of the time, or enough of the time, or at memorable times—in such a way that he created in his son an *inner* image which had some correspondence to that of the older Hitler's publicized image.

Superficially, the position in his family of the German middle-class father of the late nineteenth and the early twentieth century may have been quite similar to other Victorian versions of "life with Father." But patterns of education are elusive. They vary in families and persons; they may remain latent only to appear during memorable crises; they may be counteracted by determined attempts to be different.

I shall present here an impressionistic version of what I consider one pattern of German fatherhood. It is representative in the sense in which

Galton's blurred composites of photography are representative of what they are supposed to show.

When the father comes home from work, even the walls seem to pull themselves together (*"nehmen sich zusammen"*). The mother—although often the unofficial master of the house—behaves differently enough to make a baby aware of it. She hurries to fulfill the father's whims and to avoid angering him. The children hold their breath, for the father does not approve of "nonsense"—that is, neither of the mother's feminine moods nor of the children's playfulness. The mother is required to be at his disposal as long as he is at home; his behavior suggests that he looks with disfavor on that unity of mother and children in which they had indulged in his absence. He often speaks to the mother as he speaks to the children, expecting compliance and cutting off any answer. The little boy comes to feel that all the gratifying ties with his mother are a thorn in the father's side, and that her love and admiration—the model for so many later fulfillments and achievements—can be reached only without the father's knowledge, or against his explicit wishes.

The mother increases this feeling by keeping some of the child's "nonsense" or badness from the father—if and when she pleases; while she expresses her disfavor by telling on the child when the father comes home, often making the father execute periodical corporal punishment for misdeeds, the details of which do not interest him. Sons are bad, and punishment is always justified. Later, when the boy comes to observe the father in company, when he notices his father's subservience to superiors, and when he observes his excessive sentimentality when he drinks and sings with his equals, the boy acquires that first ingredient of *Weltschmerz:* a deep doubt of the dignity of man—or at any rate of the "old man." All this, of course, exists concurrently with respect and love. During the storms of adolescence, however, when the boy's identity must settle things with his father image, it leads to that severe German *Pubertät* which is such a strange mixture of open rebellion and "secret sin," cynical delinquency and submissive obedience, romanticism and despondency, and which is apt to break the boy's spirit, once and for all.

In Germany, this pattern had traditional antecedents. It always just happened to happen, although it was, of course, not "planned." Indeed, some fathers who had resented the pattern deeply during their own boyhood wished desperately not to inflict it on their boys. But this wish again and again traumatically failed them in periods of crisis. Others tried to repress the pattern, only to augment both their and their children's neuroticisms. Often the boy sensed that the father himself was unhappy about his inability to break the vicious circle; for this emotional impotence the boy felt pity and disgust.

What, then, made this conflict so universally fateful? What differentiates—in an unconscious but decisive way—the German father's aloofness and harshness from similar traits in other Western fathers? I think the difference lies in the German father's essential lack of true inner authority—that authority which results from an integration of cultural ideal and educational method. The emphasis here definitely lies on *German* in the sense of *Reichs-German*. So often when discussing things German, we think and speak of well-preserved German *regions*, and of "typical" yet isolated instances where the German father's inner authority seemed deeply justified, founded as it was on old rural and small urban *Gemütlichkeit*; on urban *Kultur*; on Christian *Demut*; on professional *Bildung*; or on the spirit of social *Reform*. The important point is that all of this did not assume an integrated meaning on a national scale as the imagery of the Reich became dominant and industrialization undermined the previous social stratification.

Harshness is productive only where there is a sense of obligation in command, a sense of dignity in voluntary obedience. This, however, only an integrating cause can provide: a cause that unites past and present in accord with changes in the economic, political, and spiritual institutions.

The other Western nations had their democratic revolutions. They, as Max Weber demonstrated, by gradually taking over the privileges of their aristocratic classes, had thereby identified with aristocratic ideals. There came to be something of the French chevalier in every Frenchman, of the Anglo-Saxon gentleman in every Englishman, and of the rebellious aristocrat in every American. This something was fused with revolutionary ideals and created the concept of "free man"—a concept which assumes inalienable rights, indispensable self-denial, and unceasing revolutionary watchfulness. For reasons which we shall discuss presently, in connection with the problem of *Lebensraum*, the German identity never quite incorporated such imagery to the extent necessary to influence the unconscious modes of education. The average German father's dominance and harshness was not blended with the tenderness and dignity which comes from participation in an integrating cause. Rather, the average father, either habitually or in decisive moments, came to represent the habits and the ethics of the German top sergeant and petty official who—"dress'd in a little brief authority"—would never be more but was in constant danger of becoming less; and who had sold the birthright of a free man for an official title or a life pension.

In addition, there was the breakdown of the cultural institution which had taken care of the adolescent conflict in its traditional—and regional—forms. In the old days, for example, the custom of *Wan-*

derschaft existed. The boy left home in order to be an apprentice in foreign lands at about the age—or a little later—at which Hitler announced his opposition, and at which Hitler's father had run away from home. In the immediate pre-Nazi era, some kind of break either still took place, with parental thunder and maternal tears; or it was reflected in more moderate conflicts which were less effective because more individualized and often neurotic; or it was repressed, in which case not the father-boy relation, but the boy's relation to himself, was broken. Often the—exclusively male—teachers had to bear the brunt of it; while the boy extended his idealistic or cynical hostility over the whole sphere of *Bürgerlichkeit*—the German boy's contemptible world of "mere citizens." The connotation of this word *Bürger* is hard to transmit. It is not identical with the solid burgher; nor with the glutted bourgeois of the class-conscious revolutionary youth; and least of all with the proud citoyen or the responsible citizen, who, accepting his equal obligations, asserts his right to be an individual. Rather it means a kind of adult who has betrayed youth and idealism, and has sought refuge in a petty and servile kind of conservatism. This image was often used to indicate that all that was "normal" was corrupt, and that all that was "decent" was weak. As "Wanderbirds," adolescent boys would indulge in a romantic unity with Nature, shared with many co-rebels and led by special types of youth leaders, professional and confessional adolescents. Another type of adolescent, the "lone genius," would write diaries, poems, and treatises; at fifteen he would lament with Don Carlos' most German of all adolescent complaints: "Twenty years old, and as yet nothing done for immortality!" Other adolescents would form small bands of intellectual cynics, of delinquents, of homosexuals, and of race-conscious chauvinists. The common feature of all these activities, however, was the exclusion of the individual fathers as an influence and the adherence to some mystic-romantic entity: Nature, Fatherland, Art, Existence, etc., which were super images of a pure mother, one who would not betray the rebellious boy to that ogre, the father. While it was sometimes assumed that the mother would openly or secretly favor, if not envy, such freedom, the father was considered its mortal foe. If he failed to manifest sufficient enmity, he would be deliberately provoked: for his opposition was the life of the experience.

At this stage, the German boy would rather have died than be aware of the fact that this misguided, this excessive initiative in the direction of utter utopianism would arouse deep-seated guilt and at the end lead to stunned exhaustion. The identification with the father which in spite of everything had been well established in early childhood would come to the fore. In intricate ways treacherous Fate (=reality) would finally make a *Bürger* out of the boy—a "mere citizen" with an eternal sense of sin for having sacrificed genius for Mammon and for a mere wife and mere children such as anyone can have.

Naturally, this account is made typical to the point of caricature. Yet I believe that both the overt type and the covert pattern existed, and that, in fact, this regular split between precocious individualistic rebellion and disilllusioned, obedient citizenship was a strong factor in the political immaturity of the German: this adolescent rebellion was an abortion of individualism and of revolutionary spirit. It is my belief that the German fathers not only did not oppose this rebellion, but, indeed, unconsciously fostered it, as one sure way of maintaining their patriarchal hold over youth. For once a patriarchal superego is firmly established in early childhood, you can give youth rope: they cannot let themselves go far.

In the Reichs-German character, this peculiar combination of idealistic rebellion and obedient submission led to a paradox. The German conscience is self-denying and cruel; but its ideals are shifting and, as it were, homeless. The German is harsh with himself and with others; but extreme harshness without inner authority breeds bitterness, fear, and vindictiveness. Lacking coordinated ideals, the German is apt to approach with blind conviction, cruel self-denial, and supreme perfectionism many contradictory and outright destructive aims.

After the defeat and the revolution of 1918 this psychological conflict was increased to the point of catastrophe in the German middle classes; and the middle classes anywhere significantly include the worker class in so far as it aspires to become middle-class. Their servility toward the upper class, which had lost the war, was now suddenly robbed of any resemblance to a meaningful subordination. The inflation endangered pensions. On the other hand, the groping masses were not prepared to anticipate or usurp either the role of free citizens or that of class-conscious workers. It is clear that only under such conditions could Hitler's images immediately convince so many—and paralyze so many more.

I shall not claim, then, that Hitler's father, as described in derogatory accounts, was, in his manifestly rude form, a typical German father. It frequently happens in history that an extreme and even atypical personal experience fits a universal latent conflict so well that a crisis lifts it to a representative position. In fact, it will be remembered here that great nations are apt to choose somebody from just beyond the borders to become their leader: as Napoleon came from Corsica, Stalin came from Georgia. It is a universal childhood pattern, then, which is the basis for the deep wonderment which befell the German man who read about Hitler as a youth. "No matter how firm and determined my father might be . . . his son was just as stubborn and obstinate in rejecting an idea which had little or no appeal for him. I did not want to become an official." This combination of personal revelation and shrewd propaganda (together with loud and determined action) at last carried with it that universal conviction for which the smoldering rebellion in German youth had been waiting: that no old man, be he father, emperor, or god, need stand in the way of his love for his mother Germany. At the same time it proved to the grown-up men that by betraying their rebellious adolescence they had become unworthy of leading Germany's youth, which henceforth would "shape its own destiny." Both fathers and sons now could identify with the Führer, an adolescent who never gave in.

Psychologists overdo the father attributes in Hitler's historical image; Hitler the adolescent who refused to become a father by any connotation, or, for that matter, a kaiser or a president. He did not repeat Napoleon's error. He was the Führer: a glorified older brother, who took over prerogatives of the fathers without overidentifying with them: calling his father "old while still a child," he reserved for himself the new position of the one who remains young in possession of supreme power. He was the unbroken adolescent who had chosen a career apart from civilian happiness, mercantile tranquillity, and spiritual peace: a gang leader who kept the boys together by demanding their admiration, by creating terror, and by shrewdly involving them in crimes from which there was no way back. And he was a ruthless exploiter of parental failures.

"The question of my career was to be settled more quickly than I had anticipated. . . . When I was thirteen my father died quite suddenly. My mother felt the obligation to continue my education for the career of an official." Thus thwarted, Hitler developed a severe pulmonary illness, and "all that I had fought for, all that I had longed for in secret, suddenly became reality. . . ." His mother had to grant the sick boy what she had denied the healthy and stubborn one: he could now go and prepare to be an artist. He did—and failed the entrance examination to the national art school. Then his mother died, too. He was now free—and lonely.

Professional failure followed that early school failure which in retrospect is rationalized as character strength and boyish toughness. It is well known how in picking his sub-leaders Hitler later redeemed similar civilian failures. He got away with this only because of the German habit of gilding school failure with the suspicion of hidden genius: "humanistic" education in Germany suffered all along from the severe split of fostering duty and discipline while glorifying the nostalgic outbreaks of poets.

In his dealings with the "old" generation inside or outside Germany, Hitler consequently played a role as stubborn, as devious, and as cynical as he reports his to have been in relation to his father. In fact, whenever he felt that his acts required public justification and apology, he was likely to set the stage as he did in the first chapter of *Mein Kampf.* His tirades were focused on one foreign leader—Churchill or Roosevelt—and described him as a feudal tyrant and a senile fool. He then created a second image, that of the slick, rich son and decadent cynic: Duff-Cooper and Eden, of all men, are the ones he selected. And, indeed, Germans acquiesced to his broken pledges, as long as Hitler, the tough adolescent, seemed merely to be taking advantage of other men's senility.

Mother

". . . the mother devoting herself to the cares of the household and looking after her children with eternally the same loving care."

Beyond this continuation of his fairy tale, Hitler says little of his mother. He mentions that she was sometimes lovingly worried about the fights he, the boy hero, got into; that after the father's death, she felt "obliged"—out of duty rather than inclination—to have him continue his education; and that soon she, too, died. He had respected his father, he says, but loved his mother.

Of "her children" there is no further word. Hitler never was the brother of anyone.

That Hitler, the histrionic and hysterical adventurer, had a pathological attachment to his mother, there can be little doubt. But this is not the point here. For, pathological or not, he deftly divides his mother image into the two categories which are of the highest propagandistic value: the loving, childlike, and slightly martyred cook who belongs in the warm and cozy background—and the gigantic marble or iron virgin, the monument to the ideal. In contrast to the sparsity of reference to his personal mother, then, there is an abundance of superhuman mother figures in his imagery. His Reichs-German fairy tale does not simply say that Hitler was born in Braunau because his parents lived there; no, it was "Fate which designated my birthplace." This happened when it happened not because of the natural way of things; no, it was an "unmerited mean trick of Fate" that he was "born in a period between two wars, at a time of quiet and order." When he was poor, "Poverty clasped me in her arms"; when sad, "Dame Sorrow was my foster mother." But all this "cruelty of Fate" he later learned to praise as the "wisdom of Providence," for it hardened him for the service of Nature, "the cruel Queen of all wisdom."

When the World War broke out, "Fate graciously permitted" him to become a German foot soldier, the same "inexorable Goddess of Fate, who uses wars to weigh nations and men." When after the defeat he stood before a court defending his first revolutionary acts, he felt certain "that the Goddess of History's eternal judgment will smilingly tear up" the jury's verdict.

Fate, now treacherously frustrating the hero, now graciously catering to his heroism and tearing up the judgment of the bad old men: this is the infantile imagery which pervades much of German idealism; it finds its most representative expression in the theme of the young hero who becomes great in a foreign country and returns to free and elevate the "captive" mother: the romantic counterpart to the saga of King Oedipus.

Behind the imagery of superhuman mothers there thus lurks a two-faced image of maternity: the mother at one time appears playful, childlike, and generous; and at another, treacherous, and in league with sinister forces. This, I believe, is a common set of images in patriarchal societies where woman, in many ways kept irresponsible and childlike, becomes a go-between and an in-between. It thus happens that the father hates in her the elusive children, and the children hate in her the aloof father. Since "the mother" regularly becomes and remains the unconscious model for "the world," under Hitler the ambivalence toward the maternal woman became one of the strongest features of German official thinking.

The Führer's relationship to motherhood and family remained ambiguous. In elaboration of a national fantasy he saw in himself a lonely man fighting and pleasing superhuman mother figures which now try to destroy him, now are forced to bless him. But he did not acknowledge women as companions up to the bitter end, when he insisted on making an honest woman out of Eva Braun, whom he presently shot with his own hands—or so the legend ends. But the wives of other men gave birth to their children in the shelter of the chancellery, while he himself, according to his official biographer, "is the embodiment of the national will. He does not know any family life; neither does he know any vice."

Hitler carried this official ambivalence toward women over into his relationship to Germany as an image. Openly despising the masses of his countrymen, who, after all, constitute Germany, he stood frenziedly before them, and implored them with his fanatical cries of "Germany, Germany, Germany" to believe in a mystical national entity.

But then, the Germans have always been inclined to manifest a comparable attitude of ambivalence toward mankind and the world at large. That the world is essentially perceived as an "outer world" is true for most tribes or nations. But for Germany the world is constantly changing its quality—and always to an extreme. The world is experienced either as vastly superior in age and wisdom, the goal of eternal longing and *Wanderlust;* or as a mean, treacherous, encircling encampment of enemies living for one aim—namely, the betrayal of Germany; or as a mysterious *Lebensraum* to be won by Teutonic courage and to be used for a thousand years of adolescent aggrandizement.

Note

1. Adolf Hitler, *Mein Kampf,* Reynal & Hitchcock edition, New York, 1941, by arrangement with Houghton-Mifflin Company.

6

Woodrow Wilson and Colonel House: Research Note

ALEXANDER L. GEORGE AND JULIETTE L. GEORGE

The first edition of the authors' psychobiography of Woodrow Wilson was written in 1956, when psychohistory hardly existed as a discipline. Deliberately avoiding the use of even a minimal technical vocabulary, the authors explain the dynamics of Wilson's personality in relation to his policies.

This work should be contrasted with the two important studies on peacemaking by Arno Mayer, Politics and the Diplomacy of Peacemaking, *and* Political Origin of the New Diplomacy 1917–1918, *both of which treat Wilson's behavior as governed by his rejection of Bolshevik ideology. The Georges, in contrast, emphasize that Wilson's public actions were largely the result of private needs.*

It was inevitable that, sooner or later, specialists in psychology should turn their attention to the intriguing puzzle of Wilson's personality and career. Freud himself collaborated in a study of Wilson which is as yet unpublished. The extraordinary role of "conscience" and "stubbornness" in Wilson's political behavior, noted by numerous of his contemporaries and biographers, will certainly kindle the interest of students of personality and raise the question as to how far their specialized theories about such matters are applicable to Wilson. The interest of the psychologically oriented biographer is also likely to be aroused by the discerning observation of a gifted man of letters, Edmund Wilson, who said of Woodrow Wilson's career:

> As President of the United States, he repeated after the War his whole tragedy as president of Princeton—with Lodge in the role of

From *Woodrow Wilson and Colonel House: A Personality Study* (New York: Dover, 1964), 317-322.

> West, the League of Nations in the place of the quad system, and the Senate in the place of the Princeton trustees. It is possible to observe in certain lives, where conspicuously superior abilities are united with serious deficiencies, not the progress in a career or vocation that carries the talented man to a solid position or a definite goal, but a curve plotted over and over again and always dropping from some flight of achievement to a steep descent into failure. ("Woodrow Wilson at Princeton," *Shores of Light*, N.Y.: Farrar, Straus and Young, Inc., 1952, 322.)

Our own research on Wilson dates back to 1941 when the senior author prepared a paper on Wilson's personality for a graduate course on "Personality and Politics," given at the University of Chicago by Dr. Nathan Leites. Receiving encouragement from Leites, Dr. Harold D. Lasswell and others, he prepared a second version of the study, which was presented before the Society for Social Research at the University of Chicago in 1949. More recently, in September, 1956, at the annual meeting of the American Political Science Association, we gave a paper on problems of data collection and interpretation encountered in the study. These papers, especially the first two, were technical in character and terminology. In this book, however, we present our findings in relatively nontechnical language, hoping thereby to achieve better communication with general readers as well as with the many diversely oriented specialists who share an interest in political leadership.

There have been important modifications of the study since its inception. The initial characterization of Wilson as sharing traits associated with the compulsive character type, while helpful in many ways, had important limitations. As with most diagnoses confined merely to identification of deeper layers of motivation, it was static, and did not identify the specific types of situations in which his behavior was narrowly circumscribed in range and flexibility.

Our initial impression of Wilson's "compulsive" personality underwent considerable revision when we began to examine his entire career in detail. We were confronted by evidence of an unusual flexibility of behavior in many situations; a knack of selecting as his political goals only those projects which were ripe for realization; and finally, a skill in political maneuver and in the tactics of leadership which were at times both shrewd and inventive.

Though burdened with serious, at times crippling, temperamental defects, Wilson was capable in many types of situations of behaving expediently in the pursuit of his political objectives and of acting creatively and constructively in political life. The impressive successes which Wilson was able to achieve as President of Princeton, Governor of

New Jersey and President of the United States, it emerged, were due in no small measure to the fact that he was able to harness and adapt the driving ambition and energy engendered by personal maladjustment into an effective pattern of leadership. Though forced to operate within a governmental system of divided powers and checks and balances, Wilson's driving, essentially autocratic leadership was for a number of years politically acceptable and successful. This achievement was due in large measure of course, to the character of the situation at the time, which favored political reforms and strong leadership. But it owed something also to his ability to adapt his desire to function as a prime minister to conditions as he found them and to rationalize the type of leadership he offered the country in terms of democratic theory and the national interest.

We have tried, therefore, to identify the many facets of Wilson's personality and to study them in the context of his life history. This approach reflects a growing trend in the investigation of personality and character within the psychological sciences. The complexity of personality organization, the important role of ego functioning, and the variety of ways in which given personality factors may express themselves in a political leader's behavior—all these emerge only when the career as a whole, not merely a few isolated episodes from it, is examined in detail.

The developmental analysis of political leaders—our case study of Wilson is an attempt in that direction—draws upon both genetic and dynamic propositions about personality. In recent years numerous students of personality development have felt the need to revise and broaden Freud's theory concerning the relationship of character formation to early sexual experience. As a result, the investigator who now attempts to use genetic psychology for purposes of political biography is confronted with an impressive array of propositions and hypotheses which have not as yet been fully integrated. Most helpful for our purpose, therefore, has been Dr. Harold D. Lasswell's synthesis and restatement of the state of knowledge about personality development from the standpoint of its implications for the study of political leadership. [1]

The present consensus among specialists in personality development appears to be that a variety of early childhood experiences may exercise an important formative influence on basic personality structure, but that, in any case, it is an oversimplification to explain adult behavior exclusively in these terms. In the developmental biography, accordingly, the investigator must be concerned with the development of the subject's total personality throughout his formative years and, indeed, sometimes well into adult life. He attempts to trace the subject's efforts from early childhood on to cope with his anxieties. He attempts to identify not only the development of defenses against these anxieties but also the adjustive and constructive strategies devised by the individual in an effort to harness his anxieties and to avoid situations in which they might have severely disruptive effects. In tracing the individual's elaboration and structuring of a personality system and his development of an outlook on life, the investigator pays particular attention to his familial, cultural, and social milieu. For it is in interaction with his milieu that the individual "finds himself" and learns ways of expressing himself in a satisfying manner. It is from this standpoint that the biographer examines the development of the subject's interest in politics and in leadership, and attempts to account for the subject's selection of a particular political role for himself. It is from this standpoint, too, that he studies the subject's efforts to develop the skills appropriate to the political role which he has chosen.

In a developmental biography the interaction between personality and situational factors throughout the subject's career is studied chronologically and cross-sectionally. Important episodes and actions in the life history are selected for intensive analysis; in these cross-sectional analyses of behavior, the individual's previous life history is regarded as a set of learning experiences which have structured predispositions operative in the present situation.

The general purpose of situational analysis of personality functioning is to identify the dynamics of the subject's political behavior and to characterize his ego functioning. It may be relatively easy to identify a personal value (power, approval, affection, deference, security, rectitude, etc.) for which the subject seeks some satisfaction in political life. But few political leaders who are at all successful in a democratic environment, even those who, as Wilson, are noticeably power-oriented from an early age, pursue a single value in political life to the exclusion of others.

In the case of someone like Wilson, certainly a multi-valued political personality, the task of establishing underlying motivational forces is difficult and complex. For it becomes necessary to assess the *relative strength* of individual value demands, the ways in which competing or conflicting value demands are *reconciled* in choosing one's goals, and the *conditions* under which one or another value or value pattern has primacy in motivation. Not only is the strength of the demand for some values perhaps greater than that for others, but their relative importance and operative role in specific situations may vary with the subject's shifting *expectations* as to the possibility of satisfying them.*

As a result of a detailed analysis of Wilson's career we have formulated what we hope is a consistent set of interrelated observations about the dynamics of his personality and political behavior. . . . We also seek to explain some of the contradictory aspects of Wilson's behavior, when his career is viewed as a whole, by distinguishing between Wilson the power seeker and Wilson the power holder, by distinguishing between political objectives which enlisted his aspirations for great achievement and those which did not, and by differentiating some of the conditions under which he did and did not consult.

We recapitulate here in somewhat more general terms the analysis of Wilson's political functioning in order to illustrate problems encountered in a developmental analysis. The basic hypothesis concerning the dynamics of Wilson's political behavior is that power was for him a compensatory value, a means of restoring the self-esteem damaged in childhood. (This general hypothesis—evidently of wide application in the study of political leaders—is stated and elaborated by Lasswell, *Power and Personality*, pp. 39 ff. . . .)

But power was not the only operative value in Wilson's political behavior. He did not—evidently could not—seek naked domination over others. He could indulge his hidden desire to dominate only by "purifying" his leadership, by committing it to political projects which articulated the highest moral and idealistic aspirations of the people. His desire for power was mitigated by a simultaneous need for approval, respect and, especially, for feeling virtuous.

To succeed in dominating others and in achieving great works in chosen field of politics was necessary for Wilson if he was to gain external bolstering of his self-esteem. This requirement of success was no doubt reinforced by the emphasis in his religion upon "good works" and "service." The faith in which he was reared perhaps also served to spur

*Thus, for example, Wilson also sought satisfaction in the political arena for his pronounced need for affection and approval. But the operative role of these value demands was muted for several reasons. He seems to have realized that the masses are a highly unreliable source of approval and affection; and, perhaps, he was concerned at times lest to seek popular approval and affection interfere with his overriding need to be "right" and to dominate. While he was delighted at evidences of the public's affection and approval, he continued to rely throughout his life upon family and friends as a more reliable source of the continuous supply of affection and approval which he needed.

him to bring his desire for domination into consonance with his need for approval, deference, and a feeling of righteousness. In any case, Wilson hit upon the highly constructive strategy—constructive both from his standpoint and that of the nation—of committing his desire for domination and his ambition for great accomplishments only to reform projects which already enjoyed considerable support and were within reasonable possibility of achievement. By doing so, the vast energies unleashed by his personal involvement in politics were committed to political objectives both desirable and feasible.

This strategy was a constructive one insofar as it reduced the likelihood that, if fastened to political projects which did not command widespread support, Wilson's underlying need for domination would encounter political opposition which, in turn, would rouse his anxieties and lead him into stubborn, self-defeating behavior.

Wilson entered each of his executive positions at a time when reform was the order of the day, and with a substantial fund of good will to draw upon. The Princeton Board of Trustees, the New Jersey State Legislature, and the United States Congress under Democratic control were in each case willing to give him a chance and to follow his leadership. In each position, Wilson was initially highly successful in driving through a series of reform measures, only to encounter equally impressive political deadlocks or setbacks later on.

In the last analysis, therefore, the constructive strategy proved unavailing. Why was this so? The explanation seems to lie in three factors. First, there was Wilson's demand for *immediate* compliance with his desires. This characteristic was of a piece with Wilson's unmistakably oratorical temperament, a need for quick domination once he had committed himself to a major reform project.

Second, there was Wilson's insatiable ambition. He was unable to derive normal gratification and pleasure from his achievements (". . . I am so constituted that, for some reason or other, I never have a sense of triumph.") Success never long satisfied him. No sooner did Wilson put through one reform plan than he would discover another great work calling for his attention. He was soon pressing it upon legislators as something urgently and immediately to be accepted. His ambition, in other words, was compulsive. As a result, he found it difficult to pace his political demands prudently in order to assure a continued, though slower, series of achievements. The demand for immediate and complete domination on each single issue together with his compulsive drive for reform upon reform, achievement upon achievement, generated in time the opposition of others who shared in the power of decision. The cycle tended to repeat itself in each of his three executive posts.

There is some evidence that Wilson sensed the dangers implicit in his compulsive ambition. To House, Wilson spoke of nightmares in which he relived his struggles at Princeton, and of his fear that the pattern of success-defeat might repeat itself in the Presidency. He spoke anxiously, too, of the difficulty of maintaining during the last two years of his (first) term the level and pace of achievement he had accomplished in 1913–14.[2]

There is also some evidence that Wilson was casting about for ways of avoiding a repetition of his highly distressing experience as a reformer at Princeton. Thus, for a while, he cultivated the notion that with the passage of his major legislative program of 1913–14 the task of reforming American economic life along progressive principles had been completed. Such a thesis, which Wilson publicly stated in November, 1914, was unrealistic from a political standpoint; not surprisingly, it puzzled and dismayed leaders of progressive opinion.[3] Its political naiveté makes Wilson's thesis all the more interesting from the standpoint of ego functioning. The implication that he had already made his major political contribution suggests a rudimentary effort to find a means of protecting himself—through resignation or, more likely, refusal of a second term—against the compulsive ambition which was causing anxiety.

Third, Wilson was unable to develop within the American system of government a means for resolving his power conflicts with the legislature before disruptive anxieties, which opposition to his will generated, came into full play. In other respects, Wilson did much to transform the Presidency into an instrument of party leadership and a vehicle for legislative leadership, to bring it closer to the British system of Cabinet government which he had admired from an early age.

At the very beginning of his first term Wilson had recognized that, in undertaking this creative transformation of the Presidency, some means would have to be found for breaking deadlocks between the President and the legislature and for holding the President responsible in a manner comparable to that in which a prime minister is answerable to the legislative branch. "Sooner or later," he wrote, "it would seem he [the President] must be made answerable to opinion in a somewhat more informal and intimate fashion, answerable, it may be, to the Houses whom he seeks to lead, either personally or through a Cabinet, as well as to the people for whom they speak." But, he concluded, "that is a matter to be worked out—as it will be inevitably—in some natural American way which we cannot yet even predict."[4]

But the problem, which Wilson correctly identified, proved more difficult of solution than he had imagined. His own efforts in this direction failed; yet they are of particular interest because they go to the kernel of the personal problem of his leadership. Because he generally fastened his aspirations for leadership to projects which articulated the moral and political aspirations of the people, he was able to assert with some plausibility that he directly represented the will of the people. Thereby, he justified to himself and to others his efforts to force Congress to do his will.

His need for achieving a feeling of rectitude, however, could not be so easily satisfied. He was ever sensitive to charges that he harbored autocratic tendencies and seems subconsciously to have feared this was the case. On several occasions he revealed his own concern in the matter by arguing in his self-defense that the pressure he was exerting on Congress on behalf of his legislative proposals could not be considered evidence of autocratic behavior because, after all, Congress would not yield to him unless public opinion favored the measure. It was not pressure from him—so he wanted to believe—but the pressure of the nation back of him which really caused Congress to pass what he wanted.

What Wilson needed for peace of mind, when political deadlocks with his opponents developed, was a practical device which would enable him to "test" his contention that he better represented the will of the people than did Congress (or, in other situations, the Princeton Board of Trustees, the New Jersey Legislature, the Allied negotiators at Paris), a device which, therefore, would serve as a psychological and political safety valve against any autocratic tendencies within him. The device which he most often used for this purpose was the "appeal to the people."

That "public opinion" could be made the immediate arbiter in his power conflicts with his opponents was indeed a comforting thesis. It served to relieve Wilson of the responsibility to compromise when deadlock was reached. He could seek to impose his will in such situations, without meeting the need for compromise inherent in our system of divided and shared power, by self-righteously relying upon public opinion to uphold him—or, by defeating him, to save him from being guilty of autocratic behavior. The eagerness with which he turned to the device of an appeal to the people, and the poor judgment and unrealism he often displayed in so doing, testify to the highly personal function of the device in his hands.

In practice, as we have noted, the "appeal to the people" was for Wilson a poor substitute for the "vote of confidence" lacking in our system of government. Another alternative open to a prime minister in a Cabinet system of government—his resignation when defeated by parliament on an important vote—Wilson seems never to have seriously considered, though it is said that he spoke of the possibility on several occasions.[5] For the President to resign in such circumstances was obviously useless in a system in which Congress would not at the same time be dissolved in order to give the nation an opportunity to pass on the issue.

In his effort, through personal leadership rather than constitutional amendment, to transform the role of President into that of a prime minister, therefore, Wilson failed precisely at the point at which he most needed institutional safeguards against the disruptive tendencies of his personality and leadership.

Notes

1. See his *Power and Personality*, New York, W. W. Norton, 1948; especially Chapter III, "The Political Personality"; see also his "The Selective Effect of Personality on Political Participation" in Richard Christie and Marie Jahoda, eds. *Studies In the Scope and Method of "The Authoritarian Personality,"* Glencoe, Illinois, The Free Press, 1954.

2. House diary entries 11/12/13, 12/12/13, 9/28/14 in Charles Seymour, *The Intimate Papers of Colonel House* (Boston and New York: Houghton Mifflin Co., 1926), I, 119-120, 295-296; the last of these is quoted at the beginning of chapter IX.

3. Arthur Stanley Link, *Woodrow Wilson and the Progressive Era, 1910-1917* (New York: Harper and Brothers, 1954), 79-80.

4. Woodrow Wilson to representative A. Palmer Mitchell, 2/13/13, quoted in H. J. Ford, *Woodrow Wilson, The Man and His Work* (New York: A. Appleton & Co., 1916), 323-324.

5. Ray Stannard Baker, *Woodrow Wilson: Life and Letters* (Garden City, N.Y.: Doubleday, Page & Co., 1927), IV, 415; David Lawrence, *The True Story of Woodrow Wilson* (New York: George H. Doran Co., 1924), 310-311.

PART THREE

The History of Childhood

7

The Evolution of Childhood

LLOYD DEMAUSE

As the author explains in the introductory section of this article, his work has an independent history of its own, for, in addition to providing a comprehensive review of childhood history and a theoretical scheme based on this material, it is also a kind of manifesto proclaiming the history of childhood to be a field of major importance. DeMause marshalls his extraordinary mass of evidence with the skill of a good field general and the zeal of a dedicated missionary. Such a combination of qualities—rare in any work that can pass muster as competent scholarship—conveys an exciting sense of participation in deMause's psychohistorical discovery of childhood.

On a more formal level it is clear that exploration of his hypotheses will require several years. Yet is equally evident that his formulations will inform the direction of research and discussion not only of the history of childhood, but also of the dynamics of historical change.

The history of childhood is a nightmare from which we have only recently begun to awaken. The further back in history one goes, the lower the level of child care, and the more likely children are to be killed, abandoned, beaten, terrorized, and sexually abused. It is our task

This article is a somewhat condensed version of a paper that appeared in *History of Childhood Quarterly* 1 (Spring 1974); 503–575 and has been published as the introductory chapter of *The History of Childhood,* edited by Lloyd deMause (New York: The Psychohistory Press, 1974).

Author's note: I wish to express my sincerest thanks for comments on this paper to my wife Gladys, to John Benton, Edward Shorter, Henry Ebel, Rudolph Binion, and William Dresden.

here to see how much of this childhood history can be recaptured from the evidence that remains to us.

That this pattern has not previously been noticed by historians is because serious history has long been considered a record of public not private events. Historians have concentrated so much on the noisy sandbox of history, with its fantastic castles and magnificent battles, that they have generally ignored what is going on in the homes around the playground. And where historians usually look to the sandbox battles of yesterday for the causes of those today, we instead ask how each generation of parents and children creates those issues which are later acted out in the arena of public life.

At first glance, this lack of interest in the lives of children seems odd. Historians have been traditionally committed to explaining continuity and change over time, and ever since Plato it has been known that childhood is a key to this understanding. The importance of parent-child relations for social change was hardly discovered by Freud; St. Augustine's cry, "Give me other mothers and I will give you another world," has been echoed by major thinkers for fifteen centuries without affecting historical writing. Since Freud, of course, our view of childhood has acquired a new dimension, and in the past half century the study of childhood has become routine for the psychologist, the sociologist, and the anthropologist. It is only beginning for the historian. Such determined avoidance requires an explanation.

Historians usually blame the paucity of the sources for the lack of serious study of childhood in the past. Peter Laslett wonders why the "crowds and crowds of little children are strangely missing from the written record. . . . There is something mysterious about the silence of all these multitudes of babes in arms, toddlers and adolescents in the statements men made at the time about their own experience. . . . We cannot say whether fathers helped in the tending of infants. . . . Nothing can as yet be said on what is called by the psychologists toilet training. . . . It is in fact an effort of mind to remember all the time that children were always present in such numbers in the traditional world, nearly half the whole community living in a condition of semi-obliteration."[1] As the family sociologist James Bossard puts it: "Unfortunately, the history of childhood has never been written, and there is some doubt whether it ever can be written [because] of the dearth of historical data bearing on childhood."[2]

This conviction is so strong among historians that it is not surprising that this book began not in the field of history at all but in applied psychoanalysis. Five years ago, I was engaged in writing a book on a psychoanalytic theory of historical change, and, in reviewing the results of half a century of applied psychoanalysis, it seemed to me that it had failed to become a science mainly because it had not become evolutionary. Since the repetition compulsion, by definition, cannot explain historical change, every attempt by Freud, Roheim, Kardiner, and others to develop a theory of change ultimately ended in a sterile chicken-or-egg dispute about whether childrearing depends on cultural traits or the other way around. That childrearing practices are the basis for adult personality was proven again and again. Where they originated stumped every psychoanalyst who raised the question.[3]

In a paper given in 1968 before the Association for Applied Psychoanalysis, I outlined an evolutionary theory of historical change in parent-child relations, and proposed that since historians had not as yet begun the job of writing childhood history, the Association should sponsor a team of historians who would dig back into the sources to uncover the major stages of childrearing in the West since antiquity. This book is the outcome of that project.

The "psychogenic theory of history" outlined in my project proposal began with a comprehensive theory of historical change. It posited that the central force for change in history is neither technology nor economics, but the "psychogenic" changes in personality occurring because of successive generations of parent-child interactions. This theory involved several hypotheses, each subject to proof or disproof by empirical historical evidence:

1. That the evolution of parent-child relations constitutes an independent source of historical change. The origin of this evolution lies in the ability of successive generations of parents to regress to the psychic age of their children and work through the anxieties of that age in a better manner the second time they encounter them than they did during their own childhood. The process is similar to that of psychoanalysis, which also involves regression and a second chance to face childhood anxieties.

2. That this "generational pressure" for psychic change is not only spontaneous, originating in the adult's need to regress and in the child's striving for relationship, but also occurs independent of social and technological change. It therefore can be found even in periods of social and technological stagnation.

3. That the history of childhood is a series of closer approaches between adult and child, with each closing of psychic distance producing fresh anxiety. The reduction of this adult anxiety is the main source of the childrearing practices of each age.

4. That the obverse of the hypothesis that history involves a general improvement in child care is that the further back one goes in history,

the less effective parents are in meeting the developing needs of the child. This would indicate, for instance, that if today in America there are less than a million abused children,[4] there would be a point back in history where most children were what we would now consider abused.

5. That because psychic structure must always be passed from generation to generation through the narrow funnel of childhood, a society's childrearing practices are not just one item in a list of cultural traits. They are the very condition for the transmission and development of all other cultural elements, and place definite limits on what can be achieved in all other spheres of history. Specific childhood experiences must occur to sustain specific cultural traits, and once these experiences no longer occur the trait disappears.

Now it is obvious that any evolutionary psychological theory as ambitious as this one is cannot really be tested in a single book, and our goal in this book has been the more modest one of reconstructing from what evidence remains what it felt like to be a child and a parent in the past. Whatever evidence there is for actual evolutionary patterns for childhood in the past will only emerge as we set forth the fragmentary and often confusing story we have uncovered of the lives of children during the past two thousand years in the West.

Previous Works on Children in History

Although I think this book is the first to examine seriously the history of childhood in the West, historians have undeniably been writing about children in past ages for some time.[5] Even so, I think that the study of the history of childhood is just beginning, since most of these works so badly distort the facts of childhood in the periods they cover. Official biographers are the worst offenders; childhood is generally idealized, and very few biographers give any useful information about the subject's earliest years. The historical sociologists manage to turn out theories explaining changes in childhood without ever bothering to examine a single family, past or present.[6] The literary historians, mistaking books for life, construct a fictional picture of childhood, as though one could know what really happened in the nineteenth-century American home by reading *Tom Sawyer.*[7]

But it is the social historian, whose job it is to dig out the reality of social conditions in the past, who defends himself most vigorously against the facts he turns up.[8] When one social historian finds widespread infanticide, he declares it "admirable and humane."[9] When another describes mothers who regularly beat their infants with sticks while still in the cradle, she comments, without a shred of evidence, that "if her discipline was stern, it was even and just and leavened with kindness."[10] When a third finds mothers who dunk their infants into ice water each morning to "strengthen" them, and the children die from the practice, she says that "they were not intentionally cruel," but simply "had read Rousseau and Locke."[11] No practice in the past seems anything but benign to the social historian. When Laslett finds parents regularly sending their children, at age seven, to other homes as servants, while taking in other children to serve them, he says it was actually kindness, for it "shows that parents may have been unwilling to submit children of their own to the discipline of work at home."[12] After admitting that severe whipping of young children with various instruments "at school and at home seems to have been as common in the seventeenth century as it was later," William Sloan feels compelled to add that "children, then as later, sometimes deserved whipping."[13] When Philippe Ariès comes up with so much evidence of open sexual molesting of children that he admits that "playing with children's privy parts formed part of a widespread tradition,"[14] he goes on to describe a "traditional" scene where a stranger throws himself on a little boy while riding in a train, "his hand brutally rummaging inside the child's fly," while the father smiles, and concludes: "All that was involved was a game whose scabrous nature we should beware of exaggerating."[15] Masses of evidence are hidden, distorted, softened, or ignored. The child's early years are played down, formal educational content is endlessly examined, and emotional content is avoided by stressing child legislation and avoiding the home. And if the nature of the author's book is such that the ubiquity of unpleasant facts cannot be ignored, the theory is invented that "good parents leave no traces in the records". . . .

Of all the books on childhood in the past, Philippe Ariès's book *Centuries of Childhood* is probably the best known; one historian notes the frequency with which it is "cited as Holy Writ."[16] Ariès's central thesis is the opposite of mine: he argues that while the traditional child was happy because he was free to mix with many classes and ages, a special condition known as childhood was "invented" in the early modern period, resulting in a tyrannical concept of the family which destroyed friendship and sociability and deprived children of freedom, inflicting upon them for the first time the birch and the prison cell.

To prove this thesis, Ariès uses two main arguments. He first says that a separate concept of childhood was unknown in the early Middle Ages. "Medieval art until about the twelfth century did not know childhood or did not attempt to portray it" because artists were "unable to depict a child except as a man on a smaller scale."[17] Not only does this leave the art of antiquity in limbo, but it ignores voluminous evidence that medieval artists could, indeed, paint realistic children.[18] His etymological argument for a separate concept of childhood being unknown is also untenable.[19] In any case, the notion of the "invention of childhood" is so fuzzy that it is surprising that so many historians have recently picked it up.[20] His second argument, that the modern family restricts the child's freedom and increases the severity of punishment, runs counter to all the evidence.

Far more reliable than Ariès is a quartet of books, only one of them written by a professional historian: George Payne's *The Child in Human Progress*, G. Rattray Taylor's *The Angel Makers*, David Hunt's *Parents and Children in History*, and J. Louise Despert's *The Emotionally Disturbed Child—Then and Now*. Payne, writing in 1916, was the first to examine the wide extent of infanticide and brutality toward children in the past, particularly in antiquity. Taylor's book, rich in documentation, is a sophisticated psychoanalytic reading of childhood and personality in late eighteenth-century England. Hunt, like Ariès, centers mostly on the unique seventeenth-century document, Heroard's diary of the childhood of Louis XIII, but does so with great psychological sensitivity and awareness of the psychohistorical implications of his findings. And Despert's psychiatric comparison of child mistreatment in the past and present surveys the range of emotional attitudes toward children since antiquity, expressing her growing horror as she uncovers a story of unremitting "heartlessness and cruelty."[21]

Yet despite these four books, the central questions of comparative childhood history remain to be asked, much less answered. In the next two sections of this chapter, I will cover some of the psychological principles that apply to adult-child relations in the past. The examples I use, while not untypical of child life in the past, are not drawn equally from all time periods, but are chosen as the clearest illustrations of the psychological principles being described. It is only in the three succeeding sections, where I provide an overview of the history of infanticide, abandonment, nursing, swaddling, beating, and sexual abuse, that I begin to examine how widespread the practice was in each period.

Psychological Principles of Childhood History: Projective and Reversal Reactions

In studying childhood over many generations, it is most important to concentrate on those moments which most affect the psyche of the next generation: primarily, this means what happens when an adult is face to face with a child who needs something. The adult has, I believe, three major reactions available: (1) He can use the child as a vehicle for projection of the contents of his own unconscious (projective reaction); (2) he can use the child as a substitute for an adult figure important in his own childhood (reversal reaction); or (3) he can empathize with the child's needs and act to satisfy them (empathic reaction).

The projective reaction is, of course, familiar to psychoanalysts under terms which range from "projection" to "projective identification," a more concrete, intrusive form of voiding feelings into others. The psychoanalyst, for instance, is thoroughly familiar with being used as a "toilet-lap"[22] for the massive projections of the patient. It is this condition of being used as a vehicle for projections which is usual for children in the past.

Likewise, the reversal reaction is familiar to students of battering parents.[23] Children exist only to satisfy parental needs, and it is always the failure of the child-as-parent to give love which triggers the actual battering. As one battering mother put it: "I have never felt loved all my life. When the baby was born, I thought he would love me. When he cried, it meant he didn't love me. So I hit him."

The third term, empathic reaction, is used here in a more limited sense than the dictionary definition. It is the adult's ability to regress to the level of a child's need and correctly identify it without an admixture of the adult's own projections. The adult must then be able to maintain enough distance from the need to be able to satisfy it. It is an ability identical to the use of the psychoanalyst's unconscious called "free-floating attention," or, as Theodor Reik terms it, "listening with the third ear."[24]

Projective and reversal reactions often occurred simultaneously in parents in the past, producing an effect which I call the "double image," where the child was seen as both full of the adult's projected desires, hostilities, and sexual thoughts, and at the same moment as a mother or father figure. That is, it is *both* bad *and* loving. Furthermore, the further back in history one goes, the more "concretization" or reification one finds of these projective and reversal reactions, producing progressively more bizarre attitudes toward children, similar to those of contemporary parents of battered and schizophrenic children.

The first illustration of these closely interlocking concepts which we will examine is in an adult-child scene from the past. The year is 1739; the boy, Nicolas, is four years old. The incident is one he remembers and has had confirmed by his mother. His grandfather, who has been rather attentive to him the past few days, decides he has to "test" him, and says, "Nicolas, my son, you have many faults, and these grieve your mother.

She is my daughter and has always obliged me; obey me too, and correct these, or I will whip you like a dog which is being trained." Nicolas, angry at the betrayal "from one who has been so kind to me," throws his toys into the fire. The grandfather seems pleased.

> Nicolas, your father loves you; do you love him?" "Yes, grand-papa!" "Suppose he were in danger and to save him it was necessary to put your hand in the fire, would you do it? Would you put it . . . there, if it was necessary?" "Yes grandpa." "And for me?" "For you? . . . yes, yes" "And for your mother?" "For mamma? Both of them, both of them!" "We shall see if you are telling the truth, for your mother is in great need of your little help! If you love her, you must prove it." I made no answer; but, putting together all that had been said, I went to the fireplace and, while they were making signs to each other, put my right hand into the fire. The pain drew a deep sigh from me. [25]

What makes this sort of scene so typical of adult-child interaction in the past is the existence of so many contradictory attitudes on the adult's part without the least resolution. The child is loved and hated, rewarded and punished, bad and loving, all at once. That this puts the child in a "double bind" of conflicting signals (which Bateson [26] and others believe underlie schizophrenia), goes without saying. But the conflicting signals themselves come from adults who are striving to demonstrate that the child is both very bad (projective reaction) and very loving (reversal reaction). It is the child's function to reduce the adult's pressing anxieties; the child acts as the adult's defense.

It is also the projective and reversal reactions which make guilt impossible in the severe beatings which we so often encounter in the past. This is because it is not the actual child who is being beaten. It is either the adult's own projections ("Look at her give you the eye! That's how she picks up men—she's a regular sexpot!" a mother says of her battered daughter of two), or it is a product of reversal ("He thinks he's the boss—all the time trying to run things—but I showed him who is in charge around here!" a father says of his nine-month-old boy whose skull he has split). [27] One can often catch the merging of beaten and beater and therefore lack of guilt in the historical sources. An American father (1830) tells of horsewhipping his four-year-old boy for not being able to read something. The child is tied up naked in the cellar:

> I felt all the force of divine authority and express command that I ever felt in any case in all my life. . . . But under the all controlling influence of such a degree of angry passion and obstinacy, as my son

had manifested, no wonder he thought he "should beat me out," feeble and tremulous as I was; and knowing as he did that it made me almost sick to whip him. At that time he could neither pity me nor himself.[28]

It is this picture of the merging of father and son, with the father complaining that he himself is the one beaten and in need of pity, which we will encounter when we ask how beating could have been so widespread in the past. When a Renaissance pedagogue says you should tell the child when beating him, "you do the correction against your mind, compelled thereunto by conscience, and require them to put you no more unto such labour and pain. For if you do (say you) you must suffer part of the pain with me and therefore you shall now have experience and proof what pain it is unto both of us" we will not so easily miss the merging and mislabel it hypocrisy.[29]

Indeed, the parent sees the child as so full of portions of himself that even real accidents to the child are seen as injuries to the parent. Cotton Mather's daughter Nanny fell into the fire and burned herself badly, and he cried out, "Alas, for my sins the just God throws my child into the fire!"[30] He searched everything he himself had recently done wrong, but since he believed he was the one being punished, no guilt toward his child could be felt (say, for leaving her alone), and no corrective action could be taken. Soon two other daughters were badly burned. His reaction was to preach a sermon on "What use ought parents to make of disasters befallen their children."

This matter of "accidents" to children is not to be taken lightly, for in it lies hidden the clue to why adults in the past were such poor parents. Leaving aside actual death wishes, which will be discussed later, accidents occurred in great numbers in the past because little children were so often left alone. Mather's daughter Nibby would have been burned to death but for "a person accidentally then passing by the window,"[31] because there was no one there to hear her cries. A colonial Boston experience is also typical:

> After they had supped, the mother put two children to bed in the room where they themselves did lie, and they went out to visit a neighbor. When they returned . . . the mother [went] to the bed, and not finding her youngest child (a daughter about five years of age), and after much search she found it drowned in a well in her cellar. . . .[32]

The father blames the accident on his having worked on a holy day. The point is not only that it was common to leave children alone right up to the twentieth century. More important is that parents cannot be concerned with preventing accidents if guilt is absent because it is the adult's own projections that they feel have been punished. Massive projectors don't invent safety stoves, nor often can they even see to it that their children are given the simplest of care. Their projection, unfortunately, insures repetition.

The use of the child as a "toilet" for adult projections is behind the whole notion of original sin, and for eighteen hundred years adults were in general agreement that, as Richard Allestree (1676) puts it, "the newborn babe is full of the stains and pollution of sin, which it inherits from our first parents through our loins. . . ."[33] Baptism used to include actual exorcism of the devil, and the belief that the child who cried at his christening was letting out the devil long survived the formal omission of exorcism in the Reformation.[34] Even where formal religion did not stress the devil, it was there; here is a picture of a Polish Jew teaching in the nineteenth century:

> He derived an intense joy from the agonies of the little victim trembling and shivering on the bench. And he used to administer the whippings coldly, slowly, deliberately . . . he asked the boy to let down his clothes, lie across the bench . . . and pitched in with the leathern thongs . . . "In every person there is a Good Spirit and and an Evil Spirit. The Good Spirit has its own dwelling-place—which is the head. So has the Evil Spirit—and that is the place where you get the whipping."[35]

The belief that infants were felt to be on the verge of turning into totally evil beings is one of the reasons why they were tied up, or swaddled, so long and so tightly. One feels the undertone in Bartholomaeus Anglicus (c. 1230): "And for tenderness the limbs of the child may easily and soon bow and bend and take diverse shapes. And therefore children's members and limbs are bound with lystes [bandages], and other covenable bonds, that they be not crooked nor evil shapen. . . ."[36] It is the infant full of the parent's dangerous, evil projections that is swaddled. The reasons given for swaddling in the past are the same as those of present-day swaddlers in Eastern Europe: the baby has to be tied up or it will tear its ears off, scratch its eyes out, break its legs, or touch its genitals.[37] As we shall see shortly in the section on swaddling and restraints, this often includes binding up children in all kinds of corsets, stays, backboards, and puppet-strings, and even extends to tying them up in chairs to prevent them from crawling on the floor "like an animal". . . .

Even such a simple act as empathizing with children who were beaten was difficult for adults in the past. Those few educators who, prior to modern times, advised that children should not be beaten generally argued that it would have bad consequences rather than that it would hurt the child. Yet without this element of empathy, the advice had no effect whatsoever, and children continued to be beaten as before. Mothers who sent their infants to wet-nurses for three years were genuinely distressed that their children then didn't want to return to them, yet they had no capacity to locate the reason. A hundred generations of mothers tied up their infants in swaddling bands and impassively watched them scream in protest because they lacked the psychic mechanism necessary to empathize with them. Only when the slow historical process of parent-child evolution finally established this faculty through successive generations of parent-child interaction did it become obvious that swaddling was totally unnecessary. Here is Richard Steele in *The Tatler* in 1706 describing how he thought an infant felt after being born:

> I lay very quiet; but the witch, for no manner of reason or provocation in the world, takes me and binds my head as hard as she possibly could; then ties up both my legs and makes me swallow down an horrid mixture. I thought it an harsh entrance into life, to begin with taking physic. When I was thus dressed, I was carried to a bedside where a fine young lady (my mother, I wot) had like to have me hugged to death . . . and threw me into a girl's arms that was taken in to tend me. The girl was very proud of the womanly employment of a nurse, and took upon her to strip and dress me anew, because I made a noise, to see what ailed me; she did so and stuck a pin in every joint about. I still cried, upon which, she lays me on my face in her lap; and, to quiet me fell to nailing in all the pins, by clapping me on the back and screaming a lullaby. . . .[38]

I have not found a description with this degree of empathy in any century prior to the eighteenth. It was not long thereafter that two thousand years of swaddling came to an end.

One imagines that there would be all kinds of places to look to find this missing empathic faculty in the past. The first place to look, of course, is the Bible; certainly here one should find empathy toward children's needs, for isn't Jesus always pictured holding little children? Yet when one actually reads each of the over two thousand references to children listed in the *Complete Concordance to the Bible*, these gentle images are missing. You find lots on child sacrifice, on stoning children, on beating them, on their strict obedience, on their love for their parents, and on their role as carriers of the family name, but not a single one that reveals any empathy with their needs. Even the well-known saying, "Suffer little children, and forbid them not, to come unto me" turns out to be the customary Near Eastern practice of exorcising by laying on of hands, which many holy men did to remove the evil inherent in children: "Then there were brought unto him little children, that he should put his hands on them, and pray . . . he laid his hands on them, and departed thence." (Mat. 19.13.)

All of this is not to say that parents didn't love their children in the past, for they did. Even contemporary child-beaters are not sadists; they love their children, at times, and in their own way, and are sometimes capable of expressing tender feelings, particularly when the children are non-demanding. The same was true for the parent in the past; expressions of tenderness toward children occur most often when the child is non-demanding, especially when the child is either asleep or dead. . . .

It is, of course, not love which the parent of the past lacked, but rather the emotional maturity needed to see the child as a person separate from himself. It is difficult to estimate what proportion of today's parents achieve with any consistency the empathic level. Once I took an informal poll of a dozen psychotherapists and asked them how many of their patients at the beginning of analysis were able to sustain images of their children as individuals separate from their own projected needs; they all said that very few had that ability. As one, Amos Gunsberg, put it: "This doesn't occur until some way along in their analysis, always at a specific moment—when they arrive at an image of themselves as separate from their own all-enveloping mother."

Running parallel to the projective reaction is the reversal reaction, with the parent and child reversing roles, often producing quite bizarre results. Reversal begins long before the child is born—it is the source of the very powerful desire for children one sees in the past, which is always expressed in terms of what children can give the parent, and never what the parent can give them. . . .

Once born, the child becomes the mother's and father's own parent, in either positive or negative aspect, totally out of keeping with the child's actual age. The child, regardless of sex, is often dressed in the style of clothes similar to that worn by the *parent's mother*, that is, not only in a long dress, but in one out of date by at least a generation.[39] The mother is literally reborn in the child; children are not just dressed as "miniature adults" but quite clearly as miniature *women*, often complete with décolleté.

The idea that the grandparent is actually reborn in the baby is a common one in antiquity,[40] and the closeness between the word "baby" and the various words for grandmother (baba, Babe) hints at similar beliefs.[41] But evidence exists for more concrete reversals in the past, ones that are virtually hallucinatory. For instance, the breasts of little infants were often kissed or sucked on by adults. Little Louis XIII often had both his penis and nipples kissed by people around him. Even though Heroard, his diarist, always made him the active one (at thirteen months "he makes M. de Souvre, M. de Termes, M. de Liancourt, and M. Zamet kiss his cock")[42], it later becomes evident that he was being passively manipulated: "He never wants to let the Marquise touch his nipples, his nurse had said to him: "Sir, do not let anyone touch your nipples or your cock; they'll cut them off.'"[43] Yet the adults still couldn't keep their hands and lips off his penis and nipples. Both were the mothers's breast returned.

Another instance of the "infant as mother" was the common belief that infants had milk in their breasts which had to be expelled. The fourteenth-century Italian *balia* (wet-nurse) was instructed to "be sure and press his breasts often—to get out any milk there because it bothers him."[44] There actually is a slight rationalization for this belief, since a newborn will on rare occasions show a drop of milky fluid on its breasts as a result of a carryover of female hormone from the mother. Yet there was a difference between this and "the unnatural but common practice of forcibly squeezing the delicate breasts of a newborn infant, by rough hand of the nurse, which is the most general cause of inflammation in these parts," as the American pediatrician Alexander Hamilton still had to write in 1793.[45]

Kissing, sucking, and squeezing the breast are but a few of the uses to which the "child as breast" is put; one finds a variety of practices such as the one this pediatrician warned of at the beginning of the nineteenth century:

> But a practice of the most injurious and disgusting nature, is that of many nursery maids, aunts and grandmothers, who suffer the child to suck their lips. I had an opportunity of observing the decay of a blooming infant, in consequence of having sucked the lips of its sickly grandmother for upwards on half a year.[46]

Children have always taken care of adults in very concrete ways. Ever since Roman times, boys and girls waited on their parents at table, and in the Middle Ages all children except royalty acted as servants, either at home or for others, often running home from school at noon to wait on their parents.[47] I will not discuss here the whole topic of children's work, but it should be remembered that children did much of the work of the world long before child labor became such an issue in the nineteenth century, generally from the age of four or five.

The reversal reaction is shown most clearly, however, in the emotional interaction between child and adult. Present day social workers who visit "battering" mothers are often astonished at how responsive little children are to the needs of their parents:

> I remember watching an eighteen-month-old soothe her mother, who was in a high state of anxiety and tears. First she put down the bottle she was sucking. Then she moved about in such a way that she could approach, then touch, and eventually calm her mother down (something I had not been able to begin to do). When she sensed her mother was comfortable again, she walked across the floor, lay down, picked up her bottle, and started sucking it again.[48]

This role was frequently assumed by children in the past. One child was "never known to cry or be restless . . . frequently, when a babe in her mother's arms, at these seasons, would reach up her little hand and wipe the tears from her mother's cheek. . . ."[49] Doctors used to try to entice mothers into nursing their infants themselves instead of sending them out to wet-nurse by promising that "in recompence whereof, he endeavors to show her a thousand delights . . . he kisses her, strokes her hair, nose and ears, he flatters her. . . ."[50] Along the same theme, I have catalogued over five hundred paintings of mothers and children from every country, and found that the paintings showed the child looking at, smiling at and caressing the mother at a date prior to the ones showing the mother looking at, smiling at and caressing the child, rare actions for a mother in any painting. . . .

The need of the parent for mothering placed an enormous burden on the growing child. It was sometimes even the cause of its death. One of the more frequent reasons given for infant death was "overlaying," or suffocation in bed, and although this was often just an excuse for infanticide, pediatricians admitted that when it was genuine it was due to the mother's refusal to put the child in a separate bed when she went to sleep; "not wanting to let go of the child, [she] holds him even tighter as she sleeps. Her breast closes off the nose of the child."[51] It was this reversal image of the child-as-security-blanket that was the reality behind the common medieval warning that parents must be careful not to coddle their children "like the ivy that certainly kills the tree encircled by it, or the ape that hugs her whelps to death with mere fondness."[52]

Psychological Principle: The Double Image

The continuous shift between projection and reversal, between the child as devil and as adult, produces a "double image" that is responsible for much of the bizarre quality of childhood in the past. We have already seen how this shift from the adult image to the projected image is a precondition for battering. But we can see a richer picture of the double image by examining in some detail an actual childhood in the past. The most complete record of childhood prior to modern times is the diary of Héroard, doctor of Louis XIII, with almost daily entries about what he saw the child and those around him do and say. The diary often allows us to glimpse the shifting double image as it occurs in Héroard's own mind, as his picture of the baby shifts between projective and reversal images.

The diary opens with the dauphin's birth in 1601. Immediately, his adult qualities appear. He came out of the womb holding his umbilical cord "with such force that she had trouble getting it back from him." He was described as "strongly muscled," and his cry was so loud that "he didn't sound at all like a child." His penis was carefully examined, and he was declared "well provided for."[53] Since he was a dauphin, one skips over these first projections of adult qualities as simple pride in a new king, but soon the images begin piling up, and the double image of his being both an adult and a voracious child grows.

> The day after his birth . . . his cries in general sound not at all like an infant's cries and they never did, and when he sucks at the breast it was with such mouthfuls, and he opens his jaws so wide, that he takes at one time as much as others do in three. Consequently, his nurse was almost always dry. . . . He was never satisfied.[54]

The image of the week-old dauphin as alternately an infant Hercules, who strangled the snakes, and a Gargantua, who needed 17,913 cows to nurse him, is totally at odds with the actual sickly, weak, swaddled infant who emerges from Héroard's record. Despite the dozens of people who were assigned to care for him, no one was able to provide for his simplest needs for food and rest. There were constant unnecessary changes in wet-nurses and continuous outings and long trips.[55] By the time the dauphin was two months old he was close to death.

When the dauphin was almost ten months old, leading-strings were tied to his robe. Leading-strings were supposed to be used to teach the infant to walk, but they were more often used to manipulate and control the child like a puppet. This, combined with Héroard's projective reactions, makes it difficult to understand what was actually happening, and what is being manipulated by those around little Louis. For instance, when he was eleven months old he was said to enjoy fencing with Héroard, and liked it so much that "he pursues me laughing through the whole chamber." But a month later Héroard reported that he "begins to move along with sturdiness, held under the arms."[56] It is obvious he was being carried or swung along on leading-strings earlier when he was said to "pursue" Héroard. . . . Héroard was actually hallucinating when he reports that someone came to see the fourteen-month-old dauphin, who "turns around and looks at all those who are lined up at the balustrade, goes to choose him and holds out his hand to him, which the prince then kisses. M. d'Haucourt enters and says he has come to kiss the robe of the dauphin; he turns around and says to him it isn't necessary to do that."[57]

During this same time he was pictured as being extremely active sexually. The projective basis of ascribing adult sexual behavior to the child is apparent in Héroard's descriptions: "the dauphin [at twelve months] calls the page back and with a 'Ho!' lifts up his shirt to show him his cock . . . he makes every one kiss his cock . . . in the company of the little girl, he pulls up his shirt, shows her his cock with such ardor that he is completely beside himself. . . .[58]

Only rarely did Héroard reveal that the dauphin was actually passive in these sexual manipulations: "The marquise often puts her hand under his jacket; he has himself put into his bed by the nurse where she plays with him, often putting her hand under his coat."[59] More often, he was simply depicted as being stripped, taken to bed with the King, the Queen, or both, or with various servants, and involved in sexual manipulations from the time he was an infant until he was at least seven years old.

Another example of the double image was in circumcision. As is well known, Jews, Egyptians, Arabs, and others circumcised the foreskin of boys. The reasons given for this are manifold, but all of them can be covered by the double image of projection and reversal. To begin with, such mutilations of children by adults always involve projection and punishment to control projected passions. As Philo put it in the first century, circumcision was for "the excision of passions, which bind the mind. For since among all passions that of intercourse between man and woman is greatest, the lawgivers have commanded that the instrument, which serves this intercourse, be mutilated, pointing out, that these powerful passions must be bridled, and thinking not only this, but all passions would be controlled through this one."[60] Moses Maimonides agrees:

> The true purpose of circumcision was to give the sexual organ that kind of physical pain as not to impair its natural function or the potency of the individual, but to lessen the power of passion and of too great desire.[61]

Infanticide and Death Wishes toward Children

In a pair of books rich in clinical documentation, the psychoanalyst Joseph Rheingold examined the death wishes of mothers[62] toward their children, and found that they are not only far more widespread than is commonly realized, but also that they stem from a powerful attempt to "undo" motherhood in order to escape the punishment they imagine their own mothers will wreak upon them. Rheingold shows us mothers giving birth and begging their own mothers not to kill them, and traces the origin of both infanticidal wishes and post-partum depression states as not due to hostility toward the child itself, but rather to the need to sacrifice the child to propitiate their own mothers. Hospital staffs are well aware of these widespread infanticidal wishes, and often allow no contact between the mother and child for some time. Rheingold's findings, seconded by Block, Zilboorg, and others,[63] are complex and have far-reaching implications; here we can only point out that filicidal impulses of contemporary mothers are enormously widespread, with fantasies of stabbing, mutilation, abuse, decapitation, and strangulation common in mothers in psychoanalysis. I believe that the further back in history one goes, the more filicidal impulses are acted out by parents.

The history of infanticide in the West has yet to be written, and I shall not attempt it here. But enough is already known to establish that, contrary to the usual assumption that it is an Eastern rather than a Western problem, infanticide of both legitimate and illegitimate children was a regular practice of antiquity, that the killing of legitimate children was only slowly reduced during the Middle Ages, and that illegitimate children continued regularly to be killed right up into the nineteenth century.[64]

Infanticide during antiquity has usually been played down despite literally hundreds of clear references by ancient writers that it was an accepted, everyday occurrence. Children were thrown into rivers, flung into dung-heaps and cess trenches, "potted" in jars to starve to death, and exposed on every hill and roadside, "a prey for birds, food for wild beasts to rend" (Euripides, *Ion*, 504). To begin with, any child that was not perfect in shape and size, or cried too little or too much, or was otherwise than is described in the gynecological writings on "How to Recognize the Newborn That is Worth Rearing,"[65] was generally killed. Beyond this, the first-born was usually allowed to live,[66] especially if it was a boy. Girls were, of course, valued little, and the instructions of Hilarion to his wife Alis (1 B.C.) are typical of the open way these things were discussed: "If, as may well happen, you give birth to a child, if it is a boy let it live; if it is a girl, expose it."[67] The result was a large imbalance of males over females which was typical of the West until well into the Middle Ages, when the killing of legitimate children was probably much reduced. (The killing of illegitimate children does not affect the sex ratio, since both sexes are generally killed.) Available statistics for antiquity show large surpluses of boys over girls; for instance, out of 79 families who gained Milesian citizenship about 228-220 B.C., there were 118 sons and 28 daughters; 32 families had one child, 31 had two.

The killing of legitimate children even by wealthy parents was so common that Polybius blamed it for the depopulation of Greece:

> In our own time the whole of Greece has been subject to a low birth-rate and a general decrease of the population, owing to which cities have become deserted and the land has ceased to yield fruit, although there have neither been continuous wars nor epidemics . . . as men had fallen into such a state of pretentiousness, avarice and indolence that they did not wish to marry, or if they married to rear the children born to them, or at most as a rule but one of two of them. . . .[68]

Until the fourth century A.D., neither law nor public opinion found infanticide wrong in either Greece or Rome. The great philosophers agreed. Those few passages which classicists consider as a condemnation of infanticide seem to me to indicate just the opposite, such as Aristotle's "As to exposing or rearing the children born, let there be a law that no deformed child shall be reared; but on the ground of number of children, if the regular customs hinder any of those born being exposed, there must be a limit filed to the procreation of offspring." Similarly, Musonius Rufus, sometimes called "The Roman Socrates," is often quoted as opposing infanticide, but his piece "Should Every Child That Is Born Be Raised?" quite clearly only says that since brothers are very useful they should not be killed.[69] But more ancient writers openly approved of infanticide, saying, like Aristippus, that a man could do what he wants with his children, for "do we not cast away from us our spittle, lice and such like, as things unprofitable, which nevertheless are engendered and bred even out of our own selves."[70]

The theme of exposure loomed large in myth, tragedy, and the New Comedy, which is often built around the subject of how funny infanticide is. In Menander's *Girl from Samos*, much fun is made of a man trying to chop up and roast a baby. In his comedy *The Arbitrants*, a shepherd picks up an exposed infant, considers raising it, then changes his mind, saying, "What have I to do with the rearing of children and the trouble." He gives it to another man, but has a fight over who got the baby's necklace.[71]

It must be noted, however, that infanticide was probably common since prehistoric times. Henri Vallois, who tabulated all the prehistoric fossils dug up from the Pithecanthropines to the Mesolithic peoples, found a sex ratio of 148 to 100 in favor of men.[72] The Greeks and Romans were actually an island of enlightenment in a sea of nations still in an earlier stage of sacrificing children to gods, a practice which the Romans tried in vain to stop. The best documented is Carthaginian child sacrifice, which Plutarch describes:

> with full knowledge and understanding they themselves offered up their own children, and those who had no children would buy little ones from poor people and cut their throats as if they were so many lambs or young birds; meanwhile the mother stood by without a tear or moan; but should she utter a single moan or let fall a single tear, she had to forfeit the money, and her child was sacrificed nevertheless; and the whole area before the statue was filled with a loud noise of flute and drums so that the cries of wailing should not reach the ears of the people.[73]

Child sacrifice is, of course, the most concrete acting out of Rheingold's thesis of filicide as sacrifice to the mother of the parents. It was practiced by the Irish Celts, the Gauls, the Scandinavians, the Egyptians, the Phoenicians, the Moabites, the Ammonites, and, in certain periods, the Israelites.[74] Thousands of bones of sacrificed children have been dug up by archeologists, often with inscriptions identifying the victims as first-born sons of noble families, reaching in time all the way back to the Jericho of 7,000 B.C.[75] Sealing children in walls, foundations of buildings, and bridges to strengthen the structure was also common from the building of the wall of Jericho to as late as 1843 in Germany.[76] To this day, when children play "London Bridge is Falling Down," they are acting out a sacrifice to a river goddess when they catch the child at the end of the game.[77]

Even in Rome, sacrifice of children led an underground existence. Dio said Julianus "killed many boys as a magic rite"; Suetonius said because of a portent the Senate "decreed that no male born that year should be reared"; and Pliny the Elder spoke of men who "seek to secure the leg-marrow and the brain of infants."[78] More frequent was the practice of killing your enemy's children, often in great numbers,[79] so that noble children not only witnessed infanticide in the streets but were themselves under continual threat of death depending on the political fortunes of their fathers. . . .

Although in the two centuries after Augustus, some attempts were made to pay parents to keep children alive in order to replenish the dwindling Roman population,[80] it was not until the fourth century that real change was apparent. The law began to consider killing an infant murder only in 374 A.D.[81] Yet even the opposition to infanticide by the Church Fathers often seemed to be based more on their concern for the parent's soul than with the child's life. This attitude can be seen in Saint Justin Martyr's statement that the reason a Christian shouldn't expose his children is to avoid later meeting them in a brothel: "Lest we molest anyone or commit sin ourselves, we have been taught that it is wicked to expose even newly-born children, first because we see that almost all those who are exposed (not only girls, but boys) are raised in prostitution."[82] When the Christians themselves were accused of killing babies in secret rites, however, they were quick enough to reply: "How many, do you suppose, of those here present who stand panting for the blood of Christians—how many, even, of you magistrates who are so righteous against us—want me to touch their consciences for putting their own offspring to death?"[83]

After the Council of Vaison (442 A.D.), the finding of abandoned children was supposed to be announced in church, and by 787 A.D., Dateo of Milan founded the first asylum solely for abandoned infants.[84] Other countries followed much the same pattern of evolution.[85] Despite much literary evidence, however, the continued existence of widespread infanticide in the Middle Ages is usually denied by medievalists, since it is not evident in church records and other quantitative sources. But if sex ratios of 156 to 100 (c. 801 A.D.) and 172 to 100 (1391 A.D.) are any indication of the extent of the killing of legitimate girls,[86] and if illegitimates were usually killed regardless of sex, the real rate of infanticide could have been substantial in the Middle Ages. . . . Certainly when Vincent of Beauvais wrote in the thirteenth century that a father was always worrying about his daughter "suffocating her offspring," when doctors complained of all the children "found in the frost or in the streets, cast away by a wicked mother," and when we find that in Anglo-Saxon England the legal presumption was that infants who died had been murdered if not proved otherwise, we should take these clues as a signal for the most vigorous sort of research into medieval infanticide.[87]

What is certain is that when our material becomes far fuller, by the eighteenth century,[88] there is no question that there was high incidence of infanticide in every country in Europe. As more foundling homes were opened in each country, babies poured in from all over, and the homes quickly ran out of room. Even though Thomas Coram opened his Foundling Hospital in 1741 because he couldn't bear to see the dying babies lying in the gutters and rotting on the dung-heaps of London, by the 1890s dead babies were still a common sight in London streets.[89] Late in the nineteenth century Louis Adamic described being bought up in an Eastern European village of "killing nurses," where mothers sent their infants to be done away with "by exposing them to cold air after a hot bath; feeding them something that caused convulsions in their stomachs and intestines; mixing gypsum in their milk, which literally plastered up their insides; suddenly stuffing them with food after not giving them anything to eat for two days. . . ." Adamic was to have been killed as well, but for some reason his nurse spared him. His account of how he watched her do away with the other babies she received provides a picture of the emotional reality behind all those centuries of infanticide we have been reviewing.

> In her own strange, helpless way, she loved them all . . . but when the luckless infants' parents or the latter's relatives could not or did not pay the customary small sum for their keep . . . she disposed of them. . . . One day she returned from the city with an elongated little bundle . . . a horrible suspicion seized me. The baby in the cradle was going to die! . . . when the baby cried, I heard her get up, and she nursed it in the dark, mumbling, "Poor, poor little one!" I have tried many times since to imagine how she must have felt holding to her breast a child she knew was fated to die by her hand. .. . The next morning the child was dead. . . .[90]

Once the infant in the past was born, he was regularly surrounded by the aura of death and countermeasures against death. Since ancient times, exorcisms, purifications, and magic amulets have been thought necessary to rout the host of death-dealing powers felt to lurk about the child, and cold water, fire, blood, wine, salt, and urine were used on the baby and its surroundings. . . .[91]

Urges to mutilate, burn, freeze, drown, shake, and throw the infant violently about were continuously acted out in the past. The Huns used to cut the cheeks of newborn males. Robert Pemell tells how in Italy and other countries during the Renaissance parents would "burn in the neck with a hot iron, or else drop a burning wax candle" on newborn babies to prevent "falling sickness."[92] In early modern times, the string underneath the newborn's tongue was usually cut, often with the midwife's fingernail, a sort of miniature circumcision. . . .

Throwing the swaddled child about was sometimes practiced. A brother of Henri IV, while being passed for amusement from one window to another, was dropped and killed.[93] The same thing happened to the little Comte de Marle: "One of the gentlemen-in-waiting and the nurse who was taking care of him amused themselves by tossing him back and forth across the sill of an open window. . . . Sometimes they would pretend not to catch him . . . the little Comte de Marle fell and hit a stone step below."[94] Doctors complained of parents who break the bones of their children in the "customary" tossing of infants.[95] Nurses often said that the stays children were encased in were necessary because otherwise they could not "be tossed about without them. And I remember an eminent surgeon say a child was brought to him with several of its ribs crushed inward by the hand of the person who had been tossing it about without its stays."[96] Doctors also denounced the customary violent rocking of infants, "which puts the babe into a dazed condition in order that he may not trouble those that have the care of him."[97] This was the reason that cradles began to be attacked in the eighteenth century; Buchan said he was against cradles because of the common "ill-tempered nurse, who, instead of soothing the accidental uneasiness or indisposition to sleep of her baby, when laid down to rest, is often worked up to the highest pitch of rage; and, in the excess of her folly and brutality, endeavors, by loud, harsh threats, and the impetuous rattle of the cradle, to drown the infant's cries, and to force him into slumber."[98]

Infants were also sometimes nearly frozen through a variety of customs, ranging from baptism by lengthy dipping in ice-water and rolling in the snow, to the practice of the plunge-bath, which involved regular plunging of the infant over and over again in ice cold water over its head "with its mouth open and gasping for breath."[99] Elizabeth Grant remembers in the early nineteenth century that a "large, long tub stood in the kitchen court, the ice on the top of which often had to be broken before our horrid plunge into it. . . . How I screamed, begged, prayed, entreated to be saved. . . . Nearly senseless I have been taken to the housekeeper's room. . . ."[100] Going back to the ancient custom of the Germans, Scythians, Celts, and Spartans (though not Athenians, who used other hardening methods),[101] dipping in cold rivers used to be common, and cold water dipping has since Roman times been considered therapeutic for children.[102] Even the putting of children to bed wrapped in cold wet towels was sometimes used both to harden and as therapy.[103] It is not surprising that the great eighteenth-century pediatrician William Buchan said "almost one half of the human species perish in infancy by improper management or neglect."[104]

Abandonment, Nursing, and Swaddling

Although there were many exceptions to the general pattern, up to about the eighteenth century, the average child of wealthy parents spent his earliest years in the home of a wet-nurse, returned home to the care of other servants, and was sent out to service, apprenticeship, or school by age seven, so that the amount of time parents of means actually spent raising their children was minimal. The effects of these and other institutionalized abandonments by parents on the child have rarely been discussed.

The most extreme and oldest form of abandonment is the outright sale of children. Child sale was legal in Babylonian times, and may have been quite common among many nations in antiquity.[105] Although Solon tried to restrict the right of child sale by parents in Athens, it is unclear how effective the law was.[106] Herodas showed a beating scene where a boy was told "you're a bad boy, Kottalos, so bad that none could find a good word for you even were he selling you."[107] The church tried for centuries to stamp out child sale. Theodore, Archbishop of Canterbury in the seventh century, ruled a man might not sell his son into slavery after the age of 7. If Giraldus Cambrensis is to be believed, in the twelfth century the English had been selling their children to the Irish for slaves, and the Norman invasion was a punishment from God for this slave traffic.[108] In many areas, child sale continued sporadically into modern times, not being outlawed in Russia, for instance, until the nineteenth century.[109]

Another abandonment practice was the use of children as political hostages and security for debts, which also went back to Babylonian times.[110] Sidney Painter describes its medieval version, in which it was "quite customary to give young children as hostages to guarantee an agreement, and equally so to make them suffer for their parents' bad faith. When Eustace de Breteuil, the husband of a natural daughter of Henry I, put out the eyes of the son of one of his vassals, the king allowed the enraged father to mutilate in the same way Eustace's daughter whom Henry held as hostage."[111] Similarly, John Marshall gave up his son William to King Stephen, saying he "cared little if William were hanged, for he had the anvils and hammers with which to forge still better sons," and Francis I, when taken prisoner by Charles V, exchanged his young sons for his own freedom, then promptly broke the bargain so that they were thrown in jail.[112] Indeed, it was often hard to distinguish the practice of sending one's children to serve as pages or servants in another noble household from the use of children as hostages.

Similar abandonment motives were behind the custom of fosterage, which was common among all classes of Welsh, Anglo-Saxons, and Scandinavians, wherein an infant was sent to another family to be reared to age 17, and then returned to the parents. This continued in Ireland until the seventeenth century, and the English often sent their children to be fostered by the Irish in medieval times.[113] Actually, this was just an extreme version of the medieval practice of sending noble children at the age of seven or earlier into the homes of others or to monasteries as servants, pages, ladies-in-waiting, oblates, or clerks, practices still common in early modern times.[114] As with the equivalent lower class practice of apprenticeship,[115] the whole subject of the child as laborer in the homes of others is so vast and so poorly studied that it unfortunately cannot be much examined here, despite its obvious importance in the lives of children in the past.

Besides institutionalized abandonment practices, the informal abandoning of young children to other people by their parents occurred quite often right up to the nineteenth century. The parents gave every kind of rationalization for giving their children away: "to learn to speak" (Disraeli), "to cure timidness" (Clara Barton), for "health" (Edmund Burke, Mrs. Sherwood's daughter), or as payment for medical services rendered (patients of Jerome Cardan and William Douglas). Sometimes they admitted it was simply because they were not wanted (Richard Baxter, Johannes Butzbach, Richard Savage, Swift, Yeats, Augustus Hare, and so on). Mrs. Hare's mother expresses the general casualness of these abandonments: "Yes, certainly, the baby shall be sent as soon as it is weaned; and, if anyone else would like one, would you kindly recollect that we have others."[116] Boys were of course preferred; one eighteenth-century woman wrote her brother asking for his next child: "If it is a boy, I claim it; if a girl, I will be content to stay for the next."[117]

However, it was the sending of children to wet-nurse which was the form of institutionalized abandonment most prevalent in the past. The wet-nurse is a familiar figure in the Bible, the Code of Hammurabi, the Egyptian papyri, and Greek and Roman literature, and they have been well organized ever since Roman wet-nurses gathered in the Colonna Lactaria to sell their services.[118] Doctors and moralists since Galen and Plutarch have denounced mothers for sending their children out to be wet-nursed rather than nursing them themselves. Their advice had little effect, however, for until the eighteenth century most parents who could afford it, and many who couldn't, sent their children to wet-nurse immediately after birth. Even poor mothers who could not afford sending their children out to nurse often refused to breast-feed them, and gave them pap instead. Contrary to the assumptions of most historians, the custom of not breast-feeding infants at all reaches back in many areas of Europe at least as far as the fifteenth century. One mother, who had moved from an area in northern Germany where nursing infants was more common, was considered "swinish and filthy" by Bavarian women for nursing her child, and her husband threatened he would not eat if she did not give up this "disgusting habit."[119]

As for the rich, who actually abandoned their children for a period of years, even those experts who thought the practice bad usually did not use empathic terms in their treatises, but rather thought wet-nursing bad because "the dignity of a newborn human being [is] corrupted by the foreign and degenerate nourishment of another's milk."[120] That is, the blood of the lower-class wet-nurse entered the body of the upper-class baby, milk being thought to be blood frothed white.[121]

Except in those cases where the wet-nurse was brought in to live, children who were given to the wet-nurse were generally left there from two to five years. The conditions were similar in every country. Jacques Guillimeau described how the child at nurse might be "stifled, overlaid, be let fall, and so come to an untimely death; or else may be devoured, spoiled, or disfigured by some wild beast, wolf or dog, and then the nurse fearing to be punished for her negligence, may take another child into the place of it."[122] Robert Pemell reported the rector in his parish told him it was, when he first came to it, "filled with suckling infants from London and yet, in the space of one year, he buried them all except two."[123] Yet the practice continued inexorably until the eighteenth century in England and America, the nineteenth century in France, and into the twentieth century in Germany.[124] England was, in fact, so far in advance of the continent in nursing matters that quite wealthy mothers were often nursing their children as early as the seventeenth century.[125] Nor was it simply a matter of the amorality of the rich; Robert Pemell complained in 1653 of the practice of "both high and low ladies of farming out their babies to irresponsible women in the country," and as late as 1780 the police chief of Paris estimated that of the 21,000 children born each year in his city, 17,000 were sent into the country to be wet-nursed, 2,000 or 3,000 were placed in nursery homes, 700 were wet-nursed at home and only 700 were nursed by their mothers.[126]

It is possible that by early modern times, perhaps as a result of a reduction of projective care, very long nursing was becoming less common. It is also true that statements about weaning became more accurate as children were less often relegated to the wet-nurse; Roesslin, for example, says: "Avicen advices to give the child suck two years/how be it among us most commonly they suck but one year. . . ."[127] Surely Alice Ryerson's statement that the "age of weaning was drastically reduced in actual practice in the period just preceding 1750" is too sweeping.[128] Although wet-nurses were expected to refrain from intercourse while nursing, they rarely did so, and weaning usually preceded the birth of the next child. Therefore, nursing for as much as two years might always have been exceptional in the West.

Feeding vessels of all kinds have been known since 2,000 B.C.; cows' and goats' milk were used when available, and often the infant would be put right to the teat of the animal to suck.[129] Pap, generally made of bread or meal mixed with water or milk, supplemented or replaced nursing from the earliest weeks, and sometimes was crammed down the child's throat until it vomited. Any other food was first chewed by the wet-nurse, then given to the infant.[130] Opium and liquor were regularly given to infants throughout the ages to stop them from crying.[131] The Ebers Papyrus says of the effectiveness for children of a mixture of poppy-seeds and fly-dung: "It acts at once!"

There are many indications in the sources that children as a general practice were given insufficient food. Children of the poor, of course, have often been hungry, but even children of the rich, especially girls, were supposed to be given very meager allowances of food, and little or no meat. Plutarch's description of the "starvation diet" of Spartan youth is well known, but from the number of references to scanty food, nursing babies only two or three times a day, fasts for children, and deprivation of food as discipline, one suspects that, like parents of contemporary child abusers, parents in the past found it hard to see to it that their children were adequately fed.[132] Autobiographies from Augustine to Baxter have confessed to the sin of gluttony for stealing fruit as a child; no one has ever thought to ask if they did so because they were hungry.[133]

Tying the child up in various restraint devices was a near-universal practice. Swaddling was the central fact of the infant's earliest years. Traditional swaddling is much the same in every country and age; it "consists in entirely depriving the child of the use of its limbs, by enveloping them in an endless length bandage, so as to not unaptly resemble billets of wood; and by which, the skin is sometimes excoriated; the flesh compressed, almost to gangrene; the circulation nearly arrested; and the child without the slighest power of motion. Its little waist is surrounded by stays. . . . Its head is compressed into the form the fancy of the midwife might suggest; and its shape maintained by properly adjusted pressure. . . ."[134]

Swaddling was often so complicated it took up to two hours to dress an infant.[135] Its convenience to adults was enormous—they rarely had to pay any attention to infants once they were tied up. As a recent medical study of swaddling has shown, swaddled infants are extremely passive, their hearts slow down, they cry less, they sleep far more, and in general they are so withdrawn and inert that the doctors who did the study wondered if swaddling shouldn't be tried again.[136] The historical sources confirm this picture; doctors since antiquity agreed that "wakefulness does not happen to children naturally nor from habit, i.e., customarily, for they always sleep," and children were described as being laid for hours behind the hot oven, hung on pegs on the wall, placed in tubs, and in general, "left, like a parcel, in every convenient corner."[137] Almost all nations swaddled. Even in ancient Egypt, where it is claimed children were not swaddled because paintings showed them naked, swaddling may have been practiced, for Hippocrates said the Egyptians swaddle, and occasional figurines showed swaddling clothes.[138] Those few areas where swaddling was not used, such as in ancient Sparta and in the Scottish highlands, were also areas of the most severe hardening practices, as though the only possible choice were between tight swaddling or being carried about naked and made to run in the snow without clothes.[139] The English led the way in ending swaddling, as they did in ending outside wet-nursing. Swaddling in England and America was on its way out by the end of the eighteenth century, and in France and Germany by the nineteenth century.[140]

Once the infant was released from its swaddling bands, physical restraints of all kinds continued, varying by country and period. Children were sometimes tied to chairs to prevent their crawling. Right into the nineteenth century leading strings were tied to the child's clothes to control it and swing it about. Corsets and stays made of bone, wood, or iron were often used for both sexes. Children were sometimes strapped into backboards and their feet put in stocks while they studied, and iron collars and other devices were used to "improve posture," like the one Francis Kemble described: "a hideous engine of torture of the backboard species, made of steel covered with red morocco, which consisted of a flat piece placed on my back, and strapped down to my waist with a belt and secured at the top by two epaulets strapped over my shoulders. From the middle of this there rose a steel rod or spine, with a steel collar which encircled my throat and fastened behind."[141]

Toilet Training, Discipline, and Sex

Although chairs with chamber pots underneath have existed since antiquity, there is no evidence for toilet training in the earliest months of the infant's life prior to the eighteenth century. Although parents often complained, like Luther, of their children's "befouling the corners," and although doctors prescribed remedies, including whipping, for "pissing in the bed" (children generally slept with adults), the struggle between parent and child for control in infancy of urine and feces is an eighteenth-century invention, the product of a late psychogenic stage.[142]

Children, of course, have always been identified with their excrements; newborn infants were called *ecrême,* and the Latin *merda,* excrement, was the source of the French *merdeux,* little child.[143] But it was the enema and the purge, not the potty, which were the central devices for relating to the inside of the child's body prior to the eighteenth century. Children were given suppositories, enemas, and oral purges in sickness and in health. One seventeenth-century authority said infants should be purged before each nursing so the milk wouldn't get mixed up with the feces.[144] Heroard's diary of Louis XIII is filled with minute descriptions of what goes into and comes out of Louis's body, and he was given literally thousands of purges, suppositories, and enemas during his childhood. The urine and feces of infants were often examined in order to determine the inner state of the child. David Hunt's description of this process clearly reveals the projective origin for what I have termed the "toilet-child":

> The bowels of children were thought to harbor matter which spoke to the adult world insolently, threateningly, with malice and insubordination. The fact that the child's excrement looked and smelled unpleasant meant that the child himself was somewhere deep down inside badly disposed. No matter how placid and cooperative he might appear, the excrement which was regularly washed out of him was regarded as the insulting message of an inner demon, indicating the "bad humors" which lurked within."[145]

It was not until the eighteenth century that the main focus moved from the enema to the potty. Not only was toilet training begun at an earlier age, partly as a result of diminished use of swaddling bands, but the whole process of having the child control its body products was invested with an emotional importance previously unknown. Wrestling with an infant's will in his first few months was measure of the strength of involvement by parents with their chidren, and represented a psychological advance over the reign of the enema.[146] By the nineteenth century, parents generally began toilet training in earnest in the earliest months of life, and their demands for cleanliness became so severe by the end of the century that the ideal child was described as one "who cannot bear to have any dirt on his body or dress or in his surrounding for even the briefest time."[147]

The evidence which I have collected on methods of disciplining children leads me to believe that a very large percentage of the children born prior to the eighteenth century were what would today be termed "battered children." Of over two hundred statements of advice on child-rearing prior to the eighteenth century which I have examined, most approved of beating children severely, and all allowed beating in varying circumstances except three, Plutarch, Palmieri, and Sadoleto, and these were addressed to fathers and teachers, and did not mention mothers.[148] Of the seventy children prior to the eighteenth century whose lives I have found, all were beaten except one: Montaigne's daughter. Unfortunately, Montaigne's essays on children are so full of inconsistencies that one is uncertain whether to believe even this one statement.

Beating instruments included whips of all kinds, including the cat-o'-nine-tails, shovels, canes, iron and wooden rods, bundles of sticks, the *discipline* (a whip made of small chains), and special school instruments like the flapper, which had a pear-shaped end and a round hole to raise blisters. Their comparative frequency of use may be indicated by the categories of the German schoolmaster who reckoned he had given 911,527 strokes with the stick, 124,000 lashes with the whip, 136,715 slaps with the hand, and 1,115,800 boxes on the ear.[149] The beatings described in the sources were generally severe, involved bruising and bloodying of the body, began early, and were a regular part of the child's life.

Century after century of battered children grew up and in turn battered their own children. Public protest was rare. Even humanists and teachers who had a reputation for great gentleness, like Petrarch, Ascham, Comenius, and Pestalozzi, approved of beating children.[150] Milton's wife complained she hated to hear the cries of his nephews when he was beating them, and Beethoven whipped his pupils with a knitting needle and sometimes bit them.[151] Even royalty was not exempt from battering, as the childhood of Louis XIII confirms. A whip was at his father's side at table, and as early as 17 months of age, the dauphin knew enough not to cry when threatened with the whip. At 25 months regular whippings began, often on his bare skin. He had frequent nightmares about his whippings, which were administered in the morning when he awakened. When he was king he still awoke at night in terror, in expectation of his morning whipping. The day of his coronation, when he was eight, he was whipped, and said, "I would rather do without so much obeisance and honor if they wouldn't have me whipped."[152]

Since infants who were not swaddled were in particular subjected to hardening practices, perhaps one function of swaddling was to reduce the parent's propensity for child abuse. I have not yet found an adult who beat a swaddled infant. However, the beating of the smallest of infants out of swaddling clothes occurred quite often, a sure sign of the "battering" syndrome. Susannah Wesley said of her babies: "When turned a year old (and some before), they were taught to fear the rod, and to cry softly." Giovanni Dominici said to give babies "frequent, yet not severe whippings. . . ." Rousseau said that babies in their earliest days were often beaten to keep them quiet. One mother wrote of her first battle with her 4-month-old infant: "I whipped him 'til he was actually black and blue, and until I *could not* whip him any more, and he never gave up one single inch." The examples could easily be extended.[153]

One curious method of punishment, which was inflicted on the early medieval ecclesiastic Alcuin when he was an infant, was to cut or prick the soles of the feet with an instrument which resembled a cobbler's knife. This reminds one of the Bishop of Ely's habit of pricking his young servants with a goad which he always held in one hand. When Jane Grey complained of her parents giving her "nips and bobs," and Thomas Tusser complained of "touzed ears, like baited bears,/ what bobbed lips, what jerks, what nips" it may have been the goad which was used. Should further research show that the goad was also used on children in antiquity, it would put a different light on Oedipus's killing of Laius on that lonely road, for he was literally "goaded" into it—Laius having struck him "full on the head with his two-pointed goad."[154]

Although the earliest sources are quite sketchy on the precise severity of discipline, there seems to be evidence of visible improvement in every period in the West. Antiquity is full of devices and practices unknown to later times, including shackles for the feet, handcuffs, gags, three months in "the block," and the bloody Spartan flagellation contests, which often involved whipping youths to death.[155] One Anglo-Saxon custom suggests the level of thought about children in earliest times. Thrupp says: "It was customary when it was wished to retain legal testimony of any ceremony, to have it witnessed by children, who then and there were flogged with unusual severity; which it was supposed would give additional weight to any evidence of the proceedings. . . ."[156]

References to detailed modes of discipline are even harder to find in the Middle Ages. One thirteenth-century law brought child-beating into the public domain: "If one beats a child until it bleeds, then it will remember, but if one beats it to death, the law applies."[157] Most medieval descriptions of beating were quite severe, although St. Anselm, as in so many things, was far in advance of his time by telling an abbot to beat children gently, for "Are they not human? Are they not flesh and blood like you?"[158] But it is only in the Renaissance that advice to temper childhood beatings began in earnest, although even then it was generally accompanied by approval for beatings judiciously applied. As Bartholomew Batty said, parents must "keep the golden mean," which is to say they should not "strike and buffet their children about the face and head, and to lace upon them like malt sacks with cudgels, staves, fork or fire shovel," for then they might die of the blows. The correct way was to "hit him upon the sides . . . with the rod, he shall not die thereof."[159]

Some attempts were made in the seventeenth century to limit the beating of children, but it was the eighteenth century which saw the biggest decrease. The earliest lives I have found of children who may not have been beaten at all date from 1690 to 1750.[160] It was not until the nineteenth century that the old-fashioned whipping began to go out of style in most of Europe and America, continuing longest in Germany, where 80% of German parents still admit to beating their children, a full 35% with canes.[161]

As beatings began to decrease, substitutes had to be found. For instance, shutting children up in the dark became quite popular in the eighteenth and nineteenth centuries. Children were put in "dark closets, where they were sometimes forgotten for hours." One mother shut her 3-year-old boy up in a drawer. Another house was "a sort of little Bastille, in every closet of which was to be found a culprit—some were sobbing and repeating verbs, others eating their bread and water. . . ." Children were sometimes left locked in rooms for days. One 5-year-old French boy, in looking at a new apartment with his mother, told her, "Oh no, mama, . . . it's impossible; there's no dark closet! Where could you put me when I'm naughty."[162]

The history of sex in childhood presents even more difficulty than usual in getting at the facts, for added to the reticence and repression of our sources is the unavailability of most of the books, manuscripts, and artifacts which form the basis for our research. Victorian attitudes towards sex still reign supreme among most librarians, and the bulk of works which relate to sex in history remain under lock and key in library storerooms and museum basements all over Europe, unavailable even to the historian. Even so, there is evidence enough in the sources so far available to us to indicate that the sexual abuse of children was far more common in the past than today, and that the severe punishment of children for their sexual desires in the last two hundred years was the product of a late psychogenic stage, in which the adult used the child to restrain, rather than act out, his own sexual fantasies. In sexual abuse, as in physical abuse, the child was only an incidental victim, a measure of the part it played in the defense system of the adult.

The child in antiquity lived his earliest years in an atmosphere of sexual abuse. Growing up in Greece and Rome often included being used sexually by older men. The exact form and frequency of the abuse varied by area and date. In Crete and Boeotia, pederastic marriages and honeymoons were common. Abuse was less frequent among aristocratic boys in Rome, but sexual use of children was everywhere evident in some form.[163] Boy brothels flourished in every city, and one could even contract for the use of a rent-a-boy service in Athens. Even where homosexuality with free boys was discouraged by law, men kept slave boys to abuse, so that even free-born children saw their fathers sleeping with boys. Children were sometimes sold into concubinage; Musonius Rufus wondered whether such a boy would be justified in resisting being abused: "I knew a father so depraved that, having a son conspicuous for youthful beauty, he sold him into a life of shame. If, now, that lad who was sold and sent into such a life by his father had refused and would not go, should we say that he was disobedient. . . ."[164] Aristotle's main objection to Plato's idea that children should be held in common was that when men had sex with boys they wouldn't know if they were their own sons, which Aristotle says would be "most unseemly."[165] Plutarch said the reason why freeborn Roman boys wore a gold ball around their necks when they were very young was so men could tell which boys it was not proper to use sexually when they found a group in the nude.[166]

Plutarch's statement was only one among many which indicate that the sexual abuse of boys was not limited to those over 11 or 12 years of age, as most scholars assume. Sexual abuse by pedagogues and teachers of smaller children may have been common throughout antiquity. Although all sorts of laws were passed to try to limit sexual attacks on school children by adults, the long heavy sticks carried by pedagogues and teachers were often used to threaten them. Quintillian, after many years of teaching in Rome, warned parents against the frequency of sexual abuse by teachers, and made this the basis of his disapproval of beating in schools.

The evidence from literature and art confirms this picture of the sexual abuse of smaller children. Petronius loves depicting adults feeling the "immature little tool" of boys, and his description of the rape of a seven-year-old girl, with women clapping in a long line around the bed, suggests that women were not exempt from playing a role in the process."[167] Aristotle said homosexuality often becomes habitual in "those who are abused from childhood." It has been assumed that the small nude children seen on vases waiting on adults in erotic scenes are servants, but in view of the usual role of noble children as waiters, we should consider the possibility that they may be children of the house.

For, as Quintillian said about noble Roman children: "We rejoice if they say something over-free, and words which we should not tolerate from the lips even of an Alexandrian page are greeted with laughter and a kiss . . . they hear us use such words, they see our mistresses and minions; every dinner party is loud with foul songs, and things are presented to their eyes of which we should blush to speak."[168]

Even the Jews, who tried to stamp out adult homosexuality with severe punishments, were more lenient in the case of young boys. Despite Moses's injunction against corrupting children, the penalty for sodomy with children over nine years of age was death by stoning, but copulation with younger children was not considered a sexual act, and was punishable only by a whipping, "as a matter of public discipline."[169]

It must be remembered that widespread sexual abuse of children can only occur with at least the unconscious complicity of the child's parents. Children in the past were under the fullest control of their parents, who had to agree to give them over to their abusers. Plutarch muses on how important this decision was for fathers:

> I am loathe to introduce the subject, loathe too to turn away from it . . . whether we should permit the suitors of our boys to associate with them and pass their time with them, or whether the opposite policy of excluding them and shooing them away from intimacy with our boys is correct. Whenever I look at blunt-spoken fathers of the austere and astringent type who regard intimacy with lovers as an intolerable outrage upon their sons, I am circumspect about showing myself a sponsor and advocate of the practice. [Yet Plato] declares that men who have proven their worth should be permitted to caress any fair lad they please. Lovers who lust only for physical beauty, then, it is right to drive away; but free access should be granted to lovers of the soul.[170]

The favorite sexual use of children . . . [was] anal intercourse. Martial said one should, while buggering a boy, "refrain from stirring the groin with poking hand . . . Nature has separated the male: one part has been produced for girls, one for men. Use your own part." This, he said, was because the masturbating of boys would "hasten manhood," an observation Aristotle made some time before him. Whenever a pre-pubertal boy was shown being used sexually on erotic vases, the penis was never shown erect.[171] For men of antiquity were not really homosexuals as we know them today, but a much lower psychic mode, which I think should be termed "ambisexual" (they themselves used the term "ambidextrous"). While the homosexual runs to men as a retreat from women, as a defense against the oedipal conflict, the ambisexual has never really reached the oedipal level, and uses boys and women almost without distinction.[172] In fact, as psychoanalyst Joan McDougall observes, the main purpose of this kind of perversion is to demonstrate that "there is no difference between the sexes." She says that it is an attempt to control childhood sexual traumata by reversal, with the adult now putting another child in the helpless position, and also an attempt to handle castration anxiety by proving that "castration does not hurt and in fact is the very condition of erotic arousal."[173] This well describes the man of antiquity. Intercourse with castrated children was often spoken of as being especially arousing, castrated boys were favorite "voluptates" in imperial Rome, and infants were castrated "in the cradle" to be used in brothels by men who liked buggering young castrated boys. When Domitian passed a law prohibiting castration of infants for brothels, Martial praised him: "Boys loved thee before . . . but now infants, too, love thee, Caesar."[174] Paulus Aegineta described the standard method used in castrating small boys:

> Since we are sometimes compelled against our will by persons of high rank to perform the operation . . . by compression [it] is thus performed; children, still of a tender age, are placed in a vessel of hot water, and then when the parts are softened in the bath, the testicles are to be squeezed with the fingers until they disappear.

The alternative, he said, was to put them on a bench and cut their testicles out. Many doctors in antiquity mentioned the operation, and Juvenal said they were often called upon to perform it.[175]

Christianity introduced a new concept into the discussion —childhood innocence. As Clement of Alexandria said, when Christ advised people to "become as little children" in order to enter into Heaven, one should "not foolishly mistake his meaning. We are not little ones in the sense that we roll on the floor or crawl on the ground as snakes do." What Christ means was that people should become as "uncontaminated" as children, pure, without sexual knowledge.[176] Christians throughout the Middle Ages began to stress the idea that children were totally innocent of all notions of pleasure and pain. A child "has not tasted sensual pleasures, and has no conception of the impulses of manhood . . . one becomes as a child in respect of anger; and is as the child in relation to his grief, so that sometimes he laughs and plays at the very time that his father or mother or brother is dead. . . ."[177] Unfortunately, the idea that children are innocent and cannot be corrupted is a common defense by child molesters against admitting that their abuse is harming the child, so the medieval fiction that the child is innocent only makes our sources less revealing, and proves nothing about what really went on. Abbot Guibert of Nogent said children were blessed to be without sexual thoughts or capacities; one wonders what he then was referring to when he confessed to "the wickedness I did in childhood. . . ."[178] Mostly, servants are blamed for abusing children; even a washerwoman could "work wickedness." Servants often "show lewd tricks . . . in the presence of children [and] corrupt the chief parts of infants." Nurses should not be young girls, "for many such have aroused the fire of passion prematurely as true accounts relate and, I venture to say, experience proves."[179]

That some change in the sexual use of children was going on in the Renaissance can be seen not only in the rising number of moralists who warned against it (Jean Gerson, like Louis XIII's nurse, said it was the *child's* duty to prevent others from molesting him), but also in the art of the time. Not only were Renaissance paintings full of nude *putti*, or cupids taking off blindfolds in front of nude women, but in addition real children were shown more and more often chucking the chin of the mother, or slinging one of their legs over hers, both conventional iconographic signs for sexual love, and the mother was often painted with her hand very near the genital area of the child.[180]

The campaign against the sexual use of children continued through the seventeenth century, but in the eighteenth century it took an entirely new twist: punishing the little boy or girl for touching its own genitals. That this, like early toilet-training, was a late psychogenic stage is suggested by the fact that prohibitions against childhood masturbation are found in none of the primitive societies surveyed by Whiting and Child.[181] The attitude of most people toward childhood masturbation prior to the eighteenth century can be seen in Fallopius's counsel for parents to "be zealous in infancy to enlarge the penis of the boy."[182] Although masturbation in adults was a minor sin, medieval penitentials rarely extended the prohibition to childhood; adult homosexuality, not masturbation, was the main obsession of pre-modern sexual regulation. As late as the fifteenth century Gerson complains how adults tell him they never heard that masturbation was sinful, and he instructs confessors to ask adults directly: "Friend, do you touch or do you rub your rod *as children have the habit of doing*?"[183]

But it was not until the beginning of the eighteenth century, as a climax of the effort to bring child abuse under control, that parents began severely punishing their children for masturbation, and doctors began to spread the myth that it would cause insanity, epilepsy, blindness, and death. By the nineteenth century, this campaign reached an unbelievable frenzy. Doctors and parents sometimes appeared before the child armed with knives and scissors, threatening to cut off the child's genitals; circumcision, clitoridectomy, and infibulation were sometimes used as punishment; and all sorts of restraint devices, including plaster casts and cages with spikes, were prescribed. Circumcision became especially widespread; as one American child psychologist put it, when a child of two rubs his nose and can't be still for a moment, only circumcision works. Another doctor, whose book was the bible of many an American nineteenth-century home, recommended that little boys be closely watched for signs of masturbation, and brought in to him for circumcision without anaesthetic, which invariably cured them. Spitz's graphs on different advice given for masturbation, based on 559 volumes surveyed, show a peak in surgical intervention in 1850–1879, and in restraint devices in 1880–1904. By 1925, these methods had almost completely died out, after two centuries of brutal and totally unnecessary assault on children's genitals.[184]

Meanwhile, sexual use of children after the eighteenth century was far more widespread among servants and other adults and adolescents than among parents, although when one reads of the number of parents who continued to let their children sleep with servants after previous servants had been found abusing them sexually, it is obvious that the conditions for child abuse still remained within the control of the parents. Cardinal Bernis, remembering being sexually molested as a child, warned parents that "nothing is so dangerous for morals and perhaps for health as to leave children too long under the care of chambermaids, or even of young ladies brought up in the chateaux. I will add that the best among them are not always the least dangerous. They dare with a child that which they would be ashamed to risk with a young man."[185] A German doctor said nursemaids and servants carried out "all sorts of sexual acts" on children "for fun." Even Freud said he was seduced by his nurse when he was two, and Ferenczi and other analysts since his time have thought unwise Freud's decision in 1897 to consider most reports by patients of early sexual seductions as only fantasy. As psychoanalyst Robert Fleiss puts it, "No one is ever made sick by his fantasies," and a large number of patients in analysis even today report using children sexually although only Fleiss builds this fact into his psychoanalytic theory. When one learns that as late as 1900 there were still people who believed venereal disease could be cured "by means of sexual intercourse with children," one begins to recognize the dimensions of the problem more fully.[186]

It goes without saying that the effects on the child in the past of such severe physical and sexual abuse as I have described were immense. I would here like to indicate only two effects on the growing child, one psychological and one physical. The first is the enormous number of nightmares and hallucinations by children which I have found in the sources. Although written records by adults which indicate anything at all about a child's emotional life are rare at best, whenever discovered they usually reveal recurring nightmares and even outright hallucinations. Since antiquity, pediatric literature regularly had sections on how to cure children's "terrible dreams," and children were sometimes beaten for having nightmares. Children lay awake nights terrorized by imaginary ghosts, demons, "a witch on the pillow," "a large black dog under the bed," or "a crooked finger crawling across the room."[187] In addition, the history of witchcraft in the West is filled with reports of children's convulsive fits, loss of hearing or speech, loss of memory, hallucination of devils, confession of intercourse with devils, and accusations of witchcraft against adults, including their parents. And finally, even further back in the Middle Ages, we encounter children's dancing mania, children's crusades and child-pilgrimages, subjects which are simply too vast to discuss here.[188]

A final point I wish only to touch upon is the possibility that children in the past were actually retarded physically as a result of their poor care. Although swaddling by itself usually does not affect the physical development of primitive children, the combination of tight swaddling, neglect, and general abuse of children in the past seemed often to have produced what we would now regard as retarded children. One index of this retardation is that while most children today begin to walk by 10–12 months, children in the past generally walked later.

Periodization of Modes of Parent-Child Relations

Since some people still kill, beat, and sexually abuse children, any attempt to periodize modes of childrearing must first admit that psychogenic evolution proceeds at different rates in different family lines, and that many parents appear to be "stuck" in earlier historical modes. There are also class and area differences which are important, especially since modern times, when the upper classes stopped sending their infants to wet-nurses and began bringing them up themselves. The periodization below should be thought of as a designation of the modes of parent-child relations which were exhibited by the psychogenically most advanced part of the population in the most advanced countries, and the dates given are the first in which I found examples of that mode in the sources. The series of six modes represents a continuous sequence of closer approaches between parent and child as generation after generation of parents slowly overcame their anxieties and began to develop the capacity to identify and satisfy the needs of their children. I also believe the series provides a meaningful taxology of contemporary child-rearing modes.

1. *Infanticidal Mode (Antiquity to Fourth Century A.D.)*: The image of Medea hovers over childhood in antiquity, for myth here only reflects reality. Some facts are more important than others, and when parents routinely resolved their anxieties about taking care of children by killing them, it affected the surviving children profoundly. For those who were allowed to grow up, the projective reaction was paramount, and the concreteness of reversal was evident in the widespread sodomizing of the child.

2. *Abandonment Mode (Fourth to Thirteenth Century A.D.)*: Once parents began to accept the child as having a soul, the only way they could escape the dangers of their own projections was by abandonment, whether to the wet nurse, to the monastery or nunnery, to foster families, to the homes of other nobles as servants or hostages, or by severe emotional abandonment at home. The symbol of this mode might be Griselda, who so willingly abandoned her children to prove her love for her husband. Or perhaps it would be any of those pictures so popular up to the thirteenth century of a rigid Mary stiffly holding the infant Jesus. Projection continued to be massive, since the child was still full of evil and needed always to be beaten, but as the reduction in child sodomizing shows, reversal diminished considerably.

3. *Ambivalent Mode (Fourteenth to Seventeenth Centuries)*: Because the child, when it was allowed to enter into the parents' emotional life, was still a container for dangerous projections, it was their task to mold it into shape. From Dominici to Locke there was no image more popular than that of the physical molding of children, who were seen as soft wax, plaster, or clay to be beaten into shape. Enormous ambivalence marks this mode. The beginning of the period is approximately the fourteenth century, which shows an increase in the number of child instruction manuals, the expansion of the cults of Mary and the infant Jesus, and the proliferation in art of the "close-mother image."

4. *Intrusive Mode (Eighteenth Century)*: A tremendous reduction in projection and the virtual disappearance of reversal was the accomplishment of the great transition for parent-child relations which appeared in the eighteenth century. The child was no longer so full of dangerous projections, and rather than just examine its insides with an enema, the parents approached even closer and attempted to conquer its mind, in order to control its insides, its anger, its needs, its masturbation, its very will. The child raised by intrusive parents was nursed by the mother, not swaddled, not given regular enemas, toilet trained

early, prayed with but not played with, hit but not regularly whipped, punished for masturbation, and made to obey promptly with threats and guilt as often as with other methods of punishment. The child was so much less threatening that true empathy was possible, and pediatrics was born, which along with the general improvement in level of care by parents reduced infant mortality and provided the basis for the demographic transition of the eighteenth century.

5. *Socialization Mode* (*Nineteenth to Mid-twentieth Centuries*): As projections continued to diminish, the raising of a child became less a process of conquering its will than of training it, guiding it into proper paths, teaching it to conform, socializing it. The socializing mode is still thought of by most people as the only model within which discussion of child care can proceed, and it has been the source of all twentieth-century psychological models, from Freud's "channeling of impulses" to Skinner's behaviorism. It is most particularly the model of sociological functionalism. Also, in the nineteenth century, the father for the first time begins to take more than an occasional interest in the child, training it, and sometimes even relieving the mother of child-care chores.

6. *Helping Mode* (*Begins Mid-twentieth Century*): The helping mode involves the proposition that the child knows better than the parent what it needs at each stage of its life, and fully involves both parents in the child's life as they work to empathize with and fulfill its expanding and particular needs. There is no attempt at all to discipline or form "habits." Children are neither struck nor scolded, and are apologized to if yelled at under stress. The helping mode involves an enormous amount of time, energy, and discussion on the part of both parents, especially in the first six years, for helping a young child reach its daily goals means continually responding to it, playing with it, tolerating its regressions, being its servant rather than the other way around, interpreting its emotional conflicts, and providing the objects specific to its kind of child care. From the four books which describe children brought up according to the helping mode,[189] it is evident that it results in a child who is gentle, sincere, never depressed, never imitative or group-oriented, strong-willed, and unintimidated by authority.

Psychogenic Theory: A New Paradigm for History

Psychogenic theory can, I think, provide a genuinely new paradigm for the study of history.[190] It reverses the usual "*mind as tabula rasa,*" and instead considers the "*world as tabula rasa,*" with each generation born into a world of meaningless objects which are invested with meaning only if the child receives a certain kind of care.[191] As soon as the mode of care changes for enough children, all the books and artifacts in the world are brushed aside as irrelevant to the purposes of the new generation, and society begins to move in unpredictable directions. How historical change is connected with changing child-care modes we have yet to spell out. Most of us have already begun work on articles which will extend our childhood findings into the broader area of psychohistory, and we have even initiated a new scholarly journal, *History of Childhood Quarterly: The Journal of Psychohistory*, in which to publish our future studies.

If the measure of a theory's vitality is its ability to generate interesting problems, childhood history and psychogenic theory should have an exciting future. There is still a lot to learn about what growing up in the past was really like. One of our first tasks will be to investigate why childhood evolution proceeds at different rates in different countries and different class and family lines. Yet we already know enough to be able for the first time to answer some major questions on value and behavior change in Western history. First to benefit from the theory will be the history of witchcraft, magic, religious movements, and other irrational mass phenomena. Beyond this, psychogenic theory should eventually contribute to our understanding of why social organization, political form, and technology change in specific times and directions and not in others. Perhaps the addition of the childhood parameter to history may even end the historian's century-long Durkheimian flight from psychology, and encourage us to resume the task of constructing a scientific history of human nature which was envisioned so long ago by John Stuart Mill as a "theory of the causes which determine the type of character belonging to a people or to an age."[192]

Notes

1. Peter Laslett, *The World We Have Lost* (New York, 1965), p. 104.

2. James H. S. Bossard, *The Sociology of Child Development* (New York, 1948), p. 598.

3. Geza Roheim, "The Study of Character Development and The Ontogenetic Theory of Culture," in *Essays Presented to C. G. Seligman*, E. E. Evans-Pritchard, et al., eds. (London, 1934), p. 292; Abram Kardiner, ed., *The Individual and His Society* (New York, 1939), p. 471; in *Totem and Taboo*, Freud side-stepped the problem by positing an "inheritance of psychic disposition"; Sigmund Freud, *The Standard Edition of the Complete Psychological Works of Sigmund Freud*, vol. 13, James Strachey, ed. (London, 1955), p. 158.

4. Enid Nemy, "Child Abuse: Does It Stem From the Nation's Ills and Its

Culture?" *New York Times,* August 16, 1971, p. 16; some estimates reach as high as 2.5 million abused children, see Vincent J. Fontana, *Somewhere a Child Is Crying* (New York, 1973), p. 38.

5. An evaluation of some of the most recent works can be found in John C. Sommerville, "Towards a History of Childhood and Youth," *Journal of Interdisciplinary History,* 3 (1972), 438–47; and Edward Saveth, "The Problem of American Family History," *American Quarterly,* 21 (1969), 311–29.

6. See especially Neil J. Smelser, *Social Change in the Industrial Revolution: An Application of Theory of the British Cotton Industry* (Chicago, 1959); Fred Weinstein and Gerald Platt, *The Wish to Be Free: Society, Psyche, and Value Change* (Berkeley and Los Angeles, 1969); and Talcott Parsons and Robert F. Bales, *Family, Socialization, and Interaction Process* (New York, 1955).

7. See Peter Coveney, *The Image of Childhood: The Individual and Society: A Study of the Theme in English Literature* (Baltimore, 1967); Gillian Avery, *Nineteenth Century Children: Heroes and Heroines in English Children's Stories 1780–1900* (London, 1965); F. J. Harvey Darton, *Children's Books in England: Five Centuries of Social Life* (Cambridge, 1966); and Paul Hazard, *Books, Children & Men* (Boston, 1944).

8. The best childhood histories include: Grace Abbott, *The Child and the State,* 2 vols. (Chicago, 1938); Abt-Garrison, *History of Pediatrics* (Philadelphia, 1965); Philippe Ariès, *Centuries of Childhood: A Social History of Family Life* (New York, 1962); Sven Armens, *Archetypes of the Family in Literature* (Seattle, 1966); David Bakan, *Slaughter of the Innocents* (San Francisco, 1971); Howard Clive Barnard, *The French Tradition in Education* (Cambridge, 1922); Rosamond Bayne-Powell, *The English Child in the Eighteenth Century* (London, 1939); Frederick A. G. Beck, *Greek Education: 450–350 B.C.* (London, 1964); Jessie Bedford (pseud., Elizabeth Godfrey), *English Children in the Olden Time* (London, 1907); H. Blumner, *The Home Life of the Ancient Greeks,* Alice Zimmern, trans. (New York, 1966); Bossard, *Sociology;* Robert H. Bremner et al., eds., *Children and Youth in America: A Documentary History,* 3 vols., (Cambridge, Massachusetts, 1970); Elizabeth Burton, *The Early Victorians at Home 1837–1861* (London, 1972); M. St. Clare Byrne, *Elizabethan Life in Town and Country* (London, 1961); Ernest Caulfield, *The Infant Welfare Movement in the Eighteenth Century* (New York, 1931); Oscar Chrisman, *The Historical Child* (Boston, 1920); Phillis Cunnington and Anne Boch, *Children's Costume in England: From the Fourteenth to the End of the Nineteenth Century* (New York, 1965); John Demos, *A Little Commonwealth: Family Life in Plymouth Colony* (New York, 1970); J. Louise Despert, *The Emotionally Disturbed Child—Then and Now* (New York, 1967); George Duby, *La Société aux XIe et XIIe Siècles dans la Région Maçonnaise* (Paris, 1953); Alice Morse Earle, *Child Life in Colonial Days* (New York, 1899); Jonathan Gathorne-Hardy, *The Rise and Fall of the British Nanny* (London, 1972); Willystine Goodsell, *A History of Marriage and the Family* (New York, 1934); Sister Mary Rosaria Gorman, *The Nurse in Greek Life: A Dissertation* (Boston, 1917); E. H. Hare, "Masturbatory

Insanity: The History of an Idea," *Journal of Mental Science*, 108 (1962); 2–25; Edith Hoffman, *Children in the Past* (London, n.d.); Christina Hole, *English Home-Life, 1450 to 1800* (London, 1947); David Hunt, *Parents and Children in History* (New York, 1970); Anne L. Kuhn, *The Mother's Role in Childhood Education: New England Concepts 1830–1860* (New Haven, 1947); W. K. Lacey, *The Family in Classical Greece* (Ithaca, New York, 1968); Marion Lochhead, *Their First Ten Years: Victorian Childhood* (London, 1956); Alan Macfarlane, *The Family Life of Ralph Josselin: A Seventeenth-Century Clergyman* (Cambridge, 1970); Morris Marples, *Princes in the Making: A Study of Royal Education* (London, 1965); H. I. Marrou, *A History of Education in Antiquity* (New York, 1956); Roger Mercer, *L'enfant dans la société du XVIIIe siècle* (Dakar, 1951); Edmund S. Morgan, *The Puritan Family: Religion & Domestic Relations in Seventeenth-Century New England* (New York, 1966); George Henry Payne, *The Child in Human Progress* (New York, 1916); Lu Emily Pearson, *Elizabethans at Home* (Stanford, California, 1957); Albrecht Peiper, *Chronik der Kinderheilkunde* (Leipzig, 1966); Henricus Pecters, *Kind en juegdige in het begin van de modern tijd* (Antwerpen, 1966); Ivy Pinchbeck and Margaret Hewitt, *Children in English Society*, Vol. 1: *From Tudor Times to the Eighteenth Century* (London, 1969); Chilton Latham Powell, *English Domestic Relations, 1487–1653* (New York, 1917); F. Gordon Roe, *The Georgian Child* (London, 1961); F. Gordon Roe, *The Victorian Child* (London, 1959); John Ruhrah, ed., *Pediatrics of the Past: An Anthology* (New York, 1925); Alice Ryerson, "Medical Advice on Child Rearing," Ed.D. thesis, Harvard University Graduate School of Education, 1960; Paul Sangster, *Pity My Simplicity: The Evangelical Revival and the Religious Education of Children 1738–1800* (London, 1963); Levin L. Schucking, *The Puritan Family* (London, 1969); Rene A. Spitz, "Authority and Masturbation: Some Remarks on a Bibliographical Investigation," *The Psychoanalytic Quarterly*, 21 (1952), 490–527; George Frederic Still, *The History of Paediatrics* (London, 1931); Karl Sudhoff, *Erstlinge der Padiatrischen Literatur: Drei Wiegendrucke über Heilung und Pflege des Kindes* (Munich, 1925); Gordon Rattray Taylor, *The Angel-Makers: A Study in the Psychological Origins of Historical Change 1750–1850* (London, 1958); Bernard Wishy, *The Child and the Republic: The Dawn of Modern American Child Nurture* (Philadelphia, 1968).

9. Charles Seltman, *Women in Antiquity* (London, 1956), p. 72.

10. Daniel R. Miller and Guy E. Swanson, *The Changing American Parent: A Study in the Detroit Area* (New York, 1958), p. 10.

11. Bayne-Powell, *English Child*, p. 6.

12. Laslett, *World*, p. 12; E. S. Morgan agrees that Puritan parents sent their children away at a young age only because they were "afraid of spoiling them by too great affection," *Puritan Family*, p. 77.

13. William Sloane, *Children's Books in England and America in the Seventeenth Century* (New York, 1955), p. 19.

14. Ariès, *Centuries of Childhood*, p. 103.

15. Ibid., p. 105.

16. Frank E. Manuel, "The Use and Abuse of Psychology in History," *Daedalus,* 100 (1971), 203.

17. Ariès, *Centuries of Childhood,* pp. 33, 10.

18. An enormous bibliography and many examples of paintings of the child in early medieval art can be found in Victor Lasareff, "Studies in the Iconography of the Virgin," *Art Bulletin,* 20 (1938), pp. 26–65.

19. Natalie Z. Davis, "The Reasons of Misrule," *Past and Present,* 50 (1971), 61–62. Frank Boll, *Die Lebensalter: Ein Beitrag zur antiken Ethologie und zur Geschichte der Zahlen* (Leipzig and Berlin, 1913) has the best bibliography on "Ages of Man"; for all the variations in Old English on the word "child," see Hilding Back, *The Synonyms for "Child," "Boy," "Girl" in Old English* (London, 1934).

20. Richard Sennett, *Families Against the City* (Cambridge, Massachusetts, 1970); Joseph F. Kett, "Adolescence and Youth in Nineteenth-Century America," *The Journal of Interdisciplinary History,* 2 (1971), 283–99; John and Virginia Demos, "Adolescence in Historical Perspective," *Journal of Marriage and the Family,* 31 (1969), 632–38.

21. Despert, *Emotionally Disturbed Child,* p. 40.

22. Donald Meltzer, *The Psycho-Analytical Process* (London, 1967); Herbert A. Rosenfield, *Psychotic States: A Psychoanalytical Approach* (New York, 1965).

23. Brandt F. Steele, "Parental Abuse of Infants and Small Children," in E. James Anthony and Therese Benedek, eds., *Parenthood: Its Psychology and Psychopathology* (Boston, 1970); David G. Gil, *Violence Against Children: Physical Child Abuse in the United States* (Cambridge, Massachusetts, 1970); Brandt F. Steele and Carl B. Pollock, "A Psychiatric Study of Parents Who Abuse Infants and Small Children," in Ray E. Helfer and C. Henry Kempe, eds., *The Battered Child* (Chicago, 1968), pp. 103–45; Richard Galdston, "Dysfunctions of Parenting: The Battered Child, the Neglected Child, the Exploited Child," in John G. Howells, ed., *Modern Perspectives in International Child Psychiatry* (New York, 1971), pp. 571–84.

24. Theodor Reik, *Listening With the Third Ear* (New York, 1950); also see Stanley L. Olinick, "On Empathy, and Regression in Service of the Other," *British Journal of Medical Psychology,* 42 (1969), 40–47.

25. Nicholas Restif de la Bretonne, *Monsieur Nicolas; or, The Human Heart Unveiled,* Vol. 1, R. Crowder Mathers, trans. (London, 1930), p. 95.

26. Gregory Bateson, *Steps to an Ecology of Mind* (New York, 1972).

27. Barry Cunningham, "Beaten Kids, Sick Parents," *New York Post,* February 23, 1972, p. 14.

28. Samuel Arnold, *An Astonishing Affair!* (Concord, 1830), pp. 73–81.

29. Powell, *Domestic Relations,* p. 110.

30. Cotton Mather, *Diary of Cotton Mather,* vol. 1 (New York, n.d.), p. 283.

31. Ibid., p. 369.

32. Carl Holliday, *Woman's Life in Colonial Boston* (Boston, 1922), p. 25.

33. Richard Allestree, *The Whole Duty of Man* (London, 1676), p. 20.

34. Keith Thomas, *Religion and the Decline of Magic* (New York, 1971), p. 479; Beatrice Saunders, *The Age of Candlelight: The English Social Scene in the 17th Century* (London, 1959), p. 88; Traugott K. Oesterreich, *Possession, Demoniacal and Other Among Primitive Races, in Antiquity, the Middle Ages, and Modern Times* (New York, 1930); Grunewald's "St. Cyriakus" shows a girl being exorcised, her mouth being forced open to let the devil out.

35. Shmarya Levin, *Childhood in Exile* (New York, 1929), pp. 58–59.

36. G. G. Coulton, *Social Life in Britain: From the Conquest to the Reformation* (Cambridge, 1918), p. 46.

37. Ruth Benedict, "Child Rearing in Certain European Countries," *American Journal of Orthopsychiatry*, 19 (1949), 345–46.

38. Asa Briggs, ed., *How They Lived*, vol. 3 (New York, 1969), p. 27.

39. Ariès, *Centuries of Childhood*, p. 57; Christian Augustus Struve, *A Familiar Treatise on the Physical Education of Children* (London, 1801), p. 299.

40. Agnes C. Vaughan, *The Genesis of Human Offspring: A Study in Early Greek Culture* (Menasha, Wisconsin, 1945), p. 107; James Hastings, ed., *A Dictionary of Christ and the Gospels* (New York, 1911), p. 533.

41. Kett, *Adolescence*, pp. 35, 230.

42. E. Soulié and E. de Barthelemy, eds., *Journal de Jean Héroard sur l'Enfance et la Jeunesse de Louis XIII*, vol. 1 (Paris, 1868), p. 35.

43. Ibid., p. 76.

44. Francesco da Barberino, *Reggimento e costume di donne* (Torino, 1957), p. 189.

45. Alexander Hamilton, *The Family Female Physician: Or, A Treatise on the Management of Female Complaints, and of Children in Early Infancy* (Worcester, 1793), p. 287.

46. Struve, *Treatise*, p. 173.

47. W. Warde Fowler, *Social Life at Rome in the Age of Cicero* (New York, 1926), p. 177; Edith Rickert, ed., *The Babee's Book: Medieval Manners for the Young* (London, 1908) p. xviii; Mrs. E. M. Field, *The Child and His Book* (London, 1892), reprint (Detroit, 1968), p. 91; Frederick J. Furnivall, ed., *Early English Meals and Manners* (1868), reprint (Detroit, 1969), p. 229; Pearson, *Elizabethans*, p. 172.

48. Elizabeth L. Davoren, "The Role of the Social Worker," in Ray E. Helfer and C. Henry Kempe, eds., *The Battered Child* (Chicago, 1968), p. 155.

49. Ruby Ann Ingersoll, *Memoir of Elizabeth Charlotte Ingersoll Who Died September 18, 1857 Aged 12 Years* (Rochester, New York, 1858), p. 6.

50. Jacques Guillimeau, *The Nursing of Children* (London, 1612), p. 3.

51. Most, *Mensch*, p. 74.

52. Charron, *Wisdom*, p. 1338; Robert Cleaver, *A godlie forme of household government . . .* (London, 1598), p. 296.

53. Soulié, *Héroard*, pp. 2–5.

54. Ibid., pp. 7–9.

55. Ibid., p. 11.

56. Ibid., pp. 32, 34.

57. Ibid., p. 36.

58. Ibid., pp. 34, 35.

59. Ibid., p. 45. This sexual use of the dauphin cannot be solely to imbibe his royal charisma, since the king and queen also participate.

60. Felix Bryk, *Circumcision in Man and Woman: Its History, Psychology and Ethnology* (New York, 1934), p. 94.

61. Ibid., p. 100.

62. Joseph C. Rheingold, *The Fear of Being a Woman: A Theory of Maternal Destructiveness* (New York, 1964); and Rheingold, *The Mother, Anxiety, and Death: The Catastrophic Death Complex* (Boston, 1967).

63. Dorothy Bloch, "Feelings That Kill: The Effect of the Wish for Infanticide in Neurotic Depression," *The Psychoanalytic Review*, 52 (1965); Bakan, *Slaughter;* Stuart S. Asch, "Depression: Three Clinical Variations," in *Psychoanalytic Study of the Child*, vol. 21 (1966) pp. 150–71; Morris Brozovsky and Harvey Falit, "Neonaticide: Clinical and Psychodynamic Considerations," *Journal of Child Psychiatry*, 10 (1971); Wolfgang Lederer, *The Fear of Women* (New York, 1968); Galdston, "Dysfunctions," and the bibliography in Rheingold.

64. For bibliographies, see, Abt-Garrison, *History of Pediatrics;* Bakan, *Slaughter;* William Barclay, *Educational Ideas in the Ancient World* (London, 1959), Appendix A; H. Bennett, "Exposure of Infants in Ancient Rome," *Classical Journal*, 18 (1923), pp. 341-45; A. Cameron, "The Exposure of Children and Greek Ethics," *Classical Review*, 46 (1932), 105–14; Jehanne Charpentier, *Le Droit de l'enfance Abandonée* (Paris, 1967); A. R. W. Harrison, *The Law of Athens: The Family and Property* (Oxford, 1968); William L. Langer, "Checks on Population Growth: 1750-1850," *Scientific American* (1972), 93–99; Francois Lebrun, "Naissances illégitimes et abandons d'enfants en Anjou au XVIIIE siècle," *Annales: Economies, Sociétiés, Civilisations*, 27 (1972); A. J. Levin, "Oedipus and Sampson, the Rejected Hero-Child," *International Journal of Psycho-Analysis*, 38 (1957), 103–10; John T. Noonan, Jr., *Contraception: A History of Its Treatment by the Catholic Theologians and Canonists* (Cambridge, Massachusetts, 1965); Payne, *Child;* Juha Pentikainen, *The Nordic Dead-Child Traditions* (Helsinki, 1968); Max Raden, "Exposure of Infants in Roman Law and Practice," *Classical Journal*, 20 (1925), 342-43; Edward Shorter, "Illegitimacy, Sexual Revolution, and Social Change in Modern Europe," *The Journal of Interdisciplinary History* 2 (1971), 237–72; Edward Shorter, "Infanticide in the Past," *History of Childhood Quarterly: The Journal of Psychohistory* 1 (1973), 178–80; Edward Shorter, "Sexual Change and Illegitimacy: The European Experience," in *Modern European Social History*, ed., Robert Bezucha (Lexington, Massachusetts, 1972), pp. 231-69; John Thrupp, *The Anglo-Saxon Home: A History of the Domestic Institutions and Customs of England. From the Fifth to the Eleventh Century* (London, 1862); Richard Trexler, "Infanticide in Florence," *History of Childhood Quarterly: The Journal of Psychohistory*, 1 (1973), 98–117; La Rue Van Hook, "The Exposure of Infants

at Athens," *American Philogical Association Transactions and Proceedings*, 51, (1920), pp. 36–44; Oscar H. Werner, *The Unmarried Mother in German Literature* (New York, 1966); G. Glotz, *L'Exposition des Enfants, Etudes Sociales et Juridiques sur l'antiquité grecque* (Paris, 1906); Y. B. Brissaud, "L'infanticide à la fin du moyen âge, ses motivations psychologiques et sa répression," *Revue historiqué de droit français et étranger*, 50 (1972), 229–56; M. de Gouroff (Antoine J. Duguer), *Essai sur l'histoire des enfants trouvés* (Paris, 1885); William L. Langer, "Infanticide: A Historical Survey," *History of Childhood Quarterly: The Journal of Psychohistory* 1 (1973), 353-67.

65. Soranus, *Gynecology*, p. 79.

66. Lacey, *Family*, p. 164.

67. John Garrett Winter, *Life and Letters in the Papyri* (Ann Arbor, Michigan, 1933); p. 56; Naphtali Lewis and Meyer Reinhold, *Roman Civilization: Source Book 2* (New York, 1955), p. 403; *Gunnlaugs saga ormstungu* in M. H. Scargill trans., *Three Icelandic Sagas* (Princeton, 1950), pp. 11–12.

68. Polybius, *The Histories*, vol. 6, W. R. Paton, trans. (London, 1927), p. 30.

69. Cora E. Lutz, "Musonius Rufus 'The Roman Socrates' " in Alfred R. Bellinger, ed., *Yale Classical Studies*, vol. 10 (New Haven, 1947), p. 101; although his pupil, Epictetus, seems more opposed to infanticide in Epictetus, *Discourses*, chapter 23. Also see legal approval of infanticide in *The Gortyna Law Tables*, IV:21, 23, R. Dareste Ed., *Recueil des Inscriptions Juridiques Grecques* (Paris, 1894), p. 365.

70. Batholomew Batty, *The Christian Mans Closet*, William Lowth, trans. (1581), p. 28.

71. Menander, *The Principal Fragments*, Frances G. Allinson, trans. (London, 1921), p. 33; Philip E. Slater, *The Glory of Hera: Greek Mythology and the Greek Family* (Boston, 1968).

72. Henri V. Vallois, "The Social Life of Early Man: The Evidence of Skeletons," in *Social Life of Early Man*, Sherwood L. Washburn, ed. (Chicago, 1961), p. 225.

73. Plutarch, *Moralia*, Frank C. Babbitt, trans. (London, 1928), p. 493.

74. E. Wellisch, *Isaac and Oedipus* (London, 1954), pp. 11–14; Payne, *Child*, pp. 8, 160; Robert Seidenberg, "Sacrificing The First You See," *The Psychoanalytic Review*, 53 (1966), 52–60; Samuel J. Beck, "Abraham's Ordeal: Creation of a New Reality," *The Psychoanalytic Review*, 50 (1963), 175-85; Theodore Thass-Thienemann, *The Subconscious Language* (New York, 1967), pp. 302–6; Thomas Platter, *Journal of a Younger Brother*, Jean Jennett, trans. (London, 1963), p. 85; Tertullian, "Apology," *The Anti-Nicene Fathers*, Vol. 3 (New York, 1918), p. 25; P. W. Joyce, *A Social History of Ancient Ireland*, Vol. 1, 3rd ed. (London, 1920), p. 285; William Burke Ryan, M.D., *Infanticide: Its Law, Prevalence, Prevention, and History* (London, 1862), pp. 200-20; Eusebius Pamphili, *Ecclesiastical History* (New York, 1955), p. 103; J. M. Robertson, *Pagan Christs* (New York, 1967), p. 31; Charles Picard, *Daily Life in Carthage*, A. E. Foster, trans. (New York, 1961), p. 671; Howard

H. Schlossman, "God the Father and His Sons," *American Imago*, 29 (1972), 35–50.

75. William Ellwood Craig, "Vincent of Beauvais, On the Education of Noble Children," University of California at Los Angeles, Ph.D. thesis, 1949, p. 21; Payne, *Child*, p. 150; Arthur Stanley Riggs, *The Romance of Human Progress* (New York, 1938), p. 284; E. O. James, *Prehistoric Religion* (New York, 1957), p. 59; Nathaniel Weyl, "Some Possible Genetic Implications of Carthaginian Child Sacrifice," *Perspectives in Biology and Medicine*, 12 (1968), 69–78; James Hastings, ed., *Encyclopedia of Religion and Ethics*, Vol. 3 (New York, 1951), p. 187; Picard, *Carthage*, p. 100.

76. H. S. Darlington, "Ceremonial Behaviorism: Sacrifices For the Foundation of Houses," *The Psychoanalytic Review*, 18 (1931); Henry Bett, *The Games of Children: Their Origin and History* (London, 1929), pp. 104–5; Joyce, *Social History*, p. 285; Payne, *Child*, p. 154; Anon., "Foundations Laid in Human Sacrifice" *The Open Court*, t. 23 (1909), 494–501.

77. Henry Bett, *Nursery Rhymes and Tales; Their Origin and History* (New York, 1924), p. 35.

78. *Dio's Roman History*, Vol. 9, Earnest Cary, trans. (London, 1937), p. 157; Suetonius, *The Lives of the Twelve Caesars*, Joseph Gavorse, ed. (New York, 1931), p. 108; Pliny, *Natural History*, vol. 8, H. Rockham, trans. (Cambridge, Massachusetts, 1942), p. 5.

79. Suetonius, *Caesars*, p. 265; Livy, *Works*, vol. 12, Evan T. Sage, trans. (Cambridge, Massachusetts, 1938), p. 9; Tacitus, *The Annals of Tacitus*, Donald R. Dudley, trans. (New York, 1966), pp. 186, 259.

80. Lewis and Reinhold, *Roman Civilization*, pp. 344, 483.

81. Noonan, *Contraception*, p. 86.

82. St. Justin Martyr, *Writings* (New York, 1949), p. 63; also Dio Chrysostom, *Discourses*, p. 151; Tertullian, *Apology*, p. 205; Lactantius, *The Divine Institutes*, Books 1-8 (Washington, D.C. 1964), p. 452.

83. Tertullian, *Apologitical Works* (New York, 1950), p. 31.

84. Hefele-Leclercq, *Histoire des conciles*, t.II, pt. 1 (Paris, 1908), pp. 459–60; St. Magnebode (606–654) may have established an earlier foundling hospital, according to Leclercq.

85. *Dictionnaire d'archéologie chrétienne et de liturgie* (Paris, 1907–1951), tome I, article on "Alumni" by H. Leclercq, pp. 1288–1306; Thrupp, *Anglo-Saxon Home*, p. 81.

86. Emily R. Coleman, "Medieval Marriage Characteristics: A Neglected Factor in the History of Medieval Serfdom," *The Journal of Interdisciplinary History*, 2 (1971); 205–20; Josiah Cox Russell, *British Medieval Population* (Albuquerque, New Mexico, 1948), p. 168.

87. Craig, "Vincent of Beauvais," p. 368; Thomas Phayer, *The Regiment of Life, including the Boke of Children* (1545); Thrupp, *Anglo-Saxon Home*, p. 85; William Douglass, *A Summary, Historical and Political, of the First Planting, Progressive Improvements, and Present State of the British Settlements in North America*, vol. 2 (London, 1760), p. 202.

88. Shorter, "Sexual Change"; Bakan, *Slaughter;* Shorter, "Illegitimacy";

Shorter, "Infanticide"; Charpentier, *Droit;* Robert J. Parr, *The Baby Farmer* (London, 1909); Lebrun, *Naissances;* Werner, *Mother;* Brownlow, *Memoranda;* Ryan, *Infanticide;* Langer, "Checks;" and an enormous bibliography Langer has to support this article, but which is only in mimeograph form, although it is partially reproduced in his article "Infanticide: A Historical Survey," *History of Childhood Quarterly: The Journal of Psychohistory,* 1 (1974), 353–65.

89. C. H. Rolph, "A Backward Glance at the Age of 'Obscenity,' " *Encounter,* 32 (June, 1969), 23.

90. Louis Adamic, *Cradle of Life: The Story of One Man's Beginnings* (New York, 1936), pp. 11, 45, 48.

91. Royden Keith Yerkes, *Sacrifice in Greek and Roman Religions and Early Judaism* (New York, 1952), p. 34; Ernest Jones, *Essays in Applied Psycho-Analysis,* vol. 2 (New York, 1964), pp. 22–109; Gorman, *Nurse,* p. 17.

92. Margaret Deanesly, *A History of Early Medieval Europe* (London, 1956), p. 23; Robert Pemell, *De Morbis Puerorum, or, A Treatise of the Diseases of Children . . .* (London, 1653), p. 8, a practice reminding one of the Japanese practice of burning children's skin with moxa, which is still used for health as well as disciplinary purposes; see Edward Norbeck and Margaret Norbeck, "Child Training in a Japanese Fishing Community," in Douglas C. Haring, ed., *Personal Character and Cultural Milieu* (Syracuse, 1956), pp. 651–73.

93. Graham, *Children,* p. 110.

94. Nancy Lyman Roelker, *Queen of Navarre: Jeanne d'Albret* (Cambridge, Massachusetts, 1969), p. 101.

95. Ruhrah, *Pediatrics,* p. 216; Bayne-Powell, *English Child,* p. 165; William Buchan, *Advice to Mothers* (Philadelphia, 1804), p. 186; *The Mother's Magazine,* 1 (1833), 41; Paxton Hibben, *Henry Ward Beecher: An American Portrait* (New York, 1927), p. 28.

96. James Nelson, *An Essay on the Government of Children* (Dublin, 1763), p. 100; Still, *History of Paediatrics,* p. 391.

97. W. Preyer, *Mental Development in the Child* (New York, 1907), p. 41; Thomas Phaire, *The Boke of Chyldren* (Edinburgh, 1965), p. 28; Pemell, *De Morbis,* 23; Most, *Mensch,* p. 76; Dr. Heinrich Rauscher, "Volkskunde des Waldviertels," *Das Waldviertel,* 3 Band (Volkskunde), Verlag Zeitschrift "Deutsches Vaterland," (Vienna, n.d.), 1–116.

98. Buchan, *Advice,* p. 192; Hamilton, *Female Physician,* p. 271.

99. Scevole de St. Marthe, *Paedotrophia; or The Art of Nursing and Rearing Children,* H. W. Tytler, trans. (London, 1797), p. 63; John Floyer, *The History of Cold-Bathing,* Sixth ed. (London, 1732); William Buchan, *Domestic Medicine,* revised by Samuel Griffitts (Philadelphia, 1809), p. 31; Ruhrah, *Pediatrics,* p. 97; John Jones, M.D., *The arts and science of preserving bodie and soule in healthe* (1579), Univ. Microfilms, 14724, p. 32; Alice Morse Earle, *Customs and Fashions in Old New England* (Detroit, 1968), orig. published 1893, p. 2; *The Common Errors in the Education of Children and Their Consequences* (London, 1744), p. 10; William Thomson,

Memoirs of the Life and Gallant Exploits of the Old Highlander Serjeant Donald Macleod (London, 1933), p. 9; Morton Schatzman, *Soul Murder: Persecution in the Family* (New York, 1973), p. 41; Hitchcock, *Memoirs*, p. 271.

100. Elizabeth Grant Smith, *Memoirs of a Highland Lady* (London, 1898), p. 49.

101. Aristotle, *Politics*, H. Rackham, trans. (Cambridge, Massachusetts, 1967), p. 627; Robert M. Green, trans., *A Translation of Galen's 'Hygiene' (De Sanitate Tuendà)* (Springfield, Illinois, 1951), p. 33; Peiper, *Chronik*, p. 81.

102. Horace, *Satires, Epistles, Ars Poetica*, H. Rushton Fairclough, trans. (Cambridge, Massachusetts, 1961), p. 177; Floyer, *Cold-Bathing;* Jean Jacques Rousseau, *Emile*, Barbara Foxley, trans. (London, 1911), p. 27; Earle, *Child Life*, p. 25; Richter, *Levana*, p. 140; Dorothy Canfield Fisher, *Mothers and Children* (New York, 1914), p. 113; Marian Harland, *Common Sense in the Nursery* (New York, 1885), p. 13; Earle, *Customs*, p. 24; Mary W. Montagu, *The Letters and Works of Lady Mary Wortley Montagu*, vol. 1 (London, 1861), p. 209; Nelson, *Essay*, p. 93.

103. Isaac Deutscher, *Lenin's Childhood* (London, 1970), p. 10; Yvonne Kapp, *Eleanor Marx, vol. 1–Family Life* (London, 1972), p. 41; John Ashton, *Social Life in the Reign of Queen Anne* (Detroit, 1968), p. 3.

104. Buchan, *Domestic*, p. 8.

105. Robert Frances Harper, trans., *The Code of Hammurabi King of Babylon about 2250 B.C.* (Chicago, 1904), p. 41; Payne, *Child*, pp. 217, 279–91; Bossard, *Sociology*, pp. 607–8; Aubrey Gwynn, *Roman Education: From Cicero to Quintillian* (Oxford, 1926), p. 13; Fustel de Coulanges, *The Ancient City* (Garden City, New York, n.d.), pp. 92, 315.

106. Harrison, *Law*, p. 73.

107. Herodas, *The Mimes and Fragments* (Cambridge, 1966), p. 117.

108. Thrupp, *Anglo-Saxon Home*, p. 11; Joyce, *History*, pp. 164–5; William Andrews, *Bygone England: Social Studies in Its Historic Byways and Highways* (London, 1892), p. 70.

109. John T. McNeill and Helena M. Gamer, *Medieval Handbooks of Penance* (New York, 1938), p. 211; a late American child sale auction is described in Grace Abbott, *The Child and the State*, vol. 2 (Chicago, 1938), p. 4.

110. Georges Contenau, *Everyday Life in Babylon and Assyria* (New York, 1966), p. 18.

111. Sidney Painter, *William Marshall: Knight-Errant, Baron, and Regent of England* (Baltimore, 1933), p. 16.

112. *Ibid.*, p. 14; Graham, *Children*, p. 32.

113. Joyce, *History*, vol. 1, pp. 164–5; vol. 2, pp. 14–19.

114. Marjorie Rowling, *Everyday Life in Medieval Times* (New York, 1968), p. 138; Furnivall, *Meals and Manners*, p. xiv; Kenneth Charlton, *Education in Renaissance England* (London, 1965), p. 17; Macfarlane, *Family Life*, p. 207; John Gage, *Life in Italy at the Time of the Medici* (London, 1968), p. 70.

115. O. Jocelyn Dunlop, *English Apprenticeship and Child Labour* (London, 1912); M. Dorothy George, *London Life in the Eighteenth Century* (New York, 1964).

116. Augustus J. C. Hare, *The Story of My Life*, vol. 1 (London, 1896), p. 51.

117. Betsy Rodgers, *Georgian Chronicle* (London, 1958), p. 67.

118. Harper, *Code of Hammurabi;* Winter, *Life and Letters;* I. G. Wickes, "A History of Infant Feeding," *Archives of Disease in Childhood*, 28 (1953), p. 340; Gorman, *Nurse;* A Hymanson, "A Short Review of the History of Infant Feeding," *Archives of Pediatrics*, 51 (1934), 2.

119. Green, *Galen's Hygiene*, p. 24; Foote, "Infant Hygiene," p. 180; Soranus, *Gynecology*, p. 89; Jacopo Sadoleto, *Sadoleto On Education* (London, 1916), p. 23; Horkan, *Educational Theories*, p. 31; John Jones, *The art and science of preserving bodie and soule in healthe* (London, 1579), p. 8; Juan de Mariana, *The King and the Education of the King* (Washington, D.C., 1948), p. 189; Craig R. Thompson, trans., *The Colloquies of Erasmus* (Chicago, 1965), p. 282; St. Marthe, *Paedotrophia*, p. 10; Most, *Mensch*, p. 89; John Knodel and Etienne Van de Walle, "Breast Feeding, Fertility and Infant Mortality: An Analysis of Some Early German Data," *Population Studies* 21 (1967), pp. 116–20.

120. Foote, "Infant Hygiene," p. 182.

121. Clement of Alexandria, *The Instructor*, Ante-Nicene Christian Library, vol. 4 (Edinburgh, 1867), p. 141; Aulus Gellius, *The Attic Nights of Aulus Gellius*, vol. 2 (Cambridge, Massachusetts, 1968), p. 357; Clement of Alexandria, *Christ the Educator* (New York, 1954), p. 38.

122. Guillimeau, *Nursing*, p. 3.

123. Wickes, "Infant Feeding," p. 235.

124. Hitchcock, *Memoirs*, pp. 19, 81; Wickes, "Infant Feeding," p. 239; Bayne-Powell, *English Child*, p. 168; Barbara Winchester, *Tudor Family Portrait* (London, 1955), p. 106; Taylor, *Angel-Makers*, p. 328; Clifford Stetson Parker, *The Defense of the Child by French Novelists* (Menasha, Wisconsin, 1925), pp. 4-7; William Hickey, *Memoirs of William Hickey* (London, 1913), p. 4; Jacques Levron, *Daily Life at Versailles in the Seventeenth and Eighteenth Centuries*, Elxiane Engel, trans. (London, 1968), p. 131; T. G. H. Drake, "The Wet Nurse in the Eighteenth Century," *Bulletin of the History of Medicine*, 8 (1940), 934–48; Luigi Tansillo, *The Nurse, A Poem*, William Roscoe, trans. (Liverpool, 1804), p. 4; Marmontel, *Autobiography*, vol. 4 (London, 1829), p. 123; Th. Bentzon, "About French Children," *Century Magazine*, 52 (1896), 809; Most, *Mensch*, pp. 89-112; John M. S. Allison, ed., *Concerning the Education of a Prince: Correspondence of the Princess of Nassau-Saarbruck 13 June-15 November, 1758* (New Haven, 1941), p. 26; Mrs. Alfred Sidgwick, *Home Life in Germany* (Chatauqua, New York, 1912), p. 8.

125. Lucy Hutchinson, *Memoirs of Colonel Hutchinson* (London, 1968), p. 13–15; Macfarlane, *Family Life*, p. 87; Lawrence Stone, *The Crisis of the Aristocracy: 1558-1641* (Oxford, 1965), p. 593; Kenneth B. Murdock, *The*

Sun at Noon (New York, 1939), p. 14; Marjorie H. Nicolson, ed., *Conway Letters* (New Haven, 1930), p. 10; Countess Elizabeth Clinton, *The Countesse of Lincolness Nurserie* (Oxford, 1622).

126. Wickes, "Infant Feeding," p. 235; Drake, "Wet Nurse," p. 940.

127. Euch Roesslin, *The byrth of mankynde* (London, 1540), p. 30.

128. Ryerson, "Medical Advice," p. 75.

129. Wickes, "Infant Feeding," pp. 155–8; Hymanson, "Review," pp. 4–6; Still, *History of Paediatrics*, pp. 335–6; 459; Mary Hopkirk, *Queen Over the Water* (London, 1953), p. 1305; Thompson, *Colloquies*, p. 282.

130. *The Female Instructor: or Young Woman's Companion* (Liverpool, 1811), p. 220.

131. W. O. Hassal, *How They Lived: An Anthology of Original Accounts Written Before 1485* (Oxford, 1962), p. 105.

132. John Spargo, *The Bitter Cry of the Children* (Chicago, 1968), Xenophon, *Minor Writings*, E. C. Marchant, trans. (London, 1925), p. 37; Hopkirk, *Queen*, pp. 130–5; Plutarch, *Moralia*, p. 433; St. Basil, *Ascetical Works* (New York, 1950), p. 266; Gage, *Life in Italy*, p. 109; St. Jerome, *The Select Letters of St. Jerome*, F. A. Wright, trans. (Cambridge, Massachusetts, 1933), pp. 357–61; Thomas Platter, *The Autobiography of Thomas Platter: A Schoolmaster of the Sixteenth Century*, Elizabeth A. McCoul Finn, trans. (London, 1847), p. 8; Craig, "Vincent of Beauvais," p. 379; Roesslin, *Byrth*, p. 17; Jones, *Arts*, p. 40; Taine, *Ancient Regime*, p. 130; D. B. Horn and Mary Ranson, eds., *English Historical Documents, vol. 10, 1714–1783* (New York, 1957), p. 561; Lochhead, *First Ten Years*, p. 34; Eli Forbes, *A Family Book* (Salem, 1801), pp. 240–1; Leotine Young, *Wednesday's Children: A Study of Child Neglect and Abuse* (New York, 1964), p. 9.

133. St. Augustine, *Confessions* (New York, 1963); Richard Baxter, *The Autobiography of Richard Baxter* (London, 1931), p. 5; Augustine previously mentioned having to steal food from the table, p. 18.

134. William P. Dewees, *A Treatise on the Physical and Medical Treatment of Children* (Philadelphia, 1826), p. 4; for further bibliography on swaddling, see Wayne Dennis, "Infant Reactions to Restraint: an Evaluation of Watson's Theory," *Transactions New York Academy of Science*, Ser. 2, vol. 2 (1940); Erik H. Erikson, *Childhood and Society* (New York, 1950); Lotte Danziger and Liselotte Frankl, "Zum Problem der Functions-reifung," *A. für Kinderforschung*, 43 (1943); Boyer, "Problems," p. 225; Margaret Mead, "The Swaddling Hypothesis: Its Reception," *American Anthropologist*, 56 (1954); Phyllis Greenacre, "Infant Reactions to Restraint," in Clyde Kluckholm and Henry A. Murray, eds., *Personality in Nature, Society and Culture*, 2nd ed. (New York, 1953), pp. 513–14; Charles Hudson, "Isometric Advantages of the Cradle Board: A Hypothesis," *American Anthropologist* 68 (1966), pp. 470–4.

135. Hester Chapone, *Chapone on the Improvement of the Mind* (Philadelphia, 1830), p. 200.

136. Earle L. Lipton, Alfred Steinschneider, and Julius B. Richmond, "Swaddling, A Child Care Practice: Historical Cultural and Experimental Observations," *Pediatrics*, Supplement, 35, part 2 (March, 1965), 521–67.

137. Turner Wilcox, *Five Centuries of the American Costume* (New York, 1963), p. 17; Rousseau, *Emile*, p. 11; Christian A. Struve, *A Familiar View of the Domestic Education of Children* (London, 1802), p. 296.

138. *Hippocrates*, trans. W. H. S. Jones (London, 1923), p. 125; Steffen Wenig, *The Woman in Egyptian Art* (New York, 1969), p. 47; Erich Neumann, *The Great Mother: An Analysis of the Archetype* (New York, 1963), p. 32.

139. James Logan, *The Scotish Gael; or, Celtic Manners. As Preserved Among the Highlanders* (Hartford, 1851), p. 81; Thompson, *Memoirs*, p. 8; Marjorie Plant, *The Domestic Life of Scotland in the Eighteenth Century* (London, 1952), p. 6.

140. Cunnington, *Children's Costume*, pp. 68–69; Magdelen King-Hall, *The Story of the Nursery* (London, 1958), pp. 83, 129; Chapone, *Improvement*, p. 199; St. Marthe, *Paedotrophia*, p. 67; Robert Sunley, "Early Nineteenth-Century Literature on Child Rearing," in *Childhood in Contemporary Cultures*, Margaret Mead and Martha Wolfenstein, eds. (Chicago, 1955), p. 155; Kuhn, *Mother's Role*, p. 141; Wilcox, *Five Centuries;* Alice M. Earle, *Two Centuries of Costume in America*, vol. 1(New York, 1903), p. 311; Nelson, *Essay*, p. 99; Lipton, "Swaddling," pp. 529-32; Culpepper, *Directory*, p. 305; Hamilton, *Female Physician*, p. 262; Morwenna Rendle-Short and John Rendle-Short, *The Father of Child Care: Life of William Cadogan (1711–1979)* (Bristol, 1966), p. 20; Caulfield, *Infant Welfare*, p. 108; Ryerson, "Medical Advice," p. 107; Bentzon, "French Children," p. 805; Most, *Mensch*, p. 76; Struve, *View*, p. 293; Sidgwick, *Home Life*, p. 8; Peiper, *Chronik*, p. 666.

141. Cunnington, *Children's Costume*, pp. 70–128; Tom Hastie, *Home Life*, p. 33; Preyer, *Mind*, p. 273; Earle, *Costume*, pp. 316–17; Mary Somerville, *Personal Recollections, From Early Life to Old Age, of Mary Somerville* (London, 1873), p. 21; Aristotle, *Politics*, p. 627; Schatzman, *Soul Murder;* Earle, *Child Life*, p. 58; Burton, *Early Victorians*, p. 192; Joanne Richardson, *Princess Mathilde* (New York, 1969), p. 10; Bentzon, "French Children," p. 805; Stephanie de Genlis, *Memoirs of the Countess de Genlis*, 2 vols. (New York, 1825), p. 10; Kemble, *Records*, p. 85.

142. T. B. L. Webster, *Everyday Life in Classical Athens* (London, 1969), p. 46; J. T. Muckle, trans., *The Story of Abelard's Adversities: Historia Calamitatum* (Toronto, 1954), p. 30; Roland H. Bainston, *Women of the Reformation in Germany and Italy* (Minneapolis, 1971), p. 36; Pierre Belon, *Les Observations, de plusieurs singularitez et choses memorables trouvées en Grèce, Judée, Egypte, Arabie, et autres pays éstranges* (Antwerp, 1555), pp. 317–18; Phaire, *Boke*, p. 53; Pemell, *De Morbis*, p. 55; Peckey, *Treatise*, p. 146; Elizabeth Wirth Marvick, "Heroard and Louis XIII," *Journal of Interdisciplinary History*, in press; Guillimeau, *Nursing*, p. 80; Ruhrah, *Pediatrics*, p. 61; James Benignus Bossuet, *An Account of the Education of the Dauphine, In a Letter to Pope Innocent XI* (Glasgow, 1743), p. 34.

143. Thass-Thienemann, *Subconscious*, p. 59.

144. Hunt, *Parents and Children*, p. 144. Hunt's section on purges is his most perceptive.

145. Ibid., pp. 144–5.

146. Nelson, *Essay*, p. 107; Chapone, *Improvement*, p. 200; Ryerson, "Medical Advice," p. 99.

147. Stephen Kern, "Did Freud Discover Childhood Sexuality?", *History of Childhood Quarterly: The Journal of Psychohistory*, 1 (Summer, 1973), p. 130; Preyer, *Mental Development*, p. 64; Sunley, "Literature," p. 157.

148. Plutarch, "The Education of Children," in Moses Hadas, trans., *Plutarch: Selected Essays on Love, the Family, and the Good Life* (New York, 1957), p. 113; F. J. Furnivall, ed., *Queen Elizabethes Achademy*, Early English Text Society Extra Series no. 8 (London, 1869), p. 1; William Harrison Woodward, *Studies in Education During the Age of the Renaissance 1400–1600* (Cambridge, Massachusetts, 1924), p. 171.

149. Preserved Smith, *A History of Modern Culture*, vol. 2 (New York, 1934), p. 423.

150. Morris Bishop, trans. *Letters From Petrarch* (Bloomington, Ind., 1966), p. 149; Charles Norris Cochrane, *Christianity and Classical Culture* (London, 1940), p. 35; James Turner, "The Visual Realism of Comenius," *History of Education*, 1 (June, 1972), p. 132; John Amos Comenius, *The School of Infancy* (Chapel Hill, N.C., 1956), p. 102; Roger DeGuimps, *Pestalozzi: His Life and Work* (New York, 1897), p. 161; Christian Bec, *Les marchands écrivains: affaires et humanisme à Florence 1375–1434* (Paris, 1967), pp. 288–97; Renee Neu Watkins, trans., *The Family in Renaissance Florence* (Columbia, S.C., 1969), p. 66.

151. Christina Hole, *The English Housewife in the Seventeenth Century* (London, 1953), p. 149; Editha and Richard Sterba, *Beethoven and His Nephew* (New York, 1971), p. 89.

152. Soulié, *Héroard*, pp. 44, 203, 284, 436; Hunt, *Parents and Children*, pp. 133ff.

153. Giovanni Dominici, *On The Education of Children*, Arthur B. Cote, trans. (Washington, D.C., 1927), p. 48; Rousseau, *Emile*, p. 15; Sangster, *Pity*, p. 77.

154. Thrupp, *Anglo-Saxon Home*, p. 98; Furnivall, *Meals and Manners*, p. vi; Roger Ascham, *The Scolemaster* (New York, 1967), p. 34; H. D. Traill and J. S. Mann, *Social England* (New York, 1909), p. 239; Sophocles, *Oedipus The King: 808.*

155. Herodas, *Mimes*, p. 117; Adolf Erman, *The Literature of the Ancient Egyptians* (London, 1927), pp. 189–91; Peiper, *Chronik*, p. 17; Plutarch, *Moralia*, p. 145; Plutarch, *The Lives of the Noble Grecians and Romans*, John Dryden, trans. (New York, n.d.), p. 64; Galen, *On the Passions and Errors of the Soul*, Paul W. Harkins, trans., Ohio State University Press p. 56.

156. Thrupp, *Anglo-Saxon Home*, p. 100.

157. Peiper, *Chronik*, p. 309.

158. Eadmer, R. W. Southern, trans. *The Life of St. Anselm—Archbishop of Canterbury* (Oxford, 1962), p. 38.

159. Batty, *Christian*, pp. 14–26; Charron, *Wisdom*, pp. 1334–9; Powell, *Domestic Relations*, passim; John F. Benton, ed., *Self and Society in Medieval France: The Memoirs of Abbot Guibert of Nogent* (New York, 1970), pp. 212–

41; Luella Cole, *A History of Education: Socrates to Montessori* (New York, 1950), p. 209; Comenius, *School*, p. 102; Watkins, *Family*, p. 66.

160. Bossuet, *Account*, pp. 56–7; Henry H. Meyer, *Child Nature and Nuture According to Nicolaus Ludwig von Zinzindorf* (New York, 1928), p. 105; Bedford, *English Children*, p. 238; King-Hall, *The Story of the Nursery*, pp. 83-11; John Witherspoon, *The Works of John Witherspoon, D.D.* Vol. 8 (Edinburgh, 1805), p. 178; Rev. Bishop Fleetwood, *Six Useful Discourses on the Relative Duties of Parents and Children* (London, 1749).

161. See the final chapter in this book for bibliography on England and France; see Lyman Cobb, *The Evil Tendencies of Corporal Punishment as a Means of Moral Discipline in Families and Schools* (New York, 1847), and Miller, *Changing American Parent*, pp. 13-14, for American Conditions; see Walter Havernick, *Schläge als Strafe* (Hamburg, 1964), for Germany today.

162. Smith, *Memoirs*, p. 49; Richard Heath, *Edgar Quinet: His Early Life and Writings* (London, 1881), p. 3; Lord Lindsay, *Lives of the Lindsays: or, a Memoir of the Houses of Crawford and Barcarros*, vol. 2 (London, 1849), p. 307; L. H. Butterfield, ed., *Letters of Benjamin Rush, vol. 1: 1761–1792* (Princeton, 1951), p. 511; Bentzon, "French Children," p. 811; Margaret Blundell, *Cavalier: Letters of William Blundell to his Friends, 1620–1698* (London, 1933), p. 46.

163. For bibliographies, see Hans Licht, *Sexual Life in Ancient Greece* (New York, 1963); Robert Flaceliere, *Love in Ancient Greece*, James Cleugh, trans. (London, 1960); Pierre Grimal, *Love in Ancient Rome*, Arthur Train, Jr., trans. (New York, 1967); J. Z. Eglinton, *Greek Love* (New York, 1964); Otto Kiefer, *Sexual Life in Ancient Rome* (New York, 1962); Arno Karlen, *Sexuality and Homosexuality: A New View* (New York, 1971); Vanggaard, *Phallos;* Wainwright Churchill, *Homosexual Behavior Among Males: A Cross-Cultural and Cross-Species Investigation* (New York, 1967).

164. Lutz, "Rufus," p. 103.

165. Aristotle, *Politics*, p. 81.

166. Grimal, *Love*, p. 106; Karlen, *Sexuality*, p. 33; Xenophon, *Writings*, p. 149.

167. Petronius, *The Satyricon and The Fragments* (Baltimore, 1965), p. 43.

168. Aristotle, *The Nicomachean Ethics* (Cambridge, 1947), p. 403; Quintilian, *Institutio*, p. 43; Ove Brusendorf and Paul Henningsen, *A History of Eroticism* (New York, 1963), plate 4.

169. Louis M. Epstein, *Sex Laws and Customs in Judaism* (New York, 1948), p. 136.

170. Plutarch, "Education," p. 118.

171. Martial, *Epigrams*, vol. 2, Walter C. A. Kerr, trans. (Cambridge, Massachusetts, 1968), p. 255; Aristotle, *Historia Animalium*, trans. R. Cresswell (London, 1862), p. 180.

172. Vanggaard, *Phallos*, pp. 25, 27, 43; Karlen, *Sexuality*, pp. 33–34; Eglinton, *Greek Love*, p. 287.

173. Joyce McDougall, "Primal Scene and Sexual Perversion," *International Journal of Psycho-Analysis*, 53 (1972), p. 378.

174. Hans Licht, *Sexual Life in Ancient Greece* (New York, 1963), p. 497; Peter Tomkins, *The Eunuch and the Virgin* (New York, 1962), pp. 17–30; Vanggaard, *Phallos*, p. 59; Martial, *Epigrams*, pp. 75, 144.

175. Paulus Aegineta, *Aegeneta*, pp. 379–81.

176. Clement of Alexandria, *Christ*, p. 17.

177. Origen, "Commentary on Mathew," *The Ante-Nicene Fathers*, vol. 9, Allan Menzies, ed. (New York 1925), p. 484.

178. Benton, *Self*, pp. 14, 35.

179. Craig, "Vincent of Beauvais," p. 303; Cleaver, *Godlie*, pp. 326–7; Dominici, *Education*, p. 41.

180. Ariès, *Centuries of Childhood*, pp. 107-8; Johannes Butzbach, *The Autobiography of Johannes Butzbach: A Wandering Scholar of the Fifteenth Century* (Ann Arbor, 1933), p. 2; Horkan, *Educational Theories*, p. 118; Jones, *Arts*, p. 59; James Cleland, *The Instruction of a Young Nobleman* (Oxford, 1612), p. 20; Sir Thomas Elyot, *The Book Named the Governor* (London, 1962), p. 16; Erwin Panofsky, *Studies in Iconology: Humanistic Themes in the Art of the Renaissance* (New York, 1972), pp. 95-166; Leo Steinberg, "The Metaphors of Love and Birth in Michelangelo's Pietas," *Studies in Erotic Art*, Theodore Bowie and Cornelia V. Christenson, eds. (New York, 1970), pp. 231-339; Josef Kunstmann, *The Transformation of Eros* (London, 1964), pp. 21–23.

181. Whiting, *Child-Training*, p. 79.

182. Gabriel Fallopius, "De decoraturie trachtaties," cap. 9, *Opera Omnia*, 2 vols. (Frankfurt, 1600), pp. 336–37; Soranus, *Gynecology*, p. 107.

183. Michael Edward Goodich, "The Dimensions of Thirteenth Century Sainthood," Ph.D. dissertation, Columbia University, 1972, pp. 211–12; Jean-Louis Flandrin, "Mariage tardif et vie sexuelle: Discussions et hypotheses de recherche," *Annales: Economies Sociétés Civilisations* 27 (1972) 1351–78.

184. Hare, "Masturbatory Insanity," pp. 2–25; Spitz, "Authority and Masturbation," pp. 490-527; *Onania, or the Heinous Sin of Self-Pollution*, 4th ed. (London, n.d.), pp. 1–19; Simon Tissot, "L'Onanisme: Dissertation sur les maladies produites par la masturbation," (Lausanne, 1764), G. Rattray Taylor, *Sex in History* (New York, 1954), p. 223; Taylor, *Angel-Makers*, p. 327; Alex Comfort, *The Anxiety Makers: Some Curious Preoccupations of the Medical Profession* (London, 1967); Ryerson, "Medical Advice," pp. 305ff; Kern, "Freud;" pp. 117-141; L. Deslander, M.D., *A Treatise on the Diseases Produced by Onanism, masturbation, self-pollution, and other excesses*, trans. from the French (Boston, 1838); Mrs. S. M. I. Henry, *Studies in Home and Child Life* (Battle Creek, Michigan, 1897), p. 74; George B. Leonard, *The Transformation* (New York, 1972), p. 106; John Duffy, "Masturbation and Clitoridectomy: A Nineteenth Century View," *Journal of the American Medical Association*, 186 (1963), p. 246; Dr. Yellowlees, "Masturbation," *Journal of Mental Science*, 22 (1876), p. 337; J. H. Kellogg, *Plain Facts for Old and Young* (Burlington, 1881), pp. 186–497; P. C. Remondino, M.D., *History of Circumcision from the Earliest Times to the Present* (Philadelphia, 1891), p. 272.

185. Restif de la Bretonne, *Monsieur Nicolas*, pp. 86, 88, 106; *Common Errors*, p. 22; Deslander, *Treatise*, p. 82; Andre Parreaux, *Daily Life in England in the Reign of George III*, Carola Congreve, trans. (London, 1969), pp. 125–26; Bernard Perez, *The First Three Years of Childhood* (London, 1885), p. 58; *My Secret Life*, (New York, 1966), pp. 13-15, 61; Gathorne-Hardy, *Rise and Fall*, p. 163; Henri E. Ellenberger, *The Discovery of the Unconscious* (New York, 1970), p. 299; Joseph W. Howe, *Excessive Venery, Masturbation and Continence* (New York, 1893), p. 63; C. Gasquoine Hartley, *Motherhood and the Relationships of the Sexes* (New York, 1917), p. 312; Bernis, *Memoirs*, p. 90.

186. Dr. Albert Moll, *The Sexual Life of Children* (New York, 1913), p. 219; Max Schur, *Freud: Living and Dying* (New York, 1972), pp. 120–32; Robert Fleiss, *Symbol, Dream and Psychosis* (New York, 1973), pp. 205-29.

187. Mrs. Vernon D. Broughton, ed., *Court and Private Life in the Time of Queen Charlotte: Being the Journals of Mrs. Papendiek, Assistant Keeper of the Wardrobe and Reader to Her Majesty* (London, 1887), p. 40; Morley, *Cardan*, p. 35; Origo, *Leopardi*, p. 24; Kemble, *Records*, p. 28; John Greenleaf Whittier, ed., *Child Life in Prose* (Boston, 1873), p. 277; Walter E. Houghton, *The Victorian Frame of Mind, 1830–1870* (New Haven, 1957), p. 63; Harriet Martineau, *Autobiography*, vol. 1 (Boston, 1877), p. 11; John Geninges, *The Life and Death of Mr. Edmund Geninges, Priest* (1614), p. 18; Thompson, *Religion*, p. 471.

188. Chadwick Hansen, *Witchcraft at Salem* (New York, 1970); Ronald Seth, *Children Against Witches* (London, 1969); H. C. Erik Midelfort, *Witch Hunting in Southwestern Germany* (Stanford, 1972), p. 109; Carl Holliday, *Woman's Life in Colonial Days* (Boston, 1922), p. 60; Jeffrey Burton Russell, *Witchcraft in the Middle Ages* (Ithaca, New York, 1972), p. 136; George A. Gray, *The Children's Crusade* (New York, 1972).

189. A. S. Neill, *The Free Child* (London, 1952); Paul Ritter and John Ritter, *The Free Family: A Creative Experiment in Self-Regulation for Children* (London, 1959); Michael Deakin, *The Children on the Hill* (London, 1972); and my own book on my son, which is not yet in press.

190. Despite the single line of evolution described, the psychogenic theory of history is not uni-linear but multi-linear, for conditions outside the family also affect to some extent the course of parent-child evolution in each society. There is no claim here for reducing all other sources of historical change to the psychogenic. Rather than being an example of psychological reductionism, psychogenic theory is actually an intentional application of "methodological individualism," as described by F. A. Hayek, *The Counter-Revolution of Science* (Glencoe, Illinois, 1952); Karl R. Popper, *The Open Society and Its Enemies* (Princeton, 1950); J. W. N. Watkins, "Methodological Individualism and Non-Hempelian Ideal Types," in Leonard I. Krimerman, ed., *The Nature and Scope of Social Science* (New York, 1969), pp. 457-72. See also J. O. Wisdom, "Situational Individualism and the Emergent Group Properties," *Explanation in the Behavorial Sciences*, Robert Borger and Frank Cioffi, eds., (Cambridge, Massachusetts, 1970), pp. 271–96.

191. The quotes are from Calvin S. Hall, "Out of a Dream Came the Faucet," *Psychoanalysis and the Psychoanalytic Review*, 49 (1962).

192. See Maurice Mandelbaum, *History, Man and Reason: A Study in Nineteenth Century Thought* (Baltimore, 1971), chapter 11, for Mill's abortive attempt to invent a historical science of human nature.

8

Developmental Perspectives on the History of Childhood

JOHN DEMOS

Starting with a discussion of how social scientists have been able to link culture and personality together through the concept of "modal personality," Demos suggests that theories of individual development may be employed to analyze further the childhood roots of modal personality. His formal treatment of Erikson's theory of development is then amplified and illustrated by applying it to the everyday life of seventeenth-century New England Puritans. He finds that what has often been called the "Puritan ethic" had its real psychological origins in certain childrearing practices, most notably, a diligent attack on willfulness which usually began when the child was about two years old. Moreover, typical adult behavior patterns of the Puritans are shown to be quite in line with what Erikson's theory would predict as the consequences of their early experience. Along with several instructive comments on the methodological pitfalls of psychohistorical analysis, Demos also provides some valuable closing remarks indicating how childhood history can enhance our understanding of the forces involved in cultural change.

Among the shifting currents of scholarly inquiry it is possible to discern a growing interest in the study of childhood in times past. A number of historians have undertaken detailed research into particular aspects of this subject; some of their projects are now complete, others are still in progress.[1] The major professional organizations have recently included such work in the programs of their annual meetings, and, in March

From *The Journal of Interdisciplinary History* 2 (1971), 315-327. Reprinted by permission of the author, the journal, and The M.I.T. Press, Cambridge, Mass.

1970, the first conference devoted entirely to the investigation of "childhood and youth in history" was held at Clark University in Worcester, Massachusetts.

The sources of this trend are many and complex. But, as often happens in such cases, a single book seems to have exerted a very special influence. I refer to the seminal work of Ariès.[2] Few recent studies are better known, and there is no need to summarize the contents here. Nor is there space to enter the controversy that has arisen over some particular parts of the book. But it may be worthwhile to examine briefly the kind of approach to the study of childhood that Ariès so brilliantly seems to represent.

In analyzing childhood across a span of nearly a millennium, Ariès illuminated a vast territory of social and intellectual history. He examined with great imagination portraits of children, medical treatises on the care of infants, pedagogical tracts, toys and games, and a variety of other materials, in order to reveal certain core elements of medieval and early modern society, and of the transition between the two. It is clear, however, that he has concentrated not so much on the actual life-experience of children in the past as on the prevalent attitudes *toward* and *about* these children. His work is founded on the important and incontrovertible assumption that much can be learned about a culture by investigating the way it regards its young. In this sense, *Centuries of Childhood* is primarily about adults—those who commissioned and painted the portraits, wrote and read the medical treatises, and designed and maintained the schools. By extrapolating from Ariès one can imagine a whole range of detailed studies with the same underlying purpose. Attitudes toward childhood become, then, a kind of yardstick for measuring historical trends of the most profound consequence. And work of this type exhibits an obvious resemblance to other studies of basic cultural attitudes: attitudes toward death, for example, or love, or nature.

Here is a vitally important area of inquiry—and an area, too, in which much work remains to be done. This essay, however, will deal with *another* form of the study of childhood—related, and yet significantly different in both purpose and method. There is no easy way to designate this approach, for it has scarcely been contemplated, let alone attempted, by historians before now. But what I have in mind is an effort to find certain underlying themes in the experience of children in a given culture or period in order to throw some light on the formation of later personality.[3] The approach assumes that ironic truth that "the child is father to the man"; it also assumes that each culture fosters the development of certain dominant character traits or styles. It requires, in short, something like the concept of "modal personality," which has shaped a very broad range of anthropological and psychological studies.[4]

It is well to bring the anthropologists directly into this discussion, for they have long elaborated many of the chief theoretical issues. There is no way to summarize all of the relevant literature; but perhaps the most valuable work, from the standpoint of historians, is associated with the so-called culture and personality school, in which names like Abram Kardiner, Ralph Linton, Margaret Mead, Clyde Kluckhohn, and George P. Murdock might reasonably be joined—and with important contributions from the side of psychology by men like Erik Erikson, Henry Murray, and T. W. Adorno. Kardiner's formulation of the issues is especially clear, and is useful here by way of example. He defines modal personality as "that constellation of personality characteristics which would appear to be congenial with the total range of institutions comprised within a given culture."[5] And he divides the institutions into two broad categories. "Primary institutions" are the major force for shaping personality; but they also have an important influence on other aspects of culture—political and economic systems, mythic and religious belief—which he terms "secondary." Chief among the "primary institutions" are customary practices and commitments in the area of childrearing. To be sure, the Kardiner definitions have been criticized by other anthropologists,[6] and the priorities implied in the terms "primary" and "secondary" seem especially questionable. Kluckhohn and Murray present a more cautious viewpoint, stating simply: "The members of any organized group tend to manifest certain personality traits more frequently than do other groups."[7]

Every practitioner of the "culture and personality" approach has perforce made certain assumptions about human psychology; and in practice much of this work has been deeply infused with one form or another of psychoanalytic theory. It seems likely, in my opinion, that most serious historical inquiry along these lines will be similarly organized. At any rate, it seems clear that we will need *some* theoretical viewpoint from which to approach the subject. This requires emphasis since virtually all prior comment by historians has implied a static, largely undifferentiated model of childhood. We have settled for general notions on the order of "Puritan children were subjected to severe and repressive discipline," or "slave parents regarded their children with considerable indifference."[8]

Moreover, the source materials bearing on the history of childhood form a large, diverse, and fairly inchoate mass. Simply in order to organize them, one must find some principles for distinguishing the important from the trivial—the events which strengthen, or expand, or inhibit, or traumatize the growing personality from those which leave no lasting impression. In this sense I am urging a "developmental" approach to the subject, and it is indeed from developmental psychology that we may borrow some further procedural guidelines.

Broadly speaking, there are two different but interrelated ways of carving up our materials. One may be called "vertical," since it examines the child's development through time, and the other "horizontal," in that it separates out the different areas of the child's experience.

The "vertical" dimension requires a theory of "phases" or "stages" through which the individual proceeds from his first days of life to full maturity. (Indeed, such theory should logically extend to the adult years, and even to death itself, though this is not of direct concern in the present context.) One valuable contribution of this type—and, in my opinion, the *most* valuable—is Erikson's developmental model of the "eight stages of man."[9] "Basic trust vs. mistrust," "autonomy vs. shame and doubt," "initiative vs. guilt," "industry vs. inferiority," "identity vs. role diffusion": here, according to Erikson, are the critical periods in the life of every young and growing person. The stages are not, of course, rigidly programmed across the board, and no two individuals experience them in exactly the same way. Nonetheless, each one presents certain vital "tasks" that cannot really be avoided; indeed, each one involves a measure of "crisis" that is rooted in common psychosocial determinants.

If we take this kind of theory seriously, we are obliged to investigate how a culture manages on its own terms to distinguish between different periods of childhood. We cannot be content with knowing that discipline was generally harsh, or that parents were often indifferent to their young. We must try to determine whether such tendencies were more manifest at one stage of development than another, whether there was a kind of uneven curve of repressiveness or indifference with visible peaks and valleys over time.

But even this is not enough. We must also ask whether repressiveness, or indulgence, or indifference was more effective in some areas of the child's experience than in others. Most cultures do make certain distinctions among the various human instincts, drives, emotions—however they may be named and defined. A good theoretical picture of these issues can be found in the work of the cross-cultural anthropologists Whiting and Child. Their studies are organized around a five-part division of child development, including sex, aggression, dependency, orality, and anality.[10] They have applied this scheme in the analysis of more than fifty contemporary cultures around the world, and a similar effort might well be made by historians.

Once we are committed in this direction, however, some new difficulties arise. There are many varieties of theory available in the developmental field, and it is difficult to reconcile or choose among them in a systematic way. Erikson may strike some of us as being particularly useful, but others may well form a different set of preferences. I believe, however, that the use of almost *any* developmental model—any serious attempt to differentiate among the varied experiences of childhood on either a "vertical" or a "horizontal" basis—will represent progress for the historian.

Let us consider some substantive ideas about one particular historical setting as a way of exemplifying the larger, "developmental" approach. The ideas presented in the next few paragraphs are based entirely on materials left by those seventeenth-century "Puritans" who founded the colonies of New England. There is no intention here to produce a rounded view of Puritan culture—nor is there space to provide the appropriate sort of documentation. But, hopefully, these comments will serve to characterize a certain way of thinking about historical problems, and to reveal both the gains and the drawbacks inherent in such an approach.

Here, then, are some tentative conclusions about particular aspects of Puritan practice in the treatment of infants and very young children. For the sake of clarity they are separated into seven distinct statements: [11]

1. All infants were breast-fed for the first twelve to sixteen months of life.

2. The clothing of infants was light and loosely fitted; there is no evidence in early American materials of the custom of swaddling.

3. Very young infants often slept in the bed of one or both of their parents. Later they might be transferred to a cradle, or, in some cases, to a trundle-bed shared with one or more older siblings.

4. Their immediate surroundings were animated, warm, and intimate. Puritan families tended to be quite large,[12] and most infants would have from the start a number of siblings. At the same time, the houses of this period were small, with most daytime activities being confined to the room known as the "hall." One imagines, therefore, an infant lying in a cradle, which is set near the fireplace for warmth, and with a variety of familiar shapes and faces moving constantly around him. This is, to some degree, conjectural, but there is a fit about it all that seems persuasive. In short, we may conclude that for the first year or so, the Puritan child had a relatively comfortable and unrestricted mode of life. But consider what followed.

5. As previously noted, breast-feeding ended after twelve to sixteen months. We know little enough about the usual manner of weaning in this culture, but there is fragmentary evidence to suggest that it may have been quite abrupt. Apparently in some instances a bitter substance was applied to the breast so as to curb the infant's wish to suckle. And certain mothers may actually have left the household for a few days in order to make a clean break. Particularly suggestive in this connection is the appearance of weaning as a metaphor in a wide range of Puritan literature. Experiences of misfortune and disappointment were often described as "weaning dispensations," and obviously this usage was meant to convey a poignant sense of loss.

6. When the child was about two, a new baby would arrive. Most Puritan mothers gave birth at remarkably regular intervals of twenty-two to twenty-six months. The reason for this was the powerful contraceptive influence of lactation. We can, thus, recognize that for many infants in this culture the second year of life was bounded by experiences of profound loss—at the beginning by the loss of the breast (with all that this implies for *emotional* as well as physical sustenance), and at the end by the loss of the mother's special care and attention.

7. Puritan writings which deal in some direct way with childrearing share one central theme: The child's inherent "willfullness" must be curbed—indeed, it must be "broken" and "beaten down"—as soon as it begins to appear.[13] All other aspects of character development are dependent on this procedure. Here, for Puritans, lay *the central task* of parenthood; and, in a profound sense, they regarded it as involving a direct confrontation with "original sin."

None of the extant literature specifies the precise age at which such will-training should begin, but most likely it was some time during the second year. For this is the age when every child becomes, for the first time, able to express his own wishes in an organized and effective way. He develops a variety of motor skills: he walks and runs, and he rapidly improves the coordination of hand and eye. He begins to learn speech. And, more generally, he becomes acutely aware of the difference between "I" and "you," "mine" and "yours." Even under the mildest sort of disciplinary regime there is bound to be some degree of conflict with authority, parental or otherwise, for a significant part of the child's new assertiveness is expressed as anger and aggression. This, after all, is the phase which Benjamin Spock discusses under the general rubric "the terrible twos."

And what does the psychologist have to say about it? For Erikson, this is the second of the major developmental stages, the one in which the central task is the formation of "autonomy." "This stage," he writes, "becomes decisive for the ratio between love and hate, for that between freedom of self-expression and its suppression. From a sense of *self-control without loss of self-esteem* comes a lasting sense of autonomy and pride." Moreover, while the goal of this stage is "autonomy," its negative side—and its specific vulnerability—is the possible fixation of lasting shame and doubt. It is absolutely vital that the child receive support in "his wish to 'stand on his own feet,' lest he be overcome by that sense of having exposed himself prematurely and foolishly which we call shame, or that secondary mistrust, that 'doubletake' which we call doubt."[14]

Let us return now to the Puritans, in order to pull together these varied materials on their childrearing patterns. We have, first, a period of perhaps twelve months when the infant is for the most part treated indulgently—followed, in the second year of life, by weaning, by the arrival of a younger sibling, and by a radical shift toward a harsh and restrictive style of discipline. It is necessary to emphasize, above all, the last of these events, since, in Erikson's terms, the determination to crush the child's will is nothing less than an effort to deprive him of a chance to develop a lasting and confident sense of autonomy.

Clinical experience would argue that these patterns must have exerted a profound influence on all of the people who lived through them. Our next task is to survey some of the larger areas of Puritan life in which such influence can be discerned. Let us consider the whole field of interpersonal behavior—the style of relating to one another that was characteristic of this culture. It presents, in fact, a strikingly two-sided aspect. On the one hand, the Puritans placed a tremendous emphasis on the value of harmony, unity, and concord; one could cite as evidence literally countless sermons, essays, official decrees, and pronouncements. At the level of aspirations, nothing was more important for these people.[15] On the other hand, if one examines in detail the actual record of life in these communities—through various court and personal records—one discovers an extraordinary atmosphere of contentiousness and outright conflict. "Harmony" was always the preeminent value; yet, in trying to attain it, the Puritans constantly disappointed themselves. There is no paradox here; there is only the core of a pervasive ambivalence, something that was deeply rooted in the people themselves. To a very considerable degree, the inner life of Puritanism turned on a kind of axis between the opposite poles of conflict and conciliation, anger and love, aggression and submissiveness. And *all* of this, I suggest, is a plausible outcome of the pattern of childhood experience as previously described.

Moreover, we must attempt to assess the specific causes of the many conflicts in which Puritans became enmeshed, and the manner in which such conflicts were resolved. Disputes over boundaries were a constant source of trouble in these communities—boundaries between one man's land and his neighbor's, or often between whole townships that were adjacent to one another. A second, closely-related category of actions involved "trespass" of some sort; and here, too, the court cases are very numerous. More generally, many cases in which the immediate problem was something else—debt, or theft, or breach of contract—seem to have been experienced *emotionally*, by those directly involved, as a form of personal "trespass." We may conclude, in short, that "boundaries" were an immensely potent issue for Puritan culture—and that this, in psychological terms, was tightly bound up with the question of autonomy.

We can also investigate these patterns from the *negative* side of the Eriksonian model, recalling that the reverse of autonomy is the distress created by deep inner trends of shame and doubt. Consider the large number of slander and defamation cases in the records which reveal an extreme sensitivity to the threat of public exposure and humiliation. Some of the most common forms of punishment imposed by legally-constituted authorities in these settlements were sitting in the stocks, branding, or being forced to wear badges of infamy. It seems clear that the pain which these punishments inflicted was above all due to the element of shame. As to Erikson's notion of "doubt," once again the Puritans appear to make a striking fit. Traditionally, of course they have been pictured as smug, dogmatic, self-righteous, and intolerant—and indeed they often did wear this appearance. But how deeply did it penetrate? If one reads a few of the spiritual diaries and autobiographies left by Puritans with this question in mind, something very much like "doubt"—doubt of their faith, of their "standing" in the eyes of God—emerges as the primary *leit-motif* of such documents. If they sometimes acted smugly and self-satisfied, this was perhaps a kind of false front—a defense against profound inner anxieties from which they could never truly escape.

Here we have made a direct contact with their religious experience, and this might well be a particularly fruitful field in which to develop the same line of analysis. Let us consider for a moment some of the most familiar imagery of Puritan belief: the God who was by turns infinitely loving and overwhelmingly angry, and a God, too, who had the very special power to "see" every human action, no matter how secret, and to make the sinner feel deeply shamed; Heaven pictured as the place of total harmony, Hell as the place of everlasting strife; a moral universe in which each man was to struggle to achieve his personal salvation, though God had already entirely predestined the outcome of that struggle. It is tempting, indeed, to regard Puritan religious belief as a kind of screen on which all of their innermost concerns—autonomy, shame, doubt, anger—were projected with a very special clarity.

In order to become persuasive, these interpretations will require an extended treatment, much more so than is possible here. Therefore I propose, in conclusion, simply to point out some of the strategic and theoretical problems that are likely to arise in any analysis of this sort. We must be careful not to underestimate them.

There is, in the first place, an obvious need for work on the other developmental stages besides the earliest ones—work that finally presents childhood as a long and continuing sequence of growth and change. Character is not fixed at age two or three; later socialization is also a major consequence. With respect to the Puritans, one can surmise that there was much in the experience of later childhood to reinforce the training of the first few years. Any overt display of aggression or willfulness would elicit a stern parental response. Shaming was employed as a disciplinary technique, to an extent that directly enhanced the early sensitivities in this area.[16] The religious education of young persons stressed their utter dependence on God, their need to obliterate all traces of selfhood in order to become worthy of salvation. Traditional folklore underscored these lessons; stories of witchcraft, for example, conveyed with particular vividness the aura of danger that clung to manifestly hostile behavior.[17] There was also the general influence imparted by observing one's elders engaged in countless everyday transactions with each other—in which, of course, the same themes were repeatedly elaborated.

We need not contend, therefore, that all of Puritan culture was determined by traumas occurring during the second year of life, or that there is a simple "linear" connection between autonomy issues in early childhood and later adult behavior. At the same time we can believe that what happened during the second year was critical in the development of these people—that "autonomy" was *the* characteristic Puritan conflict, and that all of this was reflected in a variety of important social and cultural forms.

But are there not other, preferable explanations for the same range of phenomena? Perhaps we should look instead to certain features of Puritan social structure or political process—fields of inquiry with which historians are generally more familiar and more comfortable. It might be argued, for example, that chronic quarreling over boundaries resulted from the entirely "natural" concerns of peasants and yeomen in an overwhelmingly agricultural society. But this interpretation seems dubious for two reasons. First, there are many agricultural societies in which boundaries are not nearly so troublesome an issue; and, second, the empty lands of the New World should, from a practical standpoint, have lessened any competitive pressures of this type.[18]

Another sort of alternative explanation might be developed from our data on shame. Perhaps the frequency of trials for slander and defamation should be viewed as a necessary concomitant of life in little communities. Where so much human interchange was on a face-to-face basis, a man would have to protect his good reputation in order to obtain rewarding work and social contacts. There is substantial merit in this idea, but it need not be construed as opposed to a more psychological mode of explanation. Indeed, these two factors, the psychological and the practical, lock neatly together. One can even see a measure of gain for the people who endured such a harsh system of discipline: when they emerged as adults, they were conditioned to respond to precisely those cues which would ensure their practical welfare. In this respect, Puritan childrearing was functionally appropriate to the wider Puritan culture.

But to use the word "Puritan" is simply to beg some further questions. How widely should such interpretations be applied? What groups of people can they reasonably be made to cover? We may agree perhaps that the above analysis treats real problems and issues in the lives of New England Puritans of the seventeenth century. But are we concerned here *only* with New England Puritans? Or can the same patterns be found among New Englanders in general, among settlers in other parts of the colonies, among Puritans in both the Old World and the New, among all English-speaking people—or, indeed, throughout all of "Western civilization" in early modern times? In short, the problem is to determine the extension of a particular line of analysis in terms of both historical time and cultural space. Until there is good comparative data on other communities from roughly the same period, we cannot be sure to what extent Puritan childrearing and Puritan personality development were, in fact, distinctively Puritan.

There are, finally, some special methodological problems in this kind of study: they are not by any means insurmountable problems, but it is best to be explicit about what they involve. There is, first, a style of "proof" or "verification" which may seem somewhat novel when set against traditional canons of historical scholarship. We have, on the one hand, certain information about the prescribed method of disciplining young children, and, on the other, certain information about adult behavior in this society—court cases, methods of punishment, statements of ultimate value, and styles of religious concern. The connection between these two matters is not something that we can follow along a visible chain of evidence. Indeed, we can scarcely link them at all except through a process of analogy and inference, and the basis for this process is what we know from clinical experience in our own time. Moreover, because we are dealing in inference, there is a sense in which each side of the sequence confirms the other. That is: if Puritan adults were especially concerned about "boundaries" and "trespass," and especially vulnerable to shame, then we can say that they *must* have been roughly treated at an early age for their assertive and aggressive strivings. Similarly, if handled this way in childhood, then they *must* have behaved more or less as described later on. This may sound like circular reasoning to the historian—but not to the psychologist, who can adduce countless clinical observations to verify the correlation of the critical variables. It is, after all, less a case of circularity, and more a matter of internal consistency.

The second problem can be presented in the form of a warning. Historians are, officially at least, well aware of the pitfalls created by their own bias; but it is sometimes unclear as to how serious they are about this. In any event, the study of childhood and the family, the exploration of the whole inner world of human personality, is particularly open to various forms of projective distortion—vastly more so, for example, than the study of political, economic, or diplomatic history. Political bias or intellectual preferences are relatively easy to recognize and deal with. But the kinds of psychological baggage that we all carry within us—the outcome, in large part, of our own experience as children, as siblings, and as parents—are both much more powerful and much less conscious.

Yet the gains made possible by adopting a developmental approach remain substantial. What I hope I am doing in my own research is reinterpreting, or at least reordering, some of the most significant elements in early American life; and a similar strategy could certainly be applied in the analysis of other historical periods and other cultures. In the effort to make this strategy work, the study of childhood necessarily assumes a central place. It serves to bring into view certain themes which may not have been clearly recognized before, and, more broadly, it adds analytic depth to the entire research enterprise. We might refer once again to the distinction suggested earlier between the two basic types of approach to our subject. In the first instance we can point to Ariès, and no doubt many others who will be following the course he has marked out—scholars who study the child as a kind of mirror which focuses and reflects back cultural themes of central importance. But in the second instance—what I have been trying to outline here—something else is involved: The child becomes not just a mirror, not only the creature, but also the creator of culture, and, in this sense, a dynamic force in his own right.

Notes

1. See, for example, David Hunt, ***Parents and Children in History: The Psychology of Family Life in Early Modern France*** (New York, 1970); Bernard Wishy, ***The Child and the Republic: The Dawn of Modern American Child Nurture*** (Philadelphia, 1967); Robert H. Bremmer, et al., ***Childhood and Youth in America*** (Cambridge, Mass., 1970-71), I–II.

2. Philippe Ariès (trans. Robert Baldick), ***Centuries of Childhood: A Social History of Family Life*** (New York, 1962).

3. A book which *does* foreshadow many of the concerns of this paper is David M. Potter, ***People of Plenty: Economic Abundance and the American Character*** (Chicago, 1954), esp. Ch. 9. See also Hunt, ***Parents and Children in History***, Chs. 6–9.

4. For an excellent summary of this work, see Alex Inkeles and Daniel J. Levinson, "National Character: The Study of Modal Personality and Sociocultural Systems," in Gardner Lindzey and Elliott Aronson (eds.), ***The Handbook of Social Psychology*** (Reading, Mass., 1969; 2nd ed.), IV, 418-506. See also Milton Singer, "A Survey of Culture and Personality Theory and Research," in Bert Kaplan (ed.), ***Studying Personality Cross-Culturally*** (New York, 1961), 9-90.

5. Abram Kardiner, ***The Individual and His Society*** (New York, 1939), 24.

6. Some of these criticisms are outlined in Inkeles and Levinson, "National Character," 424-425.

7. Clyde Kluckhohn and Henry A. Murray (eds.), ***Personality in Nature, Society, and Culture*** (New York, 1962; rev. ed.), 57. On this general topic see also Anthony F. C. Wallace, ***Culture and Personality*** (New York, 1961). It is not necessary in this paper to enter the controversy over the proper meaning, and usage, of the concept of "modal personality." I am willing for present purposes to accept a very minimal definition, such as the one quoted above from Kluckhohn and Murray.

8. These statements—not actual quotations—are intended to represent viewpoints widely prevalent in previous historical literature.

9. The best summary of this scheme is in Erik H. Erikson, ***Identity and the Life Cycle*** (New York, 1959), 50–100.

10. See John W. M. Whiting and Irvin L. Child, ***Child Training and Personality: A Cross-Cultural Study*** (New Haven, 1953). Erikson's model also lends itself to a "horizontal" breakdown, since each of the eight stages involves a "task" that is of lasting importance throughout an individual life.

11. These matters are presented at greater length in John Demos, ***A Little Commonwealth: Family Life in Plymouth Colony*** (New York, 1970), esp. 46–49, 131-144.

12. Completed families in colonial New England averaged roughly eight children apiece. For a detailed analysis of this point, see Demos, ***A Little Commonwealth***, 68-69, 192; Philip J. Greven, Jr., ***Four Generations: Population, Land, and Family in Colonial Andover, Massachusetts*** (Ithaca, 1970), 30-31, 111–112.

13. See, for example, certain statements in Robert Ashton (ed.), *The Works of John Robinson* (Boston, 1851), I, 246–247. See also Cotton Mather, "Some Special Points, Relating to the Education of My Children," reprinted in Perry Miller and Thomas H. Johnson (eds.), *The Puritans* (New York, 1963), II, 724–727.

14. Erikson, *Identity and the Life Cycle*, 68.

15. This aspect of Puritan life has been the subject of two recent studies: Kenneth A. Lockridge, *A New England Town: The First Hundred Years* (New York, 1970); Michael Zuckerman, *Peaceable Kingdoms* (New York, 1970). These authors have brilliantly portrayed the *ideal* of community in early New England—and to this extent I am much in their debt. My own analysis, however, diverges somewhat from theirs in finding a large amount of actual conflict-behavior among the individual people in question.

16. Note the following attributed to John Ward, in Cotton Mather, *Magnalia Christi Americana* (Hartford, 1853), I, 522: "Of young persons he would himself give this advice: 'Whatever you do, be sure to maintain shame in them; for if that be once gone, there is no hope that they'll ever come to good.' " In his essay, "Some Special Points, Relating to the Education of My Children," Mather writes: "I cause them to understand, that it is an *hurtful* and a *shameful* thing to do amiss. I aggravate this, on all occasions; and lett them see how *amiable* they will render themselves by well doing. The *first chastisement*, which I inflict for an ordinary fault is, to lett the child see and hear me in an astonishment, and hardly able to beleeve that the child could do so *base* a thing, but beleeving that they will never do it again" (725–726). The shaming effects of this procedure are impossible to miss.

17. See John Demos, "Underlying Themes in the Witchcraft of Colonial New England," *The American Historical Review*, LXXV (1970), 1311–1326.

18. This point can be clarified by exploring the contrary case as well. If the concern with boundaries is to be explained in terms of *psychological* functioning, then it is quite plausible that the whole issue should have been sharpened by the literally "unbounded" character of the American wilderness.

9

Childhood and Adolescence among the Thirteenth-Century Saints

MICHAEL GOODICH

In a remarkable analysis based on thorough examination of primary sources, the article informs us of both the social patterns and developmental experiences leading to sainthood. The dynamics involved were usually played out against a background including family wealth, rejection by one or both parents, and some period of commitment to a monastic order. In addition, Goodich applies modern psychological studies of conversion experiences to the phenomena of sainthood. Consequently, this essay stands as an unusual combination of material drawn from the history of medieval childhood and psychological investigations of religion.

The most neglected period in the history of European childhood has been the middle ages. Medievalists in the past have been content to study institutional, legal, or economic history, and have only recently turned to social history. Still, while the techniques of quantification and computer technology have been successfully applied in a number of areas—demography and agrarian history, for example—a psychohistorical study of the period has yet to be attempted. Historians of medieval religion have likewise been even more lax and have concentrated largely on church structure and ideology to the detriment of the psychology of religion. Nevertheless, a wealth of untapped sources are available with which to begin a study of the mental constitution of this period. Although autobiographies are sparse until the Renaissance, there remains a substantial body of first-hand documentation con-

From *History of Childhood Quarterly* 1 (Fall 1973), 283–309.

cerning the behavior patterns of medieval man, and even in that most obscure region of all, his childhood.[1] In this paper I have isolated one particular psychological "type," the thirteenth-century saint, who in many ways personified the social ideals of the age. For it was his or her allegedly pious behavior which became the paragon against which all human action was measured, whose character was presented to the young as an ideal worthy of emulation. Among those raised either officially or unofficially to the honors of veneration are kings and queens, philosophers, diplomats, martyrs, social activists, and recluses. The list encompasses such well-known figures as Francis of Assisi, Thomas Aquinas, Dominic and Louis IX of France, alongside such relatively unknown saints as the servant girl Radegund of Augsburg, and the lifelong hermit, Leonard of Camaldoli.

One of the difficulties involved in the collection of data dealing with the formative years of the saint, or any other figure of the middle ages, lies in the differing concerns of medieval biographers and hagiographers.[2] For them, the essence of the saint's mission resides in the period after his conversion to the religious life, and his biography is not so much the celebration of one individual, but of the entire value system or style of life which he personifies. In a large number of contemporary biographies, the early years are given in the barest outline, purely as an introduction to the miracles and virtues practiced by the saint in adulthood. If the work has been composed under the patronage of the saint's family, a long digression will describe his illustrious parentage, or the etymological source and connotations of his name, and then skip to late adolescence and his ecclesiastical career. Thus, evidence concerning the formative years must often be perceived indirectly through amplification upon otherwise apparently offhand remarks. Of the over five hundred saints who became the objects of local or universal cults from 1215 to about 1334, perhaps no more than ten percent possess reliable data concerning their early years and an even smaller number left autobiographical material of one kind or another: letter, apologiae, visions, etc. Nevertheless, some broad emotional patterns common to strongly motivated religious figures in all ages also appear among these Catholic saints: childhood neglect or deprivation, resentment against an absent or allegedly cruel father, and a period of emotional stress in late adolescence which is resolved through religious commitment.[3]

The vast majority of the saints came from families of the wealthy noble and urban elite which governed Europe in the thirteenth century. Consequently, considering the childrearing practices which prevailed in this milieu, a significant number experienced emotionally deprived childhoods, with either one or both parents away on Crusade or other professional duties, maintaining separate households, or sending their children away to nurses, relatives, or monasteries for rearing. Furthermore, families were large, often exceeding ten children. The result was that the sensitive child could be easily lost or neglected; while the insecurities and frequent wars or pestilence of the time carried away one or both parents, leaving many an orphan with only the church as a substitute parent. Particularly among the wealthy, marriages of convenience were common, with children becoming engaged at seven and married at twelve or thirteen.[4] Thus the responsibilities of adulthood were often thrust upon children at an extremely young age. In adulthood, after such a scarred childhood, the saint might react with a violent rejection of those parents or values which he perceived as the source of his misery.

The standard hagiographical legend begins with a prologue which eulogizes the saint's virtues. This is frequently followed by an account of the prenatal portents or prophecies which will help to explain the subject's pious inclinations. A frequently reiterated theme concerns the saint who was allegedly born to infertile parents after prayers to Heaven. As a result of their good fortune, the thankful parents destine their son or daughter for a religious career.[5] Some mothers are provided with supernatural messages which foretell their children's extraordinary future. During her pregnancy, the mother of the Franciscan Francis Venimbene was unable to feel the weight of her son's body within her, which was taken as a sign of greatness.[6] Dominic's mother, Joan of Aza, reportedly dreamed before her son's birth that she was carrying a little dog who would come out bearing a torch to set the world afire; and at his birth, bees allegedly alighted upon his lips and Joan saw an imprint of the moon on the child's forehead. Both these images were taken to prophesy Dominic's enlightening mission.[7] It was likewise said that Franca Visalta's mother seemed to be carrying a dog in pregnancy, whose bark would fend off sinners.[8] Peter Celestine appeared to be clothed in ecclesiastical raiments at birth; while the mother of Francis of Siena dreamed that she would give birth to a lily.[9] Before Clare of Assisi's birth, her mother Ortolana prayed to the Virgin, asking for an easy delivery. As she knelt down, a voice came to her reporting that these fears were groundless for she would bring forth a light to illuminate the world.[10] Thomas Aquinas's mother, Theodora, was visited by a holy man who revealed that her son would be pious, that he would be baptized Thomas, and should be placed in the Benedictine monastery of Montecassino.[11]

Such auspicious signs, however, are probably more the stock literary weapons of the hagiographers, or retrospective justifications for greatness, than actual representations of reality. The biographers did, however, come closer to the truth when they described the relative gloom in which many of the saints were raised. The twelfth and thirteenth centuries were periods of greatly increased birthrate in Europe, not to be equalled again until the nineteenth century. Thus, many were raised within large families, and probably suffered from the corresponding loss of attention. Where brothers and sisters are mentioned, they often come in clusters. Peter Celestine was one of at least ten; Thomas of Cantilupe, Hedwig of Poland, and Flora, were one of seven children; Roseline of Villeneuve had at least four brothers, and James of Certaldo at least three.[12]

One of the most frequently found images of childhood among the saints is that of a child whose attitudes and behavior before the age of seven are those of an old man or woman, "quasi senex" or some such phrase. "Like an old man," Anthony Manzoni of Padua is depicted fasting, attending mass, and listening to sermons, avoiding the usual pleasures of childhood; although bearing a youthful body, Peter Nolasco was suffused with "aged prudence."[13] Richard of Chichester, Hedwig of Poland, and Gerardesca of Pisa are portrayed as pious adults in the guise of children, with little time for their playmates and childish pranks.[14] Bartholomew Buonpedoni allegedly showed such signs of greatness that when he conversed with his companions, a spark of fire was seen to come from his mouth.[15] Both Robert of Knaresborough and Rose of Viterbo spent their early years loitering about churches and monasteries, rather than in the company of their peers; while already at the age of seven, John of Alvernia fled his father's farm and his playmates in order to contemplate the passion of Christ and mortify his flesh.[16] The precocious Margaret of Citta di Castello wore a hairshirt and restricted her diet to bread and water, while Louis of Toulouse reportedly preferred to sleep on the damp ground than on his royal bed, and eschewed sweets, which children are wont to favor.[17] According to the contemporary biographer of Herman Joseph of Steinfeld, the saint was raised in poverty and always avoided childish games. "He did not have an insolent expression," the author reports, "speak blasphemous words and thrust his arms and legs about too much, practices which generally mar the majority of infants in our day." At seven, when he began his schooling, Herman avoided the games of children and frequented the church, where he often spoke with the Virgin, who provided the child with some money to purchase shoes to cover his snow-laden bare feet. . . .[18]

From the available evidence, it would appear that those saints attached to the less rigorous, more established orders like the Cistercians, Benedictines, or canons, led less turbulent childhoods, and merely fulfilled familial desires in their religious vocation. Many grew up from infancy in an environment which tended to reinforce their latent religious urges; to them, the religious life was a natural regime. Among the ruling classes, a position in the church was a common alternative to military service or commerce, and the route to sanctity and ecclesiastical preferment was therefore well-paved by relatives who occupied a similarly exalted position. This vocational choice was made early in childhood and there are few signs of reaction to the parental decision.

A significant number of saints were thus immediately related to other respected members of the church, themselves often also venerated saints. The family of Edmund Rich, Archbishop of Canterbury, boasted a host of religious personages: his brother, Robert, was a secular canon; Nicholas, a Cistercian; and an unnamed third brother retired to the monastery of Eynsham; his two sisters, Margery and Alice became nuns at Catesby. The Flemish bourgeois gentleman, Bartholomew de Vleeschewer of Aa, who became the subject of an adoring biography by his daughter Beatrice, led his daughters Sibylla, Beatrice, and Christina, and a son, Wiebert, into the religious life after the death of his wife. The noble Odrawaz family of Poland produced three saints in one generation: Hyacinth, a canon-turned-Dominican, his brother, Ceslaus, and a cousin, Bronislava, who became a Norbertine nun at Hyacinth's urging.[19]

The largest number were joined by a brother or sister in the pursuit of the religious life. This surely cemented the original resolve which had impelled the youth toward religion. The ties which bound the two siblings were sometimes so great, their lives so intertwined, that both were, on occasion, later venerated in tandem. Thus, the brothers Otto and Herman of Heidelberg are honored together, while the Scottish royalty Alexander of Foigny and Matilda of Lappion both became Cistercians in northern France. The brothers Menricus and Berthold of Westphalia were actuated by the same vision of Mary to enter religion.[20] This phenomenon of dual conversions was particularly common among women: Agnes of Liege and her sister, Juliana of Cornillon; Clare and Joan of Montefalco; the Franciscans tertiaries, Adriana and Margaret of Cortona; Gertrude the Great and Mechtild of Hackeborn.[21] Clare of Assisi, despite initial opposition, was able to entice her mother Ortolana, her sister Agnes, and her nieces Balbina and Amata de Coccorano into the cloister of Poor Clares. Similarly, Hugh of Tennenbach, Gerard of Lunel, and Douceline all followed the advice and example of older brothers in entering religion.[22]

A considerable number belonged to families which count several saints within the thirteenth century to their credit. The Andechs of central Europe produced twenty-one saints between 1150 and 1500. The royal house of Castile could boast five figures among the thirteenth century saints; while the Sienese Piccolomini and Patrizi include two each. In such instances, however, sainthood merely represents the church's desire to reward a faithful clan rather than an outstanding individual.[23]

A common practice among the upper classes was to send the younger son, who had been marked out for an ecclesiastical career, to his mother's brother for rearing. Most often, the boy then followed his uncle into the episcopate after apprenticeship as a canon, archdeacon, and dean of the cathedral to which his uncle was attached. His biographer reports that "immediately after completing the nursing period," Angelo of Furci was sent to his uncle's monastery for rearing.[24] Although Dominic's mother Joan and brother Mannes were both raised to the honors of veneration, it was his uncle, the dean of Palencia, under whose tutelage he was raised.[25] In the same way, Thomas Cantilupe and his brother Hugh were influenced at age seven by their uncle, Bishop Walter of Worcester, to follow an ecclesiastical vocation. Abbot William of Eskill was sent as a very young child (*infantulus*) to be raised by his uncle, Abbot Hugh of S. Germain des Pres; Albertus Magnus was likewise entrusted to his uncle in Paris for tutoring.[26] Among the female saints, Sperandea of Cingoli fell under the influence of her aunt and uncle, Jennaia and Sperandeo, while Roseline of Villeneuve was raised by her aunt and uncle, Saints Elzear and Delphine of Sabran.[27]

Many of the saints, on the other hand, were involved with the new mendicant orders (e.g., Franciscans, Dominicans, Augustinian hermits, and Carmelites), the beguines or reformed Benedictine congregations, all of which demanded rather severe standards of personal poverty and social service, and at first appeared to be a threat to social stability. Such saints tended to experience more turbulent childhoods, and parental neglect or absence, which yielded deep resentment or anger. Many were orphaned or lost at least one parent at an early age, usually a father. Under such conditions, the church could fill the vacuum left by the absent parent.[28] Given the frequent military campaigns and the demands of citizenship, especially in the Italian communes from which a majority of the saints came, the number of absent fathers would have been quite high, and prolonged separation a common feature of childhood. Throughout the first twleve years of Louis's life, the father of King Louis IX of France was either in the East on Crusade or fighting the Albigensians in southern France; the formative influence on Louis's character was therefore his pious and sainted mother, Blanche of Castile.[29] Both Louis of Toulouse and Lawrence O'Toole of Dublin, for example, spent part of their childhood years as hostages away from home as a result of political dealings.[30] Even Francis of Assissi's father, a wealthy cloth merchant, was absent at the time of his son's birth, probably on business in France; on his father's return the infant's name was changed from John to Francis.[31] In the life of Thomas Aquinas, his father, one of the leading noblemen of Naples, is a veritable phantom, and his mother, Theodora, plays the leading role.[32] Such fathers, who seem to play no role whatsoever in their children's upbringing, appear to be the rule rather than the exception.

While parental absence, or premature separation as the result of wet-nursing, education, or death might well be interpreted by a young man or woman as a sign of neglect, the most commonly mentioned cause of such separation was the hallowed practice of oblation, or the admission of children to monasteries before puberty. One of the most persistent controversies among canonists in the thirteenth century concerned the rules governing admission to the monastic or mendicant life.[33] Can parents destine their offspring in childhood or infancy for a monastic career without their consent? What is the lowest permissible age of profession—fourteen, eighteen, or twenty? What is the minimum length of novitiate? The frequent papal injunctions on these matters suggest that young monks were growing increasingly restive over the strict parental controls, which had allowed the system of oblation to create monasteries peopled with veritable prisoners: young women whose families could not afford a proper dowry, young men whose parents feared the excessive division of their properties or who expected at least one son to extend the family's influence in the church. All of those saints who served as canons, for example, at least seventy-five, including Dominic, were probably made oblates at an early age. According to a rule dating to 591 A.D., children placed in a monastic community by their parents were required to make profession if their parents so desired, and such oblates were considered true monks, with all the responsibilities this entailed.[34] In some instances, children were dispatched to nunneries or monasteries as early as three years old, although seven is a more common age. Nor could they leave the order under any conditions without express permission. While by the thirteenth century, fourteen eventually became the age of discretion for males and twelve for women, any youth contemplating flight in his teens, after a substantial family investment in his oblation, would probably face a grim economic prospect. Thus, many of the monks and nuns were virtual prisoners since childhood, and only acquiesced in adulthood to this captivity as the best of two poor choices. Even a girl who had reached puberty, and had then fled and borne a child, must return if her parents so ordained, for she had at one time donned the religious habit and accepted the benediction.[35] Although such harsh rules were somewhat mitigated by the institution of a one-year probationary period during which the youth might choose to leave, evidence of dissatisfaction is apparent from the frequent calls for the return of fugitive monks.[36] How might a young man or woman feel about parents who had abandoned him or her at an early age to a never-ending regime of fasts, prayer and self-denial? Since over ninety percent of the saints were attached to religious orders, we may assume that a correspondingly high number entered not so much out of personal choice, but rather as a result of a parental decision in childhood. We may thus assume that parental absence was a common phenomenon, except as in the case of Hugh of Lincoln and his father, when both child and parent joined together.[37]

Of those whose age of profession is known, twenty-five percent were clearly oblates or made profession immediately upon reaching puberty, which suggests that they were already residing in the monastery. These are concentrated within the older orders—Benedictine, Cistercian, Vallumbrosian, Camaldolensian. Most common are young noblewomen, like Imana of Loss, Margaret of Hungary, and Christina of Retters.[38] In the case of Lutgard of Aywieres, the contemporary biographer reports that when his daughter was born, Lutgard's father, "as was customary," invested twenty marks, hoping to use the profits earned in order to enhance her future dowry. Unfortunately, he lost all but one mark in this venture; when she reached marriageable age, her father permitted Lutgard to choose a religious career rather than marriage.[39]

Thus, the typical saint's vocational choice was generally the product of a parental decision, and although some evidence of emotional tension produced by parental neglect is suggested, there are few signs of overt abuse by parents of their children mentioned in these sources. Instances of such cruelty do, however, exist. Ambrose of Siena, because of a congenital deformity, was immediately sent away to a poor nurse just outside of the city.[40] His mother experienced such great grief over her son's ugliness and her attendant misfortune that she is portrayed praying to God for an end to her misery. Of course, she is more concerned about her own inconvenience than her son's discomfort. Ambrose was cured in a church, and after a year returned to the family. Perhaps some latent resentment of this treatment remained, for he resisted parental demands that he follow a secular career. Likewise, because of her blindness, Margaret of Citta was completely abandoned by her parents at seven; while Werner of Oberwesel was apparently so mistreated by his stepfather that he was forced to leave for Trier. Maltreatment of Margaret of Cortona by a wicked stepmother forced her to leave home to become the paramour of a nobleman of Montepulciano; this scar always remained with her. . . .[41]

Voiced parental hostility in the choice of vocation was especially common among those who joined the more radical orders, which were less likely to lead to ecclesiastical preferment. Such orders, stressing absolute poverty, solitude, or self-denial, represented a complete break with the affluence of the saint's upbringing, and constituted a distinct rejection of parental values.[42] Instances of parental hostility and generational conflict become almost archetypal, especially among founders of such religious orders, e.g., Francis of Assisi, Clare of Assisi, and Diana of Andalo. On an ideological plane, this tension was expressed in the increasing scorn exhibited by the young toward the prosperity of their elders, which gave birth to Utopian movements, like the Humiliati and Franciscans; to Christian fundamentalism and Joachitic apocalypticism, both of which justified attacks on clerical and civil authority. The particular interest in missionary activity of the generation following the IV Lateran Council in 1215 suggests further that the young were more acutely aware of the desperate condition of a Christendom threatened internally by heresy and externally by Mongol and Moor. The moral reform of the Alleluia of 1233, a product of this youthful enthusiasm, during which campaigns were undertaken against heresy, prostitution, abortion, and other offenders of Christian morality, corresponds with the deep penetration of the Mongols into Hungary and Poland, and the worst defeats suffered by the papacy at the hands of Frederick II.[43] Apparently, the violence of the Albigensian and eastern Crusades had not successfully counteracted the dual menace of heresy and Islam. This was most directly felt in Italy, where the young responded with a more peaceful and pious form of Christian evangelism. They often experienced a feeling of admiration mixed with hate toward their parents. This attitude, Kenneth Keniston has shown, has characterized the radical young in America;[44] in both periods, revolutionaries have come from comparable affluent milieus. And in both instances, adolescent revolt has produced movement toward economic reform with strong moral overtones.

This generational conflict was most graphically expressed by the secular Sienese poet Cecco Angiolieri (ca. 1260–1312), the son of a banker to Pope Gregory X.[45] While many of his themes are traditional, much of Cecco's poetic ire is directed against his parents' supposed miserliness. Cecco cannot woo his beloved Becchina because his father will not provide him with the funds to buy her gifts (Son. xxiii).[46] He castigates the old man for not dying and leaving his son a fat inheritance (c-cv). The death of the old skinflint leaves Cecco delirious with joy (cvii), as he tells the inhabitants of hell to make room for another resident. Suddenly, filled with fear that his hatred for the dead parent will damn him to eternal wandering (cvi), Cecco repents of his infamies against his father (cix). But this freedom is short-lived. His mother, Lisa, turns out to be as niggardly as her dead spouse, and she works in league with a certain Mino dei Tolomei to deprive Cecco of his wealth (cx-cxii). Cecco's invective against Mino is so scurrilous that most editors have refused to print it. The scorn formerly heaped on his father is now displayed by the outraged man against his mother "Medea," whom he accuses of trying to poison him (cxii, cxv).

Cecco's clashes with his parents were mirrored in his attitudes toward political authority. Although he took part in the Guelph campaigns of 1281 and 1288/89, in 1281 he was punished for leaving his post without authorization during the battle of Maremma; in 1282 and 1291 he was punished for violating the curfew. Between 1291 and 1302 Cecco was banished from Siena. It is suggested by some commentators that this exile was political. On February 25, 1313, five of his children appeared before a notary to renounce their inheritance because of their father's indebtedness. In Cecco's case, the marked estrangement of parent and child led to financial difficulties, but this may appear to mask political differences. The severity of his attacks upon his father, however, suggest deeper conflicts stemming from the childhood relations of parent and child.

Among the saints, the lives of Francis (1180–1226) and Clare of Assisi (ca. 1194–1253) became the patterns of youthful revolt against parental authority. The official biographies by Thomas of Celano particularly emphasize the element of parental disapproval. The *Vita* of Francis, well-known to all mendicants, begins with a prologue which sets the stage for a conflict between the saint and his father.[47] In keeping with the Augustinian view of sin and its genesis found in the *Confessions*, Thomas places the blame for Francis's early debauchery on the education provided by his parents, who raised their son to love the vanities of the world. The habits of adulthood, he argues, are merely the fruits of seeds planted in childhood. This addiction to sin, however, is contrary to nature; but as long as one is surrounded by evil, the task of freeing oneself from it is all the more difficult. Only in adolescence, when the young man is freed of parental constraints, can he unlearn the vices which have so long distorted his perception. Thus, Celano viewed Francis's early life as an illustration of the conflict between evil and good, with evil apparently represented by Francis's father, Peter

Bernardone, and the conspicuous wealth of his class, and good, being the ideal of poverty which Francis propounded.

At the time of Francis's birth in 1182, his father, a cloth merchant, was abroad. Francis had at least four brothers and, like many young knights of his day, devoted his time to banquets, singing and other vain pursuits, while he acquired merely the rudiments of learning. Little else is known of his early life, except that in about 1205 he had a vision of his home filled with armor, rather than the bolts of cloth with which it was usually stocked. As a result, he joined the army of Walter of Brienne in support of the pope against the Perugians. After a second vision, he returned home, and resumed his former life; but after falling ill, he began to regret this regime of supposed debauchery.

In about 1206, his father sent him to Foligno in order to sell some cloth; on the road home, he stopped at the old, partially destroyed church of S. Damiano. Here, he had a vision, which demonstrated to him the sacredness of poverty, and gave the proceeds of his cloth sale to the local parish priest. Because he had been away longer than expected, Peter went out looking for his son; when he discovered the youth in the ramshackle church, and heard that he had decided to change his former life, Peter became incensed. Fearing the ire of his father, and the derision of his friends, Francis thereupon sequestered himself in a cave for a month. Upon his return home, Celano reports, the saint was considered insane by his fellow citizens, and taunted by them for his sloth. Meanwhile, his father had grown even more angry. He locked Francis in a dark room for several days, and whipped and chained him. But the saint remained steadfast in his resolve. Even his sympathetic mother Pica's entreaties were to no avail, so she set her erring son free. When Peter returned to discover his wife's perfidy and son's continued stubbornness, he finally brought Francis before Bishop Guido II of Assisi (d. 1228) in order to force his son to return all the squandered wealth. Francis thereupon dramatically stripped naked before the bishop, symbolically denuding himself of all his possessions, and began his evangelical career. The *Legenda trium sociorum* quoted Francis as saying: "Up till now I have called my father Peter Bernardone, but because I have decided to serve God, I return to him the money about which he is concerned, and all of the clothes which I possess of him, desiring only to say: 'Our father who is in heaven.' "[48] Thus, Francis was quite explicit in disowning his natural parent and replacing him with a celestial father.

Francis was to become a great paragon of youthful revolt against his father. The turning point in his life had come in late adolescence. After years of opulence and sensuality, he began to identify with the poor and withdraw from pleasure-seeking.[49] In Rome, he went so far as to borrow the robes of a beggar, and ask for alms, until finally, he devoted himself to the care of that most downtrodden class of all, the lepers. During a 1209 interview with the bishop of Assisi, who noted the difficulties which he would encounter in his quest for absolute poverty, Francis allegedly uttered the clarion call of his movement, a protest against the environment of his parental upbringing: ". . . if we have possessions, we will need arms to protect them. From this disputes and quarrels arise, while the love of God and one's neighbor is much hindered. Consequently, we don't wish to possess any worldly goods."[50] Here Francis explicitly states that private property is the root cause of social conflict. As a result, he dedicated himself to a total rejection of the primarily materialistic values by which he believed his father lived. A similar hostility to the commercial interests of their fathers was later expressed by John Pelingotto, son of a cloth-maker of Urbino, and Anthony Manzoni of Padua.[51]

The same kind of displeasure greeted the conversion of Francis's follower, Clare of Assisi, foundress of the Poor Clares.[52] Clare was likewise born into the urban aristocracy of Assisi, whose large family had been exiled to Perugia between 1198 and 1203. Around 1210, after hearing a sermon of Francis and conversing with him privately, Clare fled with her friend Pacifica di Guelfuccio to the Benedictine house of S. Mari degli Angeli. Pursued by her family, she moved to S. Paolo at Bastia before they were reconciled to her decision. Thereafter she was joined by other daughters of the Assisian nobility, who no doubt experienced similar hostility from their families. Diana of Andalo (d. 1237), foundress of the Dominican nuns, likewise faced parental opposition to her decision to join Dominic.[53] Her father, after two marriages, had sired many children, including Diana, Loderingo, and Brancaleone, a senator of Rome. Although her grandfather was favorably disposed to the new order, both Diana's father and the bishop of Bologna opposed her. When she presented them with a *fait accompli*, she was mistreated by her family and their clients, isolated for a year, and severely beaten. . . .

If the parties were of high social standing, the pope sometimes intervened when new Dominicans were threatened by parental anger as a result of their choice of calling. In a letter of May 15, 1235 to the archbishop of Naples, Gregory IX described how, after a certain youth had entered the Dominican house at Naples, his relatives, "sons of Belial . . . and heretics," attacked the monastery, killed some of the brethren, and burned down the house. After excommunicating the wrongdoers, Gregory asked his correspondent to seek the support of the secular power in pursuing them.[54] Considering Frederick II's animosity toward the mendicants one may wonder what the outcome was. Such violence closely parallels the case of Thomas Aquinas,[55] who came from a prominent Ghibelline, i.e., anti-mendicant and anti-papal, family of southern Italy, and who chose to join the Friars Preachers at the height of Frederick's power. Thomas, son of Landulph, Count of Aquino, had at least four brothers and four or five sisters; two of his brothers were soldiers in the emperor's army, while two of the girls eventually entered religion. At five, Thomas was made an oblate at the fashionable Benedictine monastery of Montecassino, perhaps in the hope that his ecclesiastical career might be thereby enhanced. Thus, since early childhood, Thomas had been separated from his family. In 1235/37, he left the abbey, perhaps because of political turmoil in the area, to study at Naples, where he was a student of the Dominican Peter of Spain. At thirteen he joined the Dominicans (ca. 1240/44). When his family heard about the decision, his mother Theodora rushed to Naples with her retainers in order to prevent Thomas's continuance in the order. Presumably, political considerations played some role in her decision, but the brethren feared that Thomas might relent and took their young charge to Terracina. She consequently wrote her sons and asked their help in restoring Thomas to the family. When Theodora reached Rome, the Dominicans had already removed Thomas and were on the road to Bologna or Paris. But they were apprehended by Thomas's family. The Dominicans fled, and Thomas returned to his parental estate, shut up for two years at Roccasecca and Monte S. Giovanni Campano.

Because this armed attack had been made with the knowledge of the emperor, protests were lodged in Rome. Meanwhile, sequestered in the family castle, Thomas was permitted few visitors. One biographer alleges he was beaten by his brothers and seduced by his sisters. Finally, after a year, his mother relented, and Thomas was permitted to rejoin the Dominicans. A somewhat similar event occurred in the life of the Augustinian Augustino Novello, scion of the Neapolitan nobility and chancellor to King Manfred. Augustine wanted to study at Bologna, presumably with the aim of following an ecclesiastical career. But his mother opposed this, and enrolled him in Rome, where she stayed with her son.[56]

Thus, some rather clear patterns emerge concerning the childhood years of the thirteenth-century saints. The chief responsibility for childrearing lay in the hands of the mother, or in the case of well-to-do families, the wet-nurse. In many instances, the fathers play no role and only appear in early adolescence to interfere with the youth's religious impulses. Some were placed in monasteries, oblates from their earliest years, or were sent off to some ecclesiastical uncle for an education. The loss of one or both parents is equally common, thereby increasing the desire to secure a substitute parent within the church. While many of the saints grew up in an environment which cultivated pious impulses, and were related to other religious figures, a minority faced strenuous opposition to their vocations. Such encounters occur in the lives of some of the leading figures of the period—Thomas Aquinas, Francis and Clare of Assisi, Diana of Andalo. In some cases, as in the life of Salimbene, deep psychological resentment is clear; in others, ideological differences, fear over a lost heir, or marital anxieties provide the touchstone for such conflicts. Even the secular poet Cecco Angiolieri gives voice to the kind of generation gap which afflicted the urban bourgeoisie and nobility of the thirteenth century.

The research concerning the normal age of religious profession and its psychological character is confirmed in the lives of these saints. For example, one leading psychologist of religion, Edwin Starbuck,[57] sent out a questionnaire to one hundred and ninety-two Protestant Americans in an effort to establish a pattern for the conversion experience. He found that "conversion is a distinctly adolescent phenomenon" most likely to occur between the age of ten and twenty-five, during the period of most rapid physical and psychological growth, after or just before puberty. This is confirmed among our saints, who overwhelmingly experience a conversion crisis within this age period. At a time when intellectual and spiritual development coincide, Starbuck points out, motives toward conversion dominated by fear—fear of hellfire, remorse over an alleged sin, social pressures—play the largest role. This element of fear was especially emphasized by the many preachers who fanned out across Europe in the thirteenth century, and whose grim forebodings no doubt influenced many an impressionable youth, especially those without a secure family nest.[58]

As the budding youth strives for identity, Starbuck continues, instinct overrides reason; dejection and sadness, generally based on a sense of sin rather than a positive striving toward righteousness, lead to inner turmoil, and finally to a feeling of joy and peace. In all instances, there is a latent predisposition to convert which the conversion experience merely triggers. In adolescence, this religious transformation is usually regarded as a "unifying and joyful awakening" which may sometimes be associated with hallucinatory experiences and drastic behavioral changes. The largest number of such conversions among the saints, as among Starbuck's sample, occur before twenty; in men, between sixteen and nineteen; in women, between thirteen and sixteen, in the period of most rapid bodily growth.[59]

Joel Allison has suggested that many converts have used religion to replace their deficient, weak, or absent fathers with some forceful figure represented by the church or God.[60] Those with the strongest conversion experiences exhibit a marked rebelliousness toward religion following an initially pious childhood, during which a religious or highly moralistic mother served as contrast to an "immoral" or sacrilegious father. These findings seem to be confirmed among the thirteenth century saints. Maria, the mother of Pope Celestine V, Pica Bernardone, Francis's mother, and Joan of Aza, Dominic's mother, are but three such pious women who are pictured as spiritual beacons who led their children to religion.[61] On the other hand, the strong-willed secularistic father is an equally common theme in hagiography; Peter Bernardone, Clare's and Diana's father, the father of Humiliana dei Cerchi, who disowned his daughter when she refused to remarry, all exemplify this theme. We have seen that a considerable number of saints suffered the loss of at least one parent, and some of both. The grief of loss may have led many to religion in order to recreate the strong hand and sense of security which had formerly guided their lives.

Among those whose religious calling was not merely the product of a parental decision to place their children in a monastery, a vision or dream are the most frequent events which trigger the call to convert.[62] According to current wisdom, both phenomena were regarded as bearers of a prophetic message, and were especially common among melancholics or holy men and women. But while the vision is generally quite explicit and is accompanied by voices, the dream is unspecific and requires further elucidation. As Aquinas pointed out, dreams are often an agency of God's revelation, and may themselves influence the course of events by producing anxiety in the recipient. And adolescence was universally regarded as the age most receptive to dream and vision-messages.[63]

But, clearly, such dreams or visions never occur in a psychological vacuum, and merely serve to resolve conflicts which have long plagued the recipient. James Pratt,[64] a student of William James,[65] after studying some of the more well-known examples of the conversion experience, concluded that there are two types of conversion. In one, the believer is torn between discordant internal forces which strive for resolution; in the other, the convert simply accepts certain philosophical assumptions, without experiencing great emotional trauma. The anxieties with which the convert wrestles are often of a sexual nature, and the dream or vision which leads to conversion expresses this pent-up sexual guilt. Peter Celestine, for example, always displayed a strong sense of guilt over his alleged sinfulness, and made especially strenuous efforts to avoid the sight of women. In the first days of his eremitical solitude, Peter attempted to visit a neighboring hermit, and was approached by two women who tried to destroy his resolve. These two demons again visited him, this time in the nude, accompanied by all manner of beasts, in order to tempt the twenty-year-old youth.[66] When a blind woman came to Peter seeking aid, he tried to put her off because of her sex. Later in his career, knowing that Peter abhorred the sight of women, one man went so far as to clothe his ailing six-year-old niece in boy's garments in order to present her to Peter for the cures which medicine could not provide. One witness recalled during the saint's canonization trial that in his early days as a hermit, Peter particularly feared women.[67]

The most remarkable example of Peter's sexual anxieties is found in the *Autobiography*.[68] Once, following a nocturnal emission, Peter was uncertain whether or not to celebrate the mass. Some monks advised him to do so, others disagreed. He decided to seek God's counsel. That night he had a wondrous dream in which Peter saw himself ascending a mountain to reach the castle which surmounted it. As he walked he noticed a great cloister, and in the midst of the cloister stood the gate to a palace, which was surrounded by numerous cells peopled by monks dressed in white, i.e., Benedictines. Celestine was determined to enter the palace, but was frustrated by his reluctant mule. As he ascended, the animal tagged along willingly, but after a few steps, the evil beast began to defecate. Seeing this, Peter was discouraged and dared not continue. At the top of the stairway, three persons, barely distinguishable from each other, appeared. One of this Trinity, Jesus Christ, urged Peter on, saying that the creature had defecated for its own sake, not Peter's. The hermit then awoke, satisfied that his fears had been resolved through divine intervention as expressed in the language of a dream. Subsequently, Peter realized that such an involuntary emission, like the mule's natural need, carries no guilt. In one of his own writings,[69] Peter, citing Gregory the Great, pointed out that if the pollution is the product of intoxication, it is a venal sin, and is especially sinful if it derives from a consciously evil thought. If it is the result of illness or superfluity, then no sin is involved. Thus, Peter was exonerated for his act, despite the anxiety it had produced. Three popular preachers of the period, James of Vitry, Caesarius of Heisterbach, and Bartholomew of San Concordio agree in minimizing the seriousness of involuntary emission; only failure to confess results in a severe penalty.[70]

Such sexual guilt, mirrored in dream-life, seems likewise to have played a role in the conversion of the courtly novelist and poet-turned-philosopher, Raymund Lull; such prophetic and admonitory visions fortuitously visited Raymund at every turning-point in his life.

According to his *Autobiography*,[71] one night this seneschal to the King of Aragon sat down to compose a love poem to his mistress. As he reclined on his bed, he saw on his right an image of the crucified Christ; but he dozed off and forgot the incident. Eight days later, when Lull took up his composition, the image of Jesus reappeared. He again fell asleep, but the incident recurred four more times. On the final occasion, the poet concluded that God was asking him to serve the Lord, and Lull decided that he could do this best by undertaking to convert the Saracens by abandoning his secular life and studying Arabic.

While similar visions directed him to join the Franciscans, assisted him in composing his first philosophical tracts, and advised him to journey to North Africa in order to convert the heathen, this initial conversion experience was of a clearly sexual nature, and may be explained by events to which Lull does not directly allude. At the age of twelve, the scion of a noble Majorcan family, Lull had joined the court of King James of Aragon, where he became one of the leading chivalric poets of the age. Although married at about twenty-two, he continued his amorous adventures, despite his siring two children. This amoral behavior surely created severe internal conflicts which were only partially resolved as a result of the celibacy demanded by his religious call. In later life, his remorse over his youthful desire for women was overwhelming; the beauty of women was described as the "disease and perdition" of his eyes. Although the oft-repeated tale that Lull's conversion dates from seeing the cancerous breasts of one of his mistresses is probably apocryphal, one cannot doubt that guilt over his alleged past sensuality played a role. His behavior continued to be somewhat erratic even after the conversion, for he did not completely abandon his family until ten years later, and his wife, Blanche, refused, quite sensibly, to permit him to disinherit the clan by giving all his wealth to the church.[72]

This late adolescent dream or vision which actualizes a latent potentiality to convert, is a common element in the hagiographical legend of the period. The dream is often cloaked in symbolism and requires further interpretation. The vision, on the other hand, is often accompanied by the appearance of persons who explicitly point out to the recipient the preferred course of action. The character of the apparition will depend very much upon the nature of the choices faced by the visionary, and his or her predisposition to receive this particular visitor. Thus, before admission to the Dominican order, Robert of Uzes had contemplated joining the more radical Brethren of the Sack. During his first mass as a priest, Robert saw a hypocritical member of this order, as well as a Dominican who urged him to become a Preacher.[73] Silvester Gozzolini, founder of the reformed Benedictine order of Silvestrines, likewise was visited by St. Benedict, who asked him to revitalize his ancient rule.[74]

But the most frequent supernatural guest during the thirteenth century was the Virgin Mary, to whom so many churches, monasteries, lay confraternities and religious orders were dedicated.[75] The Servite order was formed by Seven members of the Florentine *Laudesi Mariae* after a vision of the Virgin on the Feast of the Assumption of Mary in 1233; their prior membership in a lay confraternity devoted to Mary indicates a predisposition to "conversion."[76] Likewise, even before receiving instructions from the Holy Mother in 1218 to establish the Mercedarians, Peter Nolasco had decided to distribute his wealth to the poor.[77] In Northern Europe, the most frequent recipients of visits from the Virgin were those saints associated with the Cistercian order, which had been founded during the flowering of Mariolatry in the twelfth century. Beguine women, who hovered between marriage and pious seclusion, were especially prone to such visitations: Beatrice of Oliva, Catherine of Parc-les-Dames, Lutgard of Aywieres, and many more. All apparently used the Virgin's advice in order to confirm their prior religious drives, which may have originally derived from the sexual demands of marriage.[78]

Among members of the newer religious orders and lay saints not officially connected to an order, the conversion crisis often represented a period of great inner turmoil which, to the outside world, took on the appearance of severe mental and/or physical illness. The dissipation of these symptoms was accompanied by a religious vision and the advent of a dominant idea or philosophical notion in the convert's mind. Thus, after his first vision, Raymund Lull was overcome by an evangelical desire to convert the pagans; Francis was impelled to carry the idea of poverty to the limit; and Peter Celestine sought utter solitude in pursuit of the eremitical ideal. In the realm of psychopathology, this phenomenon is called "logophania."[79] This "illness," which leads to a period of great creativity coupled with relative emotional stability, has been divided into four general phases, all of which are observable in the life of the thirteenth century saint: (1) a period of deep intellectual or meditative effort; (2) growing obsession with some dominant idea; (3) liberation from suffering coupled with a euphoric or enthusiastic revelation or illumination; and (4) a transformation of the personality.[80] This syndrome of creative illness is observable among mystics who experience a "dark night of the soul," writers suffering creative blockage, and shamans who withdraw voluntarily in order to perform some praiseworthy social act.[81] And the mystic, intellectual, and cult object are characteristic poses of the saints we have dealt with. As a result of this illness, the sufferer is strengthened, rather than weakened, and feels a sense of liberation.

The curative effect of conversion was already observed by Caesarius of Heisterbach, who tells of a certain knight named Ludwig who became extremely ill and was urged to convert.[82] After receiving his wife's consent, he did so, and his illness disappeared. While still a student at Paris, Caesarius relates, the abbot of Morimund failed woefully at his studies, and, as a result became severely depressed.[83] The devil, ever watchful, asked the young fellow to become his man in return for knowledge, but the youth withstood these blandishments. Satan thereupon gave him a magical stone which, if held firmly, would give him wisdom. Sure enough, during the scholarly disputations, the student confounded everyone; nevertheless, he again fell ill, called a priest, and admitted to consort with the devil. After throwing away the stone, he died. Therefore, he passed through Purgatory, but awoke from death, much to everyone's surprise. The resurrected man became a Cistercian, and was well-known for his self-mortification. An anonymous late-thirteenth-century English Dominican exemplarist[84] tells of a certain scholar of Cambridge who was suffering a high fever when the Preachers first came to England. After seeing a vision of God sitting in judgment on the damned with the aid of the Dominicans, the student recovered and became a friar. Similarly, a contemporary Franciscan collection[85] relates the story of a blind man of Assisi who heard of the miracles wrought by the Dominican preacher Nicholas of Juventio. The blind man undertook the journey to Apulia in search of light, but returned home still sightless. The devil, however, promised to restore his sight if he remained obedient to him. The man regained his sight, but lost his soul. His damnation rested upon refusal to truly convert and repent.

The saints were no less likely to experience symptoms of physical illness during the course of their conversion crises. Francis himself, according to Thomas of Celano, was overcome with sickness in the course of his youthful debaucheries.[86] During the period of recuperation, he visited his former haunts with the aid of a walking stick, but found no joy in these sites of his former happiness. Subsequently, his doubts grew stronger, leading to the conversion to mendicancy, which was accompanied by a dissipation of the symptoms of disease. The saint's fifth disciple, Morico, joined the minorities following a miraculous cure wrought by the saint;[87] while one of Clare's early followers, her cousin Amata Martini, who suffered from dropsy, was healed by Clare following the renunciation of her bethrothal.[88] The second convert made to the Franciscan order by Agnello of Pisa in

England was a mute, William of London; after his induction, he allegedly regained the power of speech;[89] similarly, the secular canon, Otto of Halberstadt, became a Franciscan after the blessed Euphemia cured him of a throat tumor.[90] Salimbene[91] reports that while John of Parma was under the care of his uncle, a priest of S. Lazare in Parma, he fell ill and was near death. One day, comforted by God, John quoted the words of Luke 118.17 to those standing by: "I shall not die, but live and declare the works of the Lord. The Lord hath chastized me sore; but he hath not given me unto death." Thereafter, John recovered, began to study with great fervor, "walked in the way of God," and joined the Franciscans.

This phenomenon is reported somewhat less frequently among saints of the other orders. After a life of crime as a highwayman near Siena, Franco Lippi suffered a sudden blindness; as a result, after hearing a sermon of Ambrose Sansedonius, he became a recluse and Carmelite *converso.*[92] Augustine Novello was wounded during the battle of Benevento in 1266; at that time, he promised to enter religion if he should be freed of his illness. He was indeed cured, and joined the Augustinian hermits.[93] Reginald of Orleans similarly was cured of sickness through a vision of the Virgin, who presented him with the Dominican habit; thereafter, he resigned his deanship and joined the preachers.[94] Bernard Tolomei founded the Olivetan order at the age of fifty-one, shortly after suffering blindness.[95]

Thus, for the vast majority of saints, the ground had been laid by late adolescence for the charismatic powers they were to exhibit. Like the shamans of Siberia or America, these hallowed figures frequently separated themselves from the community for a term of isolation, self-denial, and purgation in preparation for re-entry into society as a prophet or healer.[96] While many suffered a severe illness or sudden crisis of conversion, the grounds for such a transformation had existed since infancy. The thirteenth-century saint had characteristically experienced a deprived childhood, separated for long periods from one or both parents. The only solace in this hostile environment was the "father" abbot, "mother" abbess, or Mother Church, who provided much of the emotional sustenance and purpose which his or her parents had failed to supply. In the case of members of the new religious orders, which clearly stood for social reform or even revolution, we have seen that overt parental hostility was almost the norm: Francis, Clare, Selimbene demonstrate this fact. This generational conflict was not restricted to the religious, however; for the Sienese poet, Cecco Angiolieri, demonstrates a similar estrangement from his parents which must have afflicted other well-placed Italian clans. The voiced basis of this conflict rested on the adolescent's refusal to remain the subservient executor of his parents' wishes. The son refuses to enter the family business or follow the accepted line of ecclesiastical preferment; while the young woman fears the responsibilities of married life and chafes under the autocratic rule of her parents.

Notes

1. Georg Misch, *Geschichte der Autobiographie,* 4 vols. (Bern, 1949–1969), IV, pt. 1 deals with the medieval period. A short, valuable bibliography can be found in F. Vernet, "Autobiographies spirituelles," *Dictionnaire de spiritualite,* vol. 1 (Paris, 1960), pp. 1141–59.

2. The major source collection of saints' lives in Socii Bollandiani, eds., *Acta sanctorum quotquot toto coluntur . . .,* new ed., 66 vols. to date (Paris, 1863-1940), which is arranged by day of the saints' feasts, and is hereafter referred to as *AS.* This may be supplemented by the periodical *Analecta Bollandiana* (1882-present), referred to as *AB;* and the biographical encyclopedia, Filippo Caraffa, et al., eds., *Bibliotheca sanctorum,* 12 vols. (Rome, 1961-1970), referred to as *BS.*

3. Joel Allison, "Religious Conversion: Regression and Progression in an Adolescent Experience," *Journal for the Scientific Study of Religion* 7 (1969): 23–38; Leon Gorlow and Harold E. Schroeder, "Motives for Participation in the Religious Experience," *Journal for the Scientific Study of Religion* 7 (1968): 241-51; Henri F. Ellenberger, "The Concept of Creative Illness," *The Psychoanalytic Review* 55 (1968), 442-56; James Bissett Pratt, *The Religious Consciousness: A Psychological Study* (New York, 1921); Edwin Diller Starbuck, *The Psychology of Religion* (London, 1899).

4. For examples of such undesired youthful marriage see *AS*, 27 September VII, 577; 19 May IV, 386.

5. *AS*, 6 February I, 936; *Acta apostoliace sedis,* 2 (1910), 411–14; *AS*, 19 September XI, 260-66; *BS*, IX, 953; *AB*, 17 (1898), 319-20; *AS*, 5 April I, 443.

6. Giacinto Pagnani, "Frammenti della Cronaca del B. Francesco Venimbene da Fabriano (+1322)," *Archivum franciscanum historicum,* 52 (1952), 153–77.

7. Jordan of Saxony, *Libellus de principiis ordinis praedicatorum,* in Jacques Quetif and Jacques Echard, eds., *Scriptores ordinis praedicatorum,* 2 vols. (Paris, 1719–1923), 1, 2-3.

8. *AS*, 25 April III, 389.

9. Arsenio Frugoni, "L,Autobiografia' di Pietro Celestino," in *Celestiniana* (Rome, 1954), 46; *AS*, 16 May III, 653.

10. Thomas of Celano, *Vita*, in *AS*, 12 August II, 755.

11. Peter Calo, *Vita*, ed. Dominic Prummer, *Fontes vitae S. Thomae Aquinatis* (Toulouse, 1911), fasc. 1, 17. On this general theme, see Francesco Lanzoni, "Il songo presago della madre incinta nella letteratura medievale e

antica," *AB*, 45 (1927), 225-61, which cites some examples of this kind of prophetic guest.

12. Peter Celestine, *Autobiografia*, 56; *AS*, 2 October I, 599; 17 October VIII, 198 ff; 11 June II, 43; 11 June II, 486; 13 April II, 154.

13. *AB*, 13 (1894), 417; *AS*, 29 January III, 597; cf. also *AS*, 29 July VII, 133; 6 February I, 537: 12 June III, 106.

14. *AS*, 3 April I, 278; 17 October VIII, 224; 29 May VII, 162.

15. *Acta apostolicae sedis*, 2 (1910), 411–14.

16. *AB*, 57 (1939), 378; *AS*, 4 September II, 434; 9 August II, 461.

17. *AB*, 19 (1900), 24; 9 (1890), 282-83.

18. *AS*, 7 April I, 684-86.

19. Clifford H. Lawrence, *St. Edmund of Abingdon* (Oxford, 1960), 106–10; L. Reypens, ed., *Vita Beatricis* (Antwerp, 1964), *passim;* Raymond-J. Loenertz, "La vie de S. Hyacinthe envisagee comme source historique," *Archivum fratrum praedicatorum*, 27 (1957), 5–38; *AS*, 17 July IV, 182-99.

20. Magnus Jocham, *Bavaria sancta*, 2 vols. (Munich, 1861-1862), I, 273-276; *AS*, 3 May I, 782-83; 20 June V, 50–55.

21. *AS*, 5 April I, 435–75; Michele Faloci-Pulignani, ed., "Vita di S. Chiara da Montefalco scritta da Berengario di S. Africano," *Archivio storico per le Marche e per l'Umbria*, 1 (1884), 587 ff; *AS*, 22 February III, 304 ff; Benedictines of Solesmes, eds., *Revelationes Gertrudianae ac Mechtildiance*, 2 vols. (Paris, 1875), I.

22. Arnaldo Fortini, *Nova vita di San Francesco*, 4 vols. (Assisi, 1950), II, 315 ff. gives a thorough account of Clare and her associates; F. J. Mone, ed., "Leben des Monches Hugo von Thennebach," *Quellensammlung der badischen Landesgeschichte*, 4 (Karlesruhe, 1867), 63–75; *AS*, 25 May VI, 158; Salimbene de Adam, *Cronica*, ed., Oswald Holder-Egger, in *Monumenta germaniae historica, Scriptores.*, 32 (Hannover, 1913), 553-54.

23. Joseph Gottschalk, *St. Hedwig von Schlesien* (Cologne, 1964), *passim; AS*, 29 May VII, 162; Vittorio Spreti, et al., *Enciclopedia storico-nobiliare italiano*, 7 vols. (Milan, 1928–1935), V, 325–38, 308–9.

24. *AS*, 6 February I, 937.

25. Jordan of Saxony, *Libellus*, cap. 5.

26. *AS*, 3 October I, 599; M. Cl. Gertz, *Vita sanctorum Danorum* (Copenhagen, 1908-1912), 300; *BS*, I, 700-715; *AS*, 13 April II, 388.

27. *AS*, 11 September III, 890-913; 11 June II, 484–98; 27 September VII, 528–94.

28. For examples see *BS*, IV, 124–25; II, 1194-1202; *AB*, 13 (1894), 417; *AS*, 5 April I, 443; 3 April I, 278; 19 October VIII, 607; 25 August V, 543, 574; 16 March II, 495; 30 March III, 848; 4 May I, 541; 31 May VII, 453.

29. *BS*, VIII, 320–42.

30. *AB*, 9 (1890), 284-85; 33 (1914), 129–31.

31. Paul Sabatier, *Vie de S. Francois d'Assise* (Paris, 1926), 5.

32. Angelo Walz, *Saint Thomas Aquinas*, trans. S. Bullough (Westminster, Md., 1951), *passim*.

33. Livario Oliger, "De pueris oblatis in ordine minorum," *Archivum francisanum historicum,* 8 (1915), 389-447; 10 (1917), 271-88 discusses the relevant texts and controversies. For the canonical legislation, see Emil Friedberg and Lewis Richter, eds., *Corpus Iuris Canonici,* 2 vols. (Leipzig, 1879), *Decretales Gregorii Noni,* III. 31.

34. Ibid, III. 31. 5.

35. Ibid, 31. 12.

36. Ibid., 31. 24.

37. Decima L. Douie and Hugh Farmer, eds., *Magna Vita Sancti Hugonis,* 2 vols. (London, 1961–1962), I, 5.

38. *AS,* 5 April I, 468-475; *BS,* VIII, 796–801; IV, 340-41.

39. *AS,* 16 June III, 191.

40. *AS,* 20 March III, 181.

41. *AB,* 19 (1900), 24; *AS,* 19 April II, 698; 22 February III, 304.

42. On mendicant radicalism, see Heribert Roggen, "Die Lebensform der hl. Franziskus von Assisi in ihrem Verhältnis zur feudalen und buergerlichen Gesellschaft Italiens," *Franziskanische Studien* 46 (1964): 1–54, 287-321.

43. For an account of anti-papal prophecies in the thirteenth century, see Marjorie E. Reeves, *The Influence of Prophecy in the Later Middle Ages* (Oxford, 1969), p. 175-228; for the specific impact of this reform program on Italian law, see Andre Vauchez, "Une campagne de pacification en Lombardie autour de 1233," *Melanges d'archeologie et d'histoire* 78 (1966): 503–49.

44. Kenneth Keniston, *The Young Radicals* (New York, 1968).

45. Hans Rheinfelder, *Lebensvorgänge, Krankheit und Heilung in den Gedichten Cecco Angiolieris und anderer burlesker Dichter der Dantezeit,* in *Sitzungen der bayerischen Akademie der Wissenschaften. Philosophisch-historische Klasse,* 10 (Munich, 1960); Mario Marti, *Cecco Angiolieri e i poeti autobiografici tra il 200 e il 300* (Galatina, 1945–1946); *idem,* "Cecco Angiolieri, "*Dizionario biografico degli italiani,* III, 280-83.

46. The Roman numerals in parentheses refer to the sonnet numbers in the following edition: Cecco Angiolieri, *Il Canzoniere,* ed., Carlo Steiner (Turin, 1928).

47. The edition here referred to is Thomas of Celano, *Vita prima S. Francisci,* in *Analecta francescana,* 10 (Quaracchi, 1926–1941), fasc. 1.

48. Michele Faloci-Pulignani, "Legenda trium sociorum ex codice Fulginatensi," *Miscellanea francescana.* 7 (1898), cap. 8; Thomas of Celano, *Vita prima,* caps. 3, 6, 7.

49. Faloci-Pulignani, *Legenda,* caps. 10, 11.

50. Ibid., cap. 35.

51. *Acta apostolicae sedis,* 10 (1918), 513–16; "Vita beati Antonii Peregrini," *AB,* 13 (1894), 417-25.

52. Thomas of Celano, *Legenda S. Clarae,* in *AS,* 12 August II, 754–68; cf. also Fortini, *Nova vita,* II, 315 ff.

53. *AS,* 10 June I, 359-60.

54. Thomas Ripoll, ed., *Bullarium ordinis praedicatorum,* 8 vols. (Rome, 1729-1740), I, 74–75. For such a case among the Cistercians, see Caesarius of Heisterbach, *Die Wundergeschichte,* ed., Alfons Hilka, 2 vols. (Bonn, 1933–1937), II, 134. The immediate cause of most of the disputes was the parental fear of losing an heir. Cf. also Thomas of Cantimpre, *Bonun universale de apibus* (Douai, 1605), 222-24, which may refer to Albertus Magnus; for the case of Maurice Csaky, who was forced to marry against his will, cf. *AS,* 20 March III, 251-55.

55. The story is repeated in the *Vitae* by Bernard Gui, Peter Calo and William of Tocco, see Prummer, *Fontes,* fasc. 1 and 2; *AS,* 7 March I, 657–86.

56. *AS,* 19 May IV, 614 ff.

57. Starbuck, *Psychology, passim.*

58. For a discussion of the role of fear in the good sermon, see Humbert of Romans, *De eruditione praedicatorum,* ed., J. J. Berthier, *Opera de vita regulari,* 2 vols. (Marietti, 1956), II, 444 (c. 28); William Paraldus, *Summa de virtutibus et vitiis* (Basel, 1497), 63 ff; John of San Gimignano, *Liber de exemplis et similitudinibus rerum* (Cologne, ca. 1478), Lib. 1, c. 17; Salimbene, *Cronica,* 561-63; Stephan of Bourbon, *Anecdotes historiques, legendes et apologues,* ed. A. Lecoy de la Marche (Paris, 1877), 29–30.

59. Starbuck, *Psychology,* 28.

60. Allison, *Religious Conversion,* 23-38.

61. Peter Celestine, *Autobiografia,* 56 ff; Thomas of Celano, *Vita prima,* 13–15; M.-H. Vicaire, *Saint Dominic and His Times,* trans. Kathleen Pond (New York, 1964), 18 ff.

62. Ernst Benz, *Die Vision* (Stuttgart, 1969), 104 ff. for examples of the conversion vision.

63. Thomas Aquinas, *Summa theologiae,* III.95.6, in *Opera omnia,* ed., Pietro Fiaccadori, 25 vols. (Parma, 1852-1873). III; Simone Collin-Rosset, ed., "Le *Liber thesauri occulti* de Paschalis Romanus (un traité d'interpretation des songes due xiie siècle)." *Archives d'histoire doctrinale et littéraire du moyen âge,* 30 (1963), 111-98; R. A. Pack, ed., "De prognosticatione sompniorum Libellus Guillelmo de Aragonia adscriptus," *Archives d'histoire doctrinale et littéraire du moyen âge,* 33 (1966), 237–93; Albertus Magnus, *De somno et vigilia,* in *Opera omnia,* ed., August Borgnet, 38 vols. (Paris, 1890–1898), IX, 122-212.

64. Pratt, *Religious Consciousness, passim.*

65. William James, *The Varieties of Religious Experience* (New York, 1968). The first edition appeared in 1902.

66. Peter Celestine, *Autobiografia,* 60-61.

67. Franz Xaver Seppelt, ed., *Die Akten des Kanonisationsprozesses,* in *Monumenta Coelestiniana,* in *Quellen und Forschungen aus dem Gebiet der Geschichte,* 19 (Paderborn, 1921), 309 ("I am a sinner, I am not worthy of reaching God . . ."), 222 ("Why have you brought this woman here? Don't you know that women ought not to be here?"), 247, 233 (". . . he fled the contact of men, but especially the sight of women.")

68. Peter Celestine, *Autobiografia*, 62-63.

69. Peter Celestine, *Opusculum Nonum*, in Margarinus de la Bigne, ed., *Maxima bibliotheca verterum patrum*, 28 vols. (Lyons, 1677), XXV, 852.

70. Goswin Frenken, ed., *Die Exempla des Jakobs von Vitry*, in *Quellen und Unterschungen zur lateinischen Philologie des Mittelalters*, 5 (Munich, 1914), no. 24; Caesarius of Heisterbach, *Dialogus miraculorum*, ed., Joseph Strange, 2 vols. (Cologne, 1851), I, 114; Batholomew of San Concordio, *Summa de casibus conscientiae* (Augsburg, 1475), cap. *Pollutio*.

71. Raymund Lull, *Vita coetanea* in *Opera*, ed. Ivo Salzinger, 10 vols. (Mainz, 1721-1742), I, 1-12; for a Catalan version, probably the original, dictated by Lull to one of students in about 1313, see Salvador Bove, "Vida coetania," *Boletin de la Real Academia de Buenas Lettras de Barcelona*, 15 (1915), 89-101. A good recent account of his life and works is Armand Llinares, *Raymond Lull, philosophe de l'action* (Grenoble, 1963).

72. Llinares, *Raymond Lull*, 137-40, 86, 150 ff.

73. Jeanne Bignami-Odier, ed., "Les visions de Robert d'Uzes (d. 1296)," *Archivum praedicatorum historicum*, 24 (1954), 258-310; cf. also *AS*, 23 August IV, 719 on James of Mevania; *AS*, 29 October XIII, 152-185 on Benvenuta Bojano.

74. *BS*, XI, 1075-77.

75. For a description of visions of the Virgin, see John Alexander Herbert, *Catalogue of Romances in the Department of Manuscripts in the British Museum*, 3 vols. (London, 1910), II, 586-97.

76. Max Heimbucher, *Die Orden und Kongregationen der katholischen Kirche*, rev. ed., 3 vols. (Paderborn, 1933), I, 576-78; for other Servite visions, see *AB*, 13 (1894), 386-87; 14 (1895), 166-97; *AS*, 23 August IV, 655-719.

77. *BS*, X, 844-852.

78. *AB*, 21 (1902), 241-260; *AS*, 4 May I, 537-539; *BS*, X, 844-52.

79. Viktor von Weiszaecker, "Der Widerstand bei der Behandlung von Organkranken," *Psyche*, 2 (1949), 481-89.

80. Ellenberger, *Creative Illness*, 444 ff.

81. Evelyn Underhill, *Mysticism* (New York, 1957), 380-412; Edmond Jaloux, "L'Inspiration poetique et l'aridite," *Etudes carmelitaines*, 22, vol. 2 (1937), 31-45; Carl-Martin Edsman, ed., *Studies in Shamanism*, in *Scripta Instituti Donneriani Aboensis*, 1 (Stockholm, 1967), 17 ff.

82. Caesarius of Heisterbach, *Dialogus*, I, 30-31.

83. Ibid., 36-37.

84. Stephen L. Forte, ed., "A Cambridge Collection of Exempla in the Thirteenth Century," *Archivum fratrum praedicatorum*, 28 (1958), 138-39.

85. Livario Oliger, ed., "Liber exemplorum fratrum minorum saeculi xiii," *Antonianum*, 2 (1927), 254.

86. Thomas of Celano, *Vita prima*, 7-9.

87. Bonaventure, *Legenda maiora S. Francisci*, in *Analecta francescana*, 10 (Quaracchi, 1926-1941), 874-75.

88. *AS*, 20 February III, 169 ff.

89. Thomas of Eccleston, *Tranctatus de adventu fratrum minorum in Angliam*, ed. A. G. Little (Manchester, 1951), 14.

90. Bartholomew of Pisa, *Liber de conformitate . . .*, in *Analecta francescana*, 4 and 5 (Quarracchi, 1904-1905), IV, 328.

91. Salimbene, *Cronica*, 297.

92. *BS*, V, 1252–53.

93. *AS*, 19 May IV, 618.

94. Jordan of Saxony, *Libellus*, cap. 51 ff.

95. *AS*, 21 August IV, 464 ff.

96. Ivan A. Lopatin, *Social Life and Religion of the Indians in Kitimat, British Columbia*, in *University of Southern California Social Science Series*, no. 26 (Los Angeles, 1945), discusses the creation of the shaman within this North American tribe. These rituals closely parallel the novitiate of the Christian monk or nun. For examples of such a trial, accompanied by seizures and hallucinations which border on schizophrenia, see *AS*, 16 April II, 462–70 (William Gnoffi of Polizzi); 22 June IV, 270–454 (Christina of Stommeln).

10

The Psychohistorical Origins of the Nazi Youth Cohort

PETER LOEWENBERG

Peter Loewenberg, a young historian with training both in history and psychoanalysis, elucidates the traumatic events experienced by a whole generation of Germans who were children or adolescents during World War I. His thesis is that the experiences of this generation predisposed many of them to become followers of National Socialism.

If a common shared experience of the trenches united most of the top leadership of National Socialism, the followers—broadly speaking those born around 1900—were united by a common set of childhood traumas. These included food deprivation, absence of the father who later returned in defeat, and unstable social conditions after the war which made normal life difficult.

In addition to its importance as a substantive history, Loewenberg's article represents a major methodological advance because of its treatment of a whole generation as the object of study.

The historical relationship between the events of World War I and its catastrophic aftermath in Central Europe and the rise of National Socialism has often been postulated. The causal relationship is usually drawn from the savagery of trench warfare on the western front, the bitterness of defeat and revolution, to the spectacular series of National Socialist electoral victories beginning in 1930, as if such a relationship were historically self-evident. It is the thesis of this paper that the

This article is an extensive abridgement of the original, which appeared in *American Historical Review* 76 (December 1971), 1457-1502. Copyright by Peter Loewenberg. Reprinted by permission of the author.

Author's Note: The preparation of this essay has been facilitated by a study fellowship from the American Council of Learned Societies. I am especially indebted to the brilliant paper of Martin Wangh, "National Socialism and the relationship between the period from 1914 to 1920 and the rise and triumph of National Socialism from 1929 to 1935 is specifically generational. The war and postwar experiences of the small children and youth of World War I explicitly conditioned the nature and success of National Socialism. The new adults who became politically effective after 1929 and who filled the ranks of the SA and other paramilitary party organizations such as the Hitler-Jugend and the Bund-Deutscher-Mödchen were the children socialized in the First World War.

This essay examines what happened to the members of this generation in their decisive period of character development—particularly in early childhood—and studies their common experiences in childhood, in psychosexual development, and in political socialization that led to similar fixations and distortions of adult character. The specific factors that conditioned this generation include the prolonged absence of the parents, the return of the father in defeat, extreme hunger and privation, and a national defeat in war, which meant the loss of the prevailing political authority and left no viable replacement with which to identify.

Most explanations for the rise of National Socialism stress elements of continuity in German history. These explanations point to political, intellectual, social, diplomatic, military, and economic factors, all of which are important and none of which should be ignored. The historian and social scientist studying Nazism should be conversant with and well versed in these categories of explanation. The study of political leadership is also of unquestioned importance for the understanding of the dynamics of totalitarianism, and it should be intensively developed by historians as an approach to that understanding.

This essay, however, will focus not on the leader but on the followers, not on the charismatic figure but rather on the masses who endow him with special superhuman qualities. It will apply psychoanalytic perceptions to the problem of National Socialism in German history in order to consider the issues of change rather than continuity in history, to deal with social groups rather than individual biography, and to focus on the ego-psychological processes of adaptation to the historical, political, and socioeconomic context rather than on the instinctual biological drives that all men share. . . .

Genocide of the Jews," *International Journal of Psychoanalysis*, 45 (1964): 386–95, to Peter Merkl, who generously shared unpublished research data with me, and to Gerhard Masur for his technical advice. For their critiques of earlier versions of this paper I am indebted to Robert G. L. Waite, William Niederland, Fred Weinstein, Franklin Mendels, Herbert Moller, Heiman van Dam, and to the members of the Interdisciplinary Colloquium on the Alternation of War and Peace of the American Psychoanalytic Association.

No genuine historical understanding is possible without the perspective of self-understanding from which the historian can then move forth to deal with historical material. Likewise there can be no measure of historical understanding if we research what men said and did and fail to understand why they acted. The twentieth century has experienced the gross magnification of political and personal irrationality correlative to the exponential increment in the power of modern technology. No history will speak with relevance or accuracy to the contemporary human condition if it fails to assess realistically the profound capacity of the irrational to move men.

Psychoanalysts are concerned with many things that are relevant to the historical problem of what happens to children in a nation at war. They have studied the effects of separation from parents and have seen the long-term consequences of deprivation, material and emotional. They know the hows and whys of a child's identification with his parents. Above all, psychoanalysis as a clinical technique of investigation demonstrates that only the smallest part of human thought and conduct is rational. The world of disembodied minds acting in an emotional vacuum has no place in a psychoanalytically informed history. Too much of history is still written as though men had no feelings, no childhood, and no bodily senses. What is needed is a new kind of history, a history that tells us how men responded to and felt about the great political and economic events that shaped their lives, a history that gives due place to the irrational, the unconscious, and the emotions not only of men, but also of the child in the man.

This new kind of history requires an understanding of the dual and related concepts of fixation and regression. Sigmund Freud, in a demographic metaphor of migration, once compared human development to the progress of a people through new territory. At those points where resistance is greatest and conflict most intense the people will leave behind its strongest detachments and move on. If the advanced parties, now reduced in strength, should suffer defeat or come up against a superior enemy, they will retreat to former stopping places where support stands ready. "But," says Freud, "they will also be in greater danger of being defeated the more of their number they have left behind on their migration." Thus, the greater the strength of early fixations, the greater will be the later need for regression: "The stronger the fixations on its path of development, the more readily will the function evade external difficulties by regressing to the fixations—the more incapable, therefore, does the developed function turn out to be of resisting external obstacles in its course."[1] As in Freud's migration metaphor, when an individual who has passed through the maturational phases of development meets with persistent and intense frustration, one of the means of coping with the pain and lack of satisfaction is to revert from the more highly developed stages of mental organization to modes of functioning typical of an earlier period. The falling back, or regression, will be to phases of psychosexual development that have left areas of weakness, where the maturational step has been marked by unresolved conflicts and anxieties. Arrests of development or points of fixation occur in sexual-drive organization, ways of relating to people, fears of conscience, persistence of primitive kinds of gratification and of reacting defensively to old, no longer present, dangers. . . .

Returning to the larger historical case of the German children of the First World War, it is Germany's Great Depression, with its unemployment, governmental chaos and impotence, and widespread anxiety about the future that constituted precisely such an "external disturbance" as Freud describes. The early point of fixation was the First World War, when the peoples of Central Europe experienced prolonged hunger, war propaganda, the absence of fathers and often both parents, and the bankruptcy of all political values and norms.

The psychological symptoms of regression to phases of ego functioning "fixed" by the traumata of a childhood in war included responding to internal personal stress with externalized violence, projecting all negative antinational or antisocial qualities onto foreign and ethnic individuals and groups, and meeting frustrations that would otherwise be tolerated with patience and rationally approached for solutions with a necessity for immediate gratification. The political expression of weakened egos and superegos that fostered regression was manifest not only in turning to violence but most especially in the longing for a glorified and idealized but distant father who is all-knowing and all-powerful, who preaches the military virtues and permits his sons and daughters to identify with him by wearing a uniform and joining combat in a national cause. . . .

The seminal conceptual formulation of the generation as a force acting in history was established by Karl Mannheim in 1927 in his essay, "The Sociological Problem of Generations."[2] Here Mannheim speaks of the human mind as "stratified" or layered, with the earliest experiences being the basis, and all subsequent experience building on this primary foundation or reacting against it. The influence of psychoanalytic thought on Mannheim's conceptualization of the problem is apparent.

> The human consciousness, structurally speaking, is characterized by a particular inner "dialectic." It is of considerable importance for the formation of the consciouness which experiences happen to make those all-important "first impressions," "childhood ex-

> periences"—and which follow to form the second, third, and other "strata." Conversely, in estimating the biographical significance of a particular experience, it is important to know whether it is undergone by an individual as a decisive childhood experience, or later in life, superimposed upon other basic and early impressions. Early impressions tend to coalesce into a *natural view* of the world. All later experiences then tend to receive their meaning from this original set, whether they appear as that set's verification and fulfillment or as its negation and antithesis. . . . Mental data are of sociological importance not only because of their actual content, but also because they cause the individuals sharing them to form one group—they have a socializing effect.[3]

Mannheim then structures a further "concrete nexus" of the generation in history as "*participation in the common destiny* of [the] historical and social unit." And such groups he terms "generation units."

> *Youth experiencing the same concrete historical problems may be said to be part of the same actual generation while those groups within the same actual generation which work up the material of their common experiences in different specific ways, constitute generation units.* . . . These are characterized by the fact that they do not merely involve a loose participation by a number of individuals in a pattern of events shared by all alike though interpreted by the different individuals differently, but an identity of responses, a certain affinity in the ways in which all move with and are formed by their common experiences.[4]

This means that those of a generation who experienced the same event, such as a world war, may respond to it differently. They were all decisively influenced by it but not in the same way. Some became pacifists, others embraced international Leninism, some longed to return to the prewar, conservative, monarchist social order, and the ones we are concerned with sought personal and national solutions in a violence-oriented movement subservient to the will of a total leader. What was politically significant in the early 1930s was the facility with which individuals of this generation moved from one allegiance to the other. Mannheim's point is that although the units of a generation do not respond to a formative crisis in the same way due to a multiplicity of variables, the overriding fact is their response to that particular event. Because of this they are oriented toward each other for the rest of their lives and constitute a generation.

An organization, such as a youth group, says Mannheim, may serve to mobilize latent opinion in a generation unit. It attracts to itself those individuals who share the formative experiences and impulses of the particular generation location, thus institutionalizing and realizing collectively the potentialities inherent in the historical and social situation.[5]

Following the theoretical work of Mannheim, sociological demographers have developed the highly suggestive concept of the "cohort," a term whose Latin etymology significantly refers to a group of fighting men who made up one of the ten divisions of a legion in the Roman army. In the modern discipline of demography a cohort is the aggregate of individuals within a population who have shared a significant common experience of a personal or historical event at the same time. This is distinguished from the loose term "generation," by which historians usually mean a temporal unit of family kinship structure such as "the founding generation," or, more ambiguously, a broad and often unspecified age span during a particular institutional, political, or cultural epoch, such as "the generation of '48" or "the lost generation." An example of a cohort would be college graduates of the year 1929, who completed their education in prosperity and in their first months on the labor market experienced the onset of the Great Depression. This cohort is distinctively marked by the period-specific stimulus of the economic depression for their entire working years in the labor force so that they are to be distinguished from other cohorts, even thirty years later, by their common experience of having endured significant events simultaneously. The same may be said for those who served in the armed forces during World Wars I and II, or those who were children during a war. . . .

The concept of the birth cohort—that is, those born at the same time—implies common characteristics because of common formative experiences that condition later life. Character formation, the direction of primary drives, and the internalization of family and social values are determined in the years of infancy and childhood. Each cohort carries the impress of its specific encounter with history, be it war or revolution, defeat or national disaster, inflation or depression, throughout its life. Any given political, social, or economic event affects people of different ages in different ways. The impact of war, hunger, defeat, and revolution on a child will be of an entirely different order of magnitude than the impact on an adult. This commonplace fact suggests that the event specificity of history must be fused with the generational-age specificity of the cohort of sociological demography and the developmental-phase specificity of psychoanalysis and childhood socialization to understand hsitorical change. In this sense history may be the syncretic catalyst of qualitative longitudinal life history and the quantitative data of sociological statistical analysis.

Rather than proceeding with the story of the Nazi youth cohort chronologically and beginning with its origins, this essay will use what Marc Bloch termed the "prudently retrogressive" method of looking at the outcome first, and then tracking down the beginning or "causes" of the phenomenon. [6] This, of course, corresponds to the clinical method of examining the "presenting complaints" first and then investigating etiology. The outcome of the story in this case is the related and concomitant economic depression, the influx of German youth to the ranks of National Socialism, the political decline of the Weimar Republic, and the Nazi seizure of power.

The Great Depression hit Germany harder than any other country, with the possible exception of the United States. Germany's gross national income, which rose by 25 per cent between 1925 and 1928, sank 43 per cent from 71 billion RM in 1929 to 41 billion RM in 1932. The production index for industry in 1927–28 was halved by 1932–33. In the critical area of capital goods, production in 1933 was one-third of what it had been five years earlier. The very aspect of Nazi success at the polls in the elections of 1930 accelerated the withdrawal of foreign capital from Germany, thus deepening the financial crisis.

The greatest social impact of the economic crisis was in creating unemployment. By 1932 one of every three Germans in the labor market was without a job. This meant that even those who held jobs were insecure, for there were numerous workers available to take the place of every employee. The young people were, of course, the most vulnerable sector of the labor market. New jobs were nonexistent, and the young had the least seniority and experience with which to compete for employment. To this must be added that the number of apprenticeships was sharply diminishing for working-class youths. For example, apprenticeships in iron, steel, and metalworking declined from 132,000 in 1925 to 19,000 in 1932. [7] University graduates had no better prospects for finding employment. They soon formed an underemployed intellectual proletariat that looked to National Socialism for relief and status.

The electoral ascendancy of the Nazi party in the four years between 1928 and 1932 constitutes one of the most dramatic increments of votes and political power in the history of electoral democracy. In the Reichstag elections of May 20, 1928, the National Socialists received 810,127 votes, constituting 2.6 per cent of the total vote and 12 Reichstag seats. In the communal elections of 1929 the Nazis made decisive gains. With this election Germany had its first Nazi minister in Thuringia in the person of Wilhelm Frick, a putschist of 1923. In the next Reichstag elections of September 14, 1930, the National Socialists obtained 6,379,672 votes, for 18.3 per cent of the total and 107 seats. At the election of July 31, 1932, the National Socialists became the largest party in the country and in the Reichstag with 13,765,781 votes, giving them 37.4 per cent of the total vote and 230 parliamentary seats.[8]

This extremely rapid growth of Nazi power can be attributed to the participation in politics of previously inactive people and of those who were newly enfranchised because they had reached voting eligibility at 20 years of age. There were 5.7 million new voters in 1930.[9] The participation of eligible voters in elections increased from 74.6 per cent in 1928 to 81.41 per cent in 1930, and 83.9 per cent in 1932. In the elections of March 5, 1933, there were 2.5 million new voters over the previous year and voting participation rose to 88.04 per cent of the electorate.[10]

The German political sociologist, Heinrich Streifler, makes the point that not only were new, youthful voters added at each election, but there were losses from the voting rolls due to deaths that must be calculated. He shows that 3 million voters died in the period between 1928 and 1933. The increment of first-time, new voters in the same period was 6,500,000.[11]

In the elections of 1928, 3.5 million young voters who were eligible did not participate in the voting. "This," says Streifler, "is a reserve that could be mobilized to a much greater extent than the older nonvoters."[12] He goes on to suggest that these young nonvoters were more likely to be mobilized by a radical party that appealed to passions and emotions than to reason.

The Nazis made a spectacular and highly successful appeal to German youth. An official slogan of the party ran "National Socialism is the organized will of youth" (*Nationalsozialismus ist organisierter Jugendwille*). Nazi propagandists like Gregor Strasser skillfully utilized the theme of the battle of the generations. "Step down, you old ones!" (*Macht Platz, ihr Alten!*) he shouted as he invoked the names of the senior political leaders from Left to Right and associated them with the disappointments of the generation of the fathers and the deprivations of war, defeat, and revolution.

> Whether they are named Scheidemann and Wels, whether Dernburg or Koch, whether Bell and Marx, Stresemann and Riesser, whether Hergt and Westarp—they are the same men we know from the time before the war, when they failed to recognize the essentials of life for the German people; we know them from the war years, when they failed in the will to leadership and victory; we know them from the years of revolution, when they failed in character as well as in ability, in the need of an heroic hour, which, if it had found great men, would have been a great hour for the German people—who, however, became small and mean because its leading men were small and mean.[13]

"National Socialism," says Walter Laqueur, the historian of the German youth movement, "came to power as the party of youth."[14] The Nazi party's ideology and organization coincided with those of the elitist and antidemocratic elements of the German youth movement. The Wandervögel, while essentially nonpolitical, retreated to a rustic life on the moors, heaths, and forests where they cultivated the bonds of group life. The Nazi emphasis on a mystical union of blood and soil, of *Volk*, nation, language, and culture, appealed to the romanticism of German youth *Bünde*.

The Hitler Youth adopted many of the symbols and much of the content of the German youth movement.[15] The Nazis incorporated the uniform, the Führer principle and authoritarian organization (group, tribe, *gau*), the flags and banners, the songs, and the war games of the *Bünde*.[16] The National Socialists were able to take over the youth movement with virtually no opposition. On April 15, 1933, the executive of the Grossdeutsche Jugenbund voted to integrate with the Nazi movement. On June 17, 1933, the Jugenbund was dissolved and Baldur von Schirach was appointed the supreme youth leader by Hitler.[17] . . .

There is ample evidence that this generation of German youth was more inclined toward violent and aggressive, or what psychoanalysts call "acting-out," behavior than previous generations. At this point the explanations offered for this phenomenon are inadequate in their one-dimensionality. To say that the youth craved action or that they sought comfort in the immersion in a sheltering group is to beg the question of what made this generation of German youth different from all previous generations. What unique experiences did this group of people have in their developmental years that could induce regression to infantile attitudes in adulthood? One persuasive answer lies in fusing the knowledge we have of personality functioning from psychoanalysis—the most comprehensive and dynamic theory of personality available to the social and humanistic sciences today—with the cohort theory of generational change from historical demography and with the data on the leadership and structure of the Nazi party that we have from the researches of political scientists, historians, and sociologists.

In the half century prior to World War I Germany was transformed from an agricultural to an industrial economy, and her population grew from an agriculturally self-sufficient forty million to sixty-seven million by 1913. This mounting industrial population made her increasingly dependent on the importation of foreign foodstuffs. In the decade preceding World War I, five-sixths of Germany's vegetable fats, more than half of her dairy goods, and one-third of the eggs her people consumed were imported. This inability to be self-sufficient in foodstuffs made the German population particularly susceptible to the weapon of the blockade. The civilian population began to feel the pressure of severe shortages in 1916. The winter of 1916–17 is still known as the infamous "turnip winter," in which hunger and privation became widespread experiences in Germany. Getting something to eat was the foremost concern of most people. The official food rations for the summer of 1917 were 1,000 calories per day, whereas the health ministry estimated that 2,280 calories was a subsistence minimum. From 1914 to 1918 three-quarters of a million people died of starvation in Germany.[18]

The armistice of November 11, 1918, did not bring the relief that the weary and hungry Germans anticipated. The ordeal of the previous three years was intensified into famine in the winter of 1918–19. The blockade was continued until the Germans turned over their merchant fleet to the Allies.[19] The armistice blockade was extended by the victorious Allies to include the Baltic Sea, thus cutting off trade with Scandinavia and the Baltic states.[20] Although the Allies undertook responsibility for the German food supply under Article 26 of the Armistice Agreement,[21] the first food shipment was not unloaded in Hamburg until March 26, 1919.[22] On July 11, 1919, the Allied Supreme Economic Council decided to terminate the blockade of Germany as of the next day, July 12. Unrestricted trade between the United States and Germany was resumed three days later, on July 15.[23]

The degree of German suffering under the postwar Allied blockade is a matter on which contemporary opinions differed. Some Allied diplomats and journalists charged that the German government exaggerated the plight of her people in order to increase Allied food deliveries.[24] Today the weight of the historical evidence is that there was widespread extreme hunger and malnutrition in the last three years of the war, which was intensified by the postwar blockade. We may concur with the evaluation of two American historians that "the suffering of the German children, women, and men, with the exception of farmers and rich hoarders, was greater under the continued blockade than prior to the Armistice."[25] . . .

On the grossest level the figures show a decline in the number of live births from 1,353,714 in 1915 to 926,813 in 1918. The birth rate per 1,000 population, including stillbirths, declined from 28.25 in 1913 to 14.73 in 1918. The number of deaths among the civilian population over one year old rose from 729,000 in 1914 to 1,084,000 in 1918. While there was a decline in deaths from causes related to nutrition and caloric intake, such as diabetes mellitus, alcoholism, obesity, diseases of the gastrointestinal tract, as well as a decrease in suicides, the gross mortality of the German population increased due to malnutrition, lack of heating, and consequent weakened resistance to disease. Specific causes of death that increased sharply during the war were influenza, lung infections and pneumonia, tuberculosis, diseases of the circulatory system, diphtheria, typhus, dysentery, and diseases of the urinary and reproductive organs.[26] All these diseases indicate a population whose biological ability to maintain health and to counter infection had been seriously undermined in the war years.

Upon looking at the comparative statistics for neonates and infants, we find a decline in weight and size at birth, a decline in the ability of mothers to nurse, a higher incidence of disease, particularly rickets and tuberculosis, as well as an increase in neurotic symptoms such as bed-wetting and an increment in the death rate. In the third year of the war the weight of neonates was 50 to 100 grams less at birth than before the war. In one Munich clinic in the year 1918 the females averaged 50 grams and the males 70 grams less at birth than in peacetime.[27]

During the first year of the war more mothers nursed babies and the period of breast feeding was longer than previously, but by the winter of 1915 a decline in breast feeding had set in that was to continue through 1919. This is attributed to the war work of mothers and the "prolonged malnutrition and the damaged body of the mother due to psychic insult."[28] One chemical analysis done in Berlin found a marked decline in the quantity and quality of mother's milk resulting in the retarded development of breast-fed children and a delay in their normal weight gain. Infants fed on cow's milk also received milk that was short of nutriments, butterfat, and vitamins because of the lack of feed for the milk cows and the skimming off of cream for butter production.[29] To the shortage and inferior quality of milk must be added the almost total absence of fresh vegetables and fruit, important sources of vitamins, in the diets of children during the war and postwar period.

Not only infants but small children also were materially deprived by malnutrition. By the third year of the war children in the third year of life were up to 2.2 pounds lighter than normal body weight for their age. A study comparing 300 Berlin children in 1919 with figures from 1908–09 showed that the boys were retarded in growth to the level of children 1.5 years younger, and the girls were 1.25 years behind normal.[30]

Like the infants, young children were also particularly afflicted with rickets, tuberculosis, and parasites. A medical examination of 2,154 children between 1914 and 1921 found that 39.1 per cent had rickets. Of the children in this group who fell ill between 12 and 18 months of age, 49.2 per cent had rickets. Cases of childhood miliary tuberculosis in the state of Baden rose 50 per cent after December 1918. A comparative sample of Berlin children aged three showed 8.1 per cent infected with tuberculosis in 1918; this rose to 29.9 per cent in 1919.[31]

The pattern of increased illness and death among infants and small children in Germany carried through to children of school age. Deaths of children between 5 and 15 years of age more than doubled between 1913 and 1918. Using figures for 1913 as a base of 100, the death figures for this age group in 1918 were 189.2 for boys aged 5 to 10, and 215 for boys aged 10 to 15. Among the girls the death rates for these age groups were 207.3 and 239.9 respectively.[32]

Among the leading causes of illness and death in this age group, as with the younger children, were rickets and tuberculosis. Corresponding losses in size and weight relative to age are also recorded. The medical statistics demonstrate an increased incidence among children of gastrointestinal disorders, worms, fleas, and lice. Psychological indications of stress among school children include an "enormous increase" in bed-wetting, "nervousness," and juvenile delinquency.[33]

The evidence for deprivation is supported from Allied and neutral sources. The British war correspondent Henry W. Nevinson reported from Cologne in March 1919 that tuberculosis had more than doubled among women and children and that the death rate among girls between 6 and 16 years had tripled. Because the children were so weak, school hours were reduced from seven to two hours daily. He wrote, "Although I have seen many horrible things in the world, I have seen nothing so pitiful as these rows of babies feverish from want of food, exhausted by privation to the point that their little limbs were like slender wands, their expression hopeless, and their faces full of pain."[34]

The British medical journal *Lancet* reported comparative figures derived from official German sources showing that the effect of food scarcity on the health of the German population was felt after mid-1916 but was stilled by skillful press censorship in wartime Germany. Among children from 1 to 5 years old the mortality was 50 per cent greater in 1917 than the norm of 1913. Among the children aged 5 to 15 mortality had risen 75 per cent.[35]

A tripartite commission of doctors was appointed by the medical faculties of the Netherlands, Sweden, and Norway to examine health conditions in Germany after the cessation of hostilities. This neutral medical commission found a state so deplorable that John Maynard Keynes was moved in 1920 to ask with prescience: "Who can say how much is endurable, or in what direction men will seek at last to escape from their misfortunes?"[36]. . . World War I was the first total war in history—it involved the labor and the commitment of full energies of its participant peoples as no previous war had. The men were in the armed services, but a modern war requires a major industrial plant and increased production of foodstuffs and supplies to support the armies. Yet the number of men working in industry in Germany dropped 24 per cent between 1913 and 1917. In the state of Prussia in 1917 the number of men working in plants employing over ten workers was 2,558,000, including foreigners and prisoners of war, while in 1913 the total of men employed had been 3,387,000.[37]

In Germany this meant a shift of major proportions of women from the home and domestic occupations to war work. In the state of Prussia alone the number of women engaged in industrial labor rose by 76 per cent, from 788,100 in 1913 to 1,393,000 in 1917. For Germany as a whole 1.2 million women newly joined the labor force in medium- and large-sized plants during the war. The number of women workers in the armaments industry rose from 113,750 in 1913 to 702,100 in 1917, a gain of 500 per cent. The number of women laborers who were covered under compulsory insurance laws on October 1, 1917, was 6,750,000. The increase of adult female workers in Prussia in 1917 was 80.4 per cent over 1913. The number of women railroad workers in Prussia rose from 10,000 in 1914 to 100,000 in 1918, an increase of 1,000 per cent.[38]

Another new factor in the labor force was the youthful workers. The number of adolescents aged 14 to 16 employed in chemical manufacturing increased 225 per cent between 1913 and 1917. For heavy industry the corresponding figure was 97 per cent. Many of these were young girls aged 16 to 21. This age group constituted 29 per cent of all working women.[39]

That German women were massively engaged in war work was recognized as having resulted in the neglect of Germany's war children and damage to the health of the mothers.[40] Reports came from government offices of increased injuries to children of ages 1 to 5 years due to lack of supervision.[41] S. Rudolf Steinmetz evaluates the demoralization of youth between 1914 and 1918 as an indirect consequence of the war. He ascribes to "the absence of many fathers, the war work of many mothers" the damaged morals and morality of youth.[42]

Many of the war-related phenomena under discussion were not unique to the Central European countries. The factor of a chauvinistic atmosphere of war propaganda was certainly present in all belligerent countries. The absence of the parents in wartime service was also not unique to Germany or Austria. The children of other countries involved in the war too had absent parents and were often orphaned. French and British families undoubtedly experienced the sense of fatherlessness and desertion by the mother as much as did German and Austrian families.

Two added factors, however, make the critical difference in the constellation of the child's view of the world: the absence of German and Austrian parents was coupled with extreme and persistent hunger bordering in the cities on starvation, and when the German or Austrian father returned he came in defeat and was unable to protect his family in the postwar period of unemployment and inflation. Not only was the nation defeated, but the whole political-social world was overturned. The Kaiser of Germany had fled, and the Kaiser of Austria had been deposed. Some Germans would say that the Kaiser had deserted his people, to be replaced by an insecure and highly ambivalent republic under equivocating socialist leadership. Much more than an army collapsed—an entire orientation to the state and the conduct of civic life was under assault in 1918–19. These national factors unique to Central Europe exacerbated the familial crisis of the absence of parents and made of this wartime experience a generational crisis.

Today it is widely recognized that the emotional constellation of the childhood years is decisive for the future psychological health and normality of the adult. Modern war conditions, through the long-term breakup of family life, added in some cases to a lack of essential food and shelter, and a national atmosphere highly charged with unmitigated expressions of patriotism, hatred, and violence must inevitably distort the emotional and mental development of children, for imbalance in the fulfillment of essential psychic and bodily needs in childhood results in lasting psychological malformations. . . .

More is now known than ever before about the psychological processes and fantasies of children. There is a high level of agreement among child-guidance specialists that maternal deprivation of the child has long-ranging effects on the mental health and emotional strength of the adult. The first relationship a child forms is with his mother. His attitude to the object—in the first case, the mother—is a passive, receptive one; that is, the child is narcissistic and selfish, he wishes to be given pleasure and to have his discomforts removed. A number of British psychoanalysts of what has come to be known as the "English school" have stressed the quality of destructive oral rage that is normally present in all children. This cataclysmic world-destroying rage is, of course, intensified in cases of deprivation. . . .

Psychoanalytic theory and clinical evidence tell us that prolonged absence of the father results in intensified closeness to the mother. This in turn will heighten Oedipal conflict for the son in latency. Stimulated incestuous fantasies will increase the fear of punishment for the forbidden longings. The sharpened castration anxiety of the boy left alone with his mother results in strengthened identification with the absent idealized father and in homosexual longings for him. The homosexual feelings for the distant father are a love for him shared with the mother and a defense against heightened incestuous feelings for her.

The emancipation of women, which was accelerated greatly in World War I by the needs of a total war economy, gave to women what had been traditionally men's vocational roles and familial responsibilities. In such circumstances, in her own eyes and in the eyes of her children, the woman who works in industry and agriculture is now doing "man's" work. Thus the mother who manages the affairs of the family may acquire a "phallic" or masculine image to her children. As she is not accustomed to bearing the full responsibility for the family welfare and discipline, she might tend to become anxious. This anxiety is further exacerbated by her sexual and emotional frustration and concern for her husband. Anxieties of all kinds are immediately and inevitably communicated to children, who then become anxious as well. In her uncertainty a mother will often be more punitive than she would be under normal circumstances, both to ward off her own sexual feelings and because of anxiety about her role as disciplinarian. This heightens the passive masochism and castration anxiety in young boys.

Boys who become homosexuals are often those who were left alone with their mothers and formed an intense attachment to them that was unmediated by the father's presence and protection. The struggle against feminine identification and the regression to narcissistic object choice—that is, choosing someone who is like himself, what he was, or what he would like to be—are all greatly intensified in boys raised without fathers.[43]

If early separation and deprivation damages the frustration tolerance and reality-testing functions of children, we must look at the process of the political socialization and political-fantasy formation of normal children. Research in the field of children's concepts of politics, political leadership, and national identity indicates that many of the primary identifications of a lifetime are already formed by the second grade of elementary school, that is at age eight or nine. Children in elementary school develop predispositions for a political party, intense nationalistic chauvinism of a "we are good, they are bad" variety, and positive affectual attachment to symbols of patriotism such as the flag or the Statue of Liberty. "Affect," David O. Sears points out, "precedes information. Children express strong positive affect toward leaders, and only later acquire supporting rationalizations."[44] Familiarity with high leaders is practically at adult levels by the second grade. In Fred Greenstein's sample, 96 per cent of American children aged nine knew who the president was.[45] In Robert D. Hess's study 95 per cent of the children aged seven through nine recognized and correctly identified the president. A similarly high level of recognition was found for the national leaders in studies done in Chile, Japan, and Australia.[46]

Children tend to idealize the president and to personalize the government—that is, they see it in terms of the person of the leader rather than as an institution in which people play roles. The extent to which children exaggerate the personal power and charisma of the leader is impressive. He has God-like qualities in the child's imagery. Eighty-six per cent of second graders see the president of the United States as "running the country";[47] 76 per cent of second graders think that the president makes the laws.[48] The president is viewed by children as benevolent and protective, powerful and strong.[49] In a study of 366 children in Chicago, 60 per cent of the second graders felt that the president is "the best person in the world."[50]

The mentality of a state of war complements the child's most archaic psychic mechanisms for coping with himself and the world, the devices of splitting and projection. Splitting is what a people at war does by dividing the world into "good" and "bad" countries, those on our side who have only virtues and whom we love, and the enemy who is evil and whom we hate. We are thus enabled to get pleasure by gratifying our aggressive feelings. For the child, too, there are two kinds of men, one "good" and one "bad." In wartime the absent father-soldier is idealized. He is glorified and any hostile feelings toward him are projected onto the evil enemy on the other side. . . .

We must seek the widest possible type and range of clinical material, cultural documentation, and quantitative statistical data in our quest for historical evidence. This essay will present three bodies of historical materials, some from each of these categories of data: comparative, qualitative, and quantitative. All varieties of historical evidence have an important and complementary function in generating new hypotheses, contributing new insight, and demarking future areas for exploration.

Psychoanalytical interest was directed at the war generation almost contemporaneously with the events. As early as 1919 Paul Federn interpreted the psychological dimensions of the postwar strikes and the soldiers' and workers' councils that sprang up throughout Central Europe.[51] He viewed the loss of the national father figure, the Kaiser, who could no longer satisfy infantile fantasies of a father who is omnipotently powerful, wise, and strong, who offers absolute security and protection, as the traumatic psychological event of the war. Now the Kaisers of Germany and Austria were deprived of land, throne, power, and the ability to offer a feeling of security. Thus a fatherless society was created that no longer stood in awe of the state. For some sons of the state, Federn suggested, the disappointment came during the war when their leaders and army officers made irresponsible and sometimes impossible demands that condemned them to death. The soldiers' and workers' councils were seen as an attempt to establish a nonpatriarchal social order, a brotherhood to replace the defeated father. Such a situation is unstable, however. Federn in March 1919—the date is worth noting for it was the zenith of republicanism in Europe—predicts the demise of the republic in Central Europe and a turn to dictatorship on the psychological grounds of prevailing family patterns and man's desire to be dominated. The fatherless society will not succeed. "Among those who have now freed themselves of the social father-son relationship, the tendency toward it still remains so strong, that they only wait for a suitable newly appearing personality who embodies their father ideal, in order to again relate as a son to him."[52]

A study such as the present one, which attempts to assess the impact on children of a catastrophe like a war, should use the best clinical observations in comparative historical situations when these are available. If wartime deprivation has profound emotional effects on young children, these effects should not be limited to one time and place in the modern world. The findings in Germany should also be evident in another industrial land and for other twentieth-century wars, such as for England in World War II.

The British experience is especially valuable to the historian who would consider the emotional effect of war on children because many English children were evacuated from their homes and families in London and the other big cities during World War II, and they were helped through this trying experience by the expert guidance of such specialists in the psychology of children as Anna Freud, Dorothy T. Burlingham, and D. W. Winnicott. These psychoanalysts carried out close residential observation of the evacuated children and published detailed studies of the children's responses and adaptations to the breakup of families in wartime. These were "normal" children, they were not hospitalized, nor were they juvenile offenders. They were not so heavily traumatized by their experience that their regressive defenses resisted all modification, as is the case with most of the children who survived concentration camps.[53] The blitzed English children were provided with a homelike environment and encouraged in every way toward normal development. The fact that they were out of their homes and away from their families provides a degree of objectivity to the observations. The data were not filtered through reports of the parents; they are first-hand observations by trained professionals.

Anna Freud and Burlingham found that while a child will accept mother substitutes in the absence of its own mother, "there is . . . no father substitute who can fill the place which is left empty by the child's own father." "The infant's emotional relationship to its father begins later in life than that of its mother," they write, "but certainly from the second year onward it is an integral part of its emotional life and a necessary ingredient in the complex forces which work towards the formation of its character and its personality." [54]

The researchers found that absent parents were greatly idealized. Their letters were carried around and had to be read to the children innumerable times.[55] When the father was away in the armed services he was spoken of by his child in terms of endearment and admiration. Especially children who were in reality rejected or disappointed by their fathers formed passionate, loving, and admiring relationships to them. When a child had never known his father he would invent an idealized fantasy father who sanctioned his forbidden greedy and destructive wishes, who loved him and gave him security. [56]

When a father came home on leave, however, and thereby encroached on the existing close mother-child relationship, he was met with resentment and hostility by the child. The father was viewed as an intruder who separated the mother and son. One little boy said: "Do write to my Daddy, I don't want him to come here. I don't want to have lunch with him. Somebody else can have my Daddy." [57] But the same son and his father were best of friends when they were left alone without the mother.

When in some cases the ultimate disaster struck, Anna Freud and Burlingham report a complete inability of the children to accept their father's death. All the orphaned children talked about their dead fathers as if they were still alive. They denied the fact of death with fantasies of the father's rebirth and return from heaven. [58]

The most original psychoanalytical approach to National Socialist youth, and the one that I find conceptually most perceptive and useful, is Martin Wangh's excellent analysis of 1964.[59] He structures the psychodynamics of the First World War German children who came to the age of political effectiveness with the rise of Hitler with precision and insight. A preoccupation with guilt, Wangh points out, is also an unrecognized self-reproach for unresolved aggression against the father. Aggression toward the absent father-rival is expressed in gleeful ideas concerning his degradation and defeat. But the hostility is coupled with a longing for the idealized father that exacerbates childish homosexual wishes. These homosexual longings offer a way out of the Oedipal conflict that is heightened for sons left alone with their mothers. In these circumstances the woman is often rejected, and the incestuous wish is ascribed to someone else. These mental defenses, Wangh suggests, were renewed in the Nazi movement's deification of the Führer and its infernalization of the Jew. Homosexual tension was relieved through submission to an all-powerful leader, through turning women into "breeders" of children, and by persecuting Jews as "incestuous criminals" and "defilers of the race." The passive-masochistic inclinations that develop when boys are brought up and disciplined by mothers who are anxious and punitive may be defended against by preference for submission to a man, as this is less threatening and less castrating than submission to a woman. Self-humiliation and self-contempt were displaced onto the Jews and other supposedly inferior people, thereby assuaging feelings of unworthiness and masochistic fantasies of rejection. Since the former wartime enemies were for the time being unassailable, the Jew, who was defenseless and available, became by the mechanism of displacement the victim of those who needed a target for regressive action.

This line of research has been carried on to the contemporary problem of the children of World War II.[60] Herman Roskamp, in a clinical study of German university students born during the Second World War, emphasizes the conflict between the child's perception of the father during the war as a highly idealized fantasy object bearing his ideas of omnipotence and the way in which the father was perceived on his return in defeat.[61] While away the father had been honored and admired; he was the object of extreme hopes and expectations upon his return. It quickly became apparent that he was not what had been longed for. Instead he was a defeated, insecure father breaking into a heretofore fatherless family. Up to this time the mother had represented all aspects of reality. The father, by contrast, was now a demanding rival who left most wishes unfulfilled, who disappointed many hopes, and who set many limits where formerly there had been none.

Among the richest sources for the expression of the experience of young Germans during the war and postwar years is the literature of the period, which more than held its place amid the cultural fecundity of the Weimar epoch. Sometimes literary expression can capture for historians the essence of a generation's experience both graphically and with a depth of emotional subtlety that cannot be statistically comprehended or documented. It is possible to see, identify, and demonstrate father identification and castration anxiety without necessarily being able to computerize them. This is the appeal to the historian of both clinical insight and literary sensibility. Can one measure or compare quantitatively, for example, the degree of suffering, mourning, loss, or rage a subject feels? For this kind of emotional evidence we must rely on that most sensitive of our cultural materials—the subjective written word of literature.

When this has been said, it is nevertheless astonishing to experience the great autobiographical pacifist novel *Jahrgang 1902* by Ernst Glaeser (1902–63), which describes the author's feelings with such intensity and pathos that it often reads more like the free associations of a patient in psychoanalysis than a novel. The critic William Soskin ranked *Jahrgang 1902* with *Sergeant Grisha* and *All Quiet on the Western Front* as one of the most significant works on the First World War. [62] This book ran through six German printings during the winter of 1928–29. It sold seventy thousand copies in Germany and was translated into twenty-five languages.

The book takes its title from the year of the author's birth, which also automatically became the year of his military-service class. The class of 1902 was not to experience the war of 1914–18 on the front.[63] For that they were too young, but as Glaeser pointedly noted, "The war did not establish a moratorium on puberty." The book, he said, deals with "the tragedy of murdered minds and souls and diseased temperaments in the noncombatant social body."

As the war began the fathers left to join their regiments and the twelve-year-old boy observes that "life in our town became quieter." The boys played war games in which the French and Russians were always soundly beaten. [64] The fathers were sorely missed. They were quickly idealized and glorified. Glaeser describes the process of overestimation and identification with the father who is absent at war:

> We thought only of our fathers in these days. Overnight they had become heroes. . . . We loved our fathers with a new sublime love. As ideals. And just as we formerly used to express our admiration for the Homeric heroes or the figures of the Wars of Liberation by token symbols of clothing such as golden helmets of tin foil or Lutzow caps, so we now also began, but in far greater measure, to turn ourselves symbolically into the idealized figures of our fathers. [65]

The boys of the village went to the barber to have their hair cut in the close-cropped military style like their fathers.

> We had our hair cut. Bare. Smooth. Three millimeters high. For this is how we had seen it on our fathers as they left for the front. None of them had hair to part now.
>
> One evening late in September a group of fifteen determined

> boys went to the barber. We stood according to height and let the instrument pass over our heads. As the barber was sweeping up our hair with a broom an hour later, he said: "Now you look like recruits."
>
> We were proud of this distinction and enthusiastically paid 40 pfennings each.[66]

By the winter of 1916 the privation of the war began to be felt in the daily lives of the boys. They were always hungry. There was never enough to eat. The steady diet of turnip soup became inedible. City folk bribed and bartered away precious possessions in order to get nourishing food from the farmers. The mother gave Kathinka, the maid, one of her finest blouses so that she would bring back food when she visited her peasant parents. Faithfully Kathinka smuggled butter past the gendarmes in her woolen bloomers. Field gendarmes and controllers appeared on the roads and at the stations to search travelers for contraband foodstuffs. The children developed tactics for deceiving the gendarmes and smuggling forbidden foodstuffs home. One boy would serve as a decoy to draw the gendarme's attention while the other raced home across the fields with a sack of flour or a ham.[67]

This progression within two years from idealism to hunger and the struggle for survival is vividly described by Glaeser.

> The winter remained hard until the end. The war began to burst over the fronts and to strike the people. Hunger destroyed our unity; in the families children stole each other's rations. . . . Soon the women who stood in gray lines in front of the shops talked more about the hunger of their children than of the death of their husbands. The sensations of war had been altered.
>
> A new front existed. It was held by women. The enemies were the entente of field gendarmes and uncompromising guards. Every smuggled pound of butter, every sack of potatoes gleefully secreted by night was celebrated in the families with the same enthusiasm as the victories of the armies two years earlier. . . . It was wonderful and inspiring to outwit the gendarmes and after successfully triumphing to be honored by one's mother as a hero.[68]

Oedipal longings were heightened for the sons left alone with their mothers during years of war. Starvation led to the mobilization of unconscious wishes for a return to the oral comforts of early mother-child units. Occasionally the prolonged hunger was broken by feasting on an illegally slaughtered pig or a smuggled goose that the father sent home from the eastern front. Then an orgy of feeding took place. Gluttony reigned and undernourished bellies got sick on the rich food.

The windows had to be stuffed to keep the neighbors from smelling the meat. The adolescent boy and his mother consumed almost an entire twelve-pound goose in one night. A stolen drumstick for his girlfriend was to her the convincing symbol of love. Glaeser writes, "We scarcely spoke of the war any more, we only spoke of hunger. Our mothers were closer to us than our fathers."[69]

The fathers were not present to shield the sons from maternal seduction. One young adolescent in the novel is seduced by a motherly farmer's wife with the promise of a large ham. But, much as the pangs of his stomach and his mother's pleading letters argued for bringing the ham home, he could not do it. The great succulent ham had become an incestuous object. He had earned it from the farm wife by taking her husband's place. Now he was too guilty and too anxious to permit himself and his family to enjoy it. The pangs of guilt were stronger than the pains of hunger. As if he could "undo" his Oedipal crime, the boy laid the ham on the farm wife's bed and left. He was tearful and depressed, feelings he rationalized as being due to his injured feelings because he was really only a substitute (*Ersatz*) for the husband. He climbed into bed with his boy comrade. In the stillness of the dawn they embraced, keeping each other warm, and he shared his story of seduction and sexual discovery.[70] In this episode we see fully elaborated the heightened Oedipal conflict when the father is absent, the increased guilt and fear of retribution, and finally the rejection of the woman as a sexual object and an exacerbation of adolescent homosexuality arising from the emotional effects of the war.

By the winter of 1917 the fathers had become aliens to their sons. But they were not only unknown men, they were feared and threatening strangers who claimed rights and control over the lives of their sons. They had become distant but powerful figures who could punish and exact a terrible price for disobedience and transgressions. Glaeser recounts his reaction as a fifteen-year-old to a letter from his father on the Russian front in terms of intense castration anxiety. The adolescent boy's Oedipal victory in having displaced his father would now be terribly expiated and revenged by a towering, castrating monster of his guilt-laden fantasies. Glaeser attempts to deny that his father has any legitimate claim to control over him at all. But his father would know where to find him and the inevitable retribution would be inexorable.

> We were frightened. That was the voice of the front. That was the voice of those men who formerly were once our fathers, who now, however, removed from us for years, were strangers before us, fearsome, huge, overpowering, casting dark shadows, oppressive as a monument. What did they still know of us? They knew

where we lived, but they no longer knew what we looked like and thought.[71]

It is of biographical interest for the thesis of this essay that Glaeser went into emigration from Germany after 1933, living in Prague, Zurich, and Paris. In Zurich in 1939 he wrote a newspaper article condoning Hitler's policies and condemning his fellow emigres. Within days he received a contract from a Berlin publisher. He returned to Germany and joined the war effort, becoming a war reporter for the Luftwaffe and the editor of the military newspaper, *Adler im Süden.*[72]

Thus, as did so many others of his cohort, Glaeser was two decades later to choose to wear a uniform and to identify with his distant and glorified father. The identification with the father who went out to war served to erase the memory of the feared and hated strange father who came home in defeat. By being a patriot and submitting to authority, the ambivalence of the young boy who gleefully observed his father's humiliating defeat and degradation was denied and expiated. Now he would do obeisance to an idealized but remote leader who was deified and untouchable. . . .

The third variety of data I wish to examine is quantitative. It is a series of autobiographical essays collected in 1934 by Theodore Abel, a sociologist at Columbia University, in an essay contest offering cash prizes for "the best personal life history of an adherent of the Hitler movement."[73]

These nearly six hundred essays constitute a valuable historical source. In the first place it is a contemporary source. No set of interviews of ex-Nazis thirty-seven years later could possibly elicit the same material. The Abel autobiographies may be utilized, not as a statistical sample for generalizations, but as bases for theory building. They will serve as a cognitive prism for drawing attention to necessary variables of political behavior rather than as a monolithic statistical sample that can produce conclusive findings for the population of the Nazi party. They can tell us, however, what excited and stimulated the writers, what preoccupied their fantasies and imaginations, how they viewed themselves, their childhoods and homes, and their enemies. These data can then become referents for further theoretical conceptualization and behavioral model building, particularly with respect to emotional connotations that are not censored by the writers because they appear to be apolitical and therefore unimportant.

The most striking emotional affect expressed in the Abel autobiographies are the adult memories of intense hunger and privation from childhood. A party member who was a child of the war years recollects, "Sometimes I had to scurry around eight to ten hours

—occasionly at night—to procure a few potatoes or a bit of butter. Carrots and beets, previously considered fit only for cattle, came to be table luxuries."[74] . . .

A study of the Abel autobiographies focused on a sample from the birth cohorts 1911 to 1915, who were small children during the war, indicates the presence of the defensive mechanisms of projection, displacement, low frustration tolerance, and the search for an idealized father. For example, the essays of two sisters born in 1913 and 1915, whose father fell in 1915, clearly demonstrate that Hitler served as an idealized father figure for them. Their earliest memories are of their mother crying a great deal and of all the people wearing black. They relate their excitement at first hearing the Führer speak in person at a rally in Kassel in 1931. The sisters were so exhilarated that neither of them could sleep all night. They prayed for the protection of the Führer, and asked forgiveness for ever having doubted him. The sisters began their Nazi party activities by caring for and feeding SA men.[75]

Some of the men in the Abel Collection who lost their fathers early in life and were separated from their mothers especially valued the comradeship of the SA. One such man wrote, "It was wonderful to belong to the bond of comradeship of the SA. Each one stood up for the other."[76] Massive projection of ego-alien impulses is evident in many of the essays. One man says that bejeweled Jewesses tried to seduce him politically with cake.[77] Many of the SA men who engaged in street brawls and violence blamed others, such as the police and the Communists, for instigating the fighting and for persecuting them.[78] One man displays remarkable projection and displacement of his own murderous feelings toward a younger brother when he relates the death of that brother in an unnecessary operation performed by a Jewish doctor. "Since I especially loved my dead brother," he writes, "a grudge arose in me against the doctor, and this not yet comprehensible hatred increased with age to become an antagonism against everything Jewish."[79]

The demographic factors of massive health, nutritional, and material deprivation and parental absence in Central Europe during World War I should lead the historian to apply theoretical and clinical knowledge of the long-term effects of such a deprived childhood on personality. The anticipation of weakened character structure manifested in aggression, defenses of projection and displacement, and inner rage that may be mobilized by a renewed anxiety-inducing trauma in adulthood is validated in the subsequent political conduct of this cohort during the Great Depression when they joined extremist paramilitary and youth organizations and political parties. In view of these two bodies of data for which a psychoanalytic understanding of personality provides the essential linkage, it is postulated that a direct relationship existed between the deprivation German children experienced in World War I and the response of these children and adolescents to the anxieties aroused by the Great Depression of the early 1930s. This relationship is psychodynamic: the war generation had weakened egos and superegos, meaning that the members of this generation turned readily to programs based on facile solutions and violence when they met new frustrations during the depression. They then reverted to earlier phase-specific fixations in their child development marked by rage, sadism, and the defensive idealization of their absent parents, especially the father. These elements made this age cohort particularly susceptible to the appeal of a mass movement utilizing the crudest devices of projection and displacement in its ideology. Above all it prepared the young voters of Germany for submission to a total, charismatic leader.

But fantasy is always in the end less satisfying than mundane reality. Ironically, instead of finding the idealized father they, with Hitler as their leader, plunged Germany and Europe headlong into a series of deprivations many times worse than those of World War I. Thus the repetition was to seek the glory of identification with the absent soldier-father, but like all quests for a fantasied past, it had to fail. Hitler and National Socialism were so much a repetition and fulfillment of the traumatic childhoods of the generation of World War I that the attempt to undo that war and those childhoods was to become a political program. As a result the regressive illusion of nazism ended in a repetition of misery at the front and starvation at home made worse by destroyed cities, irremediable guilt, and millions of new orphans.

A return to the past is always unreal. To attempt it is the path of certain disaster. There was no glorified father who went to war and who could be recaptured in Hitler. He existed only in fantasy, and he could never be brought back in reality. There are no ideal mothers and fathers; there are only flawed human parents. Therefore, for a World War I generation seeking restitution of a lost childhood there was to be only bitter reality in the form of a psychotic charlatan who skillfully manipulated human needs and left destruction to Germany and Europe. What the youth cohort wanted was a fantasy of warmth, closeness, security, power, and love. What they re-created was a repetition of their own childhoods. They gave to their children and to Europe in greater measure precisely the traumas they had suffered as children and adolescents a quarter of a century earlier.

Notes

1. Sigmund Freud, "Introductory Lectures on Psycho-analysis" (1916-17), reprinted in *The Standard Edition of the Complete Psychological Works of Sigmund Freud,* tr. and ed. James Strachey *et al.* (London, 1953-), 16: 341. I am indebted to Martin L. Grotjahn and Lilla Veszy-Wagner for aid in locating this citation.

2. Karl Mannheim, "The Sociological Problem of Generations," in Paul Kecskemeti, ed., *Essays on the Sociology of Knowledge* (London, 1952), 276–320.

3. Ibid., 298, 304.

4. Ibid., 303, 304, 306; italics in original.

5. Ibid., 310.

6. Marc Bloch, *The Historian's Craft*, tr. Peter Putman (New York, 1953), 45–46.

7. Dieter Petzina, "Germany and the Great Depression," *Journal of Contemporary History*, 4 (1969): 59-74.

8. The Nazi vote declined to 11,737,000, or 33.1 per cent in the elections of November 6, 1932. At the last quasi-free election in Germany, on March 5, 1933, five weeks after Hitler's accession to power, the Nazi vote was 17,277,200 or 43.9 per cent. See Koppel S. Pinson, *Modern Germany: Its History and Civilization* (2d ed.; New York, 1966), 603–04.

9. I derived this figure by subtracting the total number of votes cast in 1928 (30,753,300) from the corresponding figure for 1930 (34,970,900), and adding the 1.5 million older voters who died in this period according to Arthur Dix, *Die Deutschen Reichstagwahlen 1871-1930 und die Wandlungen der Volksgliederung* (Tübingen, 1930), 36.

10. Pinson, *Modern Germany*, 603-604.

11. Heinrich Streifler, *Deutsche Wahlen in Bildern und Zahlen: Eine soziografische Studie uber die Reichstagswahlen der Weimarer Republik* (Düsseldorf, 1946), 16.

12. Ibid., 20.

13. Gregor Strasser, "Macht Platz, Ihr Alten!" speech delivered May 8, 1927, as quoted in Karl Dietrich Bracher, *Die Auflösung der Weimarer Republik: Eine Studie zum Problem des Machtverfalls in der Demokratie* (3d ed.; Villingen, Schwarzwald, 1960), 116 n.84.

14. Walter Z. Laqueur, *Young Germany: A History of the German Youth Movement* (London, 1962), 191.

15. Wilhelm Flitner, "Der Krieg und die Jugend," in Otto Baumgarten *et al.*, eds., *Geistige und Sittliche Wirkungen des Krieges in Deutschland* (Stuttgart, 1927), 292-302, 346-56.

16. Laqueur, *Young Germany*, 194; Bracher, *Die Auflösung der Weimarer Republik*, 131–32.

17. Laqueur, *Young Germany*, 200–02.

18. Karl Dietrich Erdmann, "Die Zeit der Weltkriege," in Bruno Gebhardt, ed., *Handbuch der Deutschen Geschichte* (Stuttgart, 1963), 4: 49, 77.

19. James A. Huston, "The Allied Blockade of Germany 1918-1919," *Journal of Central European Affairs*, 10 (1950): 161.

20. Erdmann, "Die Zeit der Weltkriege," 88.

21. *Der Waffenstillstand 1918-1919* (Berlin, 1928), 1: 49.

22. Huston, "Allied Blockade of Germany," 162.

23. United States Embassy, Paris, to War Trade Board, "Trade Resumption between the United States and Germany: Remaining Export Restrictions," telegram, July 15, 1919, in Suda Lorena Bane and Ralph Haswell Lutz, eds., *The Blockade of Germany after the Armistice 1918–1919: Selected Documents of the Supreme Economic Council, Superior Blockade Council, American Relief Administration and Other Wartime Organizations* (Stanford, 1942), 558–60.

24. James A. Logan, Jr., memorandum to Herbert Hoover, Mar. 6, 1919, in ibid., 184–88. See also "Food for Germany," *Daily News* (London and Manchester), Dec. 16, 1918; and John C. Van Den Veer, "The 'Hunger' Blockade: Truth about 'Starving Germany,' " *Sunday Times* (London), July 13, 1919, both quoted in ibid., 670–71, 796–98 respectively.

25. Bane and Lutz, introd. to ibid., v.

26. Dr. Roesle, "Die Geburts und Sterblichkeitsverhältnisse," in Franz Bumm, ed., *Deutschlands Gesundheitsverhältnisse unter dem Einfluss des Weltkrieges* (Stuttgart, 1928), 1: 15, 17, 25, 58.

27. L. Langstein and F. Rott, "Der Gesundheitsstand unter den Säuglingen und Kleinkindern," in ibid., 90.

28. Ibid., 91.

29. Ibid., 92.

30. Ibid., 93, 95.

31. Ibid., 99, 100, 102.

32. Dr. Stephani, "Der Gesundheitsstand unter den Schulkindern," in ibid., 117.

33. Ibid., 129, 122-23.

34. Henry W. Nevinson, "Babies 'Withering Away,' " *Daily News* (London and Manchester), Mar. 13, 1919; and his "Famine in Europe," *Nation* (New York), Mar. 8, 1919, both quoted in Bane and Lutz, *Blockade of Germany*, 731, 727, respectively. See also Nevinson's report carried as "Starving Europe" in *Herald* (London), Jan. 18, 1919, also quoted in ibid., 701.

35. "The European Food Situation," *Lancet* (London), Mar. 8, 1919, quoted in ibid., 726–27.

36. John Maynard Keynes, *The Economic Consequences of the Peace* (New York, 1920), 251.

37. Marie-Elisabeth Luders, *Das Unbekannte Heer: Frauen Kämpfen für Deutschland, 1914-1918* (Berlin, 1937), 85, 85 n.1.

38. Ibid., 84, 85, 86, 151, 151 n.1, 153 n.2.

39. Ibid., 85, 86.

40. Zunehmende Vernächlassigung der Kinder sowie wachsende gesundheitliche und sittliche Gefährdung der Arbeiterinnen waren unverkennbar. Ibid., 91.

41. Ibid., 128 n.1.

42. S. Rudolf Steinmetz, *Soziologie des Krieges* (Leipzig, 1929), 169.

43. I am indebted to Oscar Sachs for his discussion in a personal communication of the homosexual dynamics of the Nazi generation.

44. David O. Sears, "Political Behavior," *Handbook of Social Psychology* (2d ed.; Reading, Mass., 1969), 5: 415, 416.

45. Fred I. Greenstein, *Children and Politics* (New Haven, 1965), 32.

46. Robert D. Hess, "The Socialization of Attitudes toward Political Authority: Some Cross-National Comparisons," *International Social Science Journal* 25 (1963): 555.

47. Robert D. Hess and Judith V. Torney, *The Development of Political Attitudes in Children* (Chicago, 1967), 35.

48. David Easton and Jack Dennis, "The Child's Image of the Government" *Annals of the American Academy of Political and Social Sciences,* 361 (1965): 48.

49. Greenstein, *Children and Politics,* 37-42; Greenstein, "The Benevolent Leader: Children's Images of Political Authority," *American Political Science Review,* 54 (1960): 934-43.

50. Robert D. Hess and David Easton, "The Child's Image of the President," *Public Opinion Quarterly,* 24 (1960): 648-54.

51. Paul Federn, *Psychologie der Revolution—Die vaterlose Gesellschaft* (Vienna, 1919).

52. Ibid., 28.

53. Gerd Biermann, "Identitätsprobleme jüdischer Kinder und Jugendlicher in Deutschland," *Praxis der Kinderpsychologie und Kinderpsychiatric,* 13 (1964): 213-21.

54. Anna Freud and Dorothy Burlingham, *Infants without Families: The Case for and against Residential Nurseries* (New York, 1944), 102, 103, respectively.

55. Anna Freud and Burlingham, *War and Children,* 154-55.

56. Anna Freud and Burlingham, *Infants without Families,* 108, 110, 113.

57. Ibid., 111.

58. Ibid., 107.

59. Martin Wangh, "National Socialism and the Genocide of the Jews: A Psycho-Analytic Study of a Historical Event," *International Journal of Psycho-Analysis,* 45 (1964): 386-95; see also Wangh, "A Psycho-genetic Factor in the Recurrence of War," *International Journal of Psycho-Analysis,* 49 (1968): 319-23.

60. Alexander Mitscherlich, *Auf dem Weg zur Vaterlosen Gesellschaft: Ideen zur Sozialpsychologie* (Munich, 1963), tr. by Eric Mosbacher as *Society without the Father: A Contribution to Social Psychology* (London, 1969).

61. Herman Roskamp, "Über Identitätskonflikte bei im zweiten Weltkrieg

geborenen Studenten," *Psyche: Zeitschrift fur Psychoanalyse und ihre Anwendungen*, 23 (1969): 754-61.

62. William Soskin, as quoted in Stanley J. Kunitz and Howard Haycraft, eds., *Twentieth Century Authors* (New York, 1942), 540.

63. Ernst Glaeser, as quoted in Kunitz and Haycroft, *Twentieth Century Authors*, 540.

64. Ernst Glaeser, *Jahrgang 1902* (Berlin, 1929), 242, 250–58.

65. Ibid., 243.

66. Ibid.

67. Ibid., 292, 294-95.

68. Ibid., 292–93.

69. Ibid., 314, 342–44, 314. "Strange what part food now plays," noted a Hamburg educator and poet in his diary. "Every conversation turns on food. Whoever has hoarded supplies keeps it secret. Whoever gets anything hides it as if it were a crime. A pound of butter has become the object of a thousand questions and outpourings of envy. From where? from whom? how?" (Nov. 11, 1916). "Formerly, eating was a means to live, now it has become its purpose" (Dec. 18, 1917). Quoted in Ernst L. Loewenberg, "Jakob Loewenberg: Excerpts from His Diaries and Letters," *Leo Baeck Institute Yearbook*, 25 (1970): 192.

70. Glaeser, *Jahrgang 1902*, 317-21.

71. Wir erschraken. Das war die Stimme der Front. Das war die Stimme jener Männer, die früher einmal unsere Väter waren, jetzt aber, seit Jahren von uns entfrernt, fremd vor uns standen, beängstigend, gross, übermächtig, mit schweren Schatten, erdrückend wie ein Denkmal. Was wussten sie noch von uns? Sie wussten, wo wir wohnten, aber wie wir aussahen und dachten, das wussten sie nicht mehr. Ibid., 323.

72. Erich Stockhorst, *Funftausend Kopfe: Wer war was im Dritten Reich* (Bruchsal, Baden, 1967), 155.

73. Theodore Abel, *Why Hitler Came into Power: An Answer Based on the Original Life Stories of Six Hundred of His Followers* (New York, 1938). Republished as *The Nazi Movement* (New York, 1965). For the purpose of this study I have used the first edition.

74. Abel, *Why Hitler Came into Power*, 14.

75. AC, 41, 42.

76. Ibid., 96.

77. Ibid., 61.

78. Ibid., 86, 96, 206.

79. Ibid., 267.

PART FOUR

Group Processes and Historical Trends

11

Stranded in the Present

KENNETH KENISTON

Keniston speaks briefly but eloquently of the obsolescence that threatens people when the pace and rhythm of their lives falls behind the rapid socio-historical changes characteristic of American society. For the elderly or middle-aged, this asynchrony between matters biological and technological may ultimately be experienced as a loss of orienting control over personal meaning, and perhaps a loss of identity itself. For the young, it seems more and more frequently to mean a life style of presentism; a tendency to grasp desperately at whatever gratifications life today, or at least this week, has to offer. As Keniston clearly shows, the future appears to become less real as it becomes less predictable in the present, and the past loses meaning and quickly becomes remote as it seems irrelevant to the present. What remains, therefore, is only the detached present. The author's discussion of this condition demonstrates that psychohistorical analyses can have clear value for understanding contemporary society as well as events in the past.

Extremely rapid and accelerating social change as we know it today in America increasingly entails a psychological distancing of the past, a sense of the unknowability of the future, and a new emphasis on the present.

A man born in the beginning of this century has seen in his lifetime changes in the quality of life which no one in his youth could have

"Social Change and Youth in America," by Kenneth Keniston, from *Youth: Change and Challenge*, edited by Erik Erikson. © 1961 by the American Academy of Arts and Sciences, © 1963 by Basic Books, Inc., Publishers, New York. This revised version of "Social Change and Youth in America" appeared under the title "Stranded in the Present" in *Confrontation*, ed. Michael Wertheimer (Glenview, Ill.: Scott Foresman, 1970), 40–43. Reprinted by permission of the publishers.

anticipated or prepared him for. Changes that once took centuries—in outlook, in technology, in living conditions, in communications—now take less than a generation. Technological changes that were the science fiction of our parents are the commonplaces of our children—trips to the moon, television, speeds greater than sound, digital computers. And more important psychologically are less noticed but even more profound changes in the constitution of society—in the family, in sex roles, work and leisure.

The human capacity to assimilate such innovation is limited. Men can of course adjust to rapid change—that is, make an accommodation to it and go on living—but truly to assimilate it involves retaining some sense of connection with the past, understanding the relationship of one's position to one's origins and one's destinations, maintaining a sense of control over one's own life in a comprehensible universe undergoing intelligible transformations. This assimilation becomes increasingly difficult in a time like our own. Whatever is radically different from the present inevitably tends to lose its relevance.

As individuals, we often forget our former selves and are reminded of them only with a shock of unfamiliarity and strangeness. So, as members of a society, we increasingly feel a similar sense of unfamiliarity, about the not-so-distant past: the Flaming 20s, the Depression, even World War II now seem slightly unreal and certainly old-fashioned—as when we comment on how "out-of-date" the films of those recent years now seem. This "out-of-dateness" of even the very recent social past signals the psychological loss of a sense of connection with it, the *birth of a new sense of being stranded in the present.*

Concurrently, and for similar reasons, the future grows more distant. We cannot anticipate that the years ahead will be basically like the present. On the contrary, our best prediction is that the future will be unpredictably different. A majority of today's college graduates will be entering jobs that *did not exist* when they were born; extrapolating, it is easy to conclude that even more of the new jobs that will be available in another twenty years do not now exist and are in good part unimaginable.

Partly because of the characteristic American unwillingness to attempt to shape the future, but partly because the process of unguided technological change is *inherently* open and unpredictable, we cannot envisage the future in which we will live. "Tomorrow" tends to disappear as a center of relevance in our lives, for building toward the future means building toward the unknown.

What is left, of course, is the present, and all that can be enjoyed therein: "today" becomes the one rock of constancy in a shifting sea of change. Yesterday's solutions are often irrelevant to today's problems and no one can know what part of today's wisdom will remain valid tomorrow: an intensification of today results. Savings accounts go out of fashion (inflation, a symptom of social change, eats them up); and in similar fashion the traditional American postponing of present enjoyment for the sake of greater future reward is disappearing as well.

We have seen some of the varieties of this outlook among alienated students—the emphasis on sensation, sentience, and experience; the reluctance to make future commitments, the sense of temporal confusion; the extreme emphasis on the present; the choice of "realistic" and present-oriented values. But there are other manifestations of the cult of the present even among the unalienated.

The resulting cult of the present takes many forms—sometimes the raw hedonism of the spiritually demoralized; sometimes the quest for "kicks," speed, sex, and stimulants of the beats; often some variant on what I have called an aesthetic outlook.

Consider, for example, the question of families. Most unalienated young people want large families; they marry early and are prepared to work hard to make their marriages a success; they usually value family life far more than meaningful work. Families play a special role in American life today—and among the reasons for our increasing emphasis on them is that they provide a place where a man can be himself and enjoy himself *in the present*. A wife and children can be enjoyed in the here and now, and are dependent neither on traditional wisdom nor on future success. Furthermore, children constitute a link with the future that, unlike vocational commitment, will endure regardless of change.

The real token of a generation gap then, is not overt and visible rebellion against the previous generation, but a vision of parents and those of their generation as irrelevant, as merely old-fashioned or as "square."

Increasing numbers of young Americans find themselves so distant from their parents that they can neither emulate nor rebel against them. Instead, they "understand" them better than previous generations (whose fates were more interwoven with their parents) could afford to. Many young Americans feel toward their parents a sympathy, a compassion, and a pity that most of us can only feel toward that from which we feel ultimately detached; and with this sympathy goes a strong sense—an implicit realization—on the part of *both* parents *and* children that the two generations face such different life situations that the way parents conducted their lives may be neither good nor bad for their children, but simply irrelevant.

Generational discontinuity is a double problem. For one, the closest link between social history and individual history is the individual's sense of relationship to his own personal history as embodied in his parents, his ancestors, and all they come to represent to him. This sense of relationship defines an individual's sense of self as surely as does his work or his children.

But the tie between parents and children has a second and more immediately personal meaning: from his parents a child has traditionally learned the meaning of adulthood, of maleness and femaleness, of work, play, and social membership. By identifying with his parents, by internalizing their ways of doing things, by imitating their behavior, he has known how to become an adult.

The problem of identification is inevitably more complicated for young Americans. Partly because of the pace of social change, identifications must be cautious, selective, partial, and incomplete. Work changes; the skills essential to our parents no longer suffice for us: it is a rare (and usually unsuccessful) farmer or carpenter who does exactly what his father did. Women, too, know in their bones that the ways they were raised as children may not suffice for their own children, and anticipate that the fashions of childrearing will continue to swing as they have in the past.

Replacing the more total identifications of the past are ever more partial, selective, and incomplete identifications. To be able to identify with her mother at all, a modern woman must winnow what remains enduringly relevant about her mother from those qualities that are "old-fashioned"—a product of her mother's particular historical situation. In place of a few deeply admired and influential older people who determine the shape of the self, young Americans must increasingly have either none—as is the case with the alienated—or else many, with each of whom they identify partially and selectively. Both alternatives are difficult. With no exemplars, no objects of identifications, and an obdurate refusal to accept them, the result is often that perplexity, self-fragmentation, and confusion we see in alienated young men.

With an effort to select the most admirable and enduring qualities from *many* older men and women, great demands are made on the individual's abilities to choose, select, synthesize, and differentiate. These demands are by no means impossible; and many young Americans undoubtedly achieve a workable synthesis of selective identifications.

The pitfalls in selective identification are several. For one, given the historically determined requirement that in our society a young man or woman *must* repudiate his parents in at least some major ways, many young men and women conclude that they can emulate their fathers and mothers in *no* ways at all. The consequence, as we have seen in alienated youths, is a major problem concerning adult sexuality and adulthood in general.

Another mishap may come from selecting the wrong qualities to emulate. A young man who attempts to emulate, for example, that solidity and even rigidity of outlook which we all openly or secretly admire in our grandparents risks finding himself considered "old before his time" and will often be unable to adapt to the changing requirements of his society.

And most likely and common, an adolescent may admire a great many qualities in others that are extremely difficult to synthesize into a workable identity. The result is likely to be a diffusion of identity, a simultaneous admiration of incompatibles, and a resulting period of confusion, lack of sense of self, and wandering in search of some way of combining irreconcilable psychic possibilities.

In lives of the alienated we have seen writ small all of the large problems: the inability to find connections with the past and future, abrupt discontinuity between themselves and those of the previous generation, whom they resolutely refuse to admire; a failure of identification with their parents; a fruitless search for enduring and solid values. Each of these problems contributes to their unwillingness to accept the adult life offered by their society.

Other adaptations are of course more common. Despite its psychological difficulties, a commitment to change and flexibility mitigates many of the individual's anxieties about his own obsolescence, and is therefore an increasingly widespread solution. And in our current emphasis on home and family life, on do-it-yourself, home swimming pools, and recreation rooms, on art, music and sports, many Americans find ways of accenting the present to such an extent that their increasing lack of relatedness to past and future seldom troubles them.

Even the characteristic American phenomenon of "youth culture"—that is, the special ways and manners of young men and women who are too old to be considered children and too young to be considered full adults in our society—can be partly understood as a reaction away from parents (who because of their different generational position cannot fully prepare their children for modern life) toward peers who are more sensitive to the demands of the present.

The full list of such adaptations would be long, for there are few aspects of our lives which are not directly or indirectly touched by chronic social change. Such a catalogue would be out of place, for my point is that whatever these adaptations, they involve a heavy demand on the individual, that they are psychically taxing and strenuous, that they make adult life in America more trying and less rewarding.

And when such adaptations fail—as they inevitably do at times—the individual is confronted with central anxieties about his own role in personal and social history. Sometimes these anxieties have to do with the feeling of unrelatedness, of being adrift, of not being able to "catch hold" of anything or anyone in our rapidly shifting society—this is the anxiety of historical dislocation. At other times they have to do with a feeling of being left behind, or being out of date, no longer needed, inadequate to the modern world, of not being able to "catch up"—this is the anxiety of human obsolescence. In most of us these anxieties remain at the periphery of psychic vision (our adaptations work), but keeping them there makes our lives more difficult and our society less inviting.

12

The Making of a Murderer

HERMAN P. LANGNER

What makes this short study different from so many other investigations of war is the very concrete interaction it describes between major historical forces and an individual personality. The material concerns the senseless murder of an elderly Vietnamese farmer by an American combat medic. The author sees the psychological roots of this event as lying partly in the prevailing contempt of American soldiers for Vietnamese ("the gooks"). But this account of the medic's personal history reveals that the psychic origin of his action was in Iowa, not Vietnam. In killing the old farmer, the soldier was asserting his masculine identity and rebelling against his own farmer father.

"Why did they take my boy and do that to him? I raised him as a good boy and they made a murderer out of him."

This was the exclamation, recently quoted in the national news media, of the distraught mother of a boy who had allegedly participated in the senseless slaughter of defenseless men, women, and children at My Lai. It is shocking to realize that young Americans were capable of acts as extreme as murdering infants and mothers huddled together for protection. Yet it has become clear that such acts of brutality committed by our servicemen in Vietnam have not been unique. My experience as a psychiatrist stationed there substantiates this. It is the purpose of this paper to examine some of the factors that have allowed these atrocities to happen.

From *American Journal of Psychiatry* 127 (January 1971), 950-953.

I will begin with the case report of a young Navy corpsman named Bob. He was sent to me after he had made a serious suicide attempt by taking a massive overdose of morphine.

Case Report

Bob had been in Vietnam for six months and in the service for two years with an excellent record. Prior to entering the Navy he had graduated from high school in a small Iowa community where his father was a successful farmer. As a student, he was involved in 4-H and had many friends in school and the community. He was a slightly built, mild mannered, nonaggressive young man who had enlisted in the Navy to fulfill his service obligation. He had become a corpsman because he felt it fit his personality and because he wanted to help people. Following discharge from the Navy, he planned to return to Iowa to take over his father's farm.

After recovering from his acute medical condition, Bob said he had been despondent since his close friend had been killed in a fire fight several days before his suicide attempt. He expressed feelings of guilt at his friend's death and felt he should have died in his place. He did not remember wanting to commit suicide, however, and said he took the morphine while in a dreamlike state. Since Bob's condition did not improve despite ample opportunity to express his grief and guilt, an amobarbital (Amytal) interview was performed to explore further the motives of his attempted suicide.

Much to my surprise Bob had little or nothing to say about his friend while under the influence of amobarbital. Instead he immediately began describing a bloody military operation he had been involved in, during which his unit had swept through a village, killing all living things, including men, women, children, and livestock. He himself set fields of rice ablaze "with my Zippo lighter" and watched peasants shot down as they ran from their burning homes. At one point during the operation Bob came across an elderly injured farmer. When smilingly asked by one of his officers, "How are you going to treat him, Doc?" Bob shot and killed the harmless man lying at his feet.

He experienced deep guilt after this and felt he should be punished for his crime. When his friend, a fellow corpsman, was killed several weeks later, he wished he could have died in his place. While it is not uncommon for a man in combat to feel guilt when a comrade dies, the deeper origin of Bob's guilt was related to the massacre he was involved in. His friend's death was the "straw that broke the camel's back" and served as the precipitant for Bob's suicide attempt.

The most startling aspect of Bob's case, however, was not simply that he had been capable of involving himself in a massacre but that he had enjoyed doing so. For mixed with his feelings of guilt and sorrow, which were real and deep, were unmistakable indications of the fascination and even pleasure he had derived from the mayhem he had witnessed and participated in. This was the deepest source of his guilt—that he had derived pleasure from his crimes.

It should be noted that the operation Bob was involved in was at a company level. As with My Lai, however, I doubt whether direct orders to gun down defenseless men, women, and children were responsible for the brutalities committed. Certainly our soldiers knew that such a command was unlawful and under most circumstances would not have obeyed it if they basically had not wanted to. Bob, for instance, did not need much prompting to kill the harmless man at his feet. In addition, many other such brutalities were reported to me by different individuals. In these cases there was no question of orders being responsible for the acts committed. These individuals clearly killed because they wanted to. Why did they want to indulge in such blood lust?

Discussion

To begin, imagine the predicament in which the average young man sent to Vietnam finds himself. He is frequently immature and separated from the support and protection of his family for the first time. He is sent to a distant land where few have any desire to be. The climate and terrain are inhospitable almost to the point of being unendurable and are totally different from what he is accustomed to. He is subject to the daily fear of death and often sees comrades whom he has grown close to maimed or killed. The enemy he is fighting is elusive and rarely gives him an opportunity to vent his anger and frustration by open, direct combat. Finally, the cause he is fighting for is unpopular at best and has been called criminal by many respected national figures. These circumstances usually leave the soldier feeling insecure, frightened, frustrated, and angry.

The uniquely frustrating circumstances of this war have strongly influenced the type of psychiatric problems seen. "Shell shock" or "war neuroses," so common in the World Wars I and II, are infrequent in Vietnam. Problems related to poorly controlled aggression, however, are very common. These problems presented themselves in a number of different ways. Often a young man came in or was sent to me with the fear or threat of killing one of his superiors who he felt had harassed him or treated him unfairly. Others were sent to me after shooting holes through their "hootches" or throwing grenades around. On occasion such cases turned into incidents involving the indiscriminate killing of comrades. Fighting and "accidental" shootings among the men were frequent; they represented another way of discharging aggressions that were reaching unmanageable proportions. It should also be noted that many problems associated with poorly controlled aggressions were dealt with through disciplinary rather than psychiatric channels and therefore did not come to the psychiatrist's attention. During times of brisk combat when aggressions could be released, the overall number of such problems admitted to my service tended to diminish.

Another common focus of anger and aggression were the very people the young soldier had come to "protect." "The way to win this war," went a common joke, "is to load all the gooks in the South on boats, kill the ones in the North, and sink the boats." Freud noted that jokes, like dreams, frequently serve as wish fulfillments.

The reasons for such feelings are understandable. Instead of fighting for a happy and liberated population, the soldier meets sullen, suspicious people who regard him as an intruder and would rather he leave. These are supposedly the people he has come to fight and die for, and they represent the reason for all of the hardships and misery he is subjected to. Furthermore, they are at times more or less directly responsible for injuries and deaths among his ranks. Incidents of stepping on land mines or being ambushed by the enemy moments after talking to the natives of a "friendly" village who could have warned the soldier were not infrequent. The plight of the villager was such that if he informed, he would be killed by the Viet Cong. This is of little consolation to a boy who has been maimed or has seen a comrade killed under such circumstances. Often the brutalities of the South Vietnamese peasants against our soldiers were expressed with considerably less passivity. At times this reached the extreme of a mother sending her child wired with explosives to a group of soldiers to destroy the hated foreign intruders.

Consider finally that many of the barriers that prevent us from giving free reign to our aggressive impulses and thus becoming murderers in our own society are largely lacking in Vietnam. Death is common, and the value of life has become cheapened in this chronically war-torn country. There is, furthermore, a tendency to degrade the peasant, and he frequently is looked upon as being little better than an animal. Also, it is often difficult to prove who was responsible for someone's death or whether such a death was justified. In certain cases, such as Bob's, killing was made easier because it received group sanction. Under the impact of these pathological circumstances the grave moral imperative that tells us from early childhood, "Thou shalt not kill," is frequently swept away.

Yet not all of the young men sent to Vietnam end up murdering its defenseless citizens. There are obviously many reasons for this. For one thing, the conditions each of these men are exposed to can differ drastically. Some are exposed to extremes of provocation or placed in situations where killing can become relatively easy. Even at My Lai, however, where the general conditions were similar, there were great variations in response among each of the individuals involved. These varied from refusal to kill to killing with obvious enthusiasm and gusto. Such variations are determined by many complex factors. Often they relate to personal issues associated with the individual's previous life. To make this clearer, let me tell you more about Bob's background and some of the thoughts, both conscious and unconscious, that were in his mind as he killed the helpless farmer.

Bob was the son of a farmer. As a boy he often tended his father's fields. He did so obediently. In fact Bob was nonrebellious and was not prone to openly expressing his feelings. As any boy might, however, he resented the demands made upon him and frequently would rather have spent his time in play or leisure. In his fantasies he often wished the source of these demands removed or destroyed. As he grew older and more socialized, he repressed these fantasies even more deeply. Yet these feelings lingered on in the deeper realms of his unconscious. Killing the farmer and setting fire to his fields represented rebellion on Bob's part. Another boy under other circumstances might have rebelled in one of the many ways that are available in our society. Only extreme circumstances allowed these feelings to be expressed in such a direct and primitive way.

Other very personal needs were met in Bob's act. He was short and slightly built. He was the only boy among three girls. His father tended to be passive and his mother domineering. As is often the case, these circumstances produced a young man with considerable doubts about his masculinity. Killing another person represented in essence the destruction of everything he disliked about himself. He was, for one brief instant, the total dominant male.

Issues of rebellion and coming to terms with one's role as a male are not, of course, uncommon in young men. In fact, most young inductees into the armed forces are still struggling with these late adolescent issues. During this period, there is a great outpouring of instinctual energy. A young man at this stage in life is at his peak of sexual power. Late adolescence is, moreover, typified by a recklessness with one's own and other people's lives. It is an unstable and frequently precarious time, and causes of death at this age are usually violent—most frequently through accidents or by suicide. In fact the extremes of behavior seen in war—both in heroism and cruelty—are a reflection of the life of the adolescent.

Killing another person represents an extreme of behavior that holds particular fascination for the young man. The total subjugation of another human being and the implications this has for one's manhood seem to be one aspect of the fascination. At some deeper level, however, there seems to be some mingling of sexual pleasure at committing the most forbidden of all crimes. Men in combat, for instance, sometimes report distinct sexual pleasure associated with killing another person and at times experience erections on such occasions. Furthermore, in the midst of the slaughter of My Lai, some of our young American men allegedly sexually assaulted Vietnamese women; several are now being charged with rape.

Conclusions

It is the family's responsibility to raise its young to be healthy and secure adults capable of loving and caring for others. Yet society must lend its support to bring such feeling to fruition. A late adolescent about to leave the protection and support of his family unit is still very close to many of his primitive, instinctual impulses and continues to need much support before becoming an independent, mature, and settled adult. Various institutions exist to help in this task. In our society the university is beginning to take on this function in an increasingly important way. The Peace Corps is another example of such an institution.

The military, with its stringent rules, regulations, and strong institutional support, has also traditionally served as a place where a young man could mature into manhood. Its popularity or importance in doing so seems to be on the decline. Perhaps this is due to an increasingly sophisticated or changing ethic in our society. Be this as it may, the My Lai incident must certainly force us to consider the wisdom of sending young and immature men who continue to need guidance into a situation where they can become involved in the wholesale slaughter of defenseless people. In fact, as it affects the individual, sending a young man to Vietnam is in many ways the obverse of sending him into the Peace Corps. Instead of developing more noble sentiments toward the family of man, the pathological circumstances in many cases cause a type of regression in a person that stimulates those primitive and undesirable instincts that individual and collective education has attempted so assiduously to check.

Bob was in many ways an American Everyman. He was a boy from the heartland of America and represented those ideals and aspirations of youth that America has always cherished.

Under ordinary circumstances he would have expressed his aggressions and insecurities as most of the rest of us do in our daily dealings with our fellow man. The combination of these aggressions and insecurities and the pathological circumstances in Vietnam made him a murderer. It is to his credit that he suffered for this crime. He suffered to the point of demanding retribution from himself and almost succeeded in committing suicide.

On the day following the My Lai massacre, the son of the woman I previously quoted also seemed to seek retribution by stepping on a land mine. Many other young men I encountered who were involved in similar atrocities did not react with such guilt feelings. Ironically, those who suffered the most because of their involvement in these atrocities had taken most seriously those values that society works so hard to instill in us. They had been "raised as good boys."

13

Death-Profit, "Evil," and the Chinese Feminist Movement

LESLIE E. COLLINS

This previously unpublished article describes the subjugation and virtual enslavement of Chinese women who lived according to traditional Confucian values. The Confucian social order was so constructed as to define women as primary sources of evil who had to be kept in check by a rigorous, comprehensive network of repressive practices. Only on the death of her husband could a traditional Chinese woman attain any important degree of autonomy, hence the term "death-profit." Working from his fluent command of Chinese, as well as his knowledge of custom and tradition based both on personal experience in Asian communities and scholarly research, Leslie Collins elaborates upon the psychology of the Chinese women's movement as it emerged to oppose Confucian values. In this connection, he employs psychoanalytic concepts cautiously—as is necessary when dealing with non-European cultures—but to such good effect that one may see implications for Western culture, and also gain insight into contemporary events in the Chinese People's Republic.

Although the concept is not unique to China, women of that society have traditionally been regarded by men as somehow an "evil" influence, a belief which many of the women themselves came to share. They were generally considered somewhat less than human when it came to sociopolitical "rights," but (and this is only a seeming contradiction), something more than human in their power to do mischief. Even today, in Taiwan, Hong Kong, and in other large enclaves of overseas Chinese, remnants of this belief are visible.

What follows are a few speculations about the origins of the concept of woman as "evil" in China and the influences of that concept upon

China's women's movement (*fu-nu yun-tung*), which began around the turn of this century and ended with the establishment of the People's Republic of China.

As Ho Ping-ti has said, "For good or for evil, it was under the alien Manchu rule (1644–1912) that China became a strictly conformist 'orthodox' Confucian state."[1] This orthodoxy included a view of women based on the conservatism and passivity which characterized social and political relationships during the Ch'ing Dynasty. Women were seen as inferior to men, an evil influence in politics, narrow-minded, and disruptors of family harmony, whose only salvation lay in a strict training, beginning in infancy, in their duties to certain men in particular and their elders in general. Even so powerful a female as the Dowager Empress Tzu-hsi (1835–1908) is reported to have admonished those present at her deathbed never again to allow a woman to rule China, as it was "against the house-law of our Dynasty and should be strictly forbidden."[2]

Like all oppressed people, women were a threat to their male oppressors. This is implicitly recognized in various "books of female instruction" widely used during the nineteenth century. *Words for Women and Girls*, written by a Manchu official in the early 1800s, maintained that the family constituted the basis of government. Therefore, "universal" instruction of women was desirable, since without it there was a great potential for rearing "bad" citizens—that is, those who through the influence of ignorant mothers would not know the proper Confucian relationships of subject to ruler, son to father, husband to wife, brother to brother, and friend to friend. The basic assumption here was that women were by nature ignorant, narrow-minded, and mischievous, and that their influence, if left uncorrected by proper training, would corrupt the Confucian social order.

Another similar work, the *Female Instructor*, written by Lu Chao in the nineteenth century, listed three principal goals for instruction to women: obedience to husbands and parents-in-law; complaisance to husbands' brothers and sisters; and pleasantness to their sisters-in-law. It is not too much to say that the aim of such training was the suppression of a female's individuality. On the other hand, in speaking of the loss of independence in living with a mother-in-law in Singapore, Ann E. Wee comments that in spite of the strains of "fitting in," the young wife who passes the tests in obedience posed by her mother-in-law and makes these adjustments to her new family will never lack help when she or her baby is sick. Should anything call her away, she will not need to rely upon servants and strangers to care for her husband and the children.[3] But even this idealized picture of the rewards of a "traditional" marriage seems to an outsider small recompense for the submergence of self involved. As one Chinese female has observed with some bitterness, the male-oriented Confucian "moral demand on women for sacrifice is so great, so imperative, and so mortifying, that it reduces the lot of a woman to that of a mere slave; she may be patient, but she can never be happy; she may swallow tears and try to smile, but she can never produce genuine laughter."[4]

It is within the structure of orthodox Confucian wishes as they relate to women and the institution of "traditional" marriage that some of the roots of female "evil" may be found.

Death Imagery in Marriage: The Ceremony

Marriage, for males, represents a major step in the direction of assuming full sociopolitical rights within a society. For women in late traditional China (1860–1930), it meant the full assumption of duties toward a new husband (who most likely was a stranger to her), his siblings, his parents (in particular his mother), and all his agnatic ascendants.

Although taught from early childhood that she would someday have to leave the familiarity and security of her own family and enter one which was strange to her, and although trained in the behavioral and emotional responses expected of a filial daughter, the Chinese woman probably did not fully experience the psychic impact of this anticipated separation until shortly before or during her actual marriage.[5] At this time, she entered a series of *rites de passage* which signified the loss of her natal family.

Such rites were crucial to her future ability to function as a wife, since we know that at a psychological level images of separation, loss, and death are largely interchangeable,[6] and that inability to relate to or to manage such imagery leads to one or more of a variety of impairments in living. Robert Lifton gives as examples of such impairment paranoia, depression, inability to love and be loved, fascination with death, and urges to destroy oneself or others.[7] It is significant that in one of his studies, Dr. R. M. Ross of the Kerr Hospital, Canton, observed that thoughts about the death of a prospective groom played a prominent role in the fantasies of female mental patients.[8]

These marriage rites also provided for the working through of the ambivalence a Chinese woman felt at losing her natal parents, and at having been deserted by them. That is, marriage represented for the bride the symbolic "death" of her natal family. Keeping in mind the basic psychic interchangeability of images of death, separation, and loss, the bride in a sense became the survivor of that family. And as

Lifton points out, "The survivor is . . . torn by a fundamental ambivalence: [she] embraces the dead, pays homage to them and joins in various rituals to perpetuate [her] relationship to them; but [she] also pushes them away, considers them . . . dangerous and threatening."[9]

From the bride's perspective, any remaining emotional and social ties to her natal family represented a threat of gross failure in her duties as wife, daughter-in-law, and (potential) mother of a male heir who would continue her husband's surname line. Members of the composite family into which she was being married, on the other hand, viewed such ties to her natal family as "dangerous and threatening" because the potential failure of the bride to integrate fully into her new family could result in conflict. Although some observers have noted instances where marriage has not meant severance of natal ties, the prevailing pattern has been one of both emotional and physical separation.[10] Burton Pasternak relates a popular saying which he translates, "If affinals live close by, eyes will always be red; if they live far apart, each side will kill a chicken in celebration when they meet."[11] And, in commenting on the actual distance desired between a new bride and her natal family, Jean Pratt speculates that the preferred distance should be a little too far for a woman to be able to run home after disputes in her husband's family.[12] In other words, where surrounding economic and ethnic conditions permit, the family emphasis (identification) will be patrilineal, with the result that the bride is excluded from the security of close association with her natal kin.[13]

In one form of wedding ceremony, when the groom came to the bride's natal home to fetch her, he was subjected to ritualistic beating by members of the bride's family.[14] Also in ritualized fashion, the bride displayed reluctance to leave her home. It is significant that her brother carried the bride out of the house after her final obeisance to her natal ancestors, since a psychic balance was being struck, almost literally, among (1) her reluctance to be separated from her natal family and the benefits of its ancestors, (2) her anger at being "taken" from her family by the groom, (3) the necessity that her family relinquish jurisdiction and rights over her, symbolized by a family member physically removing her from her family's compound, and (4) her natal family's sense of guilt at "giving her away," symbolized by the sham beating of the groom. Here I would suggest that from the psychic perspective of members of her natal family, it was they and not the bride who were given the collective mantle of survivorship. Through the sham beating they relieved themselves of responsibility for the "death" (loss) of the daughter (sister, etc.) by making a particular person—the groom—the scapegoat. The unconscious emotional salve applied might have been experienced if not expressed in this manner: "You [groom], and not I, are responsible for this girl's loss of family and ancestors and for my guilty suffering. So I am not to blame for what has happened to her." There was possibly an even deeper message that said, "If I am not to blame for her separation from the security of our family and the beneficial influences of our ancestors, then my own position remains secure and my right to the help of my ancestors remains as before."

Another portion of wedding ceremonies especially anxiety-provoking for the bride was her final obeisance to her natal ancestors, since it signified a break in the strong cultural emphasis placed upon psychological continuity with her natal family's past. In other words, it signified the cessation of her past and her rights in her family's past. Only to the degree to which her early training in the moral obligations and duties to members of her "new" family was successful in helping to establish her as an integrated member of her husband's group, did her past remain significant for her.

At a personal psychological level, then, the bride's only hope for relinking herself to the symbolically expressed biological immortality of ancestor worship was through her own offspring's worship of her; once the break with her natal ancestors had been made, her "soul" could not return or be returned to her natal home. Her husband's responsibility to sacrifice to her was optional, but it was prescriptive that the responsibility of looking after her spiritual welfare fell solely to her children, and their children. A barren wife was not necessarily sacrificed to, except where she instituted a nephew or similar relative as an heir to her husband after his death.[15] This meant that until such time as she had children of her own or could institute a legal heir to her husband after his death, her soul was in danger of becoming a "hungry ghost," a spirit harmful to the living because it had not yet properly entered the world of the immortal dead. This adds a previously unconsidered dimension to the trepidation with which the new bride viewed marriage and the anxiety with which she endured her first years in her husband's family.

The Family as Psychological Arena

Briefly described so far are some aspects of the new bride's psychological ambivalence toward getting married—her sense of loss of kin and her sense of psychohistorical discontinuity, of having been cut off from her past and being thrust into an uncertain and symbolically mortal future. The new bride was faced with the problems of fulfilling all of the duties prescribed for her by the Confucian value system in general and expression of that value system by members of her husband's family in particular, thus obtaining veneration and care during her old age and reconnecting herself with a life after death.

While the family and clan in China were an important source of psychosocial security for their members, since they provided some measure of status by generation, age, and sex, as well as continued recognition through ancestral worship, a woman's access to this security was tenuous and qualified, based upon her ability to satisfy the demands of her husband and his relatives while at the same time maneuvering for position and power. The anxieties resulting from this situation are revealed in a 1941 psychiatric survey of approximately 2,500 patients of the Peiping (Peking) Municipal Hospital from 1933 to 1938, done by Bingham Dai, who observed that while the problem of making a living seemed to cause the most strain to the male patients, to the female patients the most perplexing problem was how to adjust to family situations, especially in dealing with their husbands and in-laws.[16] The previously mentioned study by Ross reported that in addition to thoughts about the death of prospective grooms, female patients were concerned about struggles between wives and concubines, mistreatment by mothers-in-law, and fears by barren wives that their husbands would take a concubine.[17]

In addition to uncertainty about psychological and material security within her "new" family, the new wife frequently faced open hostility and oppression. In her study of clan rules, Wang Liu Hui-chen comments that, "The roles of women . . . are indispensable to family harmony and solidarity. Control over married women aims at their proper adjustment, the lack of which . . . leads to domestic troubles and even a decline of the [patrilineal] family prosperity and prestige."[18]

The same clan ideology, however, also advocated a wife's adherence to ritual propriety, kindness to other family members in carrying out her respective duties to them, and encouragement of family harmony as antidotes to the wife's own "selfish" interests and those of her husband and children. This advocacy amounts to a rather open recognition of the manipulative power of the wife and her conjugal unit. In fact, the most frequently censured behaviors of a wife by clans seem to have been "usurping the roles of her husband," "lack of filial piety toward parents-in-law," and "discord with sisters-in-law."[19]

By manipulating her husband, a wife could more effectively, if not more openly, challenge the intrafamilial influence of her sisters-in-law and their husbands. By fomenting trouble with her sisters-in-law, she could cause friction between her husband and his brothers, which might well lead to a partition of the family and its property. By being disrespectful to her parents-in-law, she could increase the probability of fragmenting the extended family and forcing division of the estate into separate households. According to traditional Confucian values such a split was disastrous, since it was believed that a family divided had no hope of attaining prosperity. [20]

Of course, belief and fact frequently diverged. What is important, however, is that the traditional Chinese clan rules did not take into account that they largely limited hopes of family prosperity to the efforts of a single sex (male), and that, consequently, clans and individual families were forced to expend great amounts of time and energy in excluding females from access to power. Women with power, especially those who wielded it too openly, were always a threat to the ideological base of male supremacy within Chinese society, and thus to the foundations of male identity.

Briefly, then, it would seem that social norms governing a wife's behavior were aimed at (1) preventing her if possible from attaining a personal base of power within the composite family, and (2) muting any source of influence which might be formed. Yet it has been argued that familial conflict was based on the relationships between "a man and his father and brothers" and that the man's wife was merely a convenient scapegoat. Why would a woman want to cause mischief within a family already hostile to her and very much in control of her future?

One answer to this question lies in the nature of female-to-female relationships within a family, particularly between the wife and her mother-in-law.

Gamble's study of Ting Hsien, a rural community in northern China, contains an informative chapter on "Yang Ke and Other Recreation." *Yang-ke* ("planting songs") were actually popular plays put on by local troops of actors, some of which depicted the relationship of mother-in-law to daughter-in-law. Gamble's description is worth quoting:

> In some cases the wife may be sent away, not by the wish of her husband, but at the order of her mother-in-law. The son sacrifices his wife rather than be unfilial. Some plays show the husband having the power to sell his wife.
>
> When a girl marries, she leaves her own family and becomes a member of her husband's family. His mother has complete power over her daughter-in-law. . . . The mother-in-law is inclined never to allow her daughter-in-law to do anything that she has never done or to enjoy anything she has never enjoyed. As a result a daughter-in-law is generally depicted as hoping that her mother-in-law will die very soon so that she may be mistress of the house. And she wants to treat her daughter-in-law in the same way that she has been treated. [21]

Although the plays did not apparently show an ascended daughter-in-law as being kinder to *her* daughter-in-law than her mother-in-law had been to her when she was in the subservient position, perhaps the point was made if the play had comedic overtones. However, the plays had a "literary quality" and depicted rural life or "life as the country people would like to have it,"[22] in which case the "lesson" of the play would have been to show that by outlasting her mother-in-law, a daughter-in-law could "get even" with society by treating her daughter-in-law as she herself had been treated.

The psychological process involved appears to be "identification with the oppressor"; that is, dealing with the residual image of an awesome and fear-inspiring mother-in-law by becoming like her after her death.[23] In this connection the socially sanctioned "reward" for having been oppressed would be the chance to enjoy being an oppressor. The result was, of course, that women would perpetuate the negative image ascribed to them by men, and would in fact have to accept it for themselves.

Another crucial relationship for the in-married woman was that which existed between herself and other women of the same age-sex status. As one Chinese woman expressed it, "I could manage with the old lady all right; after all, she's getting on in years and we owe her respect. But when I think of my sisters-in-law, I get wild; we are the same generation, why should they always be interfering and making trouble?"[24]

The sisters-in-law referred to could be the wives of the speaker's husband's brothers or his unmarried female siblings. In any event, quarrels between their children, squabbles over favoritism by the mother-in-law, arguments over sharing household duties — the number of sources of conflict among the younger women was endless.

Freedman has pointed out that in composite families where there was more than one son, fissive pressures between brothers were frequently expressed through their wives' bickering over matters involving their respective children.[25] But wives could also have a positive interest in fomenting rivalry between their husbands in the hopes of being able to establish an independent conjugal family unit. They could *use* disputes between their respective children (especially male children) to exacerbate existing tensions or to create them. In terms of the wife's legal rights, it was via the removal of the grandparents and the husband, by death *or by the establishment of a separate family unit,* that a woman became the only ascendent to her son, and that her rights over him were completely activated.[26] That is, by causing the split of her conjugal unit from the composite family she removed herself from the control of her husband's parents. In addition, by removing her children from the extended family unit, the daughter-in-law removed objects of affection from the grandparents and eliminated competition for control over them, particularly over grandsons. After the split, her area of autonomous action was potentially greatly increased.

This increase of autonomous behavior was only potential, however, since it was in part dependent upon the quality of the mother's relationship with her son. In order to assess the importance of this relationship to the mother, however, we must first examine the importence of "having a son."

It is not surprising—in a society as patrilineally oriented as that of late traditional China—that all children sired by a man belong to him by law. Even a child born of adultery by a wife belonged to the adulterer. [27]

According to traditional Confucian ethics, the gravest of unfilial acts a woman could commit was failure to provide her husband and his parents with a son, since only males could care for the souls of ancestors with prescriptive certainty, thus insuring their symbolic immortality and preserving family members' sense of their own historical continuity. Although her legal status as a wife was not seriously threatened, a young wife's social status was marginal until she produced a son. Without a son, her chances for future power and influence within the family were typically reduced. And her own self-image would suffer through her sense of intense personal failure.

Since the prosperity of the family was assumed to be partially dependent upon the cooperation of male members and since a "similarity of dispositions" was an assumed natural characteristic of maleness, any disruption in the family or failure to provide heirs could easily be blamed upon the "narrow-minded" and "evil" nature of women in general and upon the barren wife in particular. Moreover, any attempts by her to resist the family's bringing in a son via a concubine would be seen by family members as compounding both sins, and not as an attempt to grasp or cling to security within her husband's group.

Comment already has been made on the personal conflict expressed by female mental patients in relation to a husband's taking a concubine or a second wife. Just as intimacy between husband and wife brought about by children could set up pressures for the conjugal group to separate from the composite family, so too the children of a concubine, and the resulting intimacy between the concubine and the husband, tended to isolate the wife from the conjugal group, regardless of the legal status of the children as the wife's legal heirs. The children of a concubine represented an avenue of affection, and thus security, away from the wife, even though upon her husband's death she had managerial rights over the children.[28] Moreover, for the concubine a possible avenue to power within the family, at the wife's expense, was through the manipulation of her sons into the good graces of the boys' grandparents. And should the wife later bear sons, any favors bestowed upon the sons of a concubine to even the partial exclusion of those of the legal wife would be cause for conflict.

In short, the failure of a young wife, while not an unmitigated disaster, nonetheless represented to her a massive personal failure. And while she legally had managerial rights over any sons by concubines and was due the formal respect of motherhood, she still could not control the affection of her husband nor his and his parents' gratitude toward the female who *had* provided an heir.

From the wife's point of view, it was through her son and on his behalf (in terms of "orthodox" values) that she could enter into more and more of the major decisions of the family. Should she have lacked male offspring, the family could have brought in a second wife or concubine, which would have threatened her position and further rise in family status and power. Assuming this test had been passed, however, how did the relationship of a mother to her son influence her personal chances for advancement within the family hierarchy?

Marion Levy, in discussing the father-daughter relationship, suggests that in the informal intimacy which often characterized the father-daughter relationship in gentry families, the father found some relaxation from his rigorously maintained role of strict and remote disciplinarian.[29] And as Margery Wolf observes in relation to "Taiwanese" children, "Fathers who used to be affectionate become distant, with a tendency to lecture . . . when their sons reach the age of 'reason' (4–6 years), fathers must withdraw to become dignified disciplinarians."[30] The mother took over the function of providing informal intimacy and affection for her sons, while the father, presumably because daughters were believed to be less important to the future prosperity of the family, did so for daughters. This situation quickly put the mother into a position of serving as a buffer between the wrongdoings of a son and the strict punishment meted out by his father should he be found out. The warmth and gratification of infancy had added to them feelings of gratitude for the protection which the mother offered. While one may agree with Wolf that for a son to fail his father induced shame before society, but to fail his mother had a much more painful psychological effect, and to achieve this control a mother had to "*compromise her husband's relationship with his sons,*" emphasis should also be placed on filiality as the basis for the father-son relationship.[31]

Thus the mother, in controlling the emotional ties of her sons, also controlled the threat of alienation of the sons from their father, and therefore the potential prosperity of the family. [32]

The unvoiced threat of alientating the sons from their father may in part explain the husband's fear of his wife's influence over him—fear expressed in terms of condemnation of women generally (with the exception of *his* mother) and of his wife in particular. By subverting the filial basis of the relationship of the son to his father, she also brought into question the *degree* to which the sons would honor their father in death, whether they would fulfill their mourning obligations to him with the minimum amount of expense and ceremony they could get by with, or raise his postmortem status, both within the community of the living and that of the dead, by a show of great solemnity and expense on those occasions where a show of respect was called for. In this fashion, the wife, with the (initially) unwitting complicity of her son(s), influenced her husband's access to an honorable and comfortable life after death.

A mother's use of her sons in this manner, however necessary to her survival and possible advancement within the ranks of her husband's group, ran directly counter to one of the most fundamental ideological tenets of orthodox Confucianism: the filial basis of a son's relationship to his father, and by extension, that of a subject to his ruler. In short, her manipulation of the bonds of affection of her son effectively put an in-married female in a position of considerable influence over family prestige and prosperity.

This brings into focus another aspect of the mother-in-law/daughter-in-law relationship. Since it was through her manipulation of the bonds of affection between herself and her son, in addition to the clan-prescribed limited jurisdiction over him, that a mother would have secured much of her power, any interloper (e.g., a daughter-in-law) constituted a direct threat to a habitual avenue of familial influence. His marriage meant the potential loss both of family power through decreased ability to manipulate him and of affection from him as his loyalties were transferred to a too-pleasing (from the mother-in-law's viewpoint) wife, and whatever family she should be able to provide him. Also, the marriage of one of her sons introduced an economic threat to the mother-in-law, since the wife could in the name of her children, like the mother-in-law herself, hold property and therefore achieve some measure of economic independence while reducing the mother-in-law's pool of resources. It should be remembered, however, that although the daughter-in-law presented a threat to her through the loss of her son's affection, the mother-in-law, on the basis of filial responsibilities, could maintain control over the daughter-in-law.

With advancing age a woman gained increased influence and the generally higher status given the elderly. Additionally, once a woman was past fifty, the disruptive potential of sexual misconduct was popularly believed to be considerably reduced.[33] Consequently, one possible source of female disruption of family harmony and loss of family prestige was thought to be eliminated.

In China, as in many other societies, wives tended to outlive their husbands. What happened, then, to a wife-mother upon the death of her husband? It was believed that a widow, if poor enough, could return to her natal group. But while this group had responsibilities for her material welfare, they were not caretakers of her soul, for her soul and soul tablet could not be returned to her natal family. Care for her in the afterlife had to be arranged for within the boundaries of her own conjugal unit. Her husband's obligation to sacrifice to her was optional, but the obligation of her children was mandatory.

If a husband and wife had established a separate conjugal unit prior to his death, the wife's control over their property could not be influenced by meddling parents-in-law. A widow could also contract for her own remarriage without interference from parents-in-law if she and her husband had split from the extended family. Thus, while such a break from the extended family was considered reprehensible according to clan ideology and more general orthodox Confucian values, there was every reason for the wife to push for just such an occurrence. With this contradiction between clan ideology and individual influence, it is small wonder that one of the ideological inputs toward family and clan cohesiveness was the belief that paternal blood relationship formed natural dispositionary bonds *exclusively* among male members.

For male members of the society death may well have been symbolized as Max Gluckman describes it—"an attack on the society of living men for it wrenches and dislocates their relationships with one another; and once it has gained a foothold, they fear it may not be content with a single victim."[34] In China, there was the additional (unconscious) awareness that with the death of a man, there usually was a woman who profited by that death through increased control over other males. With the death of her parents-in-law or their effective "removal" by the establishment of a separate household, she could exercise increased influence over her husband. With his death she gained control over her sons and their property holdings.

Death generally transforms someone who was a source of pleasure or satisfaction into a source of pain; but for the wife in late traditional Chinese society, though the death of a man may have removed a source of affection, it also removed a source of obligation and oppression. The possible exception was the death of a son, which could be met with unambiguous grief, since for a widowed mother, the death of a son meant a loss of a source of affection and status, without the compensation of profit (potential or actual) for her.

Only after succeeding her parents-in-law and her husband and maintaining control over her sons and their wives (frequently through *their* husbands—her sons) could the Chinese female dare to express herself openly and with relative impunity.

Consequently, married women in late traditional China were locked into a social structure characterized by what can be termed a system of "death-profit." This means that for Chinese women, death could, within the social system in which both men and women lived, be advantageous. And while men exacted the price of supremacy by having women be dependent upon them, they were ultimately the victims of that dependency. Thus, women were perceived as "evil" precisely because they were not always victims of death, but profited by its existence: the death of men often worked to the personal advantage of women.

Death-Profit and Social Change

From the 1860s, the scope of change in China rapidly grew more extensive. It ranged from the acquisition of linguistic skills (the vernacular or *pai-hua* movement)[35] to education to politics. The content of education moved from orthodox Confucianism toward an increasing mixture of "Western learning" and revitalized domestic concepts. The desirable forms of political institutions were altered from that of a sage "Son of Heaven" supported by an enlightened Confucian bureaucracy toward that of a Western-oriented popular republic. In 1905, the governmental Confucian examinations were abolished; in 1911, the Manchu regime was overthrown. And China's search for a "new" nationhood, uniquely Chinese and visibly equal or superior to that of other nations, continues even today.

Given these trends, one might expect that women would be interested in modifying the death-profit system and their consequent "evil" status in order to escape from the hold of survivor guilt.[36] Men would be interested in modifying the system in order to cease being "victims" of female dependency. Just one example of such interest on the part of female reformers comes from Lien Shih, an early feminist, in an editorial for the *China New Women's Journal* (*Chung-kuo hsin nu-chieh tsa-chih*). She points directly to the debilitating influence of the traditional training which women received and to the difficulty of eliminating it. "The habit of [sexual] inequality, the oppression and hardships which harm women's bodies . . . [are] almost impossible to eliminate . . . because there is no independent life (*tu-li te sheng-huo*) [for women], men's energies will be squandered from them. . . ."[37] The implication is that whether men know it or not, they pay a price for their dominance over women in the form of the burden of female economic and social dependency. Women in turn pay one of the many prices of dependency—that of being the self-denigrating, passive-aggressive, universal "kept" woman. Lien Shih comments:

> It does not matter if a nation is large or small in area . . . nor does the size of its population matter; [in all cases] women make up half of a nation's population . . . if we keep women in the Dark Ages, even though our men be very civilized, then our nation must still be considered only half civilized. Moreover, if women remain in this Dark Age, *there is no way in which men may become* [*truly*] *civilized.*[38]

In addition to the obvious appeal for "civilized" action on the part of Chinese males, there is in this statement the implicit recognition of women's power to affect the plans of men, i.e., women's ability to keep men from achieving the Western enlightenment which they believed would save them from territorial dismemberment and cultural dissolution.

In a subsequent article, this same feminist presents a parable in the form of a dream in which she is taken on a tour of a Chinese *Inferno* by a guide named "History." They come upon the "River of Blood and Sweat," which flows with the blood, sweat, and tears of thousands of years of suffering women. While standing on its shore, "History" tells her that with each passing decade the health of women worsens and that before long women may perish altogether. "We talked about the main cause [of this situation] . . . it was oppression of women. Hearing "History" say so much, my face flushed and blanched, my heart was in agony. I was angered, filled with hatred and anxious. My brain was on fire . . . my body encased in ice . . . There were so many questions I wanted to ask, but not one word would come out."[39]

One can speculate that the conflict expressed by Lien Shih—her hatred of the system of female oppression and the men who supposedly benefitted from it on the one hand, and her anxiety on the other (the conflict of "fire" and "ice") represented an inability to admit into consciousness the self-betrayal of having been and being oppressed. And there is ample evidence to show that this was not an isolated instance.[40]

However, with the crumbling of traditional "orthodox" Confucian values, recognition of self-betrayal did not lead to hopelessness in women. For example, in 1933, two school teachers made the following observation: "We, as school teachers, often visit the parents of students. Every mother seems to say, 'I am blind and am of no use to the world, but I want to send my daughter to school and let her have an equal opportunity with her brother no matter what it costs me.' "[41] Those mothers mentioned are the ones who adapted to the traditional system; they were the "good" wives and mothers of their day. But although they may have been aware of how the system would finally affect them, they nonetheless saw a more independent and autonomous future for their daughters. As another female writer of the time put it:

> If women are to be equal to men . . . then they must have the spirit to act as humans and have the reason of humans. This spirit and reason are both worldly enterprises. They must be learned; they are not innate. If they were innate, would not every one be as Yao and Hsun [sage and wise]? . . . From ancient times to today, where there have been women of note, their learning could not but have been great, their determination high, and their ability vast. . . ."[42]

Clearly, one of the goals of educating women was simply to compete and cooperate with men on an equal basis. But more than this, there was the desire for a rejuvenated female "spirit"—freedom from the mentally restricting constraints placed upon women by a largely discredited set of orthodox Confucian values, of which the system of female death-profit formed a major part.

Notes

1. Ho Ping-ti, "The Significance of the Ch'ing Period in Chinese History," in Joseph R. Levenson (ed.), *Modern China: An Interpretive Anthology* (London, The Macmillan Company, 1971), p. 22.
2. J.O.P Bland and E. Backhouse, *China Under the Empress Dowager* (Peking, Henri Veeth, 1939), p. 414.
3. Ann E. Wee, "Chinese Women of Singapore: Their Present Status in the Family and in Marriage," in Barbara E. Ward (ed.), *Women in the New Asia* (Paris, UNESCO, 1963), p. 381.
4. Sophia Chen Zen, *Symposium on Chinese Culture* (Shanghai, China Council of the Institute of Pacific Relations, 1931), p. 312.
5. Wang Liu Huei-chen, *The Traditional Chinese Clan Rules*, Monograph of the Association for Asian Studies, VII (1959), 49–50. "Filial piety . . . (is) a self-control by which children respect their parents with deep, voluntary, and lasting affection. . . . Emotionally, it is a feeling of both warmth and solemnity. . . . A (child) should revere his parent *not because he has to, but because he*

wants to." Emphasis added. Also, for reasons which will be discussed later, the abstract, generalized "Chinese woman" mentioned here should be considered as belonging to the middle or upper classes, and not to the majority peasant class.

6. Freud was first to examine these relationships. More recent investigators include Melanie Klein, John Bowlby, and Robert Jay Lifton, though Lifton "rather than emphasize the principle of separation or 'separation anxiety' as the basic emotion involved in what we call fear of death, . . . [takes] the reverse position that these are subsumed by more fundamental imagery around life, death, and survival—imagery unique to man as a symbolizer with knowledge of his own death." Robert Lifton, *Death in Life* (New York, Random House, 1967), pp. 485-486.

7. Ibid., pp. 479-541.

8. Herbert Lamson, *Social Pathology in China* (Shanghai, The Commercial Press, 1935), p. 423.

9. Lifton, p. 493.

10. See Maurice Freedman, *Chinese Family and Marriage in Singapore* (London, Colonial Research Studies, No. 20, 1957), p. 76 on Singapore; and Burton Pasternak, *Kinship and Community in Two Chinese Villages* (Stanford, Stanford University Press, 1972), p. 73 on a village in Taiwan, for instances where marriage has not meant severance of natal ties. For the prevailing pattern, see Pasternak, pp. 82–84; C. K. Yang, *A Chinese Village in Early Communist Transition* (Cambridge, Massachusetts Institute of Technology Press, 1959), pp. 26, 83-85; Jean A. Pratt, "Emigration and Unilineal Descent Groups: A Study of Marriage in a Hakka Village in the New Territories, Hong Kong," *Eastern Anthropologist*, 13 (1960), 147-58; and Maurice Freedman, "Ritual Aspects of Chinese Kinship and Marriage," in Maurice Freedman (ed.), *Family and Kinship in Chinese Society* (Stanford, Stanford University Press, 1970), p. 184.

11. Pasternak, p. 82.

12. Pratt, p. 152.

13. Carrie Chu Brown, "The Position of a Wife in Late Traditional China," Unpublished M.A. Thesis, Cornell University Ref. no. 1404, 1966, p. 26.

14. Much of the data on marriage ceremony cited here comes from a study of a Chinese survey of Ch'ing Dynasty customs (*The Survey of Customs,* or *Min shang shih hsi kuan t'iao ch'a pao kau lu*, Nanking, 1930), done by Carrie Chu Brown, *op. cit.*

15. Brown, p. 35.

16. Bingham Dai, "Personality Problems in Chinese Culture," *American Sociological Review*, 6 (1941), 692–693.

17. Lamson, p. 423.

18. Wang Liu, p. 47. See Pasternak, pp. 60–94, for a detailed discussion of a contemporary example of the relationship of family "harmony" to land holdings and corporate lineage prosperity.

19. Wang Liu, pp. 85-86.

20. It is doubtful, however, that a wife could do this without the support of her husband, which might be forthcoming if she already had fomented sufficient friction between her husband and his brothers or his parents to make family fission seem desirable. Of course, friction also could arise between her husband and other family members without the wife's active participation.

21. Sidney D. Gamble, *Ting Hsien: A North China Rural Community* (Stanford, Stanford University Press, 1954), p. 332–333.

22. Ibid., p. 333.

23. I do not use the more standard phrase "identification with the *aggressor*," since an assumption on the part of a daughter-in-law of aggressive behavior similar to that which a mother-in-law could exercise (e.g., verbal tongue-lashings, beating, confinement to quarters, reduced food rations, etc.) would have constituted an *open* defiance of one of her husband's parents. And this was grounds for disaffiliation of the daughter-in-law from the family. Too, keeping in mind that the potential transgressions of a daughter-in-law were many, punishment could extend from a formal tongue-lashing by the clan head before members of the lineage to local governmental punishment (e.g., beating with a bamboo rod). See Wang Liu, p. 88.

24. Wee, p. 382.

25. Maurice Freedman, *Lineage Organization in Southeastern China* (London, Athlone, 1958), p. 22.

26. Brown, p. 44.

27. The precise reference is *The Ch'ing Code* (*Ta Ch'ing lu li tseng hsiu t'ung chi ch'eng*), 1878, 33:1, as cited in Brown, p. 15.

28. Giving as her source *The Ch'ing Code*, Brown, p. 15, states that, "On the death of a man, his wife exercises managerial rights over his property before his sons reach majority, and a son born of a concubine is under the authority of the legal mother."

29. Marion Levy, *The Family Revolution in Modern China* (Cambridge, Harvard University Press, 1949), p. 181.

30. Margery Wolf, *Women and the Family in Rural Taiwan* (Stanford, Stanford University Press, 1972), p. 67.

31. Ibid., p. 160. Emphasis added. Wee, p. 398, describes one of the long term effects of Chinese mothers upon their sons (the adult search for early infant security) in the following somewhat amusing example: "Mr. Tan started life as a labourer . . . by the time of the post-war boom [W.W. II] he was . . . a well-to-do citizen. . . . His first wife was already dead . . . but from her photo on the wall it was clear that she had been a plain and homespun creature. The household was presided over by the second Mrs. Tan, English-educated and an excellent housewife. . . . Also in the household was Mrs. Tan number three, who had been a manual worker in a factory controlled by her husband. Adenoidal and with protruding teeth, she exhibited no grace, poise, or any apparent charm, while her raucous speaking voice operated in perpetual fortissimo. And yet, when she got a little home of her own it was there that Mr. Tan spent most of his time. . . . Ladies-in-the-know . . . commented, 'when he was coming up 'number two' suited him very nicely; she could entertain and her English was quite an advantage,

while he knows not a word. But he probably never felt quite easy with her; number three is much more his type, just like his mother and sisters, the sort of woman he's used to.' "

32. See page 269 for the believed relationship between family unity and prosperity.

33. Females were considered "safe" prior to puberty and after the age of fifty. The plethora of stories about free-wheeling old matrons, however, indicates that once past fifty, the sexual interest of elderly women did not necessarily abate. Interviews with women in Taiwan and Hong Kong have convinced me that such behavior is tolerated, with some amusement, by younger members of the family, and that objections are likely to be raised only if and when it appears that "the old lady's" paramour might economically benefit from the relationship, or if the relationship excessively saps the family's funds. Such occurrences are apparently rare.

34. Max Gluckman, *Politics, Law and Ritual in Tribal Society* (Chicago, Aldine, 1965), p. 8.

35. The *pai-hua* movement was, in part, an attempt on the part of a number of Western-trained or influenced reformers to bring the written form of the language into closer correspondence with the spoken form.

36. Lifton, p. 539, states that, "The survivor cannot formulate from a void. [She] requires the psychological existence of a past as well as a present, of the dead as well as the living. Without these neither mastery of [her] death encounter *nor a place in human society* is possible." Emphasis added. The point is that both China's past and its present were being challenged and defeated by foreign cultures; for those who saw China's history as corrupt and outmoded and its present domestic and international situations as intolerably "weak," only the future remained.

37. Lien Shih, "Impartial Discussion of Women's Rights," (Nu-ch'uan p'ing-i), *The China New Women's Journal* (*Chung-kuo hsin nu-chieh tsa-chih*), March, 1907, p. 1, Tokyo.

38. Ibid., pp. 2–3.

39. Lien Shih, "This Journal's Views on Women's National Duty," (*Pen-pao tui-yu nu-tzu kuo-min-chuan chih yen-shuo*), *The China New Women's Journal*, March, 1907, p. 21, Tokyo.

40. Chinese women's journals written during the first two decades of this century, such as *The Women's World* (*Nu-tzu shih-chieh*), *The China Women's Journal* (*Chung-kuo nu-pao*), *The China Women's Magazine* (*Shen-chou nu-pao*), *The Journal of Women's Studies* (*Nu-hsueh pao*), etc., are filled with articles by women attributing to themselves and their sisters (*nu-t'ung-pao*) "special qualities" (viciousness, resoluteness, moral purity, and so on) which will permit them to *surpass* their male oppressors.

41. G. Fan and S. S. Djang, "Chinese Women and Education," *Women of the Pacific*, Third Conference, Pan-Pacific Women's Association (Honolulu, Pan-Pacific Union, 1933), p. 38.

42. P'ei Kung, "What is Needed for Equality Between Men and Women" (*Nan-nu p'ing-teng te pi-yao*), *The China New Women's Journal*, March, 1907, pp. 35–36. Tokyo.

14

Violence without Moral Restraint: Reflections on the Dehumanization of Victims and Victimizers

HERBERT C. KELMAN

This paper was given by the author as his Kurt Lewin Memorial Address to the Society for the Psychological Study of Social Issues in 1973. It is informed by the new concern with historical perspectives which is now becoming prevalent in social psychology. Kelman's statements—particularly the thesis that conditions weakening moral restraints against violence may be more important than individual motives inspiring people toward violence—emphasize the historical foundation of many social phenomena. His subsequent discussion of these conditions provides a good critical review of relevant knowledge in contemporary social science and also points the way to the kind of integration between historical understanding and research on group processes that may be anticipated in the future.

The Problem of Violence

My interest in the problem of violence . . . [is] an interest in the study of war and peace, of nationalism and militarism, of nonviolent approaches to social change and conflict resolution. But within this broader context the questions raised by the Nazi Holocaust aimed at the systematic destruction of the Jewish people have confronted me most profoundly and persistently. They have special meaning for me because, as a Jew

From *Journal of Social Issues* 29 (1973), 25-61. © Society for the Psychological Study of Social Issues. Reprinted by permission of the author and publisher.

Author's Note: This paper was prepared while the author was a Visiting Fellow at the Battelle Seattle Research Center. I am very grateful to Rose Kelman and Donald Warwick for their comments on the paper.

brought up in Vienna, who managed to get out of Nazi Austria a year after the Anschluss and then to get out of Belgium a few weeks before the Nazi invasion, and who lost countless relatives and childhood friends to the gas chambers and the execution squads, I am only a step removed from the category of Holocaust "survivor," although I would not presume to arrogate to myself the authority of true survivors—those who survived the Holocaust in death camps or in hiding within Nazi territory.

The attempts at genocide, of which the Holocaust is the most extreme and grotesque but by no means the only recent manifestation, represent a profound challenge to our thinking about human nature and human society—from both a moral and a sociopsychological point of view. Indeed, I would argue, it is the most profound challenge of our century, but one with which we have barely begun to grapple. Explanations that remain entirely at the psychological level of analysis or invoke a single overarching psychological principle are less than helpful. Social-psychological or psychohistorical perspectives, however, as several diverse writings have demonstrated (Arendt, 1963; Sanford, Comstock, & Associates, 1971; Kren & Rappoport, 1972; Lifton, 1973), can contribute some of the pieces to what is necessarily a multifaceted quest for understanding, and can throw some light on the question of "how such things are possible." I see my own reflections as a modest and incomplete contribution to such an effort. I do not pretend that I have any answers; all I hope is to develop some of the terms within which questions can be formulated.

Characteristics of sanctioned massacres

My focus is on a class of violent acts that can be described as sanctioned massacres. I am speaking of indiscriminate, ruthless, and often systematic mass violence, carried out by military or paramilitary personnel while engaged in officially sanctioned campaigns, and directed at defenseless and unresisting civilians, including old men, women, and children. Though occurring in the course of officially sanctioned activities, the massacres themselves may or may not be specifically sanctioned. The larger context is usually, though not necessarily, an international or civil war, a revolutionary or secessionist struggle, a colonial or ethnic conflict, a change or consolidation of political power. The Nazi atrocities against the Jews and the U.S. atrocities against the Indochinese people are prime examples of the kind of mass violence I have in mind, but numerous other cases would clearly fit the description. Within American history, My Lai had its precursors in the Philippine War around the turn of the century (Schirmer, 1971), not to speak of the Indian massacres. Elsewhere in the world, one recalls the massacres and deportations of Armenians, the liquidation of the kulaks and the great purges in the Soviet Union, and more recently the massacres in Indonesia and Bangladesh, in Biafra and Burundi, in South Africa and Mozambique. . . .

It should also be pointed out that the different examples of violence that clearly fall within my definition are by no means entirely equivalent to one another. They may vary on a number of important dimensions. For example, the context of counterinsurgency warfare waged by a high-technology society against low-technology societies, as in the case of U.S. actions in Indochina, provides a unique set of atrocity-producing conditions (see Falk, 1972; also Lifton, 1973, p. 41), in contrast to those situations in which there are no differences in level of technology or in which such differences are less marked. Another important distinction is between massacres that are part of a deliberate policy aiming to exterminate a category of people, and those that are inevitable by-products of a policy which is not aimed at extermination but which contemplates and plans the destruction of vast population groups as a means toward other ends, such as counterinsurgency or consolidation of power. Probably the most extreme example of the former type of situation is the Nazis' "final solution" for European Jewry, in which a policy aimed at exterminating millions of people was consciously articulated and executed (see Levinson, 1973), in which such extermination was an end in itself, and in which the extermination was accomplished on a mass-production basis through the literal establishment of a well-organized, efficient death industry. United States policies in Indochina exemplify the second type of situation. Though I feel that there is overwhelming evidence that the United States has committed monstrous war crimes and crimes against humanity in Indochina (Sheehan, 1971; Browning & Forman, 1972) in pursuit of a policy that considered the Vietnamese population entirely expendable, the evidence does not suggest that extermination has been the conscious purpose of the policy. These various differences may have important moral as well as sociopsychological implications. For present purposes, however, I do not intend to dwell on such differences, but to discuss at a much more general level the common features shared by the entire class of sanctioned massacres.

The question for the social psychologist is: What are the conditions under which normal people become capable of planning, ordering, committing, or condoning acts of mass violence of this kind? Before attempting to answer this question, we must examine the special characteristics of this class of violent acts, as compared to other kinds of violence, particularly other kinds of organized violence (recognizing throughout that there are continuities between the different forms of organized violence and that no sharp line can be drawn between them). Two special features characterize this class of violence, relating to its context and its target.

The context of violence. The sanctioned massacres that we are dealing with here occur in the context of an overall policy that is genocidal in character, in the sense that it is designed to destroy all or part of a category of people defined in ethnic, national, racial, religious, or other terms. In line with the distinctions that I have already drawn, such a policy may be deliberately aimed at the systematic extermination of a population group as an end in itself, as was the case with the Nazi destruction of European Jewry. Alternatively, the policy may be aimed at an objective other than extermination—such as the pacification of the rural population of South Vietnam, as in the case of U.S. policy in Indochina—but may include the deliberate decimation of large segments of a population as an acceptable means to that end. I am not qualified to judge whether U.S. actions in Vietnam constitute genocide in the legal terms of the U.N. Convention on Genocide, but they can be said to have at least a genocidal dimension. Central to U.S. strategy in South Vietnam were such actions as unrestricted air and artillery bombardments of peasant hamlets, search-and-destroy missions by ground troops, crop denial programs, and mass deportation of rural populations. These actions (and similar actions in Laos and Cambodia) have been clearly and deliberately aimed at civilian populations, and have resulted in the death, injury, and uprooting of large numbers of that population and in the destruction of their countryside, their source of livelihood, and their social structure. These consequences have been known to the policy makers and indeed intended as part of their pacification effort; the actions were designed to clear the countryside in order to bring the rural population under control and to deprive the guerrillas of their base of operation. Thus, while extermination of the civilian population was not the end of the policy, the physical destruction of large numbers of the population and the destruction of their way of life were regarded as acceptable means. Massacres of the kind that occurred in My Lai were not deliberately planned, but they took place in an atmosphere that made it quite clear that the civilian population was expendable and that actions resulting in the indiscriminate killing of civilians were central to the strategy of the war.

The target of violence. A second feature of the class of violence under discussion is that it is directed at groups that have not themselves threatened or engaged in hostile actions toward the perpetrators of the violence. Usually, the targets of massacres belong to groups that are physically weaker than their victimizers (although massacres are often directed at minorities that may be economically more advanced than the masses of the population within which they live). By definition, the victims of this class of violence are defenseless civilians, including old men, women, and children. There are, of course, historical and situational reasons why a particular group becomes a suitable target for massacres. In this sense, it can perhaps be said that the victims provoke the violence by what they are. It cannot, however, be said, in any objectively meaningful sense, that they provoke the violence against them by what they have done. They are not being murdered because they have harmed, oppressed, or threatened their attackers. Rather, their selection as targets for massacre at a particular time can ultimately be traced to their relationship to the pursuit of larger policies. They may be targeted because their elimination is seen as a useful tool or because their continued existence is seen as an irritating obstacle in the execution of policy.

The genocidal context of this class of violence and the fact that it is directed at a target that did not provoke the violence through its own actions has some definite implications for the psychological environment within which sanctioned massacres occur. It is an environment that seems almost totally devoid of those conditions that people usually see as providing at least some degree of moral justification for violence. Neither the reason for the violence nor its purpose is of the kind that people would normally consider justifiable.

The most widely accepted justification for violence is that it occurred for reasons of self-defense against attack or the threat of attack. When this reason is extended to the international level, it may refer not only to threats to the physical existence of a nation, but also to threats to its basic values or its vital national interests. Similarly, violence—both at the interpersonal and at the intergroup level—is often seen as morally justified when it occurs in response to oppression or other forms of strong provocation. There is even a tradition that justifies violence in the face of symbolic harm, as evidenced by leniency toward the perpetrators of crimes of passion. In all of these cases, the violence is provoked by actions that cause harm or threaten harm to the perpetrator of the violence, and it is directed at the source of this provocation. Violence under these conditions—particularly organized violence in the form of warfare—is not seen as morally acceptable by everyone and at all times. People may disagree in principle about the precise point at which they would draw the line between justifiable and unjustifiable reasons for violence; in any given case, they may disagree about the justification for violence because of differences in their assessment of the nature of the provocation and the probable consequences of the response. Nevertheless, most people would agree that violence in self-defense or in response to oppression and other forms of strong provocation is at least within the realm of moral discourse; even those who consider violence unjustifiable under such conditions—in general or in any given case —would acknowledge that there is room for legitimate disagreement among moral people on this score. By contrast, violence of the kind that I have described as sanctioned massacres is entirely outside of the realm of moral discourse, in that it does not occur in response to those conditions that are normally accepted as partial or complete justification for violence.

Moral justification for violence depends not only on its reasons but also on its purposes. Again, self-defense presents the purest case. If a violent response clearly blocks an act of aggression, if by taking the life of an attacker you save your own life or the lives of other potential victims, then most people would regard it as morally justifiable. As one moves away from this rather clearcut case, particularly into the area of organized violence, the issues become much more complicated and moral consensus more difficult to attain. Nevertheless, moral justification for violence usually depends on the extent to which it is seen as serving a defensive purpose, even though that term may be given a rather broad definition. Thus the use of violence by police or troops in the control of riots or the suppression of rebellions is often considered justified even though it may lead to the killing of some innocent bystanders, but only to the extent to which it is necessary to contain the rioters or rebels. Indiscriminate or purely punitive violence would generally be considered unacceptable in this case. In the case of warfare, these considerations are written into international law. Although the rules of warfare are quite permissive even with regard to the killing of civilians, they do impose some definite limits. The degree and kind of violence used must be justified by considerations of "military necessity" (i.e., as steps required for the purpose of defeating the enemy) and the targeting of civilian populations is prohibited outright. In short, the moral justification for violence depends on the extent to which it is related to the purpose of stopping aggression or neutralizing a threat toward one's self or his group. Once again, sanctioned massacres—which are designed to destroy entire segments of a population—occur in the absence of a condition that is normally considered to provide some degree of moral justification for violence.

Whether or not the conditions for moral justification are totally absent in a given case may be subject to different interpretations. In the case of U.S. actions in Vietnam, for example, it may be argued that the killing of civilians in My Lai and elsewhere did involve a legitimate element of self-defense, since women and children were known to help the guerrillas, hiding hand grenades under their clothes. Similarly, it may be argued that air and artillery bombardments against peasant hamlets had a legitimate military purpose, in that guerrillas often used these hamlets as their bases of operation. Even if one grants these possibilities, however, and puts aside the question of what U.S. troops were doing in Vietnam in the first place, it seems clear that the destructiveness of the response was far out of proportion to the conditions that might have justified it. The quantitative relationship between provocation and response and that between ends and means each have an important bearing on the moral evaluation of the action.

I have been saying that the class of violence under discussion here differs from other types of violence in that the conditions that usually provide moral justification for violent acts are absent. This is not to say, however, that those who participate—actively or passively—in these violent acts regard them as unjustified. They may either find various justifications for them or—for various reasons to which I shall return later—fail to see the need for justification (Ball-Rokeach, 1972; Hallie, 1971). The important point is that the conditions that most people, including the perpetrators of the violence themselves, would normally regard as crucial for the moral justification of violent actions are absent in these situations. Moreover, the absence of these conditions is quite apparent to most outside observers, who are not themselves caught up in the machinery of the sanctioned massacres. These objective circumstances set the framework within which psychological analysis must proceed.

Driving forces toward violence

In searching for a psychological explanation of mass violence under conditions lacking the usual kinds of moral justification for violence, the first inclination is to look for forces that might impel people toward such murderous acts. Can we identify in these massacre situations psychological forces so powerful that they outweigh the moral restraints that would normally inhibit unjustifiable violence?

One approach would be to look for psychological dispositions within those who perpetrate these acts. This approach, however, does not offer a satisfactory explanation of the phenomenon, although it may tell us something about the types of individuals who are most readily recruited for participation in such massacres. Any explanation that has recourse to the presence of strong sadistic impulses is obviously inadequate. There is no evidence to support the notion that the majority of those who participate in these killings, in one or another way, are sadistically inclined. Speaking, for example, of the men who participated in the Nazi slaughters, Arendt (1963) points out that they "were not sadists or killers by nature; on the contrary, a systematic effort was made to weed out all those who derived physical pleasure from what they did" (p. 93). To be sure, some of the commanders and guards of concentration camps could clearly be described as sadists, but what has to be explained is the existence of concentration camps in which these individuals could give play to their sadistic fantasies. These opportunities were provided with the participation of large numbers of individuals to whom the label of sadist could not be applied. Moreover, it should also be noted that much of the sadistic behavior observed in massacre situations can be understood most readily as a consequence of participation in mass violence with its dehumanizing impact, rather than as a motivating force for it.

A more sophisticated type of dispositional approach would be one that seeks to identify certain characterological themes that are dominant within a given culture. An early example of such an approach is Fromm's (1941) analysis of the appeals of Nazism in terms of the prevalence of sadomasochistic strivings, particularly among the German lower middle class. Such an approach may be very helpful in explaining the recruitment of participants in sanctioned massacres in a given society, the specific form that these massacres take, and the ideological support for them. It would be important to explore whether similar kinds of characterological dispositions can be identified in the very wide range of cultural contexts in which sanctioned massacres have occurred. However general such dispositions turn out to be, it seems most likely that they represent states of readiness to participate in sanctioned massacres when the opportunity arises, rather than major motivating forces in their own right. Similarly, high levels of frustration within a population are probably facilitators rather than instigators of sanctioned massacres, since there does not seem to be a clear relationship between the societal level of frustration and the occurrence of such violence. Such a view would be consistent with much of the recent thinking on the relationship between frustration and aggression (see, for example, Bandura, 1973).

Another approach to identifying psychological forces directing people toward violence that are so powerful that they outweigh the moral restraints that would normally inhibit such violence is to examine the relationship between the perpetrators and the targets of the violence.

Could the class of violence under discussion here be traced to an inordinately intense hatred toward those against whom the violence is directed? The evidence does not seem to support such an interpretation. Indications are that many of the men who actively participated in the extermination of European Jews, such as Adolf Eichmann (see Arendt, 1963), did not feel any passionate hatred against Jews. One of the striking characteristics of the Nazi program, in fact, is the passionless, businesslike way in which it was carried out. There is certainly no reason to believe that those who planned and executed American policy in Vietnam felt a profound hatred against the Vietnamese population. There is no question, in both cases, that the perpetrators of the violence had considerable contempt for their victims, but the desire to injure and annihilate them was not uniformly high.

Because of the incongruity between the actions and the accompanying emotions in this class of mass violence, I originally referred to it as violence without hostility. The more I thought about it, however, the more I realized that this was a misleading designation, because hatred and rage do play a significant role in sanctioned massacres. Typically, there is a long history of profound hatred against the groups targeted for violence, which helps to establish them as suitable victims. This would hold true for the Jews in Christian Europe, for the Chinese in Southeast Asia, and for the Ibos in Northern Nigeria. There is no such history in the relationship between Americans and Vietnamese, but attitudes toward the Vietnamese were readily assimilated to a racist orientation that has deep roots in American history. Hostility also plays an important part at the point at which the killings are actually carried out, even if the official planning and the bureaucratic preparations that ultimately lead to this point are carried out in a passionless and businesslike atmosphere. For example, Lifton's (1973) descriptions of My Lai, based on eyewitness reports, suggest that the killings were accompanied by generalized rage and by expressions of anger and revenge toward the victims. Lifton points out, incidentally, that he

> encountered conflicting descriptions about the kind of emotion Americans demonstrated at My Lai. Some recollections had them gunning down the Vietnamese with "no expression on . . . [their] faces . . . very businesslike," with "breaks" for cigarettes or refreshments. Yet others described the men as having become "wild" or "crazy" in their killing, raping, and destroying. (1973, p. 51)

In short, sanctioned massacres certainly involve a considerable amount of hostility toward the victims, traceable both to historical relationships and to situational dynamics. Hostility toward the target, however, does not seem to be the instigator of the violent actions. Historical relationships provide a reservoir of hostility that can be drawn upon to mobilize, feed, and justify the violent actions, but they do not cause these actions in the immediate case. The expressions of anger in the situation itself can more properly be viewed as outcomes rather than causes of the violence. They serve to provide the perpetrators with an explanation and rationalization for their violent actions and appropriate labels for their emotional state. They also help to reinforce, maintain, and intensify the violence. But they are not the initial instigators. Hostility toward the target, both historically rooted and situationally induced, contributes heavily to the violence, but it does so largely by dehumanizing the victims—a point to which I shall return in some detail—rather than by creating powerful forces that motivate violence against these victims.

The implication of my argument so far is that the occurrence of sanctioned massacres cannot be adequately explained by the existence of psychological forces—whether these be characterological dispositions to engage in murderous violence or profound hostility against the target—so powerful that they must find expression in violent acts unhampered by moral restraints. The major instigators for this class of violence derive from the policy process, rather than from impulses toward violence as such. The question that really calls for psychological analysis is why so many people are willing to formulate, participate in, and condone policies that call for the mass killings of defenseless victims. In seeking answers to this question, I submit, we can learn more by looking, not at the motives for violence, but at the conditions under which the usual moral inhibitions against violence become weakened. To put it in Lewinian terms, we need to focus not so much on factors increasing the strength of driving forces toward violence, as on factors reducing the strength of restraining forces against violence. It is to the weakening of such restraining forces that I shall address the remainder of my remarks.

The Loss of Restraint

I would like to discuss three interrelated processes that lead to the weakening of moral restraints against violence: authorization, routinization, and dehumanization. Through processes of authorization, the situation becomes so defined that standard moral principles do not apply and the individual is absolved of responsibility to make personal moral choices. Through processes of routinization, the action becomes so organized that there is no opportunity for raising moral questions and making moral decisions. Through processes of dehumanization, the actor's attitudes toward the target and toward himself become so structured that it is neither necessary nor possible for him to view the relationship in moral terms.

Authorization

Sanctioned massacres by definition occur in the context of an authority situation. The structure of an authority situation is such that, at least for many of the participants, the moral principles that generally govern human relationships do not apply. Thus when acts of violence are explicitly ordered, implicitly encouraged, tacitly approved, or at least permitted by legitimate authorities, people's readiness to commit or condone them is considerably enhanced. The fact that such acts are authorized seems to carry automatic justification for them. Behaviorally, authorization obviates the necessity of making judgments or choices. Not only do normal moral principles become inoperative, but—particularly when the actions are explicitly ordered—a different kind of morality, linked to the duty to obey superior orders, tends to take over.

An individual in an authority situation characteristically feels obligated to obey the orders of the authorities, whether or not these correspond with his personal preferences. He sees himself as having no choice as long as he accepts the legitimacy of the orders and of the authorities who give them. Individuals differ considerably in the degree to which—and the conditions under which—they are prepared to challenge the legitimacy of an order on the grounds that the order itself is illegal, or that those giving it have overstepped their authority, or that it stems from a policy that violates fundamental societal values. Regardless of such individual differences, however, the basic structure of a situation of legitimate authority requires the individual to respond in terms of authoritative demands rather than personal preferences; he can disobey only by challenging the legitimacy of the authority. Often people obey without question even though the behavior they engage in may entail great personal sacrifice or great harm to others.

An important corollary of the basic structure of the authority situation is that the individual does not see himself as personally responsible for the consequences of his action. Again, there are individual differences, depending on one's capacity and readiness to evaluate the legitimacy of orders received. Insofar as the person sees himself, however, as having had no choice in the action, he does not feel personally responsible for it. He was not a personal agent but merely an extension of the authority. Thus when his action causes harm to others, he can feel relatively free of guilt. A similar mechanism operates when a person engages in antisocial behavior that was not ordered by the authorities but tacitly encouraged and approved by them, even if only by making it quite clear that such behavior will not be punished. In this situation, behavior that was formerly illegitimate is legitimized by the authorities' acquiescence.

In the My Lai massacre, it is likely that the structure of the authority situation contributed to the massive violence in the two ways just described, that is, by conveying both the message that acts of violence against Vietnamese villagers were *required* and the message that such acts, even if not ordered, were *permitted* by the authorities in charge. The actions at My Lai represented, at least in some respects, responses to explicit or implicit orders. Everyone agrees that Lt. Calley, the officer in immediate charge of the operation, ordered his men to shoot all of the inhabitants of the village. Whether Calley himself had been ordered by his superiors to "waste" the whole area, as he claimed, is a matter of controversy. Even if we assume, however, that he was not explicitly ordered to wipe out the village, he had reason to believe that such actions were expected by his superior officers. Indeed the very nature of the war conveyed this expectation: the principal measure of military success was the "body count"—the number of enemy soldiers killed —and any Vietnamese killed by the U.S. military was commonly defined as a "Viet Cong." Thus it was not totally bizarre for Calley to believe that what he was doing at My Lai was to increase his body count, as any good officer was expected to do.

Even to the extent that the actions at My Lai occurred spontaneously, without reference to superior orders, those committing them had ample reason to assume that such actions would not be punished and might even be tacitly approved by the military authorities. Actions similar to those at My Lai, though perhaps not on the same scale, were not uncommon in Vietnam, and the authorities had quite clearly shown a permissive attitude toward them. Not only had they failed to punish such acts in most cases, but the very strategies and tactics that they themselves consistently devised were based on the proposition that the civilian population of South Vietnam—regardless of whether it involved "hostile" or "friendly" elements—was totally expendable. Such policies as search-and-destroy missions, the establishment of free-shooting zones, the use of anti-personnel weapons, the bombing of entire villages if they were suspected of harboring guerrillas, the forced migration of masses of the rural population, and the defoliation of vast forest areas helped to legitimize acts of massive violence of the kind that occurred at My Lai.

The events at My Lai suggest an orientation to authority based on unquestioning obedience to superior orders no matter how destructive the actions called for by these orders. Such obedience is specifically fostered in the course of military training and reinforced by the structure of the military authority situation. It also reflects, however, an ideological orientation that may be widespread in general populations. It seems that such an ideology—similar to though obviously rooted in different historical experiences and probably differing in many nuances from that suggested for Nazi Germany—is accepted by large numbers of Americans. In a national survey of public reactions to the Calley trial (Kelman & Lawrence, 1972), conducted a few weeks after the conviction of Lt. Calley had been announced, we asked respondents what they thought they would do if they were soldiers in Vietnam and were ordered by their superior officers to shoot all inhabitants of a village suspected of aiding the enemy, including old men, women, and children. Fifty-one percent of our sample said that they would follow orders and shoot; thirty-three percent said that they would refuse to shoot. We cannot infer, of course, from their responses to a hypothetical question what these individuals would actually do if they found themselves in the situation described. Our data do suggest, however, that they are prepared, in principle, to engage in mass violence if faced with authoritative orders to do so. They are certainly prepared to condone such actions; they regard obedience to orders under these circumstances—even if that means shooting unarmed civilians—as the normatively expected, the required, indeed the right and moral thing for the good citizen to do. In short, the cognitive and ideological grounding for mass violence in an authority situation seems to be present in large segments of the U.S. population (and very probably of other populations as well; see, for example, Mann, 1973).

From the pattern of their responses to a variety of questions, we can gain some understanding of the differences between those who say they would follow orders and shoot in the hypothetical situation and those who say they would refuse to shoot (Kelman, 1973). Those who say they would shoot seem to feel, by and large, that the individual has no choice in the face of authoritative orders; he has neither the responsibility nor the right to question such orders. They make a sharp separation between authority situations and interpersonal situations in daily life. The moral norms that apply in the latter are, in their view, irrelevant in the former. Within authority situations, they feel unable to differentiate between circumstances under which it would be right and those under which it would be wrong to obey superior orders. Those who say they would refuse to shoot would generally agree that legitimate orders must be obeyed, but their view of the authority situation is more flexible: obedience is less automatic; the individual has both the right and the duty to make certain judgments and choices. Thus they are prepared to make certain moral distinctions even in an authority situation; they are more inclined to see that situation as continuous with normal interpersonal relationships.

Respondents who say they would follow orders and shoot, seeing themselves as totally devoid of choices in the face of authority, feel strongly that the individual cannot be held personally responsible for actions that he takes under these conditions. They seem to conceive the relationship between citizens and authorities as governed by an implicit contract. According to this contract, the citizen—at least in such areas as foreign and military policy—obeys without question. In return, the authorities accept full responsibility for the consequences of his actions. This view is consistent with a pattern of involvement in the political system that I have described elsewhere (Kelman, 1969) as normative integration, i.e., integration based primarily on adherence to system rules. Normatively integrated individuals do feel included in the system, but their inclusion is tenuous. They do not see themselves as "owners" of the system and independent agents with regard to national policy, but rather as "pawns" who are obligated to support these policies regardless of their personal preferences.

Theoretically, we would expect normative integration and the conception of the citizen-authority relationship associated with it to be most prevalent among members of the working class and perhaps the lower middle class. Given their socialization experiences and the realities of their life situations, they are not likely to develop a sense of ownership of the system and a sense of power and personal agency within it, even though they are generally integrated in the society. Our survey data are consistent with this interpretation. Respondents who say they would follow orders and shoot Vietnamese civilians and who feel the individual should not be held responsible for actions taken under authoritative orders tend to be lower on several indicators of social class, especially on educational level. Though statistically significant, these relationships are not strong and must be interpreted very cautiously (Lawrence & Kelman, 1973). In any event, our data suggest that, within the population at large, the ideology of unquestioning obedience is related to a sense of political powerlessness.

Powerlessness within the system, conducive to an attitude of unquestioning obedience to authoritative orders, may help to explain the readiness to condone sanctioned massacres among large segments of the general population and the readiness to participate in such massacres among the lower echelons of the military or bureaucratic organizations involved. Sanctioned massacres, however, require the collaboration of organizational levels across the entire chain of command. What is often striking is the degree of unquestioning obedience to orders shown by officers and functionaries at high levels in the organizational hierarchy, who certainly do not belong to the more powerless segments of the society. When asked to play their part in the murderous enterprise, they seem ready to do so without claiming the right or even feeling the need to raise questions. They too seem to assume that superior orders override the moral considerations that might apply in other situations and free them of personal responsibility for their actions.

The Senate hearings on Watergate have provided some insight into the dynamics of unquestioning obedience among those at middle or moderately high levels within an authority system. Watergate of course was not a sanctioned massacre, but it provides a vivid demonstration of the way in which processes of authorization sweep aside the usual moral restraints against participation in criminal acts. People who should have known better automatically carried out what they saw as authoritative orders without questioning the moral or legal implications. Similar processes can account for the unquestioning participation of large numbers of people, many of them clearly belonging to highly educated and powerful segments of American society, in the formulation and execution of Indochina policy.

There are, of course, many reasons why officers and officials are motivated to go along with policies prescribed by higher authorities. These have to do with holding on to or advancing in their jobs, with protecting or expanding their areas of jurisdiction, with nurturing ambitions for higher office or larger duties. In tightly managed authority systems, success often depends on being a good team player and refraining from rocking the boat. Granting the importance of such considerations, we still need to ask how the voice of conscience is subdued, why the moral restraints that would normally inhibit participation in murderous violence are so hopelessly weak in these cases. I would propose that, in the case of organizational functionaries, there are two ways in which processes of authorization help to make moral restraints inoperative, and that these may act either jointly or independently: authoritative demands may elicit an overriding obligation or invoke a transcendent mission.

In certain authority systems, the governing ideology or the operating style places the highest value on the loyalty of functionaries—to the leader as a person or to the organization. Those who are committed to such a system may well see it as their duty to follow authoritative orders regardless of their personal preferences. Within their value system, the order calls forth what they would consider a moral obligation that overrides any other moral scruples they might have. Their reaction is similar to that of the normatively integrated citizen, which I described earlier, in the sense that they also see themselves in a no-choice situation once an authoritative order has been given. The difference, however, is that they have chosen to be in that situation by making a personal commitment to the organization and its leadership. The net effect, of course, is the same in that the usual standards of morality are considered inapplicable. Like the normatively integrated, these functionaries also do not expect to be held personally responsible for the consequences of their actions, but again for a different reason: they see themselves not as helpless pawns, but as agents and extensions of the authorities and thus by definition assured of their protection. Both groups believe they have no choice but to obey: the normatively integrated because they are so far removed from the centers of power that they feel overwhelmed by the authorities; the functionaries because they are so close to the centers of power that they identify with the authority system and are caught up in its glory and mystique. The functionaries thus tend to exaggerate the moral claim that the authorities have on their loyalties. What is interesting, if this analysis is correct, is that the tendency toward unquestioning obedience is most pronounced among two extreme groups: those far removed from the centers of power and those relatively close to them.

The second way in which processes of authorization may counteract the moral scruples of functionaries is by invoking a transcendent mission. By virtue of their relative closeness to the centers of power, the functionaries may share, to a certain extent, a view sometimes held by those in power. According to this view, the authorities are agents of a larger set of corporate purposes that transcend the rules of standard morality. Thus, their actions—and their orders—cannot be judged according to the usual moral or legal criteria. In acting on these orders, the functionaries become part of that transcendent enterprise. They feel justified in overcoming their moral scruples, indeed they feel obligated to do so. The nature of the transcendent mission may be quite vague. Himmler, in giving pep talks to the men in charge of extermination procedures, emphasized that they were "involved in something historic, grandiose, unique ('a great task that occurs once in two thousand years')" (Arendt, 1963, p. 93) without much further specification. He also, incidentally, praised them for their courage and devotion to duty in carrying out repugnant acts. However vague the transcendent mission may be (other examples of vague missions are "national security" or "the containment of Communicst aggression"), once the authorities invoke them, the functionaries no longer feel bound by standard moral constraints.

The notion of a transcendent mission brings me directly to the authorities themselves, those who make the decisions and formulate the policies and plans that constitute or lead to sanctioned massacres. I would argue that they too, in their own way, may feel freed of moral restraints through the process of authorization. By virtue of their positions and of the popular mandate that has presumably placed them in those positions, they are authorized to speak for the state. According to a view that is widely held (although it has been challenged by the Nüremberg principles), the state itself is an entity that is not subject to the moral law; it is free to do anything it deems necessary to protect or promote its national interests. The central authorities, in acting for the state, are similarly not subject to moral restraints that might be operative in their personal lives. What is important to note is that, according to this view, the freedom from all restraints devolves on the central decision maker from a higher authority, the state, of which he is merely the servant. (See Kren & Rappoport, 1972, for a discussion of Bismarck's formulation of this issue.) The state is conceived as external to the decision maker, making demands that must be heeded without question. Since his authority derives from the state, whose pursuit of national interests transcends standard morality, everyday moral considerations do not apply.

According to the logic of this view, justification for the decision maker's actions parallels the justifications used by those lower in the hierarchy. He too claims that he had no choice in that he was responding to authoritative demands. He too makes a sharp separation between personal morality and the overriding requirements of authority situations. He too expects to be absolved of personal responsibility because, as head of state, he was acting under higher authority. It is interesting, in this connection, that the Nuremberg principles challenged both the claim of "superior orders" and that of "head of state" as ways of avoiding personal responsibility for war crimes (Bosch, 1970). This whole doctrine is, of course, extremely dangerous because of its total circularity. The decision makers themselves determine what the national interests are that are making unchallengeable demands on them. It becomes easy to identify their own interests and inclinations—or at least their own views of the national interest—with "the" national interest, which then acquires an independent status and can be pursued without reference to moral considerations. In effect, this doctrine authorizes central decision makers to use their power without restraint by invoking a transcendent mission that is not subject to principles of personal morality.

Routinization

Authorization processes create a situation in which the person becomes involved in an action without considering the implications of that action and without really making a decision. Once he has taken the initial step, he is in a new psychological and social situation in which the pressures to continue are quite powerful. As Lewin (1947) has pointed out, many forces that might originally have kept him out of the situation reverse direction once he has made a commitment (once he has gone through the gate region, in Lewin's terms) and now help to keep him in the situation. For example, concern about the criminal nature of the action, which might originally have inhibited him from becoming involved, may now lead to deeper involvement in efforts to justify the action and to avoid negative consequences.

Despite these forces, however, given the nature of the action involved in sanctioned massacres, one might expect moral scruples and revulsions to arise at any step of the way. To deal with such resistances, repeated authorization providing renewed justification is usually necessary. Furthermore, and very importantly, the likelihood of such resistances cropping up is greatly reduced by processes of routinization—by transforming the action into routine, mechanical, highly programmed operations. Routinization fulfills two functions. First, it reduces the necessity of making decisions, thus minimizing occasions in which moral questions may arise. Second, it makes it easier to avoid the implications of the action since the actor focuses on the details of his job rather than on its meaning. The latter effect is more easily achieved among those who participate in sanctioned massacres from a distance, that is, from the desks of their bureaus or even from the cockpits of their bombers.

Routinization operates both at the level of the individual actor and at the organizational level. At the individual level, performance of the job is broken down into a series of discrete steps, most of them carried out in automatic, regularized fashion. The bureaucrat or officer concerns himself with making out schedules, keeping accounts, writing reports, assigning personnel, and dozens of other details and trivia that are part of his normal job. It becomes easy to forget the nature of the product that emerges from this process. Even those who cannot fail to see the product may come to see their actions as routine. When Calley said of

My Lai that it was "no great deal," he probably implied that it was all in a day's work.

At the organizational level, the task is divided across different offices, each of which has responsibility for a small portion of it. Not only does this arrangement result in a diffusion of responsibility, but it reduces the amount and limits the scope of decision making that is necessary. The work flows from office to office, with each automatically setting the agenda for the one next in line (hierarchically or functionally). At each point, the only decisions that generally have to be made are operational ones. There is no expectation that the moral implications will be considered at any of these points, nor is there any opportunity to do so.

The organizational processes also help further legitimize the actions of each participant. By proceeding in routine fashion—processing papers, exchanging memos, diligently carrying out their assigned tasks—the different units mutually reinforce each other in the view that what is going on must be perfectly normal, correct, and legitimate. The shared illusion that they are engaged in a legitimate enterprise helps the participants to assimilate their activities to other purposes, thus further normalizing them. For example, they may concern themselves with the efficiency of their performance, the productivity of their unit, the prospects for personal recognition and advancement, or the cohesiveness of their group (Janis, 1971). The nature of the task becomes completely dissociated from their performance of it. As they become habituated to their assignment in a supportive organizational context, they come to treat it more and more as if it were a normal job in which one can take pride, hope to achieve success, and engage in collaborative effort.

Normalization of atrocities is more difficult to the extent that there are constant reminders of the true meaning of the enterprise. Moral inhibitions are less easily subdued if the functionaries, in their own thinking and in their communications with one another, have to face the fact that they are engaged in organized murder. Such moral constraints are augmented by prudential ones when it comes to the writing of memoranda and the issuing of communiqués. The difficulty is handled by the well-known bureaucratic inventiveness in the use of language. The SS had a set of *Sprachregelungen* or "language rules" to govern descriptions of their extermination program. As Arendt (1963) points out, the term "language rule" in itself was "a code name; it meant what in ordinary language would be called a lie" (p.80). The code names for killing and liquidation were "final solution," "evacuation," and "special treatment." The war in Indochina has produced its own set of euphemisms: "protective reaction," "pacification," "forced-draft urbanization and modernization." Whatever terms they use, participants in the sanctioned massacres are of course usually aware of what they are actually doing. The euphemisms allow them to differentiate these actions from ordinary killing and destruction and thus to avoid confrontation with their true meaning. The moral revulsion that the ordinary labels would arouse can be more readily suppressed and the enterprise can proceed on its routine course.

Dehumanization

Authorization processes override standard moral considerations; routinization processes reduce the likelihood that such considerations will arise. Still, the inhibitions against murdering fellow human beings are generally so strong that the victims must be deprived of their human status if systematic killing is to proceed in a smooth and orderly fashion. To the extent that the victims are dehumanized, principles of morality no longer apply to them and moral restraints against killing are more readily overcome.

To understand the processes of dehumanization, we must first ask what it means to perceive another person as fully human, in the sense of being included in the moral compact that governs human relationships. I would propose that to perceive another as human we must accord him identity and community, concepts that closely resemble the two fundamental modalities of existence termed "agency" and "communion" by Bakan (1966). To accord a person identity is to perceive him as an individual, independent and distinguishable from others, capable of making choices, and entitled to live his own life on the basis of his own goals and values. To accord a person community is to perceive him —along with one's self—as part of an interconnected network of individuals who care for each other, who recognize each other's individuality, and who respect each other's rights. These two features together constitute the basis for individual worth—for the acceptance of the individual as an end in himself, rather than a means toward some extraneous end. Individual worth, of necessity, has both a personal and a social referent; it implies that the individual has value and that he is valued by others.

To perceive others as fully human means to be saddened by the death of every single person, regardless of the population group or the part of the world from which he comes, and regardless of our own personal acquaintance with him. If we accord him identity, then we must individualize his death, a sentiment epitomized in the words of the Talmud:

> Therefore was a single man only first created to teach thee that whosoever destroys a single soul from the children of man, Scripture charges him as though he had destroyed the whole world, and whosoever rescues a single soul from the children of man, Scripture credits him as though he has saved the whole world. (Sanhedrin, Chapter 4, Mishnah 5)

If we accord him community, then we must experience his death as a personal loss, a sentiment expressed with beautiful simplicity by John Donne's *Any man's death diminishes me, because I am involved in mankind.*

Sanctioned massacres become possible to the extent that we deprive fellow human beings of identity and community. It is difficult to have compassion for those who lack identity and who are excluded from our community; their death does not move us in a personal way. Thus when a group of people is defined entirely in terms of a category to which they belong, and when this category is excluded from the human family, then the moral restraints against killing them are more readily overcome.

Dehumanization of the enemy is a common phenomenon in any war situation. Sanctioned massacres, however, presuppose a degree of dehumanization that is considerably more extreme. People may fear and hate an enemy; they may be sufficiently angered, provoked, or threatened by him to be prepared to take his life. They may still be reacting to him, however, as a human being; in fact, they may even respect him and feel a sense of kinship with him, regretting that clashing interests have brought them into conflict. If they kill him, it is because they perceive him as a personal threat. By contrast, in sanctioned massacres as I have characterized them the killing is not in response to the target's threats or provocations. It is not what he has done that marks him for death, but what he is—the category to which he happens to belong.

In keeping with my characterization of sanctioned massacres as occurring in the context of a genocidal policy, the victims are converted into means in the most ultimate sense possible. They are killed because their deaths serve the policy purposes of their executioners. They are the victims of policies that regard their systematic destruction as a desirable end or a fully acceptable means. They are totally expendable.

Such extreme dehumanization, as I mentioned earlier, becomes possible when the target group can readily be identified as a separate category of people who have historically been stigmatized for one or another reason. There may be a long history of exclusion, distrust, and contempt of the victims by the victimizers. Or the victims may belong to a distinct racial, religious, ethnic, or political group which is commonly regarded by the victimizers as inferior, sinister, or uncivilized. The traditions, the habits, the images, and the vocabularies for dehumanizing such groups are already well established and these can be drawn upon when the groups are selected for massacre. The use of labels helps to deprive the victims of identity and community. Terms like "gook" help to define them as subhuman, despicable, and certainly incapable of evoking empathy. Terms like "Communist" allow their total identity to be absorbed by a single category, and one that is identified by the perpetrators of the massacre as totally evil.

The dynamics of the massacre process itself further increase the participants' tendency to dehumanize their victims. Those who participate as part of the bureaucratic apparatus increasingly come to see their victims as bodies to count and enter into their reports, as faceless figures that will determine their productivity rates and promotions. Those who participate in the massacre directly—in the field, as it were—are reinforced in their perception of the victims as less than human by observing their very victimization. The only way they can justify what is being done to these people, both by others and by themselves, and the only way they can extract some degree of meaning out of the absurd events in which they find themselves participating (Lifton, 1971, 1973) is by coming to believe that the victims are subhuman and deserve to be rooted out. And thus the process of dehumanization feeds on itself.

Continuing participation in sanctioned massacres not only increases the tendency to dehumanize the victim, but it also increases the dehumanization of the victimizer himself. Dehumanization of the victimizer is a gradual process that develops out of the act of victimization itself. Zimbardo, Haney, Banks, and Jaffe (1973) have dramatically demonstrated, in a simulated prison study, the way in which subjects who were randomly assigned to a victimizer role tend to become brutalized by virtue of the situational forces to which they are subjected. In sanctioned massacres, as the victimizer becomes increasingly dehumanized through the enactment of his role, moral restraints against murder are further weakened. To the extent that he is dehumanized, he loses the capacity to act as a moral being.

The actions of the victimizer make his own dehumanization an inescapable condition of his life (Sanford & Comstock, 1971). Following my earlier distinction between identity and community, I would propose that the victimizer loses both his sense of personal identity and his sense of community.

Through his unquestioning obedience to authority and through the routinization of his job, he is deprived of personal agency. He is not an independent actor making judgments and choices on the basis of his own values and assessment of the consequences. Rather, he allows himself to be buffeted about by external forces. He becomes alienated within his task—to adapt a concept developed by Pravaz (1969) for the analysis of task groups—he is unable to distance himself from the task, to reflect about it, to recognize himself as a responsible agent. He is so caught up in the routine performance of his authorized task that he automatically slides into actions without stopping to make value decisions about them. He does of course make certain decisions, particularly if he is at a moderately high level in the hierarchy, but these focus on details of procedure and on the costs and benefits of various ways of carrying out the task. What they conspicuously fail to focus on are the truly important criteria for human decision making: what effects will these actions have on the human beings involved? From this point of view, even the high-level decision makers are alienated within their task and deprived of a sense of identity. They see themselves as personal agents, often in fact as powerful actors on a global stage, participating in a historical drama, and to a certain extent this perception may well be true. Yet insofar as they operate without consideration of the human consequences of their decisions, their agency is stunted and illusory.

This brings me to the second source of the victimizer's dehumanization: his loss of the sense of community. In dehumanizing his victims, he loses his capacity to care for them, to have compassion for them, to treat them as human beings. He develops a state of psychic numbing (Lifton, 1971, 1973) and a sense of detachment (Opton, 1971) which sharply reduce his capacity to feel. Insofar as he excludes a whole group of people from his network of shared empathy, his own community becomes more constricted and his sense of involvement in humankind declines.

In sum, processes of authorization, routinization, and dehumanization of the victim contribute to the weakening of moral restraints, not only directly, but also by furthering the dehumanization of the victimizer. As he gradually discards personal responsibility and human empathy, he loses his capacity to act as a moral being.

Prevention of Sanctioned Massacres

In conclusion, I want to address myself briefly to the implications of my analysis for the prevention of sanctioned massacres. I shall not even attempt to deal with this question in its broad outlines, but merely suggest how one might counteract the processes of authorization, routinization, and dehumanization. These processes are rooted in the structure of our political and social system and reinforced in daily life. It is there that we might concentrate some of our corrective efforts. Let me mention five targets of such corrective efforts that flow directly from the present analysis.

The habit of unquestioning obedience

The relationship of wide segments of the population to political authorities is governed by unquestioning obedience and by ideologies that support it. This habit is built into the structure of authority situations more generally, even in nonpolitical contexts, as Milgram's (1963, 1965) provocative experiments have demonstrated. To counteract this habit, it will be necessary to create the conditions for developing a sense of personal agency in wide segments of the society, which in turn implies a redistribution of power and a thorough reshaping of the mechanisms of public decision making. As more people develop a sense of personal agency, they will acquire the capacity to take personal responsibility for their actions even when these are ordered by superior authorities. Furthermore, the spread of agency and responsibility will make it more difficult for central authorities to invoke overriding loyalties and transcendent missions in the unchallenged pursuit of criminal policies.

The normalization and legitimization of violence

Our society exposes us to innumerable opportunities to observe acts of violence or preparations for violence that are treated matter-of-factly or socially approved. Recent research on aggression (e.g., Bandura, 1973; Berkowitz, 1965) suggests that the desensitizing and disinhibiting effects of such observations facilitate aggressive behavior in the observer (whether in general or toward appropriate targets). The cumulative experience with such socially sanctioned violence makes it easier for participants in sanctioned massacres to accept the normality and legitimacy of the acts they are asked to perform.

The greatest contributor to the legitimization of violence in our society is the maintenance of a massive, powerful military establishment, committed to the use of force, not as a last resort, but as a central instrument of global policy, and extending its influence into broad domains of domestic life. The cheapness of human life is further underlined by strategic thinking that calculates how many millions of deaths (within the strategist's own population) represent an acceptable risk in a nuclear bargaining move. "Enemy" lives need not be considered in the calculus at all; they can be extinguished at will just to convey a message to the other side in a negotiation exchange.

Another example of the willingness of our society to discount human lives, thus contributing to the normalization and legitimization of violence, is the incredible power of the gun lobbies in blocking meaningful gun control legislation. The claim (among others) that such legislation would interfere with the legitimate rights of hunters provides another reminder of the permissive attitude toward killing—in this case, to be sure, of nonhuman victims—that pervades our society. We have witnessed the ways in which the sport can be generalized to human game once the victims have been sufficiently dehumanized. (I might add, parenthetically, that the norms of sportsmanlike conduct on which, I suppose, good hunters pride themselves strike me as highly hypocritical; the minimum conditions for "fair combat," it seems to me, would be to allow the game free choice of participation and parity of weapons—conditions noticeably lacking in the gentlemanly sport of hunting, as they are in sanctioned massacres.)

The extent to which and the way in which violence is presented on the media, particularly on television, may well have a desensitizing and disinhibiting effect and help to diffuse the message that violence is normal and legitimate. Recent research on media effects seems consistent with this interpretation. One interesting feature of many media stories, fictional or journalistic, is the tendency to define a happy ending as one in which the hero survives, even if countless, nameless, and usually guiltless others lose their lives in the process. The message is clear that ordinary human lives are cheap and their loss merits neither sorrow nor indignation. None of these considerations justifies censorship campaigns, but serious attention to them in media programming would certainly be in order.

Violence is further legitimized by labeling processes that help to dissociate it from its true meaning. The more often we associate killing with honor, with justice, or with sport, the easier we find it to perceive massacres as acceptable and socially approved forms of conduct. Paradoxically, some of the highly selective official pronouncements against violence to which our national leaders occasionally resort only contribute to the perversion of language that helps to dissociate actions from their meaning. When the architects of mass violence in Indochina say (in criticizing ghetto riots) that there is never an excuse for violence in our society, or (in decrying abortion) that it violates the sacredness of human life, they destroy the utility of these words as aids to moral judgment. People learn to look to official definitions of actions rather than to their human consequences in assessing their legitimacy.

Corrective efforts must take the form of constant challenges to the notion that human life is cheap, that killing or participation in killing is a socially acceptable and respectable activity, that violence is a normal and legitimate enterprise. These challenges must be raised at every point and every occasion in our social and political life at which such assumptions manifest themselves, because failure to challenge them creates the very conditions for their legitimization.

The sanctioned definition of victim categories

In our society, as in many others, there are certain categories of people who are defined as fair game, whose victimization is socially sanctioned and approved. This establishment of what might be called free-fire zones—in a demographic, rather than geographic sense—lays the groundwork for the dehumanization processes that facilitate sanctioned massacres. Not only do such practices define the groups available as legitimate targets for massacre, but more generally they legitimize the concept that there are categories of people who are less than human and who are expendable.

The research by Kahn and his associates (for example, Kahn, 1972) demonstrates that large proportions of the U.S. male population sampled in their survey consider violence against hoodlums, ghetto rioters, and student protesters—in many cases violence to the point of shooting to kill—to be fully justified, even though the provocation by these target groups consisted only of property damage (as distinct from personal violence). Thus the interests of social control serve to sanction the establishment of victim categories, who are widely regarded as fair game. The consequences of such an orientation, in the context of suppressing political protest, were tragically demonstrated by the killings at Kent State University in 1970.

> Thirteen students were shot at Kent State because popular feeling, officially encouraged, held that students were fair game. The Justice Department ignored the results of its own investigation because the President, the Vice President and the Attorney General had all publicly attacked student activists as ideological hoodlums. (Powers, 1973, p. 1)

Primary responsibility for the atmosphere that made these events possible must be placed on:

> callous and irresponsible behavior of public officials who felt, and who did not hesitate in the heat of the moment to say, that students were fair game. Riding a wave of antistudent ill-feeling for which both the President and the Vice President are at least partly to

blame, these officials, from the mayor of Kent to the governor of Ohio, made no attempt to calm the situation at Kent State but instead responded eagerly with steadily escalating force completely out of proportion to the provocation. (Powers, 1973, p. 1)

In the context of law enforcement, the consequences of the sanctioned definition of victim categories have been demonstrated recently by the terror tactics and blatant violations of individual rights practiced by narcotics agents. The cases that made the headlines were ones in which respectable families were brutalized "by mistake": the agents had broken into the wrong house or followed a false tip. However, the issue is not just that totally innocent people were attacked, but that we have an official policy that defines as fair game those who are—for however valid a reason—suspected of drug violations. Tom Wicker (1973) quotes the Special Assistant Attorney General in charge of the Office for Drug Abuse Law Enforcement as saying: "Drug people are the very vermin of humanity . . . occasionally we must adopt their dress and tactics." Such statements offer concrete illustrations of the intimate link between dehumanization of the victim and the victimizer.

The victimization of protesters and suspected lawbreakers is most pronounced when these belong to demographic categories that are in themselves defined as fair game. In our society, such categories include blacks and other racial minorities, welfare recipients and other poor people, hippies and other deviants. The extent to which the black community, for example, has been treated as a free-fire zone by law enforcement officers has been demonstrated again and again, whether in raids on Black Panther headquarters, in disturbances on black campuses, or in the questioning or arrests of suspected lawbreakers or people who "behave suspiciously" in black ghettoes. The degree to which our society tolerates the killing of blacks and members of other racial minorities in the course of ordinary police operations testifies to the acceptance of their categorization as fair game. Further evidence is provided by the disproportionate application of the death penalty (which itself symbolizes the dangerous principle that society is entitled to determine which categories of individuals have forfeited the right to live) against blacks as compared to whites. The definition of blacks as fair game in our society, it must be noted, has been sanctioned not only in the domain of social control, but also in other areas, such as medical experimentation—witness the recent revelation of an Alabama study in which black men (whose informed consent, of course, had not been obtained) were deprived of treatment for a syphilitic condition so that the investigators could observe the natural course of the disease.

One type of corrective effort against the sanctioned definition of victim categories is to use every opportunity to individualize the targets of violence, at home or abroad. As long as they remain identityless and are described in terms of stereotyped categories, they can more readily be dehumanized. Furthermore, just as we must constantly protest any tendency within the society to treat violent actions as normal and legitimate, so must we protest all implications that there are groups —within our own society or outside of it—that are subhuman and fair game. No attempt to exclude from the human community a group, by whatever criteria that group may be defined, must remain unchallenged. It is particularly important to challenge such attempts when they are made by public officials, and especially by officials who speak with the highest authority. Their pronouncements contribute most heavily to creating the atmosphere and providing the legitimization that make systematic attacks against designated victim categories possible. The president and vice-president do have the right to criticize practices of which they disapprove, but to single out categories of objectionable people and define them as outside of the bounds of the community represents a dangerous abuse of their authority that must be challenged whenever it occurs.

Finally, society must establish the principle that advocacy of genocide against any group of people is not permissible. We may have to reconsider—and I say this with profound reluctance—some of our assumptions about the limits of freedom of speech or at least about the criteria for clear and present danger. The danger of genocide is very real and a permissive attitude toward its advocacy helps to legitimize it and to create the conditions for its occurrence. Whether or not there are to be legal restraints against the advocacy of genocide, we must never allow it to appear legitimate through our silent or expedient acquiescence. Whenever, wherever, and in whatever guise genocide is advocated, we must immediately identify it for what it is and unambiguously condemn it.

The glorification of violence

Beyond the disinhibiting forces I have described so far that encourage a view of violence in various contexts and against certain categories of people as normal and acceptable, there are also propelling forces that encourage a view of violence as a glorious activity and a legitimate form of self-expression.

The glorification of violence receives some of its strongest reinforcement from the traditional image of the military as a uniquely noble and honorable enterprise. Within this tradition, killing of the enemy is elevated from the status of a necessary evil to that of a commendable good; productivity and proficiency in its performance are among the marks of the military hero. In the United States, this traditional adulation of the military has suffered some setbacks during the Vietnam War. The elaborately staged homecoming of our prisoners of war was aimed, among other things, at reviving popular enthusiasm for the military by casting these men in the traditional roles of returning heroes. The men deserve our fullest sympathy, respect, and support as human beings who have been subjected to extreme suffering and who have shown a high degree of personal courage. We must also remember, however, that most of these men were not only victims, but also victimizers—active (and in some cases enthusiastic) participants in the massive bombardments of the people of Vietnam. To treat them as military heroes is to honor them in their roles as victimizers and thus to support our political and military authorities in their efforts to glorify mass violence.

At the other end of the political spectrum, some of the revolutionary rhetoric of recent years has made its own contribution to the glorification of violence (Arendt, 1969; also Kelman, 1968, Chapter 9). Terrorist acts have in some quarters been romanticized and their perpetrators elevated to the status of revolutionary heroes. A revolutionary mystique has evolved in which violence is not merely a means of struggle used as a last resort by oppressed people but a valued end in its own right. Some of the writings of Fanon (1963), in particular, are often cited as intellectual justification for the idea that violence on the part of oppressed people is in itself a vital part of the struggle, serving as a cleansing and creative force.

The glorification of violence among the rank and file—whether in a military or a revolutionary context—may well be a response to the dehumanizing experiences to which they themselves have been subjected. Both regimentation and oppression create a feeling of powerlessness, a loss of personal agency, a deprivation of the sense of identity. Violence can offer a person the illusion that he is in control, that he is able to act on his environment, that he has found a means of self-expression. It may be the only way left to him to regain some semblance of identity, to convince himself that he really exists. The sad irony is that violence is a response to dehumanization that only deepens the loss that it seeks to undo; it is an attempt to regain one's sense of identity by further destroying one's sense of community.

The appeal of doctrines (on the right or the left of the political spectrum) that glorify violence can be understood more readily if we recognize their close relationship to commonly held stereotypes of masculinity. In our culture, as in many others, violence is often taken as evidence of the toughness and aggressiveness, the lack of sentimentality, and the emotional stoicism that males are expected to demonstrate. Thus the readiness to proclaim or endorse the glories of violence is often a response to the perceived requirements of the male sex role; to shy away from violence is to fail a challenge to prove one's manliness. Similarly, those who feel particularly oppressed by their powerlessness and lack of personal agency may resort to violence because they see it as a way of regaining their lost manhood.

To counteract the glorification of violence, we must challenge the concept that killing is a heroic enterprise or a legitimate form of self-expression. We must learn to overcome the reluctance to take a firm stand against the jingoist or terrorist who declares that violence is the only way, even at the risk of appearing insufficiently patriotic or insufficiently radical as the case may be. More fundamentally, we must find ways of counteracting the rigid sex-role stereotypes that are so deeply rooted in our culture and that have a profoundly dehumanizing influence. Just as commonly held notions of the female role tend to undermine women's sense of identity by restricting them in the development and expression of personal agency, so do commonly held notions of the male role undermine men's sense of community by restricting them in the development and expression of empathy toward their fellow human beings.

The promulgation of transhuman ideologies

Both among the proponents of the status quo and among the advocates of political change, there is a widespread commitment to ideologies that, in the service of some abstract transcendent mission, discount the concrete human implications of political actions. Such ideologies create the political atmosphere in which sanctioned massacres become possible and provide automatic rationales for those who design and participate in these massacres.

This is the issue to which Albert Camus (1968) addressed himself with eloquent simplicity in his essay, "Neither Victims nor Executioners," first published in 1946. He points out that the existence of "a world where murder is legitimate, and where human life is considered trifling" poses "the great political question of our times, and before dealing with other issues, one must take a position on it" (p. 3). He goes on to ask that we:

reflect and then decide, clearly, whether humanity's lot must be made still more miserable in order to achieve far-off and shadowy ends, whether we should accept a world bristling with arms where brother kills brother; or whether, on the contrary, we should avoid bloodshed and misery as much as possible so that we give a chance for survival to later generations better equipped than we are (p. 17). All I ask [says Camus in his conclusion] is that, in the midst of a murderous world, we agree to reflect on murder and to make a choice. After that, we can distinguish those who accept the consequences of being murderers themselves or the accomplices of murderers, and those who refuse to do so with all their force and being (pp. 18–19).

References

Arendt, H. *Eichmann in Jerusalem: A report on the banality of evil.* New York: Viking, 1963.

Arendt, H. Reflections on violence. *Journal of International Affairs,* 1969, 23 (1), 1–35.

Bakan, D. *The duality of human existence.* Chicago: Rand McNally, 1966.

Ball-Rokeach, S. J. The legitimation of violence. In J. F. Short, Jr. & M. E. Wolfgang (Eds.), *Collective violence.* Chicago: Aldine-Atherton, 1972.

Bandura, A. Social learning theory of aggression. In J. F. Knutson (Ed.), *Control of aggression: Implications from basic research.* Chicago: Aldine-Atherton, 1973.

Berkowitz, L. The concept of aggressive drive: Some additional considerations. In L. Berkowitz (Ed.), *Advances in experimental social psychology.* Vol. 2. New York: Academic Press, 1965.

Bosch, W. J. *Judgment on Nuremberg: American attitudes toward the major German war-crime trials.* Chapel Hill: University of North Carolina Press, 1970.

Browning, F., & Forman, D. (Eds.) *The wasted nations: Report of the International Commission of Enquiry into United States Crimes in Indochina, June 20–25, 1971.* New York: Harper & Row, 1972.

Camus, A. *Neither victims nor executioners.* Berkeley: World Without War Council, 1968. (Translation from original French-language publication in *Combat,* 1946).

Falk, R. Introduction. In F. Browning & D. Forman (Eds.), *The wasted nations: Report of the International Commission of Enquiry into United States Crimes in Indochina, June 20–25, 1971.* New York: Harper & Row, 1972.

Fanon, F. *The wretched of the earth.* New York: Grove, 1963.

Fromm, E. *Escape from freedom.* New York: Rinehart, 1941.

Hallie, P. P. Justification and rebellion. In N. Sanford, C. Comstock, & Associates (Eds.), *Sanctions for evil: Sources of social destructiveness.* San Francisco: Jossey-Bass, 1971.

Janis, I. L. Groupthink among policy makers. In N. Sanford, C. Comstock, & Associates (Eds.), *Sanctions for evil: Sources of social destructiveness.* San Francisco: Jossey-Bass, 1971.

Kahn, R. L. The justification of violence: Social problems and social solutions. *Journal of Social Issues,* 1972, 28 (1), 155-175.

Kelman, H. C. *A time to speak: On human values and social research.* San Francisco: Jossey-Bass, 1968.

Kelman, H. C. Patterns of personal involvement in the national system: A social-psychological analysis of political legitimacy. In J. N. Rosenau (Ed.), *International politics and foreign policy: A reader in research and theory.* (Rev. ed.) New York: Free Press, 1969.

Kelman, H. C. Availability for violence: A study of U.S. public reactions to the trial of Lt. Calley. Paper presented at XIV Interamerican Congress of Psychology, Sao Paulo, Brazil, April 1973.

Kelman, H. C., & Lawrence, L. H. Assignment of responsibility in the case of Lt. Calley: Preliminary report on a national survey. *Journal of Social Issues,* 1972, 28 (1) 177–212.

Kren, G. M., & Rappoport, L. H. Morality and the Nazi camps: A historical-psychological perspective on "how such things are possible." *Western Humanities Review,* 1972, 26, 101–125.

Lawrence, L. H., & Kelman, H. C. Reactions to the Calley trial: Class and political authority. *Worldview,* 1973, **16** (6), 34–40.

Levinson, S. Responsibility for crimes of war. *Philosophy and Public Affairs,* 1973, **2**, 244-273.

Lewin, K. Group decision and social change. In T. M. Newcomb & E. L. Hartley (Eds.), *Readings in social psychology.* New York: Holt, 1947.

Lifton, R. J. Existential evil. In N. Sanford, C. Comstock & Associates (Eds.), *Sanctions for evil: Sources of social destructiveness.* San Francisco: Jossey-Bass, 1971.

Lifton, R. J. *Home from the war—Vietnam veterans: Neither victims nor executioners.* New York: Simon and Schuster, 1973.

Mann, L. Attitudes toward My Lai and obedience to orders: An Australian survey. *Australian Journal of Psychology,* 1973, **25** (1), 11-21.

Marx, G. Issueless riots. In J. F. Short, Jr. & M. E. Wolfgang (Eds.), *Collective violence.* Chicago: Aldine-Atherton, 1972.

Milgram, S. Behavioral study of obedience. *Journal of Abnormal and Social Psychology,* 1963, **67**, 371-378.

Milgram, S. Some conditions of obedience and disobedience to authority. In I. D. Steiner & M. Fishbein (Eds.), *Current studies in social psychology.* New York: Holt, 1965.

Opton, E. M., Jr. It never happened and besides they deserved it. In N. Sanford, C. Comstock, & Associates (Eds.), *Sanctions for evil: Sources of social destructiveness.* San Francisco: Jossey-Bass, 1971.

Powers, T. Review of P. Davies et al., *The truth about Kent State: A challenge to the American conscience. New York Times Book Review,* 1973 (September 2), 1, 16–17.

Pravaz, S. The group and its object: The process of alienation. Buenos Aires: 1969. (Unpublished translation of a Spanish-language article published in *Revista Argentina de Psicologia*, 1970-1971, No. 3.)

Sanford, N., & Comstock, C. Epilogue: Social destructiveness as disposition and as act. In N. Sanford, C. Comstock, & Associates (Eds.), *Sanctions for evil: Sources of social destructiveness*. San Francisco: Jossey-Bass, 1971.

Sanford, N., Comstock, C., & Associates. (Eds.) *Sanctions for evil: Sources of social destructiveness*. San Francisco: Jossey-Bass, 1971.

Schirmer, D. B. Mylai was not the first time. *The New Republic*, 1971 (April 24), 18-21.

Sheehan, N. Should we have war crime trials? *New York Times Book Review*, 1971 (March 28), 1-3, 30-34.

Wicker, T. Gooks, slopes and vermin. *New York Times*, 1973 (May 4), p. 37.

Zimbardo, P. G., Haney, C., Banks, W. C., & Jaffe, D. The mind is a formidable jailer: A Pirandellian prison. *New York Times Magazine*, 1973 (April 8), 38-60.

15

Groupthink among Policy Makers

IRVING L. JANIS

Case studies of important government policy decisions, most specifically those concerning the Vietnam war, have led the author to suggest that certain psychosocial processes which ordinarily function to maintain the cohesion and morale of small groups may also impede or prevent activities required for effective decision-making. The analysis presented here in brief, commonsense terms, is based on application of social psychological research findings to the memoirs written by former government officials, and contains a number of specific examples illustrating the consequences of what Janis calls his "groupthink hypothesis." It should be noted, furthermore, that there are a number of similarities between the material in this article and the article by Kelman concerning violence. This does not seem to be mere coincidence. Rather, it suggests that as social scientists continue to investigate group processes in the general context of psychohistory, the knowledge that they produce can have practical consequences for the conduct of important affairs. Janis, for example, discusses what should be done to prevent groupthink among policymakers.

I have been studying a series of notorious decisions made by government leaders, including major fiascos such as the Vietnam escalation decisions of the Lyndon B. Johnson administration, the Bay of Pigs invasion plan of the John F. Kennedy administration, and the Korean Crisis decision of the Harry Truman administration, which unintentionally provoked Red China to enter the war. In addition, I have examined some fiascos

From *Sanctions for Evil*, ed. Nevitt Sanford and Craig Comstock (San Francisco: Jossey-Bass, 1971), 71–89. Reprinted by permission.

by European governments, such as the policy of appeasement carried out by Neville Chamberlain and his inner cabinet during the late 1930s—a policy which turned over to the Nazis the populations and military resources of Austria, Czechoslovakia, and other small countries of Europe. In all these instances, the decision-making groups took little account of some of the major consequences of their actions, including the moral and humanitarian implications.

When we examine how each of these decisions was made, we find that it was rarely the work of just one man—even though historians may refer to it as the President's or the Prime Minister's decision. Rather, the decision was a group product, resulting from a series of meetings of a small body of government officials and advisers who constituted a cohesive group of policy makers. For example, when we look into the way the Vietnam policies of the Johnson administration were arrived at, we discover very quickly that the key decisions were made by a small cohesive group. In addition to the President, the group included McGeorge Bundy, the special White House assistant (later replaced by Walt Rostow); William Moyers, press secretary (later replaced by George Christian); Robert McNamara, secretary of defense (replaced during the last months of the Johnson administration by Clark Clifford); and Dean Rusk, secretary of state (who managed to remain in Johnson's policy-making group from the bitter beginning to the bitter end). For several years George Ball, who was undersecretary of state, also participated in the meetings. The group also included Earle Wheeler, chairman of the Joint Chiefs of Staff, and Richard Helms, director of the Central Intelligence Agency.

It was surprising for me to discover the extent to which this group and other such small groups of policy makers displayed the phenomena of social conformity regularly encountered in studies of group dynamics among ordinary citizens. For example, some of the phenomena appear to be completely in line with findings from social psychological experiments showing that powerful social pressures are brought to bear by the members of a cohesive group when a dissident begins to voice his objections to a group consensus. Other phenomena I describe are reminiscent of the shared illusions observed in encounter groups and friendship cliques when the members simultaneously reach a peak of group-y feelings. Above all, numerous indications point to the development of group norms that bolster morale at the expense of critical thinking.

To begin, I mention here the main sources for the Vietnam case study. One is an insightful article by James C. Thomson, Jr.,[1] a historian at Harvard, who spent many years as a participant observer in the government, first in the State Department and then in the White House as an assistant to Bundy. Another is a book by David Kraslow and Stuart H. Loory,[2] two journalists who interviewed many government officials involved in forming policies concerning the Vietnam war. The third is a book by Townsend Hoopes,[3] who was acting secretary of the air force in the Cabinet. Hoopes's book is especially valuable for understanding the social and political pressures put on McNamara, Clifford, and other high officials who, toward the end of the Johnson administration, became disillusioned and began to favor deescalation of the war. Using these and several other references, we can get some idea of the forces that enabled intelligent, conscientious policy makers to make the series of grossly miscalculated decisions that had such destructive effects on the people of Vietnam and such corrosive effects within our country.

One of the first things we learn from these accounts is that when the in-group of key advisers met with Johnson every Tuesday (they sometimes called themselves the Tuesday Luncheon Group), their meetings were characterized by a games theory detachment concerning the consequences of the war policies they were discussing. The members of this group adopted a special vocabulary for describing the Vietnam war, using terms such as body counts, armed reconnaissance, and surgical strikes, which they picked up from their military colleagues. The Vietnam policy makers, by using this professional military vocabulary, were able to avoid in their discussions with each other all direct references to human suffering and thus to form an attitude of detachment similar to that of surgeons. But although an attitude of detachment may have functional value for those who must execute distressing operations, it makes it all too easy for policy makers to dehumanize the victims of war and to resort to destructive military solutions without considering their human consequences.

Thomson, who has reported this tendency from close at hand, recounts a memorable meeting in late 1964 when the policy planners were discussing how much bombing and strafing should be carried out against Vietnamese villages. The issue was resolved when an assistant secretary of state spoke up saying, "It seems to me that our orchestration in this instance ought to be mainly violins, but with periodic touches here and there of brass." Thomson, in retrospect, came to realize that he had himself undergone attitude changes, that he had acquired the same sense of aloof detachment that pervaded the war policy discussions of Washington bureaucrats. Back at Harvard, after leaving his post in the White House, he was shocked to realize that the young men in front of him in the classroom were the human beings in the manpower pool he had been talking about so detachedly when discussing problems of increasing the number of draftees with the policy makers in Washington.

This dehumanization tendency is closely related to another characteristic of Johnson's policy-making group: reliance on shared stereotypes of the enemy and of the peoples of Asia. Their grossly oversimplified views overlooked the vast differences in political orientation, historic traditions, and cultural patterns among the nations of Asia. Their sloganistic thinking about the North Vietnam Communists overlooked powerful nationalistic strivings, particularly North Vietnam's efforts to ward off Chinese domination. As a historian, Thomson was shocked to realize the extent to which crudely propagandistic conceptions entered into the group's plans and policies. The policy makers, according to Thomson, were disposed to take a very hard-nosed, military stance partly because of these stereotyped notions. . . . The dominant view demonized the enemy as embodying all evils, which legitimized the use of relentlessly destructive means. These stereotypes were evidently incorporated into the norms of the policy-making group, so it was very difficult for any member to introduce a more sophisticated viewpoint.

In a cohesive group that adopts such norms, what happens when a member starts expressing his mild doubts and says, "Let's sit back for a moment and think this over; don't we need to make some distinctions here?" or "Shouldn't we talk about some of the consequences we may have overlooked?" Such questions must often go through the minds of the participants before they agree on a policy that has some obvious drawbacks. But as soon as anybody starts to speak about his doubts, he discovers, often in subtle ways, that the others are becoming somewhat irritated and that he is in the presence of powerful group pressures to be a booster, not a detractor.

Typically, a cohesive group, like the in-group of policy makers in the Johnson administration, develops a set of norms requiring loyal support of past decisions. Each member is under strong pressure to maintain his commitment to the group's decisions and to support unquestionably the arguments and justifications they have worked out together to explain away obvious errors in their judgment. Given this shared commitment, the members put pressure on each other to continue marching to the same old drum beat and to insist that sooner or later everyone will be in step with it. They become inhibited about expressing doubts to insiders as well as outsiders with regard to the ultimate success and morality of their policies.

Whenever a group develops a strong "we feeling" and manifests a high degree of solidarity, there are powerful internal as well as external pressures to conform to the group's norms. A member of an executive in-group may feel constrained to tone down his criticisms, to present only those arguments that will be readily tolerated by the others, and to remain silent about objections that the others might regard as being beyond the pale. We can surmise from studies of work teams, social clubs, and informal friendship groups that such constraints arise at least partly because each member comes to rely upon the group to provide him with emotional support for coping with the stresses of decision-making. When facing any important decision, especially during a serious crisis, a group member often develops feelings of insecurity or anxiety about risks that could adversely affect the interests of the nation or organization and that could damage his own career. Moreover, most policy decisions generate conflicts between different standards of conduct, between ethical ideas and humanitarian values on the one hand and the utilitarian demands of national or organizational goals, practical politics, and economics on the other. A platitudinous policy maker is likely to reassure his colleagues by reminding them that you can't make an omelet without breaking some eggs. Nevertheless, each man's awareness that moral and ethical values are being sacrificed in order to arrive at a viable policy can give rise to distressing feelings of shame, guilt, depression, and related emotional reactions associated with lowering of self-esteem. Given all the uncertainties and dilemmas that arise whenever one shares in the responsibility of making a vital decision, such as war policies affecting the welfare and survival of entire nations, it is understandable that the members of a decision-making body should strive to alleviate stress.

Some individuals in public office are extraordinarily self-confident and may not need the support of a cohesive group when their decisions are subject to public criticism. I think, for example, of the spirited symphony orchestra conductor Thomas Beecham, who once said, "I have made just one mistake in my entire life and that was one time when I thought I was wrong but actually I was right." Not everybody who is accustomed to putting it on the line as a decision maker is able to maintain such unassailable self-confidence, however. So, not surprisingly, most members of a cohesive policy-making group strive to develop a sense of unanimity and esprit de corps that help them to maintain their morale by reaffirming the positive value of the policies to which they are committed. And, just as in friendship cliques, they regard any deviant within the group who insists on calling attention to the defects of the policies as objectionable and disloyal.

Social psychologists have observed this tendency in studies of students' clubs and other small groups. Whenever a member says something out of line with group norms, the other members increase communication with the deviant. Attempts to influence the nonconformist member to revise or to tone down his dissident ideas continue as long as most members of the group feel reasonably hopeful about talking him into changing his mind. But if they fail after repeated attempts, the amount of communication they direct toward the deviant goes down markedly. From then on, the members begin to exclude him, often quite subtly at first and later more obviously, to restore the unity of the group. A social psychological experiment conducted by Stanley Schachter in America and replicated in seven different European countries showed that the more cohesive the group and the more relevant the issue to the goals of the group, the greater the inclination of the members to reject a recalcitrant deviant.

During Johnson's administration, when any member of the in-group began to express doubts—as some of them certainly did—they were treated in a rather standardized way that strongly resembled the research findings just described. At first, the dissenter was made to feel at home—provided that he lived up to two restrictions: that he did not voice his doubts to outsiders, which would play into the hands of the opposition; and that he kept the criticisms within the bounds of acceptable deviation, not challenging any of the fundamental assumptions that went into the prior commitments the group had made. Thomson refers to such doubters as domesticated dissenters. One domesticated dissenter was Moyers, who was described as Johnson's closest adviser. When Moyers arrived at a meeting, we are told, the President greeted him with, "Well, here comes Mr. Stop-the-Bombing." But Moyers and the other domesticated dissenters, like Ball, did not stay domesticated forever. These men appear to have become casualties of subsequent group pressures; they resigned long before the entire Johnson administration became a casualty of the Vietnam war policy, long before that startling day when Johnson appeared on television and tearfully explained why he was not going to run again.

Given the series of cautionary examples and the constant reaffirmation of norms, every dissenter is likely to feel under strong pressure to suppress his doubts, misgivings, and objections. The main norm, as I have already suggested, becomes that of sticking with the policies on which the group has already concurred, even if those policies are working out badly and have some horrible consequences that may disturb the conscience of every member. The main criterion used to judge the morality as well as the practical efficacy of the policy is group concurrence. The belief that "we are a wise and good group" extends to any decision the group makes: "Since we are a good group," the members feel, "anything we decide to do must be good."

In a sense, loyalty to the policy-making group becomes the highest form of morality for the members. That loyalty requires them to avoid raising critical issues, to avoid calling a halt to soft-headed thinking, and to avoid questioning weak arguments, even when the individual member begins to have doubts and to wonder whether they are indeed behaving in a soft-headed manner. This loyalty is one of the key characteristics of what I call groupthink.

I use the term *groupthink* as a quick and easy way to refer to a mode of thinking that people engage in when they are deeply involved in a cohesive in-group, when concurrence-seeking becomes so dominant that it tends to override critical thinking. *Groupthink* is a term of the same order as the words in the newspeak vocabulary George Orwell presents in his dismaying world of *1984*, where we find terms like *doublethink* and *crimethink*. In putting groupthink into that Orwellian class of words, I realize that it takes on an invidious connotation. Exactly such a connotation is intended since the term refers to a decline in mental efficiency and in the ability to test reality and to make moral judgments. Most of the main symptoms of groupthink arise because the members of decision-making groups avoid being too harsh in their judgments of their leader's or their colleagues' ideas. They adopt a soft line of criticism, even in their own thinking. At their meetings, all the members are amiable and seek complete concurrence on every important issue with no bickering or conflict to spoil the cozy atmosphere.

Paradoxically, however, soft-headed groups can be extraordinarily hard-hearted when it comes to dealing with out-groups or enemies. In dealing with a rival nation, policy makers in an amiable group atmosphere find it relatively easy to resort to dehumanizing solutions, such as authorizing large-scale bombing attacks on large numbers of harmless civilians in the noble cause of persuading an unfriendly government to negotiate at the peace table. An affable group of government officials is unlikely to pursue the ticklish, difficult, and controversial issues that arise when alternatives to a harsh military solution come up for discussion. Nor is there much patience for those members who call attention to moral issues, who imply that this "fine group of ours, with its humanitarianism and its high-minded principles," may be capable of adopting a course of action that is inhumane and immoral. Such cohesive groups also tend to resist new information that contradicts the shared judgments of the members. Anyone, no matter how central a member of the group, who contradicts the consensus that has already started to emerge is regarded as a deviant threatening the unity of the group.

Many other sources of human error, of course, can impair the quality of policy decisions. Some errors stem from psychological factors in the personalities of the decision makers. Also, special circumstances can create undue fatigue and other stresses that interfere with adequate decision-making. In addition, numerous institutional factors embedded in the social structure may make for inefficiency and may prevent adequate communication from knowledgeable experts. The concept of groupthink puts the finger on a source of trouble that resides neither in the single individual (as when a man's judgments suffer from his prejudices) nor in the institutional setting (as when an authoritarian leader has such enormous power over the individuals who serve on his policy-planning committees that they are intimidated into becoming sycophants). Along with these well-known sources of defective judgment, we must consider what happens whenever a small body of decision makers becomes a cohesive group. We know that group psychology has its own dynamics and that interactions within a friendly group often are not conducive to critical thinking. At times, the striving for group concurrence can become so dominant that it interferes with adequate problem-solving, prevents the elaboration of alternative courses of action, and inhibits independent judgment, even when the decision makers are conscientious statesmen trying to make the best possible decisions for their country or for all of humanity.

In my case studies of cohesive policy-making committees I have repeatedly noted eight main symptoms of groupthink, several of which I have already illustrated in the foregoing discussion: (1) a shared illusion of invulnerability, which leads to an extraordinary degree of overoptimism and risk-taking; (2) manifestations of direct pressure on individuals who express disagreement with or doubt about the majority view, making it clear that their dissent is contrary to the expected behavior of loyal group members; (3) fear of disapproval for deviating from the group consensus, which leads each member to avoid voicing his misgivings and even to minimize to himself the importance of his doubts when most of the others seem to agree on a proposed course of action; (4) a shared illusion of unanimity within the group concerning all the main judgments expressed by members who speak in favor of the majority view (partly resulting from the preceding symptom, which contributes to the false assumption that any individual who remains silent during any part of the discussion is in full accord with what the others are saying); (5) stereotyped views of the enemy leaders as evil, often accompanied by the assumption that they are too weak or too stupid to deal effectively with whatever risky attempts are made to outdo them; (6) an unquestioned belief in the inherent morality of the in-group, which inclines the members to ignore the ethical or moral consequences of their decisions; (7) the emergence of self-appointed mind guards within the group—members who take it upon themselves to protect the leader and fellow members from adverse information that may prevent them from being able to continue their shared sense of complacency about the effectiveness and morality of past decisions; and (8) shared efforts to construct rationalizations in order to be able to ignore warnings and other forms of negative feedback, which, if taken seriously, would lead the members to reconsider the assumptions they continue to take for granted each time they recommit themselves to their past policy decisions.

When most or all of these interrelated symptoms are displayed by a group of executives, a detailed study of their deliberations is likely to reveal additional symptoms that are, in effect, poor decision-making practices because they lead to inadequate solutions to the problems under discussion. Among the main symptoms of inadequate problem-solving are the following:

First, the discussions are limited to a few alternative courses of action (often only two alternatives) without an initial survey of all the various alternatives that may be worthy of consideration.

Second, the group fails to reexamine the course of action initially preferred by the majority of members from the standpoint of nonobvious risks and drawbacks that had not been considered when it was originally selected.

Third, the group fails to reexamine any of the courses of action initially rejected by the majority of members from the standpoint of nonobvious gains that may have been overlooked and ways of reducing the seemingly prohibitive costs or risks that had made these alternatives appear to be inferior.

Fourth, little or no attempt is made to obtain information from experts within the same organization who may be able to supply more precise estimates of potential losses and gains to be expected from alternative courses of actions, particularly on matters about which none of the members of the group are well informed.

Fifth, selective bias is shown in the way the group reacts to factual information and relevant judgments from the mass media or from outside experts. The members show positive interest in facts and opinions that support their initially preferred policy and take up time in their meetings to discuss them, whereas they tend to ignore facts and opions that do not support their initially preferred policy.

Sixth, the members of the group spend little time thinking about how the chosen policy or set of plans may be unintentionally hindered by bureaucratic inertia, be deliberately sabotaged by opponents, or be temporarily derailed by common accidents that happen to well laid plans; consequently, they fail to work out contingency plans to cope with setbacks that could endanger the overall success of the decision.

All six of these defects are products of groupthink. These same inadequacies can arise from other causes such as erroneous intelligence, informational overloads, fatigue, blinding prejudice, ignorance, panic. Whether produced by groupthink or by other causes, a decision that suffers from these defects has little chance of long-run success. When the group members try to implement their poorly worked out plans, they are soon shocked to find themselves caught in one new crisis after another, as they are forced to work out from scratch the solutions to vital questions about all the obstacles to be overcome—questions that should have been anticipated beforehand. Their poorly constructed decision, like a defective old auto that is starting to fall apart, is barely kept running by hastily patching it up with whatever ill-fitting spare parts happen to be at hand. For a time, the owners may loyally insist that they are still operating a solidly dependable vehicle, ignoring as long as possible each new sign that another part is starting to fail. But only extraordinary good luck can save them from the ultimate humiliation of seeing the whole thing fall so completely to pieces that it has to be abandoned as a total loss.

I am not implying that all cohesive groups necessarily suffer from groupthink. All in-groups may have a mild tendency toward groupthink, displaying one or another of the symptoms from time to time, but it need not be so dominant as to influence the quality of the final decision of the members. The term *groupthink* also does not imply that there is anything necessarily inefficient or harmful about group decisions in general. On the contrary, a group whose members have properly defined roles, with methodical procedures to follow in pursuing a critical inquiry, is probably capable of making better decisions than is any individual in the group who works on the problem alone. However, the great gains to be obtained from decision-making groups are often lost because of powerful psychological pressures that arise when the members work together, share the same set of values, and, above all, face a crisis situation where everyone is subjected to a high degree of stress. In these circumstances, as conformity pressures begin to dominate, groupthink and its attendant deterioration in the quality of decision-making set in.

Time and again in the case studies of major historic fiascos, I have encountered evidence that like-minded men working in concert have a great many assets for making adequate decisions but also are subjected to group processes that have serious liabilities. Under certain conditions, which I believe we can start to specify, the liabilities can outweigh the assets. A central theme of my analysis then can be summarized briefly in a somewhat oversimplified generalization, which I offer in the spirit of Parkinson's laws. The main hypothesis concerning groupthink is this: The more amiability and esprit de corps among the members of an in-group of policy makers the greater the danger that independent critical thinking will be replaced by groupthink, which is likely to result in irrational and dehumanizing actions directed at out-groups.

Since this groupthink hypothesis has not yet been tested systematically, we must regard it as merely a suggestive generalization inferred from a small number of historical case studies. Still, one should not be inhibited, it seems to me, from drawing tentative inferences—as long as we label them as such—concerning the conditions that promote groupthink and the potentially effective means for preventing those conditions from arising.

Can we specify the conditions that help to prevent groupthink? Certainly not with any degree of certainty at present. But strong indications from comparative studies of good versus poor governmental decisions suggest a number of relevant hypotheses. So far, I have had the opportunity to examine only a small number of policy decisions, contrasting several major fiascos with two major decisions that provide counterpoint examples. One of the latter was the course of action decided upon by the Kennedy administration in October 1962, during the Cuban missile crisis. This decision involved the same cast of characters as the Bay of Pigs fiasco in 1961. My study of the Cuban missile crisis suggests that groupthink tendencies can be prevented by certain leadership practices that promote independent thinking. Another such counterpoint example I have looked into is the work of the small planning committees in the Truman administration that evolved the Marshall Plan in 1948. Like the White House group that developed the plan for coping with the Cuban missile crisis, these groups made realistic appraisals of how the Soviet Union and other out-groups were likely to respond to the various alternatives being considered, instead of relying on crude stereotypes and slogans.

One fundamental condition that appears to have an adverse effect on the quality of many vital decisions is secrecy. Frequently, only members of a small group of high-level officials are allowed to be in on a decision concerning the use of military force. The decision-making group is insulated from the judgments of experts and other qualified associates who, as outsiders, are not permitted to know anything about the new policies under discussion until after a final decision has been made. In the United States government there is a rule that even among men who have the highest security clearance, no one should be consulted or informed when a secret policy is up for discussion unless it is absolutely essential for him to know about it.

Small groups are highly susceptible to concurrence-seeking tendencies that interfere with critical thinking during crisis periods, especially if they restrict their discussions to the group itself. The chances of encountering effective, independent evaluations are greatest when the decision is openly discussed among varying groups who have different types of expertise, all of whom examine the decision and its probable outcomes from the standpoint of somewhat different value orientations. But when a decision is closed—confined to a small group—the chances of encountering anyone who can break up a premature emerging consensus is reduced. Similarly, insulation of the decision-making group greatly reduces the chances that unwarranted stereotypes and slogans shared by members of the group will be challenged before it is too late to avert a fiasco. . . .

Here I am speaking of more than isolation from out-groups. It is a matter of isolation from other potential in-group members, such as respected associates in high positions within the government who are not members of the specific policy-making group. If brought into the meetings, these nonmembers may be capable of presenting a fresh point of view and of raising critical questions that may be overlooked by the in-group. Their comments may induce members of the group to reconsider their assumptions.

If group isolation promotes groupthink, with its consequent mindless and dehumanized policies, then we should see what may be done to help prevent insulation of the members of a policy planning group. First, each member of the planning group could be expected to discuss the deliberations with associates in his home office—assuming he has associates who can be trusted—and then to report back to the planning group the reactions obtained from this source of relatively independent thinkers.

A second safeguard is to invite to each meeting one or more outside experts or qualified colleagues who are not core members of the policy-making group, including representatives from other branches of the government who are known to be critical thinkers, sensitive to moral issues, and capable of presenting their ideas effectively. Such outsiders were, in fact, deliberately brought into the Executive Committee meetings during the Cuban missile crisis and were encouraged to express their objections openly so that the group could debate them. This atmosphere was quite different from the one that prevailed throughout the Bay of Pigs planning sessions, which were restricted to the same small group of advisers and were dominated by the two CIA leaders who had developed the ill-fated plan. On one occasion, Chester Bowles was present as undersecretary of state to replace his chief, Rusk, who had to attend a meeting abroad. But Bowles was never asked about his reactions. He sat there silently, listening with horror to a discussion based on what he regarded as incredibly foolish and dangerous assumptions. After he left the meeting, he wrote down his objections in a memorandum to Rusk, who promptly buried it in the State Department files. In this instance, Rusk took on the role of what I call a self-appointed mind guard.

Third, a multiple-group procedure can be instituted so that instead of having only a single group work on a given major policy problem from beginning to end, responsibility is assigned to several planning and evaluation groups, each carrying out its deliberations, concurrently or successively, under a different leader. At times, the separate groups can be brought together to hammer out their differences, a procedure which would also help to reduce the chances that the decision makers will evolve a consensus based on shared miscalculations and illusory assumptions.

Now we turn to factors other than isolation that determine whether groupthink tendencies will predominate in a cohesive policy-making group. In the light of my comparative case studies, the following additional prescriptions can be added to the three already mentioned as possible antidotes for counteracting groupthink.

Fourth, new leadership procedures and traditions may be established so that the leader abstains from presenting his own position at the outset to avoid setting a norm that evokes conformity before the issues are fully explored by the members. For example, the leader may deliberately absent himself from the initial policy-making discussions, as Kennedy did when the White House Executive Committee began to meet during the Cuban missile crisis. In order to introduce this corrective procedure, of course, the leader has to be willing to renounce some of his traditional prerogatives.

Fifth, at every general meeting of the group, whenever the agenda calls for evaluation of policy alternatives, at least one member can be assigned the role of devil's advocate, to function like a good lawyer in challenging the testimony of all those who advocate the majority position. During the Cuban missile crisis, Kennedy gave his brother, the attorney general, the mission of playing devil's advocate, with seemingly excellent results in breaking up a premature consensus. When this devil's advocate's role is performed well, it requires the members of the group to examine carefully the pros and cons of policy alternatives before they agree upon the best course of action.

Sixth, throughout all the group meetings, each member can be assigned the primary role of critical evaluator of policy alternatives, a role which takes precedence over any factional loyalties and over the traditional forms of deference or politeness that often incline a man to remain silent when he objects to someone else's cherished ideas. This proposed practice, which could not be instituted unless it were wholeheartedly approved, initiated, and reinforced by the President and other top executives in the hierarchy, can help to counteract the spontaneous group pressures for concurrence-seeking. It should certainly prevent an illusion of unanimity from bolstering a premature consensus.

Seventh, whenever the policy issue involves relations with a rival nation or organization, at least part of a session can be devoted to surveying recent warning signals from the rivals, using special audiovisual techniques or psychodramatic role-playing, to stimulate the policy makers to construct alternative scenarios regarding the rival's intentions. In order to counteract the members' shared illusions of invulnerability and tendency to ignore or explain away any warning signals that interfere with a complacent outlook, this special effort may be required to induce them to become sharply aware of the potential risks and the need for making realistic contingency plans.

Eighth, after a preliminary consensus is reached concerning what seems to be the best policy alternative, a special session can be held at which every member is expected to express as vividly as he can all his residual doubts and to rethink the entire issue before making a definitive choice. This second-chance meeting should be held before the group commits itself by taking a final vote.

Two main conclusions are suggested by the case studies of foreign policy decisions: along with other sources of error in decision-making, the symptoms of groupthink are likely to occur from time to time within cohesive small groups of policy makers; and the most corrosive symptoms of groupthink are preventable by eliminating group insulation, overdirective leadership practices, and other conditions that foster premature concurrence-seeking. Awareness of these tentative conclusions can be useful to those who participate in policy-making groups if it inclines them to consider introducing one or another of the antidote prescriptions just listed—providing, of course, that they are aware of the costs in time and effort and realize that they must also watch for other disadvantages before they decide to adopt any of the prescriptions as standard operating procedure. . . .

Sometimes it may even be useful for one of the policy makers to ask at the right moment, before a decision is definitely made, "Are we allowing ourselves to become victims of groupthink?" I am not proposing that this question should be place in the agenda or that the members should try to conduct a group therapy session, comparable to parlor psychoanalysis. Rather, I have in mind enabling some policy makers to adopt a psychological set that inclines them to raise critical questions whenever there are signs of undue complacency or premature consensus. One such question has to do with the consensus itself. A leader who is aware of the symptoms of groupthink, for example, may say, "Before we assume that everyone agrees with this proposed strategy, let's hear from those who haven't said anything yet, so that we can get all points of view onto the table." In addition to this commonsense application, some ingenious procedures may be worked out or spontaneously improvised so that the symptoms of groupthink are counteracted by participants who know about the groupthink hypothesis without constantly having to remind the group of it.

Notes

1. J. Thomson, "How Could Vietnam Happen: An Autopsy," *The Atlantic*, April 1968, pp. 47–53.
2. D. Kraslow and S. Loory, *The Secret Search for Peace in Vietnam* (New York: Vintage, 1968).
3. T. Hoopes, *The Limits of Intervention* (New York: McKay, 1969).

16

On America

CARL G. JUNG

Carl Gustav Jung, at one time Freud's chosen crown prince, broke with Freud primarily over the latter's emphasis on sexuality; but their differences also included interpretations of culture and personality. In contrast to Freud, Jung believed in the legitimacy of religion, faith, and tradition.

Jung's essay is an attack on mass society; the "rule of the masses" being synonymous to Jung with vulgarity and primitiveness. America represents to Jung all the forces in the modern world, from feminism to jazz, that he regards as destructive. His essay employs psychoanalytic rhetoric to defend traditional values against modernity.

The first thing I noticed in the American was the great influence of the Negro—naturally only a psychological influence without blood mixture. The emotional expressiveness of the American, in particular his laughing which may best be seen in the Society gossip columns of American newspapers; this inimitable Roosevelt [TR] laughing may be found in its original form in the American Negro. The unique walk with relatively loose joints, or the swinging hips which one can observe so frequently in American women, have their origin in the Negro. American music received its main inspiration from the Negro; the dance is Negro dance. The expressions of religious feelings, the *revival meetings* [English in original], the *holy rollers* [English in original], and other abnormalities stand strongly under the influence of the Negro—the famous American naiveté in its charming as well as in its

Translated by George M. Kren from *Der Leuchter Weltanschauung und Lebensgestaltung: Achtes Buch: Mensch und Erde*, ed. Count H. Kesyerling, Schuleder Weisheit, Otton Reichl Verlag, Darmstadt, 1927.

more unpleasant forms of expression may readily be compared with the childishness of the Negro. The generally very animated temperament is visible not only at baseball games, but above all manifests itself in an exceptional desire for verbosity, for which the unceasing and boundless gossiping in the American newspapers is the most typical example; it cannot be derived from the Germanic ancestors, but on the contrary parallels the *chattering* [English in original] of the Negro village. The almost complete absence of intimacy and the mass society which absorbs everything reminds one of primitive life in open huts with complete identity of all tribal members. It appeared to me, as if in American houses all doors always stood open, as also in the American country town no garden fences can be found. Everything appears to be street. . . . In the American hero fantasy the Indian character plays a dominant role. The American concept of sport is far removed from the European *Gemütlichkeit*. Only the Indian initiation can compare in cruelty and ruthlessness with rigorous American sports training. The total achievement of American sport is therefore remarkable. In everything that the American desires, the Indian makes his appearance; in the extraordinary concentration upon specific goals, in persistence at pursuing them, in bearing the greatest of difficulties impassively, all the legendary virtues of the Indian receive their full due.

I have noticed in my American patients that the hero figure also possesses the Indian religious aspect. The most important figure of the Indian religious form is the shaman, the medicine man who can exorcise the spirits. The first American innovation in this realm, which also has become important for Europe, is spiritualism; the second is Christian Science and other forms of Mental Healing. Christian Science is an incantation ritual in which the demons of illness are denied, the stubborn body is sung to with the appropriate formulas, and the Christian religion of a high cultural niveau is used for magic healing. The poverty of the spiritual content is frightening, but Christian Science is alive, and possesses a definite indigenous force and creates those miracles for which one would search in vain in the official churches. Thus the American offers a rare picture; a European with the manner of Negroes and an Indian soul. He shares the fate of all usurpers of alien land: certain Australian primitives maintain that one cannot conquer alien soil because ancestral spirits live in that alien soil and so the newborns will incarnate alien ancestral spirit. In this may be found a great psychological truth. The alien land assimilates the conqueror. But in contrast to the Latin conquerors of Central and South America, the North Americans have with their strong puritanism maintained the European niveau, but could not prevent the souls of their Indian enemies from becoming their own. The virgin earth everywhere demands that at least the subconscious of the conquerors will sink to the level of the independent native [autochone].

17

The Ethics of a Therapeutic Man

CLARENCE J. KARIER

Two dialectically connected myths prevail in all science, including psychoanalysis: first, that science is a value-free analysis of an objective reality, and second, that scientific research is governed by an internal logic forcing progressive movement from one truth to another, from one discovered law to the next. These myths are sharply contradicted by Karier's analysis of Jung's work, which shows that Jung's ideas were explicitly tied to his personal value system.

More concretely, Jung's values were determined by his recognition that Christian myths had lost their credibility in the twentieth century. He sought to create a new "therapeutic" set of ideals based on the primitive, prerational qualities of human nature, and became very critical of the formal, analytical thinking which had destroyed the old myths. Having judged the Nazi movement to be an eruption of elemental life forces, Jung's position brought him dangerously close to German Völkisch ideas, to anti-Semitism, and to a positive assessment of National Socialism.

The sounds of machine guns across the frozen mountain ridges of Korea had not yet faded into the stillness of history when Hermann Hesse, writing to his friends from the peace and tranquility of the Engadine,

In writing this paper I have profited from both the research and the dialogue of a number of people at the University of Illinois. I am particularly indebted to Russell Marks, Stephen Yulish, Lauren Weisberg, Paul Violas, Mobin Shorish, Chris Shea, David Hogan, Mark Sorenson, Marion Metzow, Erik Kristiansen, Brisbane Rouzan, and Micky Becker. The research reported herein was in part supported by the Spencer Foundation and in part by the College of Education at the University of Illinois, Urbana-Champaign.

reflected on the feeling of guilt that attacks men of his generation whenever they think of the peaceful times before 1914. As he said:

> Whoever has been awakened and shaken by world history since the first collapse of the peaceful world will never be entirely free from the feeling of complicity, although it is more appropriate to the young, for age and experience should have taught us that this question is the same as that of our share in original sin and should not disquiet us; we can leave it to theologians and philosophers. But since within my lifetime the world in which I live has changed from a pretty, sportive, somewhat self-indulgent world of peace to a place of horror, I will no doubt suffer occasional relapses into this state of bad conscience. [1]

Throughout his life Hesse and other intellectuals like him suffered occasional relapses into that "state of bad conscience." During those times they would feel themselves responsible for the ills of the world. They were, after all, men and women of the world, as well as in the world. As participants in the ongoing rush of events which helped structure and shape the evolving future of western culture, their remorse stemming from "bad conscience" was perhaps justified. However, as alienated observers, merely describing the chaos of the present and perhaps insightfully but prophetically predicting the impending holocaust of World War I or the rise of National Socialism, they could and often did claim innocence. For the truly sensitive artist the line between insightfully describing a social movement and becoming a functional part of that movement is necessarily subtle, thin, and often obscure. This inevitably is the case, because the more sensitively the artist describes his age, the more he and his work become the conceptual lens through which that age perceives itself. That perception, in turn, often becomes the basis for acts which significantly influence the future course of events. In many ways the truly sensitive artist who often claims to be an unpolitical man is doomed to be an unwilling prophet of a new politics for a new age. Ironically enough, the unpolitical artists who touch on those issues about which an age really cares often turn out to be far more politically significant than those who consciously set out to "change the world."

Whether guilty or innocent for the events of that world, one of the responsibilities of those who play *The Glass Bead Game* in the Castilian world of Hermann Hesse was, in the end, to forsake the world of art for art's sake and return to the world of action in order to at least give warning of impending danger. Surely then the sensitive artist who senses the fire which burns within and gives warning of the coming social conflagration cannot be held responsible for the fire itself. Nevertheless, the problem still remains. To what extent does the very analysis of both the ideal and the real form the combustible material out of which the fire developed in the first place? What, then, are the functions of knowledge, and to what extent are the producers of that knowledge accountable for the ways that knowledge is used to shape our social destiny? What are the moral responsibilities of the artist as creative thinker to the human community? To what extent, then, should the artist feel responsible for a world that went from a "world of peace to a place of horror?" These are questions not easily answered. Yet while they remain unanswered, and some might contend unanswerable, they are not easily dismissed. They are not easily dismissed because they are substantive questions which strike at the very heart of the moral function of imaginative art, whether that art appeared in the form of painting, sculpture, literature, philosophy, or psychology. The intent of this essay is to critically examine the philosophic assumptions about human nature and the social order held by selected artists in literature and psychology within an historical context, and to consider further the role these ideas may or may not have had in helping to shape a world from one of "peace to a place of horror," and to once again raise the thorny question of guilt or innocence.

Alienated from the world of bourgeois values which increasingly structured a mechanized industrial bureaucratic society, artists such as Hermann Hesse, seeking a more authentic existence, saw in the outbreak of World War I the hopeful death of the old order and the birth of the new. They therefore quickly volunteered their services to the cause.[2] For Hesse and others, however, disillusionment was just as quick. The war did not bring an end to the inauthentic, fraudulent, bourgeois world, but instead seemed to infuse new life into a decaying civilization. By 1918 the naive but desperate hope that somehow the new order might emerge from the war lay buried with the blood of ten million in the mud of the trenches somewhere in Europe.

During those nightmarish years, Thomas Mann espoused a form of *Kultur* jingoism while pronouncing in *Betrachtengen eines Unpolitischen* that he was "an unpolitical man, and proud of it."[3] Profoundly shaken by the course of world events and disillusioned with the liberal enlightenment world of political action, Mann, at a critical moment in history, moved away from the world of politics. As he put it: "I hate politics and the belief in politics, because it makes men arrogant, doctrinaire, obstinate, and inhuman."[4] Although he later changed his position and urged artists to return to politics, the course that Mann set here was essentially the same kind of course which Hesse and others like him set for themselves. In a world gone insanely barbaric, the search for meaning in life was no longer to be found in reforming social-political institutions, but rather to be found in the depths of the individual soul.

The revolt against middle-class values expressed in art, drama, literature, and youth culture at the *fin de siècle* in Europe eventually fused with the moral nihilism of World War I. As in all wars, legitimacy of authority could not withstand the corrosive effects of the lies and deception so necessary to mobilize and sustain people for the action of war. While most expressionists were repelled by the horror of the trenches[5] and the Dadaists[6] mocked the *Kultur* which led men to their deaths in the trenches, other authors such as Ernst Juenger in *Thunder of Steel*, 1919, found in the blind fury of the bloody killing the renewal of the primeval instinct, the renewal of man, indeed, the renewal of civilization itself.[7] Even though Juenger found in that bloody violence the instinctual basis for a "new man" and a "new order" that transcended the inauthentic bourgeois sense of good and evil, many more artists turned away from the war in profound disgust. Perhaps Paul Valery was the best spokesman for those disillusioned men and women when he said:

> We do not know what will be born, and we fear the future, not without reason, we hope vaguely, we dread precisely; our fears are more precise than our hopes; we confess that the charm of life is behind us, but doubt and disorder are in us and with us.[8]

Somehow men seemed to sense that this was one of those rare moments of history when a transformation of values was about to occur. What remained of the enlightenment faith in reason, whether expressed in a Comtean positivism or Spencerian science, was declared bankrupt by Ferdinand Brunetiere; and what was left of Condorcet's faith in progress was declared dead by Georges Sorel in his *Reflections on Violence.* The traditional enlightenment faith in progress, science, technology, and reason no longer sufficed. For more than a century the enlightenment faith in science and rationality had cut deeper and deeper into the Judeo-Christian mythology which had sustained western man with meaningful assumptions about his personal and collective existence for over two thousand years.[9]

Frederick Nietzsche sensed how deeply the empirical knife of the scientist has penetrated and indeed had cut into the mythical assumptions which undergirded the psyche of the westerner's soul when he announced that: "God is dead. God remains dead. And we have killed him."[10] The death of God meant more than the death of the Church as a viable institution; more important, it meant the death of the theologian as the spiritual guide to the inner depths of the human soul. In his place there emerged in the twentieth century a new high priest of the secular city, a man of science and rationality, the "psychotherapist." The authentic life of Christianity never really existed on the Church door at Wittemberg, nor in the Vatican Councils of Rome, but rather in the inner conscience of the individual. The declining role of the theologian and the ascending role of the psychotherapist as a spiritual guide to that inner conscience marks, in a very significant way, the last stand of Christianity in its extended battle with the rising national state.

Since the Renaissance the growing power of the nation state had gradually replaced the Church as the dominant institution governing men's social relations. As a consequence men would more often be asked to declare loyalty to the state rather than to the Church. So apparent is this that in most Western European countries today one would not consider it unusual to ask a person to lay down his life for his country, but surely odd to die for his Church. Institutions, like men, characteristically die with a whimper rather than a bang. They do so as the life force is drained from their existence. For most institutions that life force adheres in the capability of that institution to command a faith among its consituents in the mythological assumptions which underlie its reason for existence. By the turn of the century it was clear to Nietzsche and others that the critical mythical assumption upon which the Judeo-Christian cosmology rested was no longer tenable. While the Churches to Nietzche's "madman" would eventually become "tombs and sepulchers of God," the madman who heralded the news sensed that he had come too early. As he said:

> I come too early, my time has not come yet. This tremendous event is still on its way, still wandering—it has not yet reached the ears of man. Lightning and thunder require time, the light of the stars requires time, deeds require time even after they are done, before they can be seen and heard. [11]

When that day comes, however, the earth will be unchained from the sun, plunging:

> Backward, sideward, forward, in all directions? Is there any up or down left? Are we not straying as through an infinite nothing? Do we feel the breath of empty space? Has it not become colder? Is not night and more night coming on all the while? Must not lanterns be lit in the morning? [12]

Although the heavens did not fall, nor were lanterns lit in the morning, the problem of meaning in a universe without God emerged as an acute psychological problem for man living in the secular city of the twentieth century.[13] In a mass technological society which tends to obscure meaning, destroy identity, and degrade human value, the quest in such a society for meaning, identity, and value becomes even more significant. The individual's guide for this quest was not the theologian nor the philosopher, but the psychologist. In the past it was theologians such as St. Augustine and Jonathan Edwards who, under the old faith, defined human nature, good and evil, and psychologically ministered to the existential loneliness of the individual. Now it was the psychotherapist who defined human nature, sickness, and health, and in turn, spiritually ministered to that same existential condition within a vastly changed social environment.

Similarly, as in the past when there had emerged diverse and competing numbers of theological positions with respect to the nature of man and his place in the universe, so too, in the modern era, there emerged a wide range of psychological positions defining human nature and man's place in the universe. Competing philosophical assumptions about the nature of man and his reality lie at the base of most doctrinal disputes which divide the therapeutic community. These assumptions clearly shape the diagnosis as well as the prescribed therapy.[14] The life of the therapeutic man, whether he be a therapist or a client, was dominated by an impulse for healing, dispensing curative remedies in order to gain a sense of well-being, whereas the life of the theological man was most often dominated by an impulse for salvation. As Philip Rieff put it:

> Religious man was born to be saved; psychological man is born to be pleased. The difference was established long ago, when "I believe," the cry of the ascetic, lost precedence to "one feels," the caveat of the therapeutic. And if the therapeutic is to win out, then surely the psychotherapist will be his secular spiritual guide.[15]

In 1909 when Sigmund Freud, Carl Jung, William James, G. Stanley Hall, and others met at Clark University, the age of the "therapeutic man" was about to dawn. In that age, the psychotherapist would become the spiritual guide for the individual in a secular society. Goethe sensed the coming of that age when he said: "Speaking for myself, I too believe that humanity will win in the long run; I am only afraid that at the same time the world will have turned into one huge hospital where everyone is everybody else's humane nurse."[16] By the turn of the century, Christian theology and the mythology upon which it was based seemed to crumble, under the weight of scientific investigation.[17] While some turned to a scientific humanism as a substitute faith,[18] others vested their faith in a Comtean positivism; while still others turned to psychoanalysis. Although Freud, in an apparently anti-positivistic stance, argued that since man thinks in terms of perceptions, and everything must be translated in terms of those perceptions "which he cannot free himself . . . reality will forever be unknowable."[19] Ultimately he did place his faith in science and rationality over against what he believed were the illusions involved in religious experience. As Freud said: "No, our science is no illusion. But an illusion it would be to suppose that what science cannot give us we can get elsewhere."[20]

Carl Jung, on the other hand, based his psychology on the reality of what Freud called illusions, and argued that much of modern man's neuroses stemmed from his inability to believe in the sacred myths of religion. Speaking before the Alsatian Pastoral Conference at Strasbourg, Germany, in 1932, Jung noted that:

> courageous and upright persons . . . [had the] feeling that our religious truths have somehow become hollow. Either they cannot reconcile the scientific and the religious outlook, or the Christian tenets have lost their authority and their psychological justification. People no longer feel redeemed by the death of Christ; they cannot believe—for although it is a lucky man who *can* believe, it is not possible to compel belief.[21]

Jung had experienced this problem within his own immediate family. His father had "suffered from religious doubts,"[22] which Jung believed contributed to, if not caused, his mental illness. Few men of the cloth can suffer religious doubts without experiencing the psychological pains of derangement. Thus Jung attributed his father's debilitating psychological condition, as well as his failure as a theologian, to his growing loss of faith in the fundamental Christian tenets. Several times, under these circumstances, the elder Jung advised his son to "Be anything you like except a theologian."[23] Much of his youth, Jung recalled, was spent in trying to come to grips with the religious beliefs of his father, a father whom he grew not only to disrespect, but to "pity."[24]

Carl Jung, as a young man, had experienced what he believed was "the grace of God." He had a secret vision, a vision which set the course of his "modern consciousness" and Gnostic beliefs. He said, "My entire youth can be understood in terms of this secret."[25] His vision left little for the imagination as he said:

> I saw before me the cathedral, the blue sky. God sits on His golden throne, high above the world—and from under the throne an

> enormous turd falls upon the sparkling new roof, shatters it, and breaks the walls of the cathedral asunder.[26]

With this vision Jung had experienced "illumination." The "miracle of grace" had clarified his life. He now understood why and how his father's faith was so "empty and hollow." His father, he said:

> did not know the immediate living God who stands, omnipotent and free, above His Bible and His Church, who calls upon man to partake of His freedom, and can force him to renounce his own views and convictions in order to fulfill without reserve the command of God. In his trial of human courage God refuses to abide by traditions, no matter how sacred.[27]

Without this kind of direct experience his father would never know that God ultimately was the author of evil as well as good. Spiritually enlightened by this Gnostic illumination, Jung's fate came sharply into focus.[28] He was destined to succeed where his father had failed. Keenly sensitive to the inadequacies of his father's theology and accepting his father's admonition to stay away from theology, Carl G. Jung would not become a doctor of theology, but rather a "doctor of the soul." Traveling in his father's footsteps, he attended his father's university, joined his fraternity, and upon his father's death, occupied his room, and took over his position in the family, which gave him a feeling of "manliness and freedom."[29] Jung's divinely guided fate was to succeed where his father had failed. He believed he was spiritually called as a "doctor of the soul" to minister to the spiritual needs of the therapeutic man by cultivating a new but also very ancient Gnostic theology. Jung's mother seemed to sense this idea of a calling when shortly after her husband's death she turned to Carl and said, "He died in time for you," which Carl interpreted to mean, "You did not understand each other and he might have become a hindrance to you."[30] His father's death freed him to develop a kind of faith which rejected the traditional dogmas of his father's church by developing a system of beliefs based on the psychological experiences of religious mysticism. Some of the key tenets of his new faith had been rejected by the early Church as heresy.

Unlike Freud, who found an explanation for mysticism in repressed sexuality, Jung found it rooted in the real demands of the collective unconscious and the darker spirits of the cosmic universe.[31] Traditional Christianity at its best could successfully deal with only half a world. The other half, the side of evil, occult, and darkness, it could not interpret correctly. Evil was not as most traditional Christians defined it—as a mere absence of good. Evil, Jung believed, was to be accorded its place in the universe with good. The God of the universe was not the God of good and light alone, but of evil and darkness as well. Jung's therapeutic faith included a process by which men and women could come to accept the evil that was in their shadow as well as in their God. Through a therapeutic process men and women would overcome their alienation by becoming reunited to their true selves properly rooted in the mystical archetypes of the cosmic universe. The universe, he envisioned, was Gnostic and neo-Platonic.

As the western mind seemed to lose confidence in itself and the issue of decadence was again of viable concern, historians such as Toynbee and Spengler reached back to the past to redevelop the classical cyclical theories of history. Jung also seemed to reach back in time to the pre-Christian era to recreate his Gnostic–neo-Platonism for the modern world. Martin Buber correctly recognized that Jung's psychoreligious therapy was more than a simple process of psychological healing, but was a fundamental challenge to the Judeo-Christian tradition. As Buber put it:

> Gnosis is not to be understood as only a historical category, but as a universal one. It—and not atheism, which annihilates God because it must reject the hitherto existing images of God—is the real antagonist of the reality of faith. Its modern manifestation concerns me specifically not only because of its resumption of the Carpocratian motif. This motif, which it teaches as psychotherapy, is that of mystically deifying the instincts instead of hallowing them in faith. That we must see C. G. Jung in connection with this modern manifestation of Gnosis I have proved from his statements and can do so in addition far more abundantly. [32]

Jung's gnosticism not only challenges traditional beliefs, but, in the context of the modern world, poses a basic moral issue. The issue is this: To what extent can one be held responsible for acting out the evil will of God? Jung knew that his "new consciousness" reopened the Biblical problem of Job for himself and others who adopted his faith. [33] This problem would repeatedly recur in Jung's work as well as in Hesse's and others who had taken this particular therapeutic path to salvation.

As the therapeutic man replaced the theological man as spiritual guide to modern consciousness, the therapist defined the psychological boundaries of health and sickness in much the same way as the theologian had defined good and evil. [34] As both delineated the boundaries of the mind or soul, both had to come to grips with the way that mind or soul interacted with the world—a world often viewed as humanly destructive.

While some therapists, like Alfred Adler, advocated a kind of socialism which they thought might alleviate the psyche as well as physical suffering of humanity, other therapists took the more stoic path of Freud. To Freud happiness was not attainable, for ultimately the fault lay not with society nor with the individual, but was inherent in the very unchanging nature of man himself. All culture, he believed, was created out of libidinal restraint and sublimation. Universalizing the reality principle based on the nature of man, Freud offered little solace for the suffering soul, as he said: "A great deal will be gained if we succeed in 'transforming your hysterical misery into everyday unhappiness,' which is the usual lot of mankind."[35]

While other therapists, such as Wilhelm Reich and R. D. Laing, challenged the repressive nature of the social environment and advocated changing the reality principle itself, most therapists, in one way or another, made peace with the world by helping their clients adjust, if only in a suffering way, to the existing world. A part of that adjustment included a definition of the neurotic person as that individual who persists in suffering guilt and anxiety feelings derived from a world which he cannot control. In this sense the well-balanced individual is the kind of person who loses little sleep over the events he cannot control. The person who does is neurotic and can be treated. Hermann Hesse spoke as a therapeutic man when he said:

> Presumably this feeling of shared responsibility for the state of the world, which those who have it sometimes like to interpret as a sign of an especially sensitive conscience and a higher humanity, is only a sickness or, to be specific, a lack of innocence and faith. The completely well-balanced person will not hit upon the arrogant idea that he must share responsibility for the crimes and sickness of the world, for its inertia in peace and its barbarity in war, unless he is important and influential enough to be able to increase or lessen its suffering and guilt.[36]

What happens, however, to the unpolitical artist, alienated from society, repelled by politics, who turns inward in his search for meaning? Does he become increasingly powerless in controlling events, and less responsible for the "crimes and sickness of the world"? Under such circumstances, the more alienated a person becomes, the less he is likely to influence the course of political action, and in turn, the less guilt he should feel. The therapeutic man can thus survive the feelings of "bad conscience" which can erupt from time to time from the memories of such events as Buchenwald, Dachau, Belsen, Dresden, Hiroshima, or My Lai. This was the moral dilemma, indeed, the moral tragedy not only for Hermann Hesse, but for all imaginative artists who turned inward to find their authentic soul, and in the end, therapeutically lost their social conscience.

Therapy involves a re-education of the person at a fundamental level. It usually includes the adoption of the basic assumptions undergirding the therapist's philosophy of man, society, and nature. The kind of therapy a person undergoes is then critical in shaping what that person finds in both his inner soul and the particular perspective from which he perceives the world of action. From May, 1916, to November, 1917, Hermann Hesse underwent seventy-two therapeutic sessions with Dr. Joseph Lang, a student of C. G. Jung. The immediate literary consequence of his therapy was the writing of the prize-winning novel, *Demian*, which he is said to have written in 1917, in a matter of a few weeks.[37] Published in 1919, *Demian* exerted an electrifying influence on German youth in the early years of the Weimar Republic. As Thomas Mann put it:

> With uncanny accuracy this poetic work struck the nerve of the times and called forth grateful rapture from a whole youthful generation who believed that an interpreter of their innermost life had risen from their own midst—whereas it was a man already forty-two years old who gave them what they sought.[38]

While one might wonder just what it was that German youth in the 1920s and American youth in the 1970s found so attractive about *Demian*, it is clear that C. G. Jung's philosophy of life had profoundly shaped Hesse's perspective of his own life.

Demian is the story of Emil Sinclair's youth and his struggle to "live in accord with the promptings which came from his true self." The story exemplifies the Jungian process of individuation. The young Sinclair struggles to free himself from the "persona," or social roles, he is expected to play within a middle-class culture. In time, and with the assistance of Pistorius (Lang),[39] Sinclair confronts his "shadow" and finds the evil in his soul to be ultimately sparked by Abraxas, the Gnostic God of good and evil. Confronting his "shadow," Pistorius advises Sinclair to:

> Gaze into the fire, into the clouds, and as soon as the inner voices begin to speak, surrender to them, don't ask first whether it's permitted or would please your teachers or father, or some god. You will ruin yourself if you do that. . . . Sinclair, our god's name is Abraxas and he is God and Satan and he contains both the luminous and dark world.[40]

Young Sinclair is led to discover that he is one of the children of Cain. Cain, to be sure, murdered his brother, but he did it because he had the courage to follow his inner destiny, a destiny which God had willed. So it also was with the story of the two thieves on the cross. Certainly the so-called "good" thief was not to be respected—he was nothing but a "sniveling convert." No, the real man of character was the thief who remained a thief following his destiny to the "appointed end."[41] The children of Cain, and all who bore the inner mark of Cain, could accept evil and follow out their appointed destiny. As Sinclair's personal growth continued, he came to grips with his Anima, Frau Eva, the feminine mother archetypical figure within his own soul. Accepting the feminine, Sinclair's process of individuation continued. Eventually he came to sense, feel, and then know his personal destiny. That destiny involved the destruction of the old order and the painful birth of the new. As one of the marked children of Cain, Sinclair was prepared to face and participate in the evil and destruction involved in the death of the old and the birth of the new. He was prepared to play out his "appointed" destiny.

Just as Jung found the traditional beliefs of Christianity wanting, so too Sinclair's Demian would argue that the present Europe was dominated by the "herd instinct."

> A whole society composed of men afraid of the unknown within them! They all sense that the rules they live by are no longer valid, that they live according to archaic laws—neither their religion nor their morality is in any way suited to the needs of the present. For a hundred years or more Europe has done nothing but study and build factories! They know exactly how many ounces of powder it takes to kill a man but they don't know how to pray to God. . . .[42]

To be sure, Demian insisted the coming revolution would be bloody and could "not improve the world." It would, however, not be in vain. The bloodletting which follows would "reveal the bankruptcy of present-day ideals, there will be a sweeping away of Stone Age gods. The world, as it is now, wants to die, wants to perish—and it will."[43] At this point, there is remarkable similarity between the way Jung and Hesse both viewed their worlds. For example, in 1918 Jung prophetically predicted these coming events:

> As the Christian view of the world loses its authority, the more menacingly will the "blond beast" be heard prowling about in its underground prison, ready at any moment to burst out with devastating consequences. When this happens in the individual it

> brings about a psychological revolution, but it can also take a social form.[44]

So too Hermann Hesse's Demian sensed the imminent collapse of the present world and said:

> What will come is beyond imagining. The soul of Europe is a beast that has lain fettered for an infinitely long time. And when it's free its first movements won't be the gentlest. But the means are unimportant if only the real needs of the soul—which has for so long been repeatedly stunted and anesthetized—come to light.[45]

The new order was coming, and those marked children of Cain will be prepared to fulfill their destiny. As Demian put it:

> Then our day will come, then we will be needed. Not as leaders and lawgivers—we won't be there to see the new laws—but rather as those who are willing, as men who are ready to go forth and stand prepared wherever fate may need them. Look, all men are prepared to accomplish the incredible if their ideals are threatened. But no one is ready when a new ideal, a new and perhaps dangerous and ominous impulse, makes itself felt. The few who will be ready at that time and who will go forth—will be us. That is why we are marked—as Cain was—to arouse fear and hatred and drive men out of a confining idyl into more dangerous reaches.[46]

The future belonged to the children of Cain who were ready and willing to bloody themselves and others for the new ideal; indeed, the new order which was coming.[47] Hesse had found his Demian, his inner voice, his destiny, his "master."[48] This, then, was the expression of a philosophy of life appropriate for youth, ready and willing to ignore bloody violence in the process of giving birth to the new order. In the name of sincerity one must reject the facade of bourgeois values. While the war had shaken the political institutions of the herd, Hesse had found therapeutic salvation in a nihilistic world by listening to his inner voice echoing from the dark unconscious world which determined his fate. God really hadn't died after all. He had been rediscovered in the unconscious. He was, however, different than the traditional God. He was, as Jung also had found Him, a Gnostic God of both good and evil.

Here Hesse, like others who adopted Jung's perspective of life, ran into the same problem of Job. How, indeed, could one be held responsible for acting out the evil will of God? The idea of fate, destiny, and predetermination was a central idea in this therapeutic philosophy of life which allowed one in a humanly destructive world not only to engage in that world without suffering the pangs of what Hesse called a "bad conscience," but to further that destruction. How, then, is one to judge the ethics of this kind of therapeutic man? Is he merely following his inner voice, prophetically acting as a midwife to the evolving predetermined future? Or are his ideas, including that inner voice, the very stuff which shapes world events? The therapeutic, quasi-religious philosophy of Hesse and Jung cannot be judged in a social vacuum. In this sense, as a philosophy, it ought to be considered not only from the standpoint of the social matrix out of which it grew, but also the social forces to which it contributed.

Jung's faith was, in part at least, created out of his personal need to overcome his father's inadequate faith as he saw those inadequacies projected across the religious conscience of western man. It was further constructed out of the longing to overcome the alienation involved in the technological urban existence by returning to a more authentic rural existence where the spiritual, indeed, the occult and demonic myths, were still creditable. Late in life Jung said: "Plainly the urban world knew nothing about the country world, the real world of mountains, woods, and rivers, of animals and 'God's thoughts.' "[49]

Jung imbibed deeply that German neoromantic nectar which allowed him to appreciate the reality of the primitive and the occult in a Volkish culture which he found rooted in the chthonic qualities of the soil.[50] The divine spirits literally lived in the soil from which they spiritually, psychically, and even physically influenced the lives of men.[51] Relying on Franz Boas as an anthropological source, Jung pointed out that the American immigrant and his children undergo anatomical changes as a result of their trespassing on Indian soil when he said: "Thus the American presents a strange picture: A European with Negro behavior and an Indian soul. He shares the fate of all usurpers of foreign soil."[52] To be personally authentic, one must be rooted to the earth. As Jung put it:

> he who is rooted in the soil endures. Alienation from the unconscious and from its historical conditions spells rootlessness. That is the danger that lies in wait for the conqueror of foreign lands, and for every individual who, through one-sided allegiance to any kind of -ism, loses touch with the dark, maternal, earthy ground of his being.[53]

Freud and the Jews were examples of those rootless individuals who adopted the "ism" of materialism and lost touch with the earthy "ground of their being." The problem with the Jew, Jung argued, was twofold. First, he represented an ancient civilization with a rationalized psyche which was abstract, spent, and so thoroughly developed that he had little if any youthful vigor or potential for future development. Secondly, the Jew was a wanderer, rootless, and therefore incapable of independent culture. Without the maternal earth to gain vital spiritual sustenance the Jew inevitably existed in a parasitical fashion, requiring other nations to act as a "host for their development." Speaking in Nazi Germany in 1934, Jung characterized the Jew in this manner:

> The Jew, who is something of a nomad, has never yet created a cultural form of his own and as far as we can see never will, since all his instincts and talents require a more or less civilized nation to act as a host for their development.[54]

Given the Jew's over-developed consciousness and his "soulless rationalism," reinforced by a narrow "materialistic outlook," his dominant role as therapist for the German people could only lead to the corruption of the true German psyche.[55] Freudian Jewish psychology, Jung argued, ought to be abandoned for the more Aryan racially conscious psychotherapy which he espoused. Clearly identifying himself with the Germanic soul, Jung, as early as 1918, said:

> [Freud and Adler] are thoroughly unsatisfying to the Germanic mentality; *we* still have a genuine barbarian in us who is not to be trifled with, and whose manifestation is no comfort for *us* and not a pleasant way of passing the time. Would that people could learn the lesson of this war! The fact is *our* unconscious is not to be got at with over-ingenious and grotesque interpretations. The psychotherapist with a Jewish background awakes in the German psyche not those wistful and whimsical residues from the time of David but the barbarian of yesterday, a being for whom matters suddenly become serious in the most unpleasant way.[56]

Although Jung, after World War I, identified his soul with that of the Germans, which contained a barbarian character yet to be developed in cultural terms, after World War II, his identification had shifted. In his 1945 essay, "After the Catastrophe," he accepted the guilt which goes with being a European, but he no longer wrote in terms of *our* German soul, but rather in terms of his Swiss background. As he put it: "Living as we do in the middle of Europe, *we* Swiss feel comfortably far removed from the foul vapours that arise from the morass of German guilt."[57]

Increasingly after World War II the Jewish stereotyping which marked his earlier work tends to disappear from his writings as does his references to a Volkish Germanic soul. In its place he tended to universalize his mysticism and write in terms of archetypes appropriate for all men. Whether this shift was conscious or unconscious is unknown. Nowhere, however, does he seem seriously to entertain the possibility that the Volkish religious philosophy which he espoused was part of the broader ideological *Zeitgeist* which marked National Socialism itself. On the contrary, he often pointed to his early discovery of the "blond beast" in the German soul as a confirmation of his belief system. The beast had broken out of his underground prison and Jung had seen himself as correctly warning western man what might happen.

The events in Germany from 1932–1945 confirmed in his mind the belief about the chthonic qualities, albeit demonic qualities, imbedded in the unconscious soul of the German people. So it was that he saw Adolf Hitler as the "mirror of every German's unconscious."[58] He believed Hitler reflected the real unconscious needs of the German people when he said, "He is the first man to tell every German what he has been thinking and feeling all along in his unconscious about German fate."[59] He asserted that Hitler's power was not political, but rather "it is magic." He was a true mystic and prophet of the Third Reich with all its mystical trappings from Wotan to storm troopers. Hitler was a *true* leader, Jung argued, a charismatic leader who spoke with the divine, albeit demonic, authority of the Gnostic God which lives in the Volkish unconscious soul of the German people. As Jung said:

> Now, the secret of Hitler's power is not that Hitler has an unconscious more plentifully stored than yours or mine. Hitler's secret is twofold: first, that his unconscious has exceptional access to his consciousness, and second, that he allows himself to be moved by it. He is like a man who listens intently to a stream of suggestions in a whispered voice from a mysterious source and then acts upon them. In our case, even if occasionally our unconscious does reach us as through dreams, we have too much rationality, too much cerebrum to obey it. This is doubtless the case with Chamberlain, but Hitler listens and obeys. The true leader is always led.[60]

This kind of unconscious leadership is strikingly reminiscent of Hesse's Demian who advised the young Sinclair, as a child of Cain, to "listen within yourself" to find the voice of fate, good, and evil, his "master." The children of Cain would listen to the voice within and be prepared to act on the bloody consequences of that voice when and if it is needed. Hitler also acted on his inner voice, Jung surmised, when he made the decision to march into the Rhineland, Austria, and Czechoslovakia. In those situations, Jung argued, "Hitler's unconscious knew—it didn't guess or feel, it *knew*—that Britain would not risk war."[61] Hitler listened and obeyed his Demian. National Socialism itself was an inevitable expression of the demonic divine.

As Hitler took over Germany the attack on the Jews began in earnest. Freud and the Jews who dominated the field of psychotherapy came under direct attack. On April 6, 1933, Ernst Kretschmer, editor of the *Zentralblatt Für Psychotherapie* and president of the International Society for Psychotherapy, and all other Jewish members of his staff were forced to resign. Carl Jung, as Vice President, took over as President of the society and as editor of the Aryanized journal.[62] He did this, he later argued, to save psychotherapy from being completely wiped out as a Jewish discipline. Sharply criticized by Dr. G. Bally for his action, Jung responded by arguing that just as the totalitarian church has had its day and at present is in a state of decline, now the totalitarian state is going to have its day. Jung argued, "The 'metamorphosis of the gods' rolls rumbling on and the State becomes Lord of this world."[63] Under such inevitable circumstances men of science must learn to "adapt themselves." Indeed, he insisted:

> To protest is ridiculous—how protest an avalanche? It is better to look out. Science has no interest in calling down avalanches; it must preserve its intellectual heritage even under the changed conditions.[64]

He further argued that one should:

> render unto Caesar the things that are Caesar's and unto God the things that are God's. . . . There is no sense in us as doctors facing the National Socialist regime as if we were a party. As doctors we are first and foremost men who serve our fellows, if necessary under all aggravations of a given political situation. We are neither obliged nor called upon to make protests from a sudden access of untimely political zeal and thus gravely endanger our medical activity.[65]

A basic part of Jung's philosophy was not to protest, not to confront, but to allow the unconscious to find expression and then to moderate, if possible, the extremes.[66] Often he had counseled not to face Germany and its National Socialist movement directly. This was not so much a matter of tactics as it was a matter of philosophy. National Socialism, he believed, was an expression of the demonic religious spirit which welled up from the deeper reaches of the unconscious. Maintaining his Gnostic perspective, he commented to a friend: "Religions are not necessarily lovely or good. They are powerful manifestations of the spirit and we have no power to check the spirit."[67]

Jung's role in the Aryanization of the *Zentralblatt* was no doubt stimulated not only by his psycho-religious philosophy, which helped him see the rise of National Socialism as inevitable, but also by his own personal distaste for Freud as well as his long-standing stereotyped view of the Jews. Still more significant perhaps was the role he believed they had played in profoundly misinterpreting, and thereby corrupting, the true German spirit. In the *Zentralblatt* (Vol. 7, Nos. 1 and 2), he wrote an extensive paper, "Zur gegenwaertigen Lage der Psychotherapie" (On the Present Situation of Psychotherapy) in 1934 in which he stereotyped the Jewish unconscious and their psychology and then compared them with the Aryan unconscious with which he identified himself and his psychology. Writing in an Aryanized journal to be read in a country where Jews were being beaten, tortured, and murdered on the streets, Jung described the Jewish problem in psychotherapy in the following manner:

> Freud and Adler have beheld very clearly the shadow that accompanies us all. The Jews have this peculiarity in common with women; being physically weaker, they have to aim at the chinks in the armour of their adversary, and thanks to this technique which has been forced on them through the centuries, the Jews themselves are best protected where others are most vulnerable. Because, again, of their civilization, more than twice as ancient as ours, they are vastly more conscious than we of human weaknesses, of the shadow-side of things, and hence in this respect much less vulnerable than we are. Thanks to their experience of an old culture, they are able, while fully conscious of their frailties, to live on friendly and even tolerant terms with them, whereas we are still too young not to have "illusions" about ourselves. Moreover, we have been entrusted by fate with the task of creating a civilization—and indeed we have need of it—and for this "illusions" in the form of one-sided ideals, convictions, plans, etc., are indispensable. As a member of a race with a three-thousand-year-old civilization, the Jew, like the cultured Chinese, has a wider area of psychological consciousness than we. Consequently it is *in general* less dangerous for the Jew to put a negative value on his unconscious. The "Aryan" unconscious, on the other hand, contains explosive forces and seeds of a future yet to be born, and these may not be devalued as nursery romanticism without psychic danger. The still youthful Germanic peoples are fully capable of

creating new cultural forms that still lie dormant in the darkness of the unconscious of every individual—seeds bursting with energy and capable of mighty expansion. The Jew, who is something of a nomad, has never yet created a cultural form of his own and as far as we can see never will, since all his instincts and talents require a more or less civilized nation to act as host for their development.

The Jewish race as a whole—at least this is my experience—possesses an unconscious which can be compared with the "Aryan" only with reserve. Creative individuals apart, the average Jew is far too conscious and differentiated to go about pregnant with the tensions of unborn futures. The "Aryan" unconscious has a higher potential than the Jewish; that is both the advantage and the disadvantage of a youthfulness not yet fully weaned from barbarism. In my opinion it has been a grave error in medical psychology up till now to apply Jewish categories—which are not even binding on all Jews—indiscriminately to Germanic and Slavic Christendom. Because of this the most precious secret of the Germanic peoples—their creative and intuitive depth of soul—has been explained as a morass of banal infantilism, while my own warning voice has for decades been suspected of anti-Semitism. This suspicion emanated from Freud. He did not understand the Germanic psyche any more than did his Germanic followers. Has the formidable phenomenon of National Socialism, on which the whole world gazes with astonished eyes, taught them better? Where was that unparalleled tension and energy while as yet no National Socialism existed? Deep in the Gemanic psyche, in a pit that is anything but a garbage-bin of unrealizable infantile wishes and unresolved family resentments. A movement that grips a whole nation must have matured in every individual as well. That is why I say that the Germanic unconscious contains tensions and potentialities which medical psychology must consider in its evaluation of the unconscious.[68]

Repeatedly Jung denied the charge of anti-Semitism that Freud, Bally, Reik, and many others have made.[69] Confronted with such criticism, Jung frequently pointed out that some of his best students were Jewish. He had even written introductions for their books.[70] Adamantly he insisted he was not against the Jews, but against Freud and the application of his psychology which was Jewish to non-Jews. As he so often put it:

I am absolutely not an opponent of the Jews even though I am an opponent of Freud's. I criticize him because of his materialistic and intellectualistic and—last but not least—irreligious attitude and not because he is a Jew. Insofar as his theory is based in certain respects on Jewish premises, it is not valid for non-Jews. [71]

Although Jung thus repeatedly denied being anti-Semitic, he had throughout his life stereotyped the Jew as rootless, burned out, overly conscious, materialistic, rationalistic, intellectualistic, abstract, and parasitic, unable to commune with the chthonic qualities of the true Aryan soul. On the other hand, he had stereotyped the Aryan as barbarian, youthful, creative, powerful, dangerous, with a fantastic potential for building new cultural forms. Do these stereotypes make him anti-Jewish and pro-Aryan? Not at all, Jung argued. He was, he claimed, only describing "scientifically" the psychological characteristics of two different races and pointing out the implications those differences had for therapeutic practice. [72] Jung's racial psychology argument here turns very close to the argument which men like Arthur Jensen and Richard Herrnstein have used in America in recent years with respect to the cognitive abilities of blacks. They too claim they are not anti-black, but merely scientifically describing the cognitive differences between the races. They too disclaim any responsibility for claiming one race as superior to another, but insist the society-at-large makes that judgment by determining those values they most cherish. In a race-oriented America, not only the stereotype—in this case "cognitive ability"—is determined by the white majority, but the value of the stereotype itself is determined by that majority. In a race-oriented Germany, not only the stereotype—in this case "rootless, parasitic, old, etc."—was determined by the Aryan majority, but the value of the stereotype itself was also determined by that majority. At this point, the racial psychologist absolves his conscience of the responsibility of both the stereotype and its social value and then, under the guise of "science," proceeds to make recommendations for social action. Thus it was that in a race-oriented America which places high value on cognitive ability, Arthur Jensen recommended that we should stop trying to teach congnitive skills to black preschool children. In a parallel manner, C. G. Jung moved from his stereotype of the Jews to call for action against Jewish psychotherapy as corrupter of the German psyche.

While one can and should question the empirical validity of the stereotype being used and ask for solid evidence which demonstrates that Jews were, in fact, materialistic, rootless, etc., or blacks were, in fact, cognitively inferior, it is perhaps at least as important to raise the social question regarding what that stereotype actually means within an historic context. The social stereotype invariably carries a loaded meaning within a given culture. For a nation like Germany which had maintained a youth movement for more than three decades,[73] the stereotype of the Aryan as youthful, vigorous, alive, and creative, in juxtaposition to the Jew as rationalized, materialistic, culturally spent, and old, carried a profound if not deadly meaning. To maintain the position as Jung, Jensen, and Herrnstein have maintained, that these particular stereotypes of Jews and blacks are merely descriptive and therefore neither anti-Jew or anti-black is difficult to support. Whether or not a particular category with which a group of people are described will be positive, negative, or neutral is a function of the normative beliefs of the society in which those terms are used. Ultimately the only way to judge whether or not a particular statement about the Jew is, in effect, an anti-Semitic statement can only be established within a social context. While the author may, indeed, claim to have intended something different, the social effects of the stereotype cannot be escaped. One might give Jung the benefit of the doubt and recognize that he did not stereotype Jews so that they could be burned in ovens. It is, nevertheless, clear that he believed his stereotype of the Jew was correct, and, moreover, that he stereotyped them to show the damaging effects their psychology had when applied to the German nation. Regardless of whether or not Jung's statements about Jews were empirically true or false, or even whether or not he intended only to counteract the damaging effect Jewish psychology had upon the German nation, the statements he made in the historic context of National Socialism can only be assessed as anti-Semitic in consequence. He was, at the very least, guilty along with others of cultivating the intellectual climate through which the "final solution" was ultimately made possible.

Why did Jung act as he did? Was he carried away with the *Zeitgeist* and emotional trappings of the National Socialist movement, making personal choice contrary to his stated philosophy and lifetime work? Very little evidence indicates this to be the case. On the contrary, he said:

> The assertion that I acknowledge racial psychology only at this present juncture [1934] is incorrect. In 1927 I wrote: "Thus it is a quite unpardonable mistake to accept the conclusions of a Jewish psychology as generally valid. Nobody would dream of taking Chinese or Indian psychology as binding upon ourselves . . . and in 1928 I wrote . . . "He [the Jew] is domesticated to a higher degree than we are, but he is badly at a loss for that quality in man which roots him to the earth and draws new strength from below.

> This chthonic quality is found in dangerous concentration in the German people. . . . The Jew has too little of this quality. [74]

Built into Jung's philosophy from the very early days of his career was a racial stereotype which he had cultivated from his youthful experiences. Jung, it should be recalled, associated his father's mental weakness with his inability to defend himself and his faith "against the ridiculous materialism of the psychiatrists. . . ." His father had taken to reading Bernheim's book on suggestion in Sigmund Freud's translation. The effect of such reading was negative; as Jung said: "but his psychiatric reading made him no happier. His depressive moods increased in frequency and intensity, and so did his hypochondria."[75] During those years, Jung's relations with his father were strained. He saw him as a man whose view of himself and the world had become rationalized and sour by attempting to live a life based on indefensible dogma. Jung's stereotype of the Jews and the condition of his father's theological beliefs are strikingly similar. He objected to his father's acceptance of dogmatic theology without the direct experience of "grace." Yet after his father's death he studied dogmatic theology from his father's mentor before a series of divine interventions led him to become a "doctor of the soul," Jung also studied the dogma of the world with his adopted father, Sigmund Freud. As Jung said:

> I can still recall vividly how Freud said to me, "My dear Jung, promise me never to abandon the sexual theory. That is the most essential thing of all. You see, we must make a dogma of it, an unshakable bulwark." He said that to me with great emotion, in the tone of a father saying, "And promise me this one thing, my dear son: that you will go to church every Sunday!"[76]

Jung then publicly rejected Freud for requiring dogmatic belief in sexual theory, just as he secretly rejected his father's theological beliefs as dogmatic without grace. Shortly before the final break with Freud, Jung had a dream about an elderly man in the uniform of an Imperial Austrian custom official:

> His expression was peevish, rather melancholic and vexed. There were other persons present, and someone informed me that the old man was not really there, but was the ghost of a customs official who had died years ago. "He is one of those who still couldn't die properly." That was the first part of the dream. [77]

It was Jung's opinion, interestingly enough, that his father had not died "properly." It should also be recalled that he was "pitied." However,

Jung proceeded to analyze his own dream, interpreting the border passing as part of Freud's censorship and control over the field of psychoanalysis. He said:

> As for the old customs official, his work had obviously brought him so little that was pleasurable and satisfactory that he took a sour view of the world. I could not refuse to see the analogy with Freud.[78]

Much of this dream analysis could have applied to his own father as well as to Freud. The very words, "sour view of the world," were the same words he used to describe his father's condition shortly before he died. Jung sensed this connection when he later said:

> At that time Freud had lost much of his authority for me. But he still meant to me a superior personality, upon whom I projected the father, and at the time of the dream this projection was still far from eliminated.[79]

He then proceeded to question whether or not his own revolt against Freud's strong personal control over his own public statements included that "death-wish which Freud had insinuated I felt toward him?"[80] On two occasions—once in Bremen in 1909 and again in Munich in 1912—Freud suffered a fainting spell while Jung was speaking.[81] In both cases, the subject of patricide was part of his speech. Freud explained his fainting behavior (albeit neurotic) as reading in Jung's unconscious a death-wish for him. Although personally, Jung said, he could not find any part of himself which reflected such a wish, he was "distinctly shocked" by his dream about the Austrian custom official.

One might hypothesize that perhaps Freud was correct. It is conceivable that Jung projected a death-wish for Freud, his second father. He had some difficulty accepting his real father in both life and death. It is also conceivable that Jung unconsciously projected his death-wish for Freud to all of Jewish psychology. More than two decades after the break with Freud, Jung's father problem still appeared in his public statements. Responding to Dr. Bally's criticism of his role in helping to Aryanize the *Zentralblatt*, Jung said:

> I am grateful to my theological forebears for having passed on to me the Christian premise, and I also admit my so-called "father complex": I do not want to knuckle under to any "fathers" and never shall.[82]

Jung had refused to knuckle under to Freud and "Jewish psychology" and continued his battle with his "fathers" into the National Socialist era. Under the circumstances, he seemed to see nothing wrong with raising the question of the effect of Jewish psychology on the German psyche during one of the most virulent anti-Semitic periods of western history. As he said, "I must confess my total inability to understand why it should be a crime to speak of 'Jewish' psychology."[83] The psychologist who gave us such stereotype categories as introvert and extrovert seemed unable to understand the social consequences involved in stereotyping people. Was Jung, then, a malicious person who actively sought the destruction of the Jews? The evidence does not seem to warrant such an assertion. The evidence, however, does seem to indicate that while he did not seek the destruction of the Jews per se, he actively urged his colleagues not to protest their destruction while he also actively sought the demise of Freudian and Jewish influence in psychology in Germany. The consequences of these activities in some measure contributed to the holocaust which followed. It is clear that the Gnostic faith which Jung had developed allowed him to interpret Adolf Hitler as an expression of the demonic-divine, and therefore he cautioned against direct opposition. It is also clear that his relations, real and projected, with his "fathers" no doubt helped frame his attitude toward Jewish psychology and explains, in part, the choices he made throughout the tragic era of National Socialism. Whether one analyzes his philosophic-religious position, or one considers his personal psychological relation with his father, each analysis contributes a part of the complicated process by which men make choices and assert their freedom. In the end, however, men need not remain true to their ideological commitments or their psychological hang-ups. Even the neurotic knows that he need not act on his fear, even though he most often does. The same is true for the ideological commitment which one holds. One can choose to be non-ideological at any given moment. There are limits, however. Undoubtedly for some more than others the ideological sets and unconscious pressures generated in a repressive culture form the anesthesia which protects the individual from what Soren Kierkegaard knew as the "fear and trembling" of moral choice.[84]

The therapeutic man in the twentieth century chooses a therapy in much the same way his predecessors chose religious help. In so doing he assumed responsibility for the social consequences of his choice. He chooses, then, for others as he creates himself. As Jean-Paul Sartre once put it: "Man is nothing else but that which he makes of himself."[85] Man must choose, and as he does, he chooses himself. As Sartre further put it:

> When we say that man chooses himself, we do mean that every one of us must choose himself; but by that we also mean that in choosing

> for himself he chooses for all men. For in effect, of all the actions a man may take in order to create himself as he wills to be, there is not one which is not creative, at the same time, of an image of man such as he believes he ought to be. . . . I am thus responsible for myself and for all men, and I am creating a certain image of man as I would have him to be. In fashioning myself I fashion man.[86]

. . . Speaking as a therapeutic man, Jean-Paul Sartre argued that the root of man's illness lies imbedded not in man's nature, his soul, or his unconscious, but in the capitalist organization of society itself. Sartre found himself in fundamental agreement with Engels, who in *The Condition of the Working Classes in England* (1845) argued that capitalist industrialization inevitably develops a social system "in which a race of people could feel at home only if it were dehumanized, degraded, intellectually and morally depressed to the level of animals, and physically morbid."[87] Capitalist society, Sartre agreed, was a sick society and illness was the only possible form of life under such a system. The psychiatrist then who tries to help his client to adjust to the social ills of his world is himself ill. As Sartre said:

> In reality the psychiatrist, who is a wage earner, is sick like every one of us. The ruling class merely gives him the power of "cure" and of commital to institutions. It is self-evident that "cure" in our system cannot mean the *abolition* of illness: it serves exclusively the maintenance of work capacity, whereby one continues to remain ill. In our society there thus exists the healthy and the cured (two categories of the unconsciously sick who adopt to norms of production) and on the other hand the avowedly sick, those whom aimless rebellion incapacitates for work and who are delivered over to the psychiatrist.[88]

The psychotherapist, Sartre argued, who leads his clients to adjust to such a system serves as a "policeman" for that system whereas the psychotherapist who seeks a real cure meaning the "abolition of the illness" itself must become a social revolutionary.

The psychological therapy, philosophy, and religion, indeed, the life style one chooses has important consequences as to what one becomes individually and what influence one has collectively. Neither the Gnostic faith, Volkish mysticism, occult beliefs, Jewish stereotypes of Jung, nor the Gnostic Demian of Hesse's children of Cain were neutral concepts. Within the historical context of the twentieth century, these concepts contributed to and were functionally useful parts of the ideological *Zeitgeist* that culminated in National Socialism. To the extent that these concepts were freely chosen and to the extent that these ideas actually influenced people to act as they did act is the extent to which Jung's therapeutic man was responsible for helping move that world from one of "peace to a place of horror." While it is difficult, indeed, if not presumptuous to ascribe guilt for those crimes which plague humanity, it is clear that in the twentieth century neither art nor the artist was, as he so often claimed, "unpolitical."

The artist's values, attitudes, and beliefs about himself, his universe and even his God often were part of the plague which engulfed the western man. While some might, indeed, debate whether or not the fascination with the occult, magic, Volkish mysticism, Gnostic faith, and racial psychology were the disease or merely the symptoms of a deeper malaise that affects all western culture, it was clear that these ideas, movements, and trends were all part of the syndrome. Considering Albert Camus' warning that the plague could be expected to return, one might reflect more seriously on the current resurge of interest in the words of C. G. Jung, Hermann Hesse, and Volkish mysticism, magic, the occult, and the theme of the "children of Cain," as found in such music as the Jefferson Airplane.[89] We might, then, turn back in time to the peace and tranquility of the Engadine and wonder, along with Hermann Hesse, whether or not that "bad conscience" which affects the intellectual in the modern age was, or is, deserved.

Notes

1. Hermann Hesse, *Autobiographical Writings* (New York: Farrar, Straus and Giroux, 1972), p. 286.

2. Although Hesse had been living in Switzerland for over two years, he immediately went to the German consulate in Berne to volunteer for military service. See Bernhard Zeller, *Portrait of Hesse* (New York: Herder and Herder, 1971), p. 80.

3. Peter Gay, *Weimar Culture: The Outsider as Insider* (New York: Harper Torchbooks, 1968), p. 73. For further impact of the war see George L. Mosse, *The Crisis of German Ideology* (New York: Grosset and Dunlap, 1964); George L. Mosse, *Nazi Culture* (New York: Grosset and Dunlap, 1966); George L. Mosse, *Germans and Jews* (New York: Howard Fertig, 1970), p. 213; George L. Mosse, *The Culture of Western Europe* (Chicago: Rand McNally Co., 1961); Erick Eyck, *A History of the Weimar Republic*, Vol. I (New York: Atheneum, 1970); Hans Kohn, *The Mind of Germany* (New York: Charles Scribner's Sons, 1960).

4. As quoted in Gay, *Weimar Culture*, p. 74.

5. The expressionist film, "The Cabinet of Dr. Caligari," as it was originally created by Hans Janowitz and Carl Mayer, was focused explicitly on the issue of legitimacy of all authority. As the play, however, came under the direction

of Robert Wiene, the focus of the film was changed to only *one* kind of authority. See Gay, *Weimar Culture*, pp. 102–105; also Otto Friedrich, *Before the Deluge* (New York: Harper and Row, 1972).

6. The Dadaist of World War I might be favorably compared to the American Crazies during the Vietnam War. Both represented the fundamental mocking of the existing dominant culture.

7. See Mosse, *The Culture of Western Europe*, p. 297.

8. As quoted in Hans Kohn, *Making of the Modern Mind* (New York: D. Van Nostrand Co., 1955), p. 79.

9. Myth is being used in this essay as a sociological term. A *myth* in this sense is defined as any idea or cluster of ideas which people believe in enough to use as a rationale for action. The critical question, then, is not whether the myth is true or false, but whether or not it works in shaping behavior.

10. Walter Kaufmann, *The Portable Nietzsche* (New York: The Viking Press, 1954), p. 95.

11. Kaufmann, *The Portable Nietzsche*, p. 96.

12. Ibid., p. 95.

13. A good example of both a person who as a psychologist deals with the spiritual problems of the therapeutic man and at the same time suffers the anxiety of a universe without meaning is William James. In a personal letter to his son, James admitted that the case of the Frenchman which he described so vividly in *The Varieties of Religious Experience: A Study in Human Nature* (New York: Collier, 1961), p. 138, was, in fact, James himself. For confirmation see Gay Wilson Allen, *William James, A Biography* (New York: The Viking Press, 1967), p. 165. In the case of the Frenchman, James goes on to suggest that the problem was one of pervasive "fear of the universe," fear of a universe without meaning or God. James' God turned out to be something "more" existing in the unconscious which satisfied his need for something "more" to overcome his existential loneliness. James' God served a therapeutic function. In American Letters, James was one of the key therapeutic men who represents that critical cross-over from religion to psychology.

14. Consider, for example, the competing philosophic assumptions implicit in such twentieth century therapeutic approaches as those practiced by Sigmund Freud, R. D. Laing, George H. Mead, or B. F. Skinner.

15. Philip Rieff, *The Triumph of the Therapeutic* (New York: Harper and Row, 1966), pp. 24–25. Also see Philip Rieff, *Freud: The Mind of the Moralist* (rev. ed.) (New York, 1961), pp. 361–93. Throughout this essay I am using the term "therapeutic" as a broad category in much the same way as Philip Rieff uses the term to include such very diverse therapists who sought remedies for the diseased western mind as Freud, Jung, Reich, and Lawrence. For the purpose of this paper, however, our focus will be restricted to only one kind of therapeutic man, namely C. G. Jung, and the way that therapy is reflected in the work of others such as Hermann Hesse.

16. As quoted in Ibid., p. 24.

17. See C. G. Jung, *Psychology and Religion West and East* (London: Routledge and Kegan, 1958).

18. For example, see John Dewey, *A Common Faith* (New Haven: Yale University Press, 1934).

19. As quoted in Mosse, *The Culture of Western Europe*, p. 268.

20. Sigmund Freud, *The Future of an Illusion* (revised) (New York: Anchor Books, Doubleday & Co., 1964), p. 92.

21. C. G. Jung, *Psychology and Religion, West and East*, p. 337.

22. C. G. Jung, *Memories, Dreams, Reflections* (Recorded and edited by Aniela Jaffe) (New York: Vintage Books, 1963), p. 92.

23. Ibid., p. 75.

24. Ibid., p. 55.

25. Ibid., p. 41.

26. Ibid., p. 39.

27. Ibid., p. 40.

28. After this vision there were also a number of other divine signs which steered him toward his chosen profession. One sign was the cracking of a solid walnut table, while another was the breaking of a bread knife by mystical occult forces into several pieces. The latter event, which occurred in 1898, helped him to decide not to be a surgeon. For his description of these events see Ibid., pp. 104–109. For a picture of the knife which he saved all his life see C. G. Jung, *Letters*, Vol. 1 (Princeton: Princeton University Press, 1973), p. 181.

29. Jung, *Memories, Dreams, Reflections*, pp. 94-96.

30. Ibid., p. 96.

31. While Jung interpreted his vision of God on a throne, etc., as a message from the divine, Freud would probably have interpreted it in terms of Jung's conflict with his father. The difference between the two positions is profound.

32. Martin Buber, *Eclipse of God* (New York: Harper Torchbook, 1952), pp. 136-137.

33. See Jung, *Psychology and Religion West and East*, "Answer to Job," pp. 357–470.

34. See R. D. Laing, *The Politics of Experience* (New York: Random House, 1967).

35. As quoted by Herbert Marcuse, *Eros and Civilization* (Boston: The Beacon Press, 1955), pp. 246-247.

36. Hesse, *Autobiographical Writings*, p. 286.

37. See Joseph Mileck, *Hermann Hesse and His Critics* (Chapel Hill: University of North Carolina Press, 1958), p. 298; also see Clarence Boersma, "The Educational Ideal in the Major Works of Hermann Hesse" (Unpublished Ph.D. Dissertation, University of Michigan, 1948), p. 28; also Hesse, *Autobiographical Writings*, p. xxiii.

38. Hermann Hesse, *Demian* (New York: Bantam Books, 1970), p. ix.

39. Most literary authorities agree that Sinclair is Hesse and Pistorius was his Jungian therapist, Dr. Lang.

40. Hesse, *Demian*, p. 93.

41. Ibid., p. 52.

42. Ibid., p. 115.

43. Ibid., pp. 115-116.

44. C. G. Jung, *Civilization in Transition*, "The Role of the Unconscious" (London: Routledge and Kegan, 1964—first pub. in 1918), p. 13.

45. Hesse, *Demian*, p. 124.

46. Ibid., p. 124.

47. Hermann Hesse was not a pacifist as some seem to think. He had attempted to volunteer for World War I and was rejected. Later he became disillusioned with the consequences of the war and publicly advocated a kind of detachment for the artist in order to preserve culture. For this he was severely criticized. However in 1914 in *If the War Goes On*, he said: "Since shooting is the order of the day, let there be shooting—not, however, for its own sake and not out of hatred for the execrable enemy but with a view of resuming as soon as possible a higher and better type of activity." Hermann Hesse, *If the War Goes On* (New York: Farrar Straus and Giroux, 1970), p. 12.

48. Hesse, *Demian*, p. 141.

49. Jung, *Memories, Dreams, Reflections*, p. 100.

50. I am using Volkish as George Mosse defined the term in *The Crisis of German Ideology* (New York: Grosset and Dunlap, 1964), p. 4. As Mosse said: " 'Volk is one of those perplexing German terms which connotes far more than its specific meaning. 'Volk' is a much more comprehensive term than 'people,' for to German thinkers ever since the birth of German romanticism in the late eighteenth century 'Volk' signified the union of a group of people with a transcendental 'essence.' This 'essence' might be called 'nature' or 'cosmos' or 'mythos,' but in each instance it was fused to man's innermost nature, and represented the source of his creativity, his depth of feeling, his individuality, and his unity with other members of the Volk."

51. Jung's doctoral thesis was entitled, "On the Psychology and Pathology of So-called Occult Phenomena," 1902.

52. Jung, *Civilization in Transition*, p. 49.

53. Ibid., p. 49.

54. Ibid., p. 166.

55. The abstract materialism with which he stereotyped the Jew and Jewish psychology also appeared in his association with his father's problem of faith. He said: "He could not even defend himself [Jung's father] against the ridiculous materialism of the psychiatrists. This, too, was something one had to believe, just like theology, only in the opposite sense." Jung, *Memories, Dreams, Reflections*, p. 74.

56. Jung, *Civilization in Transition*, p. 14. (Italics for emphasis added.)

57. Ibid., p. 196. (Italics for emphasis added.)

58. H. R. Knickerbocker, "Diagnosing the Dictators," *Hearst's International Cosmopolitan*, January, 1939, p. 116.

59. Ibid., p. 116.

60. Ibid., p. 116.

61. Ibid., p. 116.

62. For a sympathetic treatment of Jung's role in this event, see Ernest Harms, "Carl Gustav Jung—Defender of Freud and the Jews," *Psychiatric*

Quarterly, April, 1946, pp. 199–230. For a more critical review, see Edward Glover, *Freud or Jung* (New York: Meridian Books, 1956), pp. 141–153. For personal letters relevant to the issue at hand, see Gerhard Adler and Aniela Jaffe, *C. G. Jung Letters*, Vol. I (Princeton: Princeton University Press, 1973), pp. 131–165.

63. Jung, *Civilization in Transition*, p. 537.

64. Ibid., p. 538. It should be noted that Hermann Hesse did not protest either. Under the circumstances the Third Reich neither banned nor burned his books. During the period 1933 to 1945 Hesse had twenty books in print in Germany selling a total of 481,000 copies. See Bernard Zeller, *Portrait of Hesse*, pp. 131–132.

65. Ibid., p. 539.

66. While the *Zentralblatt* was reorganized during his presidency of the International Medical Society for Psychotherapy, Jung was also instrumental in getting the international association to adopt an enabling clause which allowed German Jewish doctors to become members of other national groups. See C. G. Jung's letter to J. H. Van der Hoop; Adler and Jaffe, *C. G. Jung Letters*, p. 149.

67. Ibid., Letters from Jung to Leslie Hollingsworth, April 21, 1934, p. 159.

68. Jung, *Civilization in Transition*, pp. 165–166.

69. See Sigmund Freud, "History of the Psychoanalytic Movement." Also see Dr. G. Bally, "Deutschstammige Psychotherapie" No. 343 (February 27) Neue Zurcher Zeitung (CLV 1934); also Glover, *Freud Or Jung;* also Erika Freeman, "Theodore Reik," *Psychology Today*, April, 1972, p. 50; as well as Jung's *Letters.*

70. Erich Neumann was one such example. See Adler and Jaffe, *C. G. Jung Letters*, p. 167, C. E. Benda, June 19, 1934.

71. Ibid., p. 154, Letter to B. Cohen, March 26, 1934.

72. Throughout this discussion I am using the term *stereotype* not in a pejorative sense but rather in a sociological sense as a fixed ideological matrix into which groups of people are categorized and objectified.

73. See David Crawford Poteet, "The Nazi Youth Movement, 1920–1927" (Unpublished Ph.D. Dissertation, University of Georgia, 1972). Also see Walter Z. Laqueur, *Young Germany* (New York: Basic Books, 1962); and George L. Mosse, *Germans and Jews* (New York: Howard Fertig, 1970).

74. Jung, *Civilization in Transition*, p. 544.

75. Jung, *Memories, Dreams, Reflections*, p. 94.

76. Ibid., p. 150.

77. Ibid., p. 163.

78. Ibid., p. 163.

79. Ibid., p. 163.

80. Ibid., p. 164.

81. Ibid., pp. 156–157.

82. Jung, *Civilization in Transition*, p. 540.

83. Ibid., p. 541. One is reminded here of current statements by Arthur Jensen and Richard Herrnstein to a similar effect.

84. Jean-Paul Sartre in his essay on "Self-Deception" warns about the use of the unconscious as a way of escaping the burden of choice. George Mosse also correctly points out that the danger involved in doing psychohistory is found not only in the tendency to move to a single cause, but to also fall into a pre-determination analysis. See George L. Mosse, "Commentary," *History of Childhood Quarterly*, Fall, 1973, Vol. 1, No. 2, pp. 230-233.

85. Walter Kaufmann, *Existentialism from Dostoevsky to Sartre* (New York: Meridian Books, 1963), p. 291.

86. Ibid., pp. 291-292.

87. As quoted in the Foreword written by Sartre in the "Socialist Patients Collective," mimeographed pamphlet, 1972, p. 3.

88. Ibid., p. 3.

89. The lyrics for much of the music of the Jefferson Airplane is revealing, for example: "Whatever you think is totally irrelevant Both to us now and to you. We are the present We are the future You are the past . . . We're something new . . . Open your eyes there's a New world a-coming Open your eyes there's a New world today." Paul Kanter, Grace Slick, Joey Covington (words) "Mau Mau Amerikon" *Jefferson Airplane*, God Tunes, 1970. Another example is: "Surprise civilized man You were keeper to me Now your animal is free And now you're free to die. . . ." Grace Slick (words) "Sunrise" *Jefferson Airplane*, God Tunes, 1970.

Index

Abel, T., 241
Adamic, L., 143
Adler, A., 342
Adolescence, 105-110, 202-217
Adorno, T. W., 68, 182
Alexander, L., 67
Alienation, 41, 67, 253-256
  psychological dimension of, 69
Allison, J., 207
Annales, 46, 56
Anti-Semitism
  and Jung, 352-355
Apprenticeship, 105, 127, 146, 198, 225
Arendt, H., 297
Ariès, P., 8, 27, 53, 72, 181, 190
Aron, R., 47
Authoritarian Personality, The (Adorno), 68
Authority
  in families, 34, 104, 202, 234-235
  in Jung, 355-356
  in military, 232, 294-295
  in organizations, 227
  in theory, 84
  in Woodrow Wilson, 116

Ball, G., 316
Baptism, 144
Barraclough, G., 4
Bay of Pigs invasion, 325
Bettelheim, B., 69-70
Biography
  Dilthy and, 43
  Jaspers on, 20
  origins of, 7
  psycho-, 8, 58, 81-119
  transference in, 23
Birth control, 22
Black Panther Party, 31, 308
Bloch, M., 225
Bodin, J., 46
Bolshevism, 84-85
Bombings
  atomic, 30, 34
  Hiroshima, 67
  Vietnam, 317
Bonaparte, M., 49
Bossard, J., 124
Brown, N. O., 66
Buber, M., 341
Buchan, W., 144
Bundy, McG., 316
Burlingham, D. T., 235-236

Camus, A., 311
Capitalism, 357
Carr, E. H., 24

Central Intelligence Agency, 316
Centuries of Childhood (Ariès), 8, 27, 72, 181
Childhood, 123-247
  abandonment in, 145-147
  cohorts in, 119-127
  experiences of, 88
  history of, 8, 71, 123-179
  infanticide, 139
    in antiquity, 139-142
    in Renaissance, 142-144
  labor in, 135-146, 231
  mortality and, 230
  personality and, 181-183
  politicization and, 233
Childhood and Society (Erikson), 19
Childrearing, 137
  modes of, 160-161, 184-190
  punishments in, 151-152
  religion and, 131
  toilet training, 149-150
  weaning, 185
Children
  cruelty to, 72, 126, 131, 153, 200
  disturbed, 70
  roles of
    as innocent, 156
    as parent, 136
China
  feminist movement in, 164-181
  Pye on, 35
Christian, G., 316
Circumcision, 138, 158
Civilization and Its Discontents (Freud), 12
Clifford, C., 316
Cohen, E., 67
Cohn, N., 31
Confucianism, 265-281
  ancestors in, 268
  family life and, 265-266, 270-276
  marriage and, 265-268
  sex role and, 269
Countertransference. *See* Transference
Cuban missile crisis, 325

Dadaists, 336
Dai, B., 269
Decline of the West (Spengler), 8
Demography, 34
  birthrate, 228
  family composition, 50, 196
  psychological aspects of, 56, 242-243
  saints and, 194-196
  sex ratio, 140, 142
Déscartes, R., 48
Despert, J. L., *The Emotionally Disturbed Child—Then and Now*, 128
Dilthy, W., 42-45, 59, 64
Disease. *See* Health

Easy Rider, 32
Edwards, J., 338
Ego theory, 50
Empathic reaction, 129, 133
Engels, F., *The Condition of the Working Classes in England*, 357
Erikson, E., 99-110
  analytic method of, 50, 83, 182
  challenged, 24
  on life history, 18-22, 47-48, 88-89
    on Gandhi, 22-51
    on Hitler, 99-110
    on Luther, 23, 44-45
Eros and Civilization (Marcuse), 12
Existentialism and psychology, 52-53
Explorations in Personality (Murray), 87

Family
  history and, 25-26, 50, 71
  nationality and
    Chinese, 264-281
    German, 104
  parental role in, 102-103, 108, 125, 205, 232, 236, 240, 261
  Puritanism and, 184-190
  See also Childhood; Authority

Febvre, L., 42, 44, 46, 50, 58
Federn, P., 234
Female Instructor (Lu Chao), 265
Foucault, M., 46-47
Franklin, B., 85-97
Freud, A., 235-236
Freud, S., 1, 12, 32, 42, 45, 221
  on historical limits, 65
  on jokes, 260
  on psychobiography, 8
  on psychohistory, 48
  on values, 59
Fromm E., 68
Future of an Illusion (Freud), 66

Geertz, C., 24
Genocide, 31, 33, 282-284
George, A. L., 49,111-119
George, J. L., 49, 111-119
Gandhi's Truth (Erikson), 19, 22
Glaeser, E., 238-241
Glass Bead Game, The (Hesse), 334-335
Gluckman, M., 275
Gnosticism, 340-341
Goclenius of Marburg, 42
Goethe, 41, 338
Goodman, P., 67
Greenstein, F., 233
Groups, 251-363
  decision making in, 316-317
  dehumanization in, 326
  political, 316-329
  psychological factors in, 321-324
Gunsberg, A., 134

Hall, G. S., 339
Hamilton, A., 135
Hayden, T., 30
Health
  Black Death, 28, 58
  childhood and, 241
  malnutrition, 229, 239
Hegel, G. F., 41, 52, 59
Helms, R., 316
Herder, J. G., 41
Hess, R. D., 234
Hesse, H., 334-335, 343-345
Hitler, A., 99-110, 348
Hoffman, A., 32
Holland, N., 33
Homosexuality
  in antiquity, 154
  Oedipal conflict and, 155, 236-237
  Plutarch on, 155
Hoopes, T., 317
Hughes, S., 55
Huizinga, J., 45
Hunt, D., 27, 72.
  Parents and Children in History, 128

Indians (American), 12, 331-332
Industrialization, 227
Jahrgang 1902 (Glaeser), 238
James, W., 207
Jaspers, K., 20
  Psychologie der Weltanschauungen, 44
Johnson, L., 317
Jokes, 260
Jones, E., 82, 84
Juenger, E., 336
Jung, C., 12, 58
  analyzed by Karier, 339-358
  anti-Semitism and, 352-355
Juvenile delinquency, 230

Kardiner, A., 182
Keniston, K., 33, 201
Kennedy, J. F., 327
Kent State University, killings at, 307
Keynes, J.M., 230
Kluckhohn, C., 182
Kraslow, D., 317
Kren, G. M., 298
Kris, E., 49

Laing, R. D., 342
Langer, W., "The Next Assignment," 1, 28, 32, 35, 55, 64, 81

Laslett, P., 124
Lasswell, H., 49, 112, 115
Leites, N., 84–85, 112
Lifton, R. J., 67, 226, 290
Linton, R., 182
Literature
  as emotional evidence, 238-239, 271
  and psychoanalysis, 33
Loory, S. H., 317
Lovejoy, A., 58
Lu Chao, 265
Luther, M., 8, 23

McNamara, R., 316
Maimonides, M., 138
Manchu dynasty, 265
Mandrou, R., 46
Mann, T., 343
Mannheim, K., 222–224
Manuel, F., 64
Marcuse, H., 12, 47, 66
Marriage, Confucian, 265-268

Marx, K., 3, 21, 41-42, 52–54
Masturbation, 157
Mazlish, B., 55
  "Inside the Whales," by, 18
Mead, M., 182
Mein Kampf (Hitler), 99
Meiss, M., 58
Michelet, J., 41
Milieu therapy, 70
Mill, J. S., 162
Moses and Monotheism (Freud), 1, 48, 66
Motivation
  among groups, 18
  Erikson on, 51
  subject of history, 4, 54
Moyers, W., 316
  "Mr. Stop-the-Bombing," 320
Murdock, G. P., 247
Murray, H., 87
My Lai, 69, 257-263, 283-285

National Socialism
  Fromm on, 68–69
  Hesse prediction of, 334
  Jung on, 350–351
  paranoia and, 67
  personality and, 68, 219-247
Negroes, 12, 66, 330–332
Nietzsche, F., 38, 43, 336
Nuremberg principles, 298
Nursing. *See* Wet-nursing
Nutrition. *See* Health

Oedipus complex
  history and, 26–28
  Hitler and, 67, 100–101
  homosexuality and, 155-156, 232, 236
Orwell, G., 321

Paranoia, 66, 67
Parents and Children in History (Hunt), 27, 72
Pasternak, B., 267
Payne, B., "The Child in Human Progress", 128
Peace Corps, 262
Personality
  cult of, 20
  historians and, 54
  industrialization and, 227
  modal, 182
  politics and, 13
  Wilson, 112-119
Piaget, J., 71
Pinel, P., 50
Policy making, 315-329
  foreign policy
    Cuba, 325
    Vietnam, 315-316
  groups and, 316-317
  norms and, 318
Politics
  decisions in groups, 315-329
  personality and, 13, 335
Pratt, James, 207

Pratt, Jean, 267
Projection, 129, 242
Psychobiography. *See* Biography
Puritan childrearing, 184-190
Pye, L., 35

Racism, 290, 308
Ranke, L. van, 53
Rappoport, L., 298
Reflections on Violence (Sorel), 336
Regression, 222, 227
Reich, W., 342
Reik, T., 129
Religion
  in America, 330–332
  childrearing and, 131, 185, 193–218
  Christian science, 331
  Dilthy and, 43
  psychotherapy and, 337
  Wilson, W., 115
  See also Confucianism
Reversal reaction, 129, 134, 136
Rheingold, J., 139
Rickert, H., 65
Rieff, P., 338
Roosevelt, T. R., 330
Roskamp, G., 237
Ross, R. M., 226
Rostow, W., 316
Rusk, D., 316

St. Augustine
  on childrearing, 124
  as psychologist, 338
Sartre, J., 47, 52–53
Science
  and change, 3–4
  and unconscious, 42
  and values, 3
Scienza Nuova (Vico), 40
Sears, D. O., 233
Shame, 186
Simmel, E., 33
Snow, C. P., 30

Social change
  in China, 276–278
  and psychology, 251-256
  and science, 3
Social stratification, 104
"Sociological Problem of Generations, The" (Mannheim), 222
Sorel, G., 336
Soskin, W., 238
Spengler, 12, 42
Steele, R., 133
Sterba, R., 49
Strasser, G., 226
Streifler, H., 226
Suicide, 258
Superego, 106
Swaddling, 132, 148. *See also* Childhood; Family

Taylor, G. R., 128
Technology, effects on psychology, 252
Thomson, J. C., Jr., 316
Thunder of Steel (Juenger), 336
Totem and Taboo (Freud), 66
Transference
  and biography, 21, 23
  and families, 26

Unconscious
  concept of, 48
  science and, 42
Utility
  absolute value, 3
  of psychohistory, 13

Valery, P., 336
Values
  Freud on, 59
  history and, 4
  science and, 3
Vergin, F., 67
Vico, G., 40–41
Viet Cong, 260

Vietnam, war policy in, 315–329
  See also My Lai
Violence, 282–314
  context of, 285
  glorification of, 309–311
  police and, 287
  prevention of, 304–305
  psychological explanations of, 288
  sanctions of, 292–301
  self-defense and, 286
  society and, 284
Vries, Peter de, 22

Wallon, H., 46
Wangh, M., 236
Waning of the Middle Ages, The (Huizinga), 45
War in Vietnam, 32
Weaning, 148–149, 185
Weber, M., 104
Wet-nursing, 146–147, 198, 205
Wheeler, E., 316
White, H., 64
Whitehead, A. N., 39
Wicker, T., 308
Wilson E., 111
Wilson, W., 49, 111–119
Winnicott, D. W., 235
Witchcraft, 46, 56, 188
Women. *See* Family: Confucian marriage
Words for Women and Girls, 265

Young Man Luther (Erikson), 19, 23, 44